THE COMPLETE POETRY OF BEN JONSON

WILLIAM B. HUNTER, JR., was born in 1915 in Louisville, Kentucky. He received the A.B. from Princeton University and the M.A. and Ph.D. from Vanderbilt University. He has taught at Mary Baldwin College in Staunton, Virginia; Wofford College in Spartanburg, South Carolina; Vanderbilt University, Baylor University, and the University of Idaho; and is now Professor of English at Macalester College.

Professor Hunter is secretary of the Milton Society of America and the author of various articles, especially upon Milton's theology.

THE NORTON LIBRARY
SEVENTEENTH-CENTURY SERIES

J. MAX PATRICK, *General Editor*

The Complete Poetry
of
BEN JONSON

EDITED WITH AN INTRODUCTION,
NOTES, AND VARIANTS BY
WILLIAM B. HUNTER, JR.

The Norton Library
W · W · NORTON & COMPANY · INC ·
NEW YORK

W. W. Norton & Company, Inc. also publishes *The Norton Anthology of English Literature*, edited by M. H. Abrams et al; *The Norton Anthology of Poetry*, edited by Arthur M. Eastman et al; *World Masterpieces*, edited by Maynard Mack et al; *The Norton Reader*, edited by Arthur M. Eastman et al; *The Norton Facsimile of the First Folio of Shakespeare*, prepared by Charlton Hinman; and the Norton Critical Editions.

ISBN 0 393 00436 8

Printed in the United States of America

3 4 5 6 7 8 9 0

CONTENTS

CONTENTS

INTRODUCTION

Ben Jonson has some claim to be England's first poet lau-
reate; at least he received for his literary services a royal
pension, paid irregularly in wine and money. In his own time
his literary prestige was greater than that of either Donne or
Shakespeare; but today his fame as a poet is dim in compari-
son with theirs, though "Drink to me only with thine eyes"
retains its perennial charm. The recent success of *Volpone*
with audiences of the stage, movies, and television, however,
shows that as a writer of comedy Jonson bears comparison
with Shakespeare, and some of his poems are so similar to
Donne's that it is difficult to decide which of the two men
penned them. In his most typical writing he provides a
blunt masculine honesty hardly matched by any other author
of his day. His artistic—if not his moral—integrity carried
directly into the next generation of writers to influence
among others Herrick, Carew, Suckling, and Lovelace. It ex-
tended ultimately into the work of Milton, Dryden, and
Pope.

Throughout his life Jonson made his own way by tenacity
and hard work. The stepson of a bricklayer, he never attended
a university but after a short period of schooling was ap-
prenticed in his foster father's occupation (as his enemies
never tired of reminding him). He managed to break away
and join the army in the Low Countries, where he boasts
that he killed one of the enemy in single combat. Back in
England he became an actor and playwright, and was jailed
twice for his authorship and once for killing a fellow actor
in a duel. Somehow he gave himself a better classical educa-
tion than any of his fellow writers had managed. Personal
convictions led him to become, for a few years, a communi-
cant of the Roman Catholic Church at a time when such
membership could mean the death sentence. Nevertheless,

his dramatic activities led him to court, where with the coronation of James I he became the most popular purveyor of entertainment with his elaborate masques; for most of the remainder of his life he seems to have been well received by the nobility. But he never lost his roots in the taverns, his kinship with the common man. His gusto for life always emerges along with his enthusiasm for classical scholarship.

In his later years Jonson was a great tun of a man—a shapeless blob, he himself suggests—who became a benevolent literary dictator at the various taverns where writers met to drink and discuss their work. When he was younger the Mermaid seems to have been his favorite; later he moved to the Apollo Room of the Old Devil Inn, where he and the members of the "Tribe of Ben" held animated sessions. The biographer John Aubrey recalls that "he would many times exceed in drink. Canary was his beloved liquor. Then he would tumble home to bed; and when he had thoroughly perspired then to study. I have seen his studying chair, which was of straw, such as old women used." But years and hard living took their toll. In 1628 Jonson suffered a stroke from which he never completely recovered, although he persisted in writing and continued to see his friends until about 1635. They remained loyal: shortly after his death in 1637 they compiled a volume of tributes, *Jonsonus Virbius*. Surprisingly, there is nothing in it by Carew, Herrick, or Milton. But perhaps the finest tribute is the one on his gravestone in Westminster Abbey: "O Rare Ben Jonson."

* * *

The text which follows includes all of the poems by Jonson which survive. It closely follows the earliest editions, even where modern usage has changed. For instance, he generally spelled *lose* as *loose* and *than* as *then*; this spelling has been retained. One of the most important assets of the lyrics of his period is their music. Several contemporary musical settings are included here. From the Eragny Press edition of the songs (London, 1906) come "If all these Cupids," "It was no policie," "Yes, were the loves," "Come, my Celia, let us prove," "Still to be neat," and "Though I am young." From

Introduction

Andrew J. Sabol's *Songs and Dances for the Stuart Masque* (Brown University Press, Providence, R.I., 1959) are reprinted "So beauty on the waters stood" and "Had those that dwell in error foul." Finally, "Slow, slow, fresh fount" is reproduced from Henry Youll, *Canzonets to Three Voyces* (1608), through the kind permission of the Folger Shakespeare Library. I wish to thank especially Professors J. Max Patrick and Sanford Golding for the help which they have given me.

William B. Hunter, Jr.

March 1963

A JONSON CHRONOLOGY

June 11, 1573 (?) born in London.
1588 (?) leaves Westminster School; apprenticed as brick-layer.
1591–92 (?) soldier in the Low Countries.
November 14, 1594, marries Anne Lewis.
1597 or earlier, playwright and actor.
—— Imprisoned for acting in and for part authorship of a lost play, *The Isle of Dogs.*
1598 *The Case Is Altered* acted by a company of boys recruited from the choir school of the Chapel Royal.
—— *Every Man in his Humour* acted by the Lord Chamberlain's Men, the company of actors for whom Shakespeare also wrote.
—— Kills Gabriel Spencer, a fellow actor, in a duel; imprisoned but freed by plea of benefit of clergy. Converted in jail to Roman Catholicism.
1599–1600 *Every Man out of his Humour* acted by the Lord Chamberlain's Men at the new Globe Theater.
1600 *Cynthia's Revels* acted by the boys of the Chapel Royal.
1601 *Poetaster* acted by the boys of the Chapel Royal.
1603 *Sejanus* acted by the Lord Chamberlain's Men, now known as the King's Men.
—— First masque, *Entertainment at Althorpe.*
—— Son Benjamin dies, aged 6.
1604 or 1605 *Eastward Hoe!*, in collaboration with Chapman and Marston, acted by the boys of the Chapel Royal, now known as the Children of the Queen's Revels. All three authors imprisoned because of a supposed slight in it against King James.
1606 *Volpone* acted at Oxford and Cambridge universities and by the King's Men at the Globe Theater.

1609 *Epicœne* acted by the Children of the Queen's Revels.

1610 *The Alchemist* acted by the King's Men.

— (?) Returns to Anglican religion.

1611 *Catiline* acted by the King's Men.

1612–13 travels in France as tutor to son of Sir Walter Raleigh.

1614 *Bartholomew Fair* acted by Lady Elizabeth's Men.

1616 *The Devil is an Ass* acted by the King's Men.

— Publication of the *Works* in folio; receives royal pension.

1618–19 journeys on foot to Scotland; visits there with William Drummond.

July 17, 1619, honorary M.A. from Oxford University.

1623 teacher at Gresham College in London.

— (Oct.–Nov.) Lodgings burned, with loss of books and manuscripts.

1626 *The Staple of News* acted by the King's Men.

1628 paralyzed by a stroke.

— Appointed chronologer of the City of London (a sinecure).

1629 *The New Inn* acted by the King's Men; a complete failure.

1632 *The Magnetic Lady* acted by the King's Men.

1633 A *Tale of a Tub*, revised from an earlier play, acted by Queen Henrietta's Men.

1634 final masque, *Love's Welcome at Bolsover*.

1635 a second son named Benjamin dies.

August 6, 1637, death in Westminster; buried August 9 in Westminster Abbey.

1640–41 publication of *Works* (2 vols. folio) by Sir Kenelm Digby.

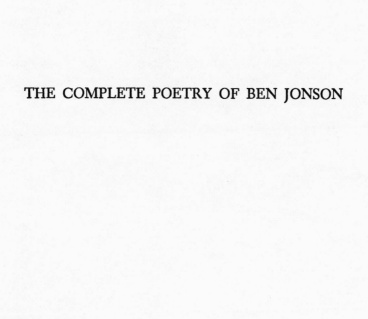

THE COMPLETE POETRY OF BEN JONSON

EPIGRAMMES

"In short and sweet poems, framed to praise or dispraise, which are called *Epigrammes*," wrote Jonson's old teacher William Camden in his *Remaines*, "our countrey men now surpasse other nations." Primarily on the model of the epigrams written by the Latin poet Martial, English poets tried, with varying success, to master this terse form—one which is now rarely used. When in 1612 or 1613 Jonson collected his verse for the folio which appeared in 1616, he ambitiously entitled a group of poems "Epigrammes. I. Booke." and in the dedication of them to the Earl of Pembroke proclaimed them to be "the ripest of my studies." A second book never appeared, although he continued to write epigrams for the rest of his life. Many appear in the later *Under-wood* and in the *Uncollected Poetry*.

Most of Jonson's poems—and his epigrams are no exception—were occasional; that is, they are connected with particular events and circumstances such as a death, a marriage, or an insult. Jonson did not, however, arrange these poems in their chronological order either of composition or of the events celebrated. Instead, the order in which he published them suggests that his aim was to vary the subject matter so as to avoid monotony. The lines themselves possess little variety since they are almost entirely in pentameter couplets. The only really long poem, the last one, is not epigrammatic at all but rather is a kind of mock epic which still offends Victorian tastes.

In Jonson's eyes the epigram should not be merely irritating but should serve a sincere moral purpose. "He that departs with his owne honesty For vulgar praise," he writes in No. 2, "doth it too dearely buy"; and again in No. 98, "Be alwayes to thy gather'd selfe the same." These poems are

forthright and masculine: Jonson gives no quarter and seeks
none. He wishes to have his work judged by capable people
like John Donne (No. 96) and is irritated by indiscriminate
praise from a parasite (Nos. 38 and 58). Through the epi-
grams Jonson provides glimpses of his friendly relations with
the great and the near-great: with King James and his cousin
Esme Stuart, with the family of Sir Philip Sidney, with
Donne and such of his friends as the Countess of Rutland
and Henry Goodyere, with scholars, translators, and musi-
cians. He invites a friend to dinner (No. 101) in lines which
more than bear comparison with Milton's Sonnet to Edward
Lawrence and with their common source in Martial (*Epig.*
V. 78, X. 48, and XI. 52). Some of his finest efforts are
reserved for the brief elegies, echoed especially in the next
generation by Robert Herrick: to his daughter Mary and his
first son Benjamin, to Margaret Ratcliffe, to a boy actor, to
Elizabeth L.H.—still tantalizingly unidentified. All but one
of these elegies are in meters other than the pentameter of
the other epigrams; without exception they convey the ten-
derness of a personal loss.

At the other extreme, Jonson attacks social corruption as
he had done in his plays. All of the satiric poems are directed
against anonymous people, but the types persist today: the
plagiarist who has a whole series directed at him (Nos. 53,
66, 81, 100, and 112), the usurer Banck, the unhappily mar-
ried couple, the lawyer with an elastic conscience, the man
who lives by pious trickery, quoting his motto, "God pays."
The *Epigrammes* are a varied group, lacking only love poetry,
which can be found in plenty in the contemporary sonnet,
a form which Jonson seems to have consciously avoided. In
their variety and in their complete sincerity and honesty the
collection offers some of the best poetry of its age. It re-
mained for a later generation of Jonson's followers to per-
fect the heroic couplet with its ideal epigrammatic qualities
and finally produce the brilliance of Pope.

TO THE GREAT EXAMPLE
OF HONOR AND VERTUE,
THE MOST NOBLE
WILLIAM, EARLE OF PEMBROKE,
L. CHAMBERLAYNE, &C.

MY LORD.[1] *While you cannot change your merit, I dare not change your title: It was that made it, and not I. Under which name, I here offer to your Lo: the ripest of my studies, my* Epigrammes; *which, though they carry danger[2] in the sound, doe not therefore seeke your shelter: For, when I made them, I had nothing in my conscience, to expressing of which I did need a cypher. But, if I be falne into those times, wherein, for the likenesse of vice, and facts,[3] every one thinks anothers ill deeds objected to[4] him; and that in their ignorant and guiltie mouthes, the common voyce is (for their securitie) Beware the Poet, confessing, therein, so much love to their diseases, as they would rather make a partie for them,[5] then be either rid, or told of them: I must expect, at your Lo: hand, the protection of truth, and libertie, while you are constant to your owne goodnesse. In thankes whereof, I returne you the honor of leading forth so many good, and great names (as my verses mention on the better part) to their remembrance with posteritie. Amongst whom, if I have praysed, unfortunately, any one, that doth not deserve; or, if all answere not, in all numbers, the pictures I have made of them: I hope it will be forgiven me, that they are no ill pieces, though they be not like the persons. But I foresee a neerer fate to my booke, then this: that the vices therein*

[1] William Herbert, Earl of Pembroke (1580–1630), son of the Countess of Pembroke who was sister of Sir Philip Sidney. Jonson also dedicated *Catiline* to Sir William.

[2] liability to punishment.
[3] crimes, as in the legal phrase, "after the fact."
[4] attributed to.
[5] support them.

*will be own'd before the vertues (though, there, I have
avoyded all particulars, as I have done names) and that some
will be so readie to discredit me, as they will have the im-
pudence to belye themselves. For, if I meant them not, it is
so. Nor, can I hope otherwise. For, why should they remit
any thing of their riot, their pride, their selfe-love, and other
inherent graces, to consider truth or vertue; but, with the
trade of the world, lend their long eares[6] against men they
love not: and hold their deare Mountebanke, or Jester, in
farre better condition, then all the studie, or studiers of hu-
manitie? For such, I would rather know them by their
visards, still, then they should publish their faces, at their
perill, in my Theater, where CATO, if he liv'd, might enter
without scandall.[7]*

Your Lo: most faithfull honorer,
BEN. JONSON

I. TO THE READER

PRay thee, take care, that tak'st my booke in hand,
To reade it well: that is, to understand.

II. TO MY BOOKE

IT will be look'd for, booke, when some but see
    Thy title, *Epigrammes*, and nam'd of mee,
Thou should'st be bold, licentious, full of gall,
    Wormewood, and sulphure,[1] sharpe, and tooth'd
                          [withall;
5   Become a petulant[2] thing, hurle inke, and wit,
    As mad-men stones: not caring whom they hit.
Deceive their malice, who could wish it so.
    And by thy wiser temper, let men know

[6] of a jackass.
[7] Martial (Book I, Letter to the Reader) forbids the stern Cato to enter the "theater" of his licentious writings since Cato would not approve of them.

II: [1] burning brimstone.

[2] rude, insolent.

Thou are not covetous of least selfe fame,
10 Made from the hazard of anothers shame:
Much lesse with lewd, prophane, and beastly phrase,
  To catch the worlds loose laughter, or vaine gaze.
He that departs with[3] his owne honesty
  For vulgar praise, doth it too dearely buy.

III. TO MY BOOKE-SELLER[1]

THou, that mak'st gaine thy end, and wisely well,
  Call'st a booke good, or bad, as it doth sell,
Use mine so, too: I give thee leave. But crave
  For the lucks sake, it thus much favour have.
5 To lye upon thy stall, till it be sought;
  Not offer'd, as[2] it made sute to be bought;
Nor have my title-leafe on posts, or walls,
  Or in cleft-sticks, advanced to make calls
For termers,[3] or some clarke-like serving-man,
10 Who scarse can spell th'hard names: whose knight
           [lesse can.
If, without these vile arts, it will not sell,
  Send it to *Bucklers-bury*,[4] there 'twill, well.

IV. TO KING JAMES

HOw, best of Kings, do'st thou a scepter beare!
  How, best of *Poets*,[1] do'st thou laurell weare!
But two things, rare, the *Fates* had in their store,
  And gave thee both, to shew they could no more.
5 For such a *Poet*, while thy dayes were greene,
  Thou wert, as chiefe of them are said t'have beene.

---

[3] gives up.
III: [1] John Stepneth.
  [2] as if.
  [3] appear as advertising for visitors in town.
  [4] an area of grocers in London, where the leaves could be used as wrapping paper.
IV: [1] James I had published *His Majesties Poetical Exercises* in 1591.

And such a Prince thou art, wee daily see,
  As chiefe of those still promise they will bee.
Whom should my *Muse* then flie to, but the best
10 Of Kings for grace; of *Poets* for my test?

V. ON THE UNION

WHen was there contract better driven by *Fate?*
  Or celebrated with more truth of state?
The world the temple was, the priest a king,
  The spoused paire[1] two realmes, the sea the ring.

VI. TO ALCHYMISTS

IF all you boast of your great art[1] be true;
Sure, willing povertie lives most in you.

VII. ON THE NEW HOT-HOUSE

WHere lately harbour'd many a famous whore,
  A purging bill, now fix'd upon the dore,
Tells you it is a hot-house:[1] So it ma',
  And still be a whore-house. Th'are *Synonima.*

VIII. ON A ROBBERY

RIdway rob'd *Duncote* of three hundred pound,
  Ridway was tane, arraign'd, condemn'd to dye;
But, for this money was a courtier found,
  Beg'd *Ridwayes* pardon:[1] *Duncote,* now, doth
              [crye;
5 Rob'd both of money, and the lawes reliefe,
  The courtier is become the greater thiefe.

V: [1] England and Scotland, united under James to the extent of having a common sovereign.
VI: [1] the transmutation of base metals into gold.
VII: [1] place for hot baths, often used to treat social diseases; or brothel.
VIII: [1] begged a pardon for Ridway.

IX. TO ALL, TO WHOM I WRITE

MAy none, whose scatter'd names honor my booke,
      For strict degrees of ranke, or title looke:
'Tis 'gainst the manners of an *Epigram:*
      And, I a *Poet* here, no *Herald* am.

X. TO MY LORD IGNORANT

THou call'st me *Poet*, as a terme of shame:
      But I have my revenge made, in thy name.

XI. ON SOME-THING, THAT WALKES SOME-WHERE

AT court I met it, in clothes brave[1] enough,
      To be a courtier; and lookes grave enough,
To seeme a statesman: as I neere it came,
      It made me a great face, I asked the name.
5   A lord, it cryed, buried in flesh, and blood,
      And such from whom let no man hope least good,
For I will doe none: and as little ill,
      For I will dare none. Good Lord, walke dead still.

XII. ON LIEUTENANT SHIFT

SHift,[1] here, in towne, not meanest among squires,
      That haunt *Pickt-hatch, Mersh-Lambeth,* and
                                          [*White-fryers,*[2]
Keepes himselfe, with halfe a man,[3] and defrayes
      The charge of that state, with this charme, god
                                                    [payes.

XI: [1] fine.   [2] disreputable districts of Lon-
XII: [1] expediency; cf. "shifty."   don.
The character also appears in   [3] supports himself and a poor
Every Man out of his Humour.   servant.

5   By that one spell he lives, eates, drinkes, arrayes
     Himselfe: his whole revennue is, god payes.
The quarter day[4] is come; the hostesse sayes,
     Shee must have money: he returnes, god payes.
The taylor brings a suite home; he it 'ssayes,[5]
10   Lookes o're the bill, likes it: and say's, god payes.
He steales to ordinaries;[6] there he playes
     At dice his borrow'd money: which, god payes.
Then takes up fresh commoditie,[7] for dayes;
     Signes to new bond, forfeits: and cryes, god payes.
15   That lost, he keepes his chamber, reades *Essayes,*
     Takes physick, teares the papers: still god payes.
Or else by water goes,[8] and so to playes;
     Calls for his stoole, adornes the stage:[9] god payes.
To every cause he meets, this voyce he brayes:
20   His onely answere is to all, god payes.
Not his poore cocatrice[10] but he betrayes
     Thus: and for his letcherie, scores, god payes.
But see! th'old baud hath serv'd him in his trim,[11]
     Lent him a pockie[12] whore. Shee hath paid him.

XIII. TO DOCTOR EMPIRICK[1]

WHen men a dangerous disease did scape,
     Of old, they gave a cock to *Æsculape:*[2]
Let me give two: that doubly am got free,
     From my diseases danger, and from thee.

---

[4] one of four days in the year on which payment of such charges as rent becomes due.

[5] tries on.

[6] taverns.

[7] "a parcel of goods sold on credit by a usurer to a needy person, who immediately raised some cash by re-selling them at a lower price, generally to the usurer himself." (NED)

[8] across the Thames to the Bankside, where several theaters and bear pits were located.

[9] Elizabethan gallants often showed themselves in public by occupying stools upon the stage while a play was being given.

[10] whore.

[11] his own fashion.

[12] syphilitic.

XIII: [1] quack.

[2] as a sacrifice for recovery offered to Aesculapius, the Greek god of medicine.

XIV. TO WILLIAM CAMDEN

CA*mden*,[1] most reverend head, to whom I owe
 All that I am in arts, all that I know.
(How nothing's that?) to whom my countrey owes
 The great renowne, and name[2] wherewith shee
  [goes.
5 Then thee the age sees not that thing more grave,
 More high, more holy, that shee more would crave.
What name, what skill, what faith hast thou in
  [things![3]
 What sight in searching the most antique springs!
What weight, and what authoritie in thy speech!
10 Man scarse can make that doubt, but thou canst
  [teach.
Pardon free truth, and let thy modestie,
 Which conquers all, be once over-come by thee.
Many of thine this better could, then I,
 But for their powers, accept my pietie.

XV. ON COURT-WORME

ALl men are wormes: But this[1] no man. In silke
 'Twas brought to court first wrapt, and white as
  [milke;
Where, afterwards, it grew a butter-flye:
 Which was a cater-piller. So t'will dye.

XVI. TO BRAYNE-HARDIE

HA*rdie*, thy braine is valiant, 'tis confest,
 Thou more; that with it every day, dar'st jest

XIV: [1] (1551–1623), Jonson's teacher in Westminster School. Jonson dedicated *Every Man in his Humour* to him.
 [2] referring to Camden's *Brit-tania* (1586) and *Remaines of a Greater Worke Concerning Brit-aine* (1605).
 [3] facts or events.
XV: [1] this is.

Thy selfe into fresh braules: when, call'd upon,
    Scarse thy weekes swearing brings thee of,[1] of one.
5 So, in short time, th'art in arrerage growne
    Some hundred quarrells, yet dost thou fight none;
Nor need'st thou: for those few, by oath releast,
    Make good what thou dar'st doe in all the rest.
Keepe thy selfe there, and thinke thy valure right,
10   He that dares damne himselfe, dares more then
                                [fight.

XVII. TO THE LEARNED CRITICK

MAy others feare, flie, and traduce thy name,
    As guiltie men doe magistrates: glad I,
That wish my poemes a legitimate fame,
    Charge them, for crowne, to thy sole censure hye.[1]
5 And, but a sprigge of bayes, given by thee,
    Shall out-live gyrlands, stolne from the chast tree.[2]

XVIII. TO MY MEERE[1] ENGLISH
CENSURER

TO thee, my way in *Epigrammes* seemes new,
    When both it is the old way, and the true.
Thou saist, that cannot be: for thou hast seene
    Davis, and *Weever*,[2] and the best have beene,
5 And mine come nothing like. I hope so. Yet,
    As theirs did with thee, mine might credit get:
If thou'ldst but use thy faith, as thou didst then,
    When thou wert wont t'admire, not censure men.
Pr'y thee beleeve still, and not judge so fast,
10   Thy faith is all the knowledge that thou hast.

XVI: [1] off.
XVII: [1] deliver them, for re-
ward, to thy sole high judgment.
  [2] the laurel, into which Daphne
was transformed in trying to
preserve her chastity from an
attack by Jupiter.

XVIII: [1] completely, abso-
lutely.
  [2] Sir John Davies (1569–
1626), whose epigrams had ap-
peared about 1590, and John
Weever (1576–1632), whose
Epigrammes were published in
1599.

XIX. ON SIR COD THE PERFUMED

THat *Cod*[1] can get no widdow, yet a knight,
    I sent[2] the cause: Hee wooes with an ill sprite.[3]

XX. TO THE SAME SIR COD

TH'expence in odours is a most vaine sinne,
    Except thou could'st, Sir *Cod*, weare them within.

XXI. ON REFORMED GAM'STER

LOrd, how is *Gam'ster* chang'd! his haire close cut![1]
    His neck fenc'd round with ruffe! his eyes halfe
                               [shut!
His clothes two fashions of,[2] and poore! his sword
    Forbidd' his side! and nothing, but the word[3]
5 Quick in his lips! who hath this wonder wrought?
    The late tane bastinado.[4] So I thought.
What severall wayes men to their calling have!
    The bodies stripes, I see, the soule may save.

XXII. ON MY FIRST DAUGHTER

HEre lyes to each her parents ruth,
Mary, the daughter of their youth:
Yet, all heavens gifts, being heavens due,
It makes the father, lesse, to rue.
5 At sixe moneths end,[1] shee parted hence
With safetie of her innocence;

XIX: [1] meaning both a perfume bag and the testicles.
[2] corrected to "scent" in 1692 ed.
[3] spirit, with a pun on the etymological sense of *spiritus*, breath.

XXI: [1] like a Puritan.
[2] off.
[3] the Bible, sole source of authority for the Puritan.
[4] the late-taken beating.

XXII: [1] The date is not known.

Whose soule heavens Queene, (whose name shee
[beares)
In comfort of her mothers teares,
Hath plac'd amongst her virgin-traine:
10   Where, while that sever'd doth remaine,[2]
This grave partakes the fleshly birth.
Which cover lightly, gentle earth.

XXIII. TO JOHN DONNE

DO*nne*, the delight of *Phœbus*, and each *Muse*,
    Who, to thy one, all other braines refuse;[1]
Whose every worke, of thy most earely wit,
    Came forth example, and remaines so, yet:
5   Longer a knowing, then most wits doe live.
        And which no affection praise enough can give!
To it,[2] thy language, letters, arts, best life,
    Which might with halfe mankind maintayne a
[strife.
All which I meant to praise, and, yet, I would;
10   But leave, because I cannot as I should!

XXIV. TO THE PARLIAMENT

THere's reason good, that you good lawes should make:
Mens manners ne're were viler, for your sake.

XXV. ON SIR VOLUPTUOUS BEAST

WHile *Beast* instructs his faire, and innocent wife,
    In the past pleasures of his sensuall life,
Telling the motions of each petticote,
    And how his *Ganimede*[1] mov'd, and how his
[goate,

[2] Soul and body will reunite at the Resurrection.
XXIII: [1] perhaps, Who reject all other brains in favor of yours. *Epig.* 96 is also addressed to Donne.
[2] i.e., Add to it.
XXV: [1] a boy kept for sexual purposes.

5   And now, her (hourely)[2] her owne cucqueane[3] makes,
      In varied shapes, which for his lust shee takes:
What doth he else, but say, leave to be chast,
      Just wife, and, to change me, make womans
            [hast.[4]

XXVI. ON THE SAME BEAST

THen his chast wife, though *Beast* now know no more,
He'adulters still: his thoughts lye with a whore.

XXVII. ON SIR JOHN ROE

IN place of scutcheons,[1] that should decke thy herse,
Take better ornaments, my teares, and verse.
      If any sword could save from *Fates, Roe's*[2] could;
      If any *Muse* out-live their spight, his can;
5   If any friends teares could restore, his would;
      If any pious life ere lifted man
To heaven; his hath: O happy state! wherein
Wee, sad for him, may glorie, and not sinne.

XXVIII. ON DON SURLY

DO*n Surly*, to aspire the glorious name
      Of a great man, and to be thought the same,
Makes serious use of all great trade he knowes.
      He speakes to men with a *Rhinocerotes*[1] nose,

[2] with a pun on "whore."
[3] female cuckold.
[4] emended to "haste," 1640 folio; but the meaning is not clear.
XXVII: [1] hatchments: funeral tablets, often containing the armorial bearings of the deceased.
[2] close friend of Jonson, born 1581, died in Jonson's arms c. 1606 of the plague. He served under Essex in Ireland and traveled to Holland and Russia. Some of his poems were printed as Donne's.
XXVIII: [1] curled up: sneering.

5   Which hee thinkes great; and so reades verses, too:
           And, that is done, as he saw great men doe.
       H'has tympanies[2] of businesse, in his face,
           And, can forget mens names, with a great grace.
       He will both argue, and discourse in oathes,
10   Both which are great. And laugh at ill made
                                                 [clothes;
       That's greater, yet: to crie his owne up neate.
           He doth, at meales, alone, his pheasant eate,
       Which is maine greatnesse. And, at his still boord,
           He drinkes to no man: that's, too, like a lord.
15   He keepes anothers wife, which is a spice
           Of solemne greatnesse. And he dares, at dice,
       Blaspheme god, greatly. Or some poore hinde beat,
           That breathes in his dogs way: and this is great.
       Nay more, for greatnesse sake, he will be one
20   May heare my *Epigrammes*, but like of none.
       Surly, use other arts, these only can
           Stile thee a most great foole, but no great man.

XXIX. TO SIR ANNUAL TILTER

T*Ilter*, the most may'admire thee, though not I:
    And thou, right guiltlesse, may'st plead to it, why?
For thy late sharpe device.[1] I say 'tis fit
    All braines, at times of triumph, should runne wit.
5   For then, our water-conduits doe runne wine;
    But that's put in, thou'lt say. Why, so is thine.

XXX. TO PERSON GUILTIE

G*Uiltie*, be wise; and though thou know'st the crimes
    Be thine, I taxe, yet doe not owne my rimes:
'Twere madnesse in thee, to betray thy fame,
    And person to the world; ere I thy name.

[2] tumors or swellings; here used   XXIX: [1] trickery. Just what
figuratively for the swelling of   Jonson is alluding to is not clear.
pride.

XXXI. ON BANCK THE USURER

BA*nck* feeles no lamenesse of his knottie gout,
    His monyes travaile[1] for him, in and out:
And though the soundest legs goe every day,
    He toyles to be at hell, as soone as they.

XXXII. ON SIR JOHN ROE[1]

WHat two brave perills of the private sword[2]
    Could not effect,[3] not all the furies doe,
That selfe-divided *Belgia*[4] did afford;
    What not the envie of the seas reach'd too,[5]
5   The cold of *Mosco*, and fat[6] *Irish* ayre,
    His often change of clime (though not of mind)
What could not worke; at home in his repaire[7]
    Was his blest fate, but our hard lot to find.
Which shewes, where ever death doth please t'appeare,
10   Seas, serenes,[8] swords, shot, sicknesse, all are
                     [there.

XXXIII. TO THE SAME

ILe not offend thee with a vaine teare more,
    Glad-mention'd *Roe:* thou art but gone before,
Whither the world must follow. And I, now,
    Breathe to expect my when, and make my how.
5   Which if most gracious heaven grant like thine,
    Who wets my grave, can be no friend of mine.

XXXI: [1] both travail and travel.
XXXII: [1] See *Epig.* 27.
  [2] As a swordsman Roe had won
two duels.
  [3] i.e., his death.
  [4] The Hapsburgs lost the Low
Countries in 1579 and Holland
came into being, but the political
and military situation remained
confused.

[5] to.
[6] moist.
[7] i.e., Roe's death, which the
cold of Moscow and damp Irish
air were unable to inflict, was the
fate which overtook him when he
repaired (returned) home.
  [8] a mist or fine rain in the eve-
ning, regarded as poisonous.

XXXIV. OF DEATH

HE that feares death, or mournes it, in the just,
Shewes of the resurrection little trust.

XXXV. TO KING JAMES

WHo would not be thy subject, *James*, t'obay
    A Prince, that rules by'example, more than sway?
Whose manners draw, more than thy powers constraine.
    And in this short time of thy happiest raigne,
5   Hast purg'd thy realmes, as[1] we have now no cause
    Left us of feare, but first our crimes, then lawes.
Like aydes 'gainst treasons[2] who hath found before?
    And than in them, how could we know god more?
First thou preserved wert, our king to bee,
10   And since, the whole land[3] was preserv'd for thee.

XXXVI. TO THE GHOST OF MARTIAL

MArtial, thou gav'st farre nobler *Epigrammes*
    To thy *Domitian*,[1] than I can my *James*:
But in my royall subject I passe thee,
    Thou flattered'st thine, mine cannot flatter'd bee.

XXXV: [1] so that.
  [2] There had been plots against James before his coronation.
  [3] The country had survived the plague of 1603, which de-layed James's arrival in London.
XXXVI: [1] Roman emperor (81–96) during whose reign Martial (40–104) wrote many of his epigrams.

XXXVII. ON CHEV'RILL THE LAWYER

NO cause, nor client fat, will *Chev'rill*[1] leese,[2]
    But as they come, on both sides he takes fees,
And pleaseth both. For while he melts his greace
    For this: that winnes,[3] for whom he holds his
                               [peace.

XXXVIII. TO PERSON GUILTIE

GU*iltie*, because I bad you late[1] be wise,
    And to conceale your ulcers, did advise,
You laugh when you are touch'd, and long before
    Any man else, you clap your hands, and rore,
5   And crie good! good! This quite perverts my sense,
    And lyes so farre from wit, 'tis impudence.
Beleeve it, *Guiltie*, if you loose your shame,
    I'le loose my modestie, and tell your name.

XXXIX. ON OLD COLT

FOr all night-sinnes, with others wives, unknowne,
  Colt,[1] now, doth daily penance in his owne.

XXXVII: [1] kid leather; used figuratively here in the sense of being very flexible.
[2] lose.
[3] i.e., while he works hard for one side, the other (by whom he is also paid) wins.
XXXVIII: [1] in *Epig.* 30.
XXXIX: [1] i.e., Lasciviousness.

XL. ON MARGARET RATCLIFFE[1]

MArble, weepe, for thou dost cover
A dead beautie under-neath thee,
R ich, as nature could bequeath thee:
G rant then, no rude hand remove her.
5   A ll the gazers on the skies
R ead not in faire heavens storie,
E xpresser truth, or truer glorie,
T hen they might in her bright eyes.
R are, as wonder, was her wit;
10   A nd like *Nectar* ever flowing:
T ill time, strong by her bestowing,
C onquer'd hath both life and it.
L ife, whose griefe was out of fashion,
I n these times. Few so have ru'de[2]
15   F ate, in a brother. To conclude,
F or wit, feature, and true passion,
E arth, thou hast not such another.

XLI. ON GYPSEE

GY*psee*, new baud, is turn'd physitian,
    And get more gold, then all the colledge[1] can:
Such her quaint[2] practise is, so it allures,
    For what shee gave, a whore; a baud, shee cures.

XLII. ON GILES AND JONE

WHo says that *Giles* and *Jone* at discord be?
    Th'observing neighbours no such mood can see.
Indeed, poore *Giles* repents he married ever.
    But that his *Jone* doth too. And *Giles* would
                                        [never,

XL: [1] daughter of Sir John
Ratcliffe; see *Epig*. 93. She died
in November 1599, mourning the
recent death of her brother Sir
Alexander in Ireland.

[2] rued.
XLI: [1] i.e., the College of
Physicians.
    [2] with a pun on the meaning of
pudendum.

5   By his free will, be in *Jones* company.
              No more would *Jone* he should. *Giles* riseth
                                                    [early,
       And having got him out of doores is glad.
              The like is *Jone*. But turning home, is sad.
       And so is *Jone*. Oft-times, when *Giles* doth find
10   Harsh sights at home, *Giles* wisheth he were
                                                    [blind.
       All this doth *Jone*. Or that his long yearn'd[1] life
              Were quite out-spun. The like wish hath his wife.
       The children, that he keepes, *Giles* sweares are none
              Of his begetting. And so sweares his *Jone*.
15   In all affections shee concurreth still.
              If, now, with man and wife, to will, and nill[2]
       The selfe-same things, a note of concord be:
              I know no couple better can agree!

XLIII. TO ROBERT EARLE OF SALISBURIE[1]

WHat need hast thou of me? or of my *Muse*?
       Whose actions so themselves doe celebrate;
Which should thy countries love to speake refuse,[2]
       Her foes enough would fame thee in their hate.
5 'Tofore, great men were glad of *Poets*: Now,
       I, not the worst, am covetous of thee.
Yet dare not, to my thought, lest[3] hope allow
       Of adding to thy fame; thine may to me,
When in my booke, men reade but *Cecill's* name,
10   And what I write thereof find farre, and free
From servile flatterie (common *Poets* shame)
       As thou stand'st cleere of the necessitie.

XLII: [1] long yarned: long spun
out.
    [2] not will.
    XLIII: [1] Robert Cecil, famous
as Secretary of State under Eliza-
beth and as Lord Treasurer under
James; created Earl of Salisbury in
May 1605. See also *Epig*. 63.
    [2] Which if thy country's love
should refuse to utter.
    [3] least.

XLIV. ON CHUFFE, BANCKS THE USURER'S KINSMAN

CH*uffe*,[1] lately rich in name, in chattels, goods,
    And rich in issue to inherit all,
    Ere blacks were bought for his owne funerall,
Saw all his race approch the blacker floods:[2]
5   He meant they thither should make swift repaire,
    When he made him executor, might be heire.[3]

XLV. ON MY FIRST SONNE

FArewell, thou child of my right hand,[1] and joy;
    My sinne was too much hope of thee, lov'd boy,
Seven yeeres tho'wert lent to me, and I thee pay,
    Exacted by thy fate, on the just day.
5   O, could I loose all father now. For why
    Will man lament the state he should envie?
To have so soone scap'd worlds, and fleshes rage,
    And, if no other miserie, yet age?
Rest in soft peace,[2] and, ask'd, say here doth lye
10   *Ben. Jonson* his best piece of *poetrie*.
For whose sake, hence-forth, all his vowes be such,
    As what he loves may never like[3] too much.

XLIV: [1] churl; or perhaps chough, a crow. On Banck, see *Epig.* 31.

[2] the river Styx, symbol of death.

[3] perhaps, "He meant that they should be hurried into mourning when he (Chuffe) made him (Banck) his executor and perhaps his heir"—perhaps his heir because any surviving relative would already owe his inheritance to Banck.

XLV: [1] The boy was named Benjamin, which means "child of the right hand" in Hebrew. He died in 1603.

[2] the familiar *Requiescat in pace.*

[3] thrive.

XLVI. TO SIR LUCKLESSE WOO-ALL

IS this the *Sir*, who, some wast[1] wife to winne,
    A knight-hood bought, to goe a wooing in?
'Tis *Lucklesse* he, that tooke up one on band[2]
    To pay at's day of marriage. By my hand
5 The knight-wright's[3] cheated then: Hee'll never pay.
    Yes, now he weares his knight-hood every day.

XLVII. TO THE SAME

SIr *Lucklesse*, troth, for lucks sake passe by one:
    Hee that wooes every widdow, will get none.

XLVIII. ON MUNGRIL ESQUIRE

HIs bought armes *Mung'*[1] not lik'd; for his first day
Of bearing them in field, he threw 'hem away:
And hath no honor lost our Due'llists say.

XLIX. TO PLAY-WRIGHT

PL*ay-wright* me reades, and still my verses damnes,
    He sayes, I want the tongue of *Epigrammes;*
I have no salt:[1] no bawdrie he doth meane.
    For wittie, in his language, is obscene.
5 *Play-wright*, I loath to have thy manners knowne
    In my chast booke: professe them in thine owne.

XLVI: [1] probably "lavish."
  [2] bond.
  [3] the person who raised him to knighthood.
XLVIII: [1] i.e., Mongrel. The "armes" are his coat-of-arms or perhaps his weapons. Thus he threw them away in his first encounter but lost no honor: he had none to lose.
XLIX: [1] wit.

L. TO SIR COD

LE*ave Cod*,[1] *tabacco*-like, burnt gummes to take,
Or fumie clysters,[2] thy moist lungs to bake:
Arsenike would thee fit for societie make.

LI. TO KING JAMES

*Upon the happy false rumour of his death, the
two and twentieth day of March,
1607.*[1]

THat we thy losse might know, and thou our love,
    Great heav'n did well, to give ill fame free wing;
Which though it did but *panick*[2] terror prove,
    And farre beneath least pause of such a king,
5   Yet give thy jealous subjects leave to doubt:
        Who this thy scape from rumour gratulate,[3]
No lesse than if from perill; and devout,
    Doe beg thy care unto thy after-state.
For we, that have our eyes still in our eares,
10   Looke not upon thy dangers, but our feares.

LII. TO CENSORIOUS COURTLING

CO*urtling*, I rather thou should'st utterly
    Dispraise my worke, then praise it frostily:
When I am read, thou fain'st a weake applause,
    As if thou wert my friend, but lack'dst a cause.
5   This but thy judgement fooles: the other way
        Would both thy folly, and thy spite betray.

L: [1] See *Epigs.* 19 and 20.
  [2] usually the medicine given in an enema; here some kind of vapor to be inhaled through a tube.

LI: [1] Jonson recounts the effects of a rumor of the death of King James. The actual date was in April 1606.
  [2] groundless.
  [3] express joy over.

LIII. TO OLD-END GATHERER

LOng-gathering *Old-End*, I did feare thee wise,
     When having pill'd[1] a booke, which no man
                                        [buyes,
Thou wert content the authors name to loose:
     But when (in place) thou didst the patrons
                                        [choose,
5   It was as if thou printed had'st an oath,
     To give the world assurance thou wert both;[2]
And that, as *puritanes* at baptisme doo,
     Thou art the father, and the witnesse too.[3]
For, but thy selfe, where, out of motly, 's hee
10   Could save that line to dedicate to thee?

LIV. ON CHEV'RIL

CH*ev'ril*[1] cryes out, my verses libells are;
     And threatens the *starre-chamber*, and the barre:
What are thy petulant[2] pleadings, *Chev'ril*, then,
     That quit'st the cause so oft, and rayl'st at men?[3]

LV. TO FRANCIS BEAUMONT

HOw I doe love thee *Beaumont*,[1] and thy *Muse*,
     That unto me dost such religion[2] use!
How I doe feare my selfe, that am not worth
     The least indulgent thought thy pen drops forth!
5   At once thou mak'st me happie, and unmak'st;
     And giving largely to me, more thou tak'st.

LIII: [1] probably "compiled," though possibly "pillaged" (stolen). Old-end has apparently put together a text out of bits of old authors.
[2] author and patron.
[3] The non-Puritan churches generally required an independent witness at baptism.

LIV: [1] See *Epig.* 37.
[2] also in the etymological sense: ready to attack.
[3] that ignore the subject so often and attack the men (*ad hominem* argument).

LV: [1] friend of Jonson and fellow dramatist (c. 1584–1616).
[2] faithfulness.

What fate is mine, that so it selfe bereaves?
  What art is thine, that so thy friend deceives?
When even there, where most thou praysest mee,
10 For writing better, I must envie thee.

LVI. ON POET-APE

POore *Poet-Ape*,[1] that would be thought our chiefe,
  Whose workes are eene the fripperie[2] of wit,
From brocage[3] is become so bold a thiefe,
  As we, the rob'd, leave rage, and pittie it.
5 At first he made low shifts, would picke and gleane,
  Buy the reversion[4] of old playes; now growne
To'a little wealth, and credit in the *scene*,
  He takes up all, makes each mans wit his owne.
And, told of this, he slights it. Tut, such crimes
10 The sluggish gaping auditor devoures;
He markes not whose 'twas first: and after-times
  May judge it to be his, as well as ours.
Foole, as if halfe eyes will not know a fleece
  From locks of wooll, or shreds from the whole
              [peece?

LVII. ON BAUDES, AND USURERS

IF, as their ends, their fruits were so, the same[1]
Baudrie', and usurie were one kind of game.

LVIII. TO GROOME[1] IDEOT

ID*eot*, last night, I pray'd thee but forbeare
  To reade my verses; now I must to heare:
For offring, with thy smiles, my wit to grace,
  Thy ignorance still laughs in the wrong place.

LVI: [1] Whom Jonson is criti-
cizing is not known. Those who
believe in the fiction of hostility
between him and Shakespeare
favor Shakespeare for the role.
[2] old clothes.

[3] dealing in old things, castoffs.
[4] rights.
LVII: [1] If their fruits were the
same as their ends (money).
LVIII: [1] probably servant; i.e.,
servile.

5   And so my sharpnesse thou no lesse dis-joynts,
               Then thou did'st late my sense, loosing my
                                                    [points.[2]
       So have I seene at *Christ*-masse sports one lost,
               And, hood-wink'd, for a man, embrace a post.

LIX. ON SPIES

SP*ies*, you are lights in state, but of base stuffe,
Who, when you'have burnt your selves downe to the
                                                    [snuffe,[1]
Stinke, and are throwne away. End faire enough.

LX. TO WILLIAM LORD MOUNTEAGLE[1]

LOe, what my countrey should have done (have rais'd
       An obeliske, or columne to thy name,
Or, if shee would but modestly have prais'd
       Thy fact,[2] in brasse or marble writ the same)
5   I, that am glad of thy great chance, here doo!
               And proud, my worke shall out-last common
                                                    [deeds,
       Durst thinke it great, and worthy wonder too,
               But thine, for which I doo't, so much exceeds!
       My countries parents I have many knowne;
10   But saver of my countrey thee alone.

LXI. TO FOOLE, OR KNAVE

THy praise, or dispraise is to me alike,
       One doth not stroke me, nor the other strike.

[2] missing my punctuation (meaning).
LIX: [1] candle-end.
LX: [1] William Parker (1575– 1622), a Catholic peer who helped uncover the Gunpowder Plot.
[2] course of conduct.

LXII. TO FINE LADY WOULD-BEE

FIne *Madame Would-Bee*, wherefore should you feare,
 That love to make so well, a child to beare?
The world reputes you barren: but I know
 Your 'pothecarie, and his drug sayes no.
5 Is it the paine affrights? that's soone forgot.
  Or your complexions losse? you have a pot,
That can restore that. Will it hurt your feature?
  To make amends, yo'are thought a wholesome
            [creature.
What should the cause be? Oh, you live at court:
10 And there's both losse of time, and losse of sport
In a great belly. Write, then on thy wombe,
  Of the not borne, yet buried, here's the tombe.

LXIII. TO ROBERT EARLE OF SALISBURIE[1]

WHo can consider thy right courses run,
 With what thy vertue on the times hath won,
And not thy fortune; who can cleerely see
 The judgement of the king so shine in thee;
5 And that thou seek'st reward of thy each act,
  Not from the publike voyce, but private fact;[2]
Who can behold all envie so declin'd
  By constant suffring of thy equall[3] mind;
And can to these be silent, *Salisburie*,
10 Without his, thine, and all times injurie?
Curst be his *Muse*, that could lye dumbe, or hid
  To so true worth, though thou thy selfe forbid.

LXIII: [1] See *Epig.* 43.   [3] fair, impartial.
  [2] course of conduct.

LXIV. TO THE SAME

Upon the accession of the Treasurer-ship to him.[1]

NOt glad, like those that have new hopes, or sutes,
 With thy new place, bring I these early fruits
Of love, and what the golden age did hold
 A treasure, art: contemn'd in th'age of gold.[2]
5 Nor glad as those, that old dependents bee,
  To see thy fathers rites[3] new laid on thee.
Nor glad for fashion. Nor to shew a fit
 Of flatterie to thy titles. Nor of wit.
But I am glad to see that time survive,
10 Where merit is not sepulcher'd alive.
Where good mens vertues them to honors bring,
 And not to dangers. When so wise a king
Contends t'have worth enjoy, from his regard,
 As her owne conscience, still, the same reward.
15 These (noblest *Cecil*) labour'd in my thought,
  Wherein what wonder see thy name hath
              [wrought?
That whil'st I meant but thine to gratulate,
 I'have sung the greater fortunes of our state.

LXV. TO MY MUSE

AWay, and leave me, thou thing most abhord
 That hast betray'd me to a worthlesse lord;
Made me commit most fierce idolatrie
 To a great image through thy luxurie.[1]

LXIV: [1] Salisbury was awarded the office in May 1608. See *Under.* 32.

[2] The former, according to Hesiod and others, was the original time of innocence and happiness; Jonson contrasts it with the mercenary present.

[3] Cecil's father, Lord Burghley, had been appointed Lord High Treasurer in 1572.

LXV: [1] excess, or perhaps lust.

5   Be thy next masters more unluckie *Muse*,
    And, as thou'hast mine, his houres, and youth
               [abuse.
    Get him the times long grudge, the courts ill will;
        And, reconcil'd, keepe him suspected still.
    Make him loose all his friends; and, which is worse,
10   Almost all wayes, to any better course.[2]
    With me thou leav'st an happier *Muse* then thee,
        And which thou brought'st me, welcome povertie.
    Shee shall instruct my after-thoughts to write
        Things manly, and not smelling parasite.
15   But I repent me: Stay. Who e're is rais'd,
        For worth he has not, He is tax'd,[3] not prais'd.

LXVI. TO SIR HENRIE CARY

THat neither fame, nor love might wanting be
    To greatnesse, *Cary*,[1] I sing that, and thee.
    Whose house, if it no other honor had,
        In onely thee, might be both great, and glad.
5   Who, to upbraid the sloth of this our time,
        Durst valour make, almost, but not a crime.
    Which deed I know not, whether were more high,
        Or thou more happie, it to justifie
    Against thy fortune: when no foe, that day,
10   Could conquer thee, but chance, who did betray.
    Love thy great losse, which a renowne hath wonne,
        To live when *Broeck* not stands, nor *Roor* doth
               [runne.[2]
    Love honors, which of best example bee,
        When they cost dearest, and are done most free,

---

[2] of action. Cf. Donne, "The Canonization": "Take you a course, get you a place."
[3] censured.
LXVI: [1] Viscount Falkland (c. 1575–1633), one of Jonson's friends.
[2] The Castle and River neere where he was taken (Jonson's note). In a battle near the confluence of the Ruhr and the Rhine an army of Dutch and English fled from a smaller Italian group. Sir Henry tried ineffectually to stem the rout and was captured.

15   Though every fortitude deserves applause,
           It may be much, or little, in the cause.
       Hee's valiant'st, that dares fight, and not for pay;
           That vertuous is, when the reward's away.

LXVII. TO THOMAS EARLE OF SUFFOLKE[1]

       SInce men have left to doe praise-worthy things,
           Most thinke all praises flatteries. But truth brings
       That sound, and that authoritie with her name,
           As,[2] to be rais'd by her, is onely fame.
5   Stand high,[3] then, *Howard*, high in eyes of men,
           High in thy bloud, thy place, but highest then,
       When, in mens wishes, so thy vertues wrought,
           As all thy honors were by them first sought:
       And thou design'd to be the same thou art,
10   Before thou wert it, in each good mans heart.
       Which, by no lesse confirm'd, then thy kings choice,
           Proves, that is gods, which was the peoples voice.

LXVIII. ON PLAY-WRIGHT

       PL*ay-wright* convict of publike wrongs to men,
           Takes private beatings, and begins againe.
       Two kindes of valour he doth shew, at ones;
           Active in's braine, and passive in his bones.

LXIX. TO PERTINAX COB[1]

       CO*b*, thou nor souldier, thiefe, nor fencer art,
           Yet by thy weapon liv'st! Th'hast one good part.

LXVII: [1] Thomas Howard (1561–1626) created Earl of Suffolk in July 1603. He helped to secure Jonson's release from prison in 1605.

[2] so that.

[3] "How" means a high place according to William Camden, *Remaines Concerning Britaine* (1637 ed.), p. 118.

LXIX: [1] Pertinax means obstinate or stiff; Cob means a big or stout man, with implication of strong sexual powers (cf. cob-swan). The joke is extended in the character Cob of *Every Man in his Humour* with further play on the meaning of cob as red herring.

LXX. TO WILLIAM ROE

WHen *Nature* bids us leave to live, 'tis late
    Then to begin, my *Roe*:[1] He makes a state
In life, that can employ it; and takes hold
    On the true causes, ere they grow too old.
5 Delay is bad, doubt worse, depending[2] worst;
    Each best day of our life escapes us, first.
Then, since we (more then many) these truths know:
    Though life be short, let us not make it so.

LXXI. ON COURT-PARRAT[1]

TO plucke downe mine, *Poll* sets up new wits still,
Still, 'tis his lucke to praise me 'gainst his will.

LXXII. TO COURT-LING

I Grieve not, *Courtling*, thou are started up
    A chamber-critick,[1] and dost dine, and sup
At *Madames* table, where thou mak'st all wit
    Goe high, or low, as thou wilt value it.
5 'Tis not thy judgement breeds the prejudice,
    Thy person only, *Courtling*, is the vice.

LXXIII. TO FINE GRAND

WHat is't, fine *Grand*, makes thee my friendship flye,
    Or take an *Epigramme* so fearefully:
As't were a challenge, or a borrowers letter?
    The world must know your greatnesse is my
                [debter.

LXX: [1] brother (1585–1667) to Sir John Roe, for whom see *Epig.* 27. Another poem to William is *Epig.* 128.
  [2] suspense.

LXXI: [1] Mark Eccles suggests that Henry Parrot, a contemporary writer of epigrams, may be meant. *RES*, XIII (1937), 388.
LXXII: [1] a private, not a public, critic.

5   *In-primis*,[1] *Grand*, you owe me for a jest;
  I lent you, on meere acquaintance, at a feast.
 Item, a tale or two, some fortnight after;
  That yet maintaynes you, and your house in
             [laughter.
 Item, the *babylonian*[2] song you sing;
10   *Item*, a faire *greeke* poesie for a ring:
 With which a learned *Madame* you belye.
  Item, a charme surrounding fearefully,
 Your *partie-per-pale*[3] picture, one halfe drawne
  In solemne cypres,[4] the other cob-web-lawne.
15 *Item*, a gulling *imprese*[5] for you, at tilt.
  Item, your mistris *anagram*, i'your hilt.
 Item, your owne, sew'd in your mistris smock.
  Item, an *epitaph* on my lords cock,
 In most vile verses, and cost me more paine,
20   Then had I made 'hem good, to fit your vaine.[6]
 Fortie things more, deare *Grand*, which you know true,
  For which, or pay me quickly', or Ile pay you.

LXXIV. TO THOMAS LORD CHANCELOR

 WHil'st thy weigh'd judgements, *Egerton*,[1] I heare,
  And know thee, then, a judge, not of one yeare;
 Whil'st I behold thee live with purest hands;
  That no affection in thy voyce commands;
5 That still th'art present to[2] the better cause;
  And no lesse wise, then skilfull in the lawes;
 Whil'st thou art certaine to thy words, once gone,
  As is thy conscience, which is alwayes one:
 The *Virgin*,[3] long-since fled from earth, I see,
10   T'our times return'd, hath made her heaven in
             [thee.

LXXIII: [1] first.
[2] probably whorish; H&S suggest confused (in language).
[3] having two contrasted qualities.
[4] black mourning fabric.
[5] emblem or motto.

[6] vanity, with pun on vein (style).
LXXIV: [1] (1540?–1617), named Lord Chancellor by James in 1603. See *Under*. 33.
[2] intent upon.
[3] Astraea, goddess of justice.

LXXV. ON LIPPE, THE TEACHER

I Cannot thinke there's that antipathy
    'Twixt *puritanes*, and *players*, as some cry;
Though *Lippe*,[1] at *Pauls*, ranne from his text away,
    T'inveigh 'gainst playes: what did he then but
                           [play?

LXXVI. ON LUCY COUNTESSE OF BEDFORD[1]

THis morning, timely rapt with holy fire,
    I thought to forme unto my zealous *Muse*,
What kinde of creature I could most desire,
    To honor, serve, and love; as *Poets* use.
5   I meant to make her faire, and free, and wise,
    Of greatest bloud, and yet more good then great;
I meant the day-starre should not brighter rise,
    Nor lend like influence from his lucent seat.
I meant shee should be curteous, facile,[2] sweet,
10   Hating that solemne vice of greatnesse, pride;
I meant each softest vertue, there should meet,
    Fit in that softer bosome to reside.
Onely a learned, and a manly soule
    I purpos'd her; that should, with even powers,
15   The rock, the spindle, and the sheeres[3] controule
    Of destinie, and spin her owne free houres.
Such when I meant to faine, and wish'd to see,
    My *Muse* bad, *Bedford* write, and that was shee.

LXXV: [1] blear-eyed   (Latin *lippus*).
LXXVI: [1] daughter (1581?–1627) of Sir John Harington, friend of many authors, including Donne. See also *Epigs.* 84 and 94.
[2] affable, courteous.
[3] emblems of the three Fates: Clotho, Lachesis, and Atropos.

LXXVII. TO ONE THAT DESIRED ME
NOT TO NAME HIM

BE safe, nor feare thy selfe so good a fame,
    That, any way, my booke should speake thy name:
For, if thou shame, ranck'd with my friends, to goe,
    I'am more asham'd to have thee thought my foe.

LXXVIII. TO HORNET

HO*rnet*,[1] thou hast thy wife drest, for the stall,[2]
    To draw thee custome: but her selfe gets all.

LXXIX. TO ELIZABETH COUNTESSE OF
RUTLAND[1]

THat *Poets* are far rarer births then kings,[2]
    Your noblest father prov'd: like whom, before,
Or then, or since, about our *Muses* springs,
    Came not that soule exhausted so their store.
5 Hence was it, that the *destinies* decreed
    (Save that most masculine issue[3] of his braine)
No male unto him: who could so exceed
    Nature, they thought, in all, that he would faine.
At which, shee happily displease'd, made you:
10   On whom, if he were living now, to looke,
He should those rare, and absolute numbers view,
    As he would burne, or better farre his booke.

LXXVIII: [1] probably also with
reference to horned: cuckolded.
  [2] in the theater.
LXXIX: [1] daughter (1584–
1612) of Sir Philip Sidney. See
also *The Forrest* 12.
  [2] See *Uncol. P.* 15, n. 28.
  [3] perhaps Sidney's novel, the
Arcadia. He had no sons.

LXXX. OF LIFE, AND DEATH

THe ports[1] of death are sinnes; of life, good deeds:
    Through which, our merit leads us to our meeds.
How wilfull blind is he then, that would stray,
    And hath it, in his powers, to make his way!
5 This world deaths region is, the other lifes:
    And here, it should be one of our first strifes,
So to front death, as men might judge us past it.
    For good men but see death, the wicked tast it.

LXXXI. TO PROULE THE PLAGIARY

FOrbeare to tempt me, *Proule*,[1] I will not show
    A line unto thee, till the world it know;
Or that I'have by two good sufficient men,
    To be the wealthy[2] witnesse of my pen:
5 For all thou hear'st, thou swear'st thy selfe didst doo.
    Thy wit lives by it, *Proule*, and belly too.
Which, if thou leave not soone (though I am loth)
    I must a libell[3] make, and cosen both.[4]

LXXXII. ON CASHIERD[1] CAPT. SURLY

SUrly's old whore in her new silkes doth swim:
    He cast,[2] yet keeps her well! No, shee keeps him.

LXXX: [1] gates.
LXXXI: [1] prowl: one who gets by petty theft.
  [2] trustworthy.
  [3] leaflet assailing your character.

[4] perhaps, defraud both wit and belly.
LXXXII: [1] cast off; also possibly "relieved of cash": cf. Bardolph's speech in *Merry Wives of Windsor* I.i.184.
  [2] rejected her.

LXXXIII. TO A FRIEND

TO put out[1] the word, whore, thou do'st me woo,
    Throughout my booke. 'Troth put out woman too.

LXXXIV. TO LUCY COUNTESSE OF BEDFORD[1]

MA*dame*, I told you late how I repented,
    I ask'd a lord a buck, and he denyed me;
And, ere I could aske you, I was prevented:[2]
    For your most noble offer had supply'd me.
5   Straight went I home; and there most like a *Poet*,
    I fancied to my selfe, what wine, what wit
I would have spent: how every *Muse* should know it,
    And *Phoebus*-selfe should be at eating it.
O *Madame*, if your grant did thus transferre mee,
10   Make it your gift.[3] See whither that will beare
                         [mee.

LXXXV. TO SIR HENRY GOODYERE

GO*odyere*,[1] I'am glad, and grateful to report,
    My selfe a witnesse of thy few dayes sport:
Where I both learn'd, why wise-men hawking follow,
    And why that bird was sacred to *Apollo*,
5   Shee doth instruct men by her gallant flight,[2]
    That they to knowledge so should toure[3] upright,

LXXXIII: [1] reject.
LXXXIV: [1] See *Epig.* 76.
   [2] anticipated.
   [3] "Grant" and "gift" are distinguished in law: the former is a conveyance by deed, the latter a transfer without any valuable consideration.

LXXXV: [1] friend (d. 1628) of Donne and minor poet.
   [2] In his verse "Letter to Henry Goodyere" (ll. 33ff.), Donne also mentions Goodyere's love of hawking.
   [3] tower: rise above the prey.

And never stoupe,[4] but to strike ignorance:
    Which if they misse, they yet should re-advance
To former height, and there in circle tarrie,
10   Till they be sure to make the foole their quarrie.
Now, in whose pleasures I have this discerned,
    What would his serious actions me have learned?

LXXXVI. TO THE SAME

WHen I would know thee *Goodyere*, my thought
                        [lookes
    Upon thy wel-made choise of friends, and bookes;
Then doe I love thee, and behold thy ends
    In making thy friends bookes, and thy bookes
                        [friends:
5 Now, I must give thy life, and deed, the voice
    Attending such a studie, such a choice.
Where, though't be love, that to thy praise doth move
    It was a knowledge, that begat that love.

LXXXVII. ON CAPTAINE HAZARD THE CHEATER

TOuch'd with the sinne of false play, in his punque,[1]
    Hazard a month forsware his; and grew drunke,
Each night, to drowne his cares: But when the gaine
    Of what shee had wrought came in, and wak'd his
                        [braine,
5 Upon th'accompt, hers grew the quicker trade.
    Since when, hee's sober againe, and all play's
                        [made.

[4] the hawk's swift descent on
its prey.   LXXXVII: [1] whore.

LXXXVIII. ON ENGLISH MOUNSIEUR

WOuld you beleeve, when you this *Mounsieur* see,
   That his whole body should speake *french*, not he?
That so much skarfe of *France*, and hat, and fether,
   And shooe, and tye, and garter should come
                                                                    [hether,
5   And land on one, whose face durst never bee
      Toward the sea, farther then halfe-way tree?[1]
That he, untravell'd, should be *french* so much,
      As *french*-men in his companie, should seeme
                                                                    [*dutch?*
Or had his father, when he did him get,
10   The *french* disease,[2] with which he labours yet?
Or hung some *Mounsieurs* picture on the wall,
      By which his damme conceiv'd him clothes and
                                                                    [all?
Or is it some *french* statue? No: 'T doth move,
      And stoupe, and cringe. O then, it needs must
                                                                    [prove
15   The new *french*-taylors motion,[3] monthly made,
      Daily to turne in *Pauls*,[4] and helpe the trade.

LXXXIX. TO EDWARD ALLEN[1]

IF *Rome* so great, and in her wisest age,
   Fear'd not to boast the glories of her stage,
As skilfull *Roscius*, and grave *Æsope*,[2] men,
   Yet crown'd with honors, as with riches, then;

LXXXVIII: [1] "Evidently a landmark on the way to Dover." (H&S)
   [2] syphilis.
   [3] puppet.
   [4] St. Paul's Churchyard, a popular social place.

LXXXIX: [1] famous actor (1566–1626), son-in-law of Philip Henslowe and partner with him in the Fortune Theater.
   [2] Roman actors, respectively of comedy and tragedy.

5   Who had no lesse a trumpet of their name,
            Then *Cicero*, whose every breath was fame:
        How can so great example dye in mee,
            That, *Allen*, I should pause to publish thee?
        Who both their graces in thy selfe hast more
10   Out-stript, then they did all that went before:
        And present worth in all dost so contract,
            As others speake, but onely thou dost act.
        Weare this renowne. 'Tis just, that who did give
            So many *Poets* life, by one should live.

XC. ON MILL. MY LADIES WOMAN

        WHen *Mill* first came to court, the unprofiting foole,
            Unworthy such a mistris, such a schoole,
        Was dull, and long, ere shee would goe to man:
            At last, ease, appetite, and example wan
5   The nicer thing to tast her ladies page;
            And, finding good securitie in his age,
        Went on: and proving him still, day by day,
            Discern'd no difference of his yeeres, or play.
        Not though that haire grew browne, which once was
                                                [amber,
10   And he growne youth, was call'd to his ladies
                                                [chamber,
        Still *Mill* continu'd: Nay, his face growing worse,
            And he remov'd to gent'man of the horse,
        Mill was the same. Since, both his body and face
            Blowne up; and he (too'unwieldie for that place)
15   Hath got the stewards chaire; he will not tarry
            Longer a day, but with his *Mill* will marry.
        And it is hop'd, that shee, like *Milo*, wull
            First bearing him a calfe, beare him a bull.[1]

XC: [1] Milo was said to have
lifted a calf every day until it grew
to be a bull.

XCI. TO SIR HORACE VERE

WHich of thy names I take, not onely beares
    A *romane* sound, but *romane* vertue weares,
Illustrous V*ere*,[1] or *Horace*; fit to be
    Sung by a *Horace*, or a *Muse* as free;
5   Which thou art to thy selfe: whose fame was wonne
    In th'eye of *Europe*, where thy deeds were done,
When on thy trumpet shee did sound a blast,
    Whose rellish[2] to eternitie shall last.
I leave thy acts, which should I prosequute[3]
10   Throughout, might flatt'rie seeme; and to be mute
To any one, were envie: which would live
    Against my grave, and time could not forgive.
I speake thy other graces, not lesse showne,
    Nor lesse in practice; but lesse mark'd, lesse
                    [knowne:
15   Humanitie, and pietie, which are
    As noble in great chiefes, as they are rare.
And best become the valiant man to weare,
    Who more should seeke mens reverence, then
                    [feare.

XCII. THE NEW CRIE

ERe cherries ripe, and straw-berries be gone,
    Unto the cryes of *London* Ile adde one;
Ripe statesmen, ripe: They grow in every street.
    At sixe and twentie, ripe. You shall 'hem meet,
5   And have 'hem yeeld no savour, but of state.
    Ripe are their ruffes, their cuffes, their beards,
                    [their gate,

XCI: [1] a noted English soldier (1565–1635). V*ere* means "truly" in Latin.   [2] musical ornament. [3] follow with honor.

And grave as ripe, like mellow as their faces.
    They know the states of *Christendome*, not the
                                            [places:
Yet have they seene the maps, and bought 'hem too,
10   And understand 'hem, as most chapmen doe.
The councels, projects, practises they know,
    And what each prince doth for intelligence owe,
And unto whom: They are the almanacks
    For twelve yeeres yet to come, what each state
                                          [lacks.
15   They carry in their pockets *Tacitus*,
    And the *Gazetti*,[1] or *Gallo-Belgicus*:[2]
And talke reserv'd, lock'd up, and full of feare,
    Nay, aske you, how the day goes, in your eare.
Keepe a *starre*-chamber sentence close, twelve dayes:[3]
20   And whisper what a Proclamation sayes.
They meet in sixes, and at every mart,
    Are sure to con' the catalogue[4] by hart;
Or, every day, some one at *Rimee's* looks,
    Or *Bils*,[5] and there he buyes the names of books.
25   They all get *Porta*,[6] for the sundrie wayes
    To write in cypher, and the severall keyes,
To ope' the character. They'have found the sleight
    With juyce of limons, onions, pisse, to write.[7]
To breake up seales, and close 'hem. And they know,
30   If the *States*[8] make peace, how it will goe
With *England*. All forbidden bookes they get.
    And of the poulder-plot,[9] they will talke yet.
At naming the *French* King, their heads they shake,
    And at the *Pope*, and *Spaine* slight faces make.

XCII: [1] contemporary news-sheets.

[2] a newssheet published in Cologne.

[3] Jonson implies that Star-Chamber decisions were widely known shortly after they had been made.

[4] an open list.

[5] Rime and Bill were well-known booksellers in London.

[6] author of *De Furtivis Literarum Notis*, a book about secret codes.

[7] "invisibly."

[8] the Low Countries.

[9] the Gunpowder Plot, 1605.

35 Or 'gainst the Bishops, for the Brethren,[10] raile,
        Much like those Brethren; thinking to prevaile
    With ignorance on us, as they have done
        On them: And therefore doe not onely shunne
    Others more modest, but contemne us too,
40   That know not so much state, wrong, as they doo.

XCIII. TO SIR JOHN RADCLIFFE

HOw like a columne, *Radcliffe,*[1] left alone[2]
    For the great marks of vertue, those being gone
Who did, alike with thee, thy house up-beare,
        Stand'st thou, to shew the times what you all
                                                    [were?
5   Two bravely in the battaile fell, and dy'd,
        Upbraiding rebells armes, and barbarous pride:[3]
    And two, that would have falne as great, as they,
        The *Belgick* fever ravished away.
    Thou, that art all their valour, all their spirit,
10   And thine owne goodnesse to encrease thy merit,[4]
    Then whose I doe not know a whiter soule,
        Nor could I, had I seene all *Natures* roule,
    Thou yet remayn'st, un-hurt in peace, or warre,
        Though not unprov'd: which shewes, thy fortunes
                                                    [are
15 Willing to expiate the fault in thee,
        Wherewith, against thy bloud,[5] they'offenders
                                                    [bee.

---

[10] some Puritan group like the Plymouth Brethren.

XCIII: [1] brother (d. 1627) of Margaret (see *Epig.* 40). He had been knighted by Essex in Ireland in 1599.

[2] In 1599 Margaret had died, mourning the loss of their brother Alexander. As later lines say, two brothers had died in Ireland and the remaining two in the Low Countries.

[3] In Ireland (Jonson's note).

[4] In the *Faerie Queene* IV.iii, when two brothers, Priamond and Diamond, die, their souls and strength enter the third brother, Triamond.

[5] i.e., of the dead relatives.

XCIV. TO LUCY, COUNTESSE OF BED-
* FORD, WITH MR. DONNES SATYRES

LU*cy*,[1] you brightnesse of our spheare, who are
 Life of the *Muses* day, their morning-starre!
If workes (not th'authors) their owne grace should
         [looke,
 Whose poems would not wish to be your booke?
5 But these, desir'd by you, the makers ends
 Crowne with their owne. Rare poemes aske rare
         [friends.
Yet, *Satyres*, since the most of mankind bee
 Their un-avoided subject, fewest see:
For none ere tooke that pleasure in sinnes sense,
10 But, when they heard it tax'd, tooke more offence.
They, then, that living where the matter is bred,
 Dare for these poemes, yet, both aske, and read,
And like them too; must needfully, though few,
 Be of the best: and 'mongst those, best are you.
15 *Lucy*, you brightnesse of our spheare, who are
 The *Muses* evening, as their morning-starre.[2]

XCV. TO SIR HENRIE SAVILE[1]

IF, my religion safe, I durst embrace
 That stranger doctrine of *Pythagoras*,[2]
I should beleeve, the soule of *Tacitus*
 In thee, most weighty *Savile*, liv'd to us:
5 So hast thou rendred him in all his bounds,
 And all his numbers, both of sense, and sounds.

XCIV: [1] See *Epig.* 76. She is
termed the "brightnesse of our
spheare" because Lucy derives
from Latin *lux*, bright.
 [2] Refrain lines such as these
two are exceptional in Jonson's
writing.

XCV: [1] Sir Henry (1549–
1622) was provost of Eton Col-
lege. He translated Tacitus, add-
ing a section entitled *The Ende
of Nero and the Beginning of
Galba*. He also edited Chrysos-
tom.
 [2] the transmigration of souls.

But when I read that speciall piece, restor'd,
    Where *Nero* falls, and *Galba* is ador'd,
To thine owne proper[3] I ascribe then more;
10   And gratulate[4] the breach, I griev'd before:
Which *Fate* (it seemes) caus'd in the historie,
    Onely to boast thy merit in supply.
O, would'st thou adde like hand, to all the rest!
    Or, better worke! were thy glad countrey blest,
15 To have her storie woven in thy thred;
    Mineruaes loome[5] was never richer spred.
For who can master those great parts like thee,
    That liv'st from hope, from feare, from faction
                          [free;
That hast thy brest so cleere of present crimes,
20   Thou need'st not shrinke at voyce of after-times;
Whose knowledge claymeth at the helme to stand;
    But, wisely, thrusts not forth a forward hand,
No more then *Salust*[6] in the *Romane* state!
    As, then, his cause, his glorie emulate.
25 Although to write be lesser then to doo,
    It is the next deed, and a great one too.
We need a man that knowes the severall graces
    Of historie, and how to apt[7] their places;
Where brevitie, where splendor, and where height,
30   Where sweetnesse is requir'd, and where weight;
We need a man, can speake of the intents,
    The councells, actions, orders, and events
Of state, and censure them: we need his pen
    Can write the things, the causes, and the men.
35 But most we need his faith (and all have you)
    That dares nor write things false, nor hide things
                          [true.

[3] gift, ability (from Latin *proprium*).
[4] express joy over.
[5] Minerva was goddess of weaving.
[6] After a military career, Sallust devoted his life to literature.
[7] adapt to.

XCVI. TO JOHN DONNE

WHo shall doubt, *Donne*,[1] where[2] I a *Poet* bee,
    When I dare send my *Epigrammes* to thee?
That so alone canst judge, so'alone dost make:
    And, in thy censures, evenly, dost take
5   As free simplicitie, to dis-avow,
        As thou hast best authoritie, t'allow.
Reade all I send: and, if I find but one
    Mark'd by thy hand, and with the better stone,[3]
My title's seal'd. Those that for claps[4] doe write,
10   Let pui'nees,[5] porters, players praise delight,
And, till they burst, their backs, like asses load:
    A man should seeke great glorie, and not broad.

XCVII. ON THE NEW MOTION

SEe you yond' Motion?[1] Not the old *Fa-ding*,[2]
    Nor Captayne *Pod*,[3] nor yet the *Eltham*-thing;[4]
But one more rare, and in the case so new:
    His cloke with orient velvet quite lin'd through,
5   His rosie tyes and garters so ore-blowne,
        By his each glorious parcell[5] to be knowne!
He wont was to encounter me, aloud,
    Where ere he met me; now hee's dumbe, or
                    [proud.
Know you the cause? H'has neither land, nor lease,
10   Nor baudie stock,[6] that travells[7] for encrease,

XCVI: [1] See *Epig.* 23.
   [2] whether.
  [3] In ancient Rome, happy days
were noted with a white stone.
   [4] applause.
   [5] inferiors.
XCVII: [1] puppet. H&S apply
this epigram to Inigo Jones,
architect and collaborator with
Jonson in staging masques.
   [2] the name of a dance, apparently Irish (NED).
   [3] a puppet-master.
   [4] a mechanical show.
   [5] part.
   [6] income-producing property:
a brothel.
   [7] travails, works.

Nor office in the towne, nor place in court,
>Nor 'bout the beares, nor noyse[8] to make lords
>>[sport.
He is no favourites favourite, no deare trust
>Of any *Madames*, hath neadd squires, and must.[9]
15 Nor did the king of Denmarke him salute,[10]
>When he was here. Nor hath he got a sute,
Since he was gone, more then the one he weares.
>Nor are the Queenes most honor'd maides by
>>[th'eares
About his forme. What then so swells each lim?
20 >Onely his clothes have over-leaven'd him.[11]

XCVIII. TO SIR THOMAS ROE

THou hast begun well, *Roe*,[1] which stand well too,[2]
>And I know nothing more thou hast to doo.
He that is round[3] within himselfe, and streight,
>Need seeke no other strength, no other height;
5 Fortune upon him breakes her selfe, if ill,
>And what would hurt his vertue makes it still.
That thou at once, then, nobly maist defend
>With thine owne course the judgement of thy
>>[friend,
Be alwayes to thy gather'd selfe the same:
10 >And studie conscience, more then thou would'st
>>[fame.
Though both be good, the latter yet is worst,
>And ever is ill got without the first.

---

[8] probably scandal.
[9] perhaps, "of any madame who has needed pimps and must have them."
[10] on his visit to England in 1606.

[11] swollen him.
XCVIII: [1] friend (1581–1644) of Jonson; knighted 1605.
[2] carry out well.
[3] honest.

XCIX. TO THE SAME

THat thou hast kept thy love, encreast thy will,
  Better'd thy trust to letters; that thy skill;[1]
Hast taught thy selfe worthy thy pen to tread,
  And that to write things worthy to be read:
5 How much of great example wert thou, *Roe*,
  If time to facts,[2] as unto men would owe?
But much it now availes, what's done, of whom:
  The selfe-same deeds, as diversly they come,
From place, or fortune, are made high, or low,
10 And even the praisers judgement suffers so.
  Well, though thy name lesse then our great ones bee,
   Thy fact is more: let truth encourage thee.

C. ON PLAY-WRIGHT

PL*ay-wright*,[1] by chance, hearing some toyes I'had
               [writ,
  Cry'd to my face, they were th'*elixir* of wit:
And I must now beleeve him: for, to day,
  Five of my jests, then stolne, past him a play.

CI. INVITING A FRIEND TO SUPPER

TO night, grave sir, both my poore house, and I
  Doe equally desire your companie:
Not that we thinke us worthy such a ghest,
  But that your worth will dignifie our feast,
5 With those that come; whose grace may make that
                [seeme
  Something, which, else, could hope for no es-
                [teeme.

XCIX: [1] "that [trust to letters]   [2] deeds (Latin *facere*).
has increased thy skill."   C: [1] See *Epig.* 49.

It is the faire acceptance, Sir, creates
 The entertaynment perfect: not the cates.
Yet shall you have, to rectifie your palate,
10 An olive, capers, or some better sallade
Ushring the mutton; with a short-leg'd hen,
 If we can get her, full of egs, and then,
Limons, and wine for sauce: to these, a coney
 Is not to be despair'd of, for our money;
15 And, though fowle, now, be scarce, yet there are
            [clarkes,
 The skie not falling, thinke we may have larkes.
Ile tell you of more, and lye, so you will come:
 Of partrich, pheasant, wood-cock, of which some
May yet be there; and godwit, if we can:
20 Knat, raile, and ruffe too.[1] How so ere, my man
Shall reade a piece of *Virgil*, *Tacitus*,
 Livie, or of some better booke to us,
Of which wee'll speake our minds, amidst our meate;
 And Ile professe no verses to repeate:
25 To this, if ought appeare, which I know not of,
 That will the pastrie, not my paper, show of.
Digestive cheese, and fruit there sure will bee;
 But that, which most doth take my *Muse*, and
            [mee,
Is a pure cup of rich *Canary*-wine,
30 Which is the *Mermaids*, now, but shall be mine:
Of which had *Horace*, or *Anacreon* tasted,
 Their lives, as doe their lines, till now had lasted.
Tabacco, *Nectar*, or the *Thespian* spring,[2]
 Are all but *Luthers* beere,[3] to this I sing.
35 Of this we will sup free, but moderately,
 And we will have no *Pooly'*, or *Parrot*[4] by;

CI: [1] The godwit, knat, raile, and ruffe are all edible birds.

[2] Tobacco was often said to be drunk; the Thespian spring was associated with the Muses.

[3] German beer, considered inferior to English wine.

[4] two informers, identified by Mark Eccles with Robert Poley and perhaps Henry Parrot (cf. *Epig.* 71). RES, XIII (1937), 385–97. Poley witnessed the stabbing of Christopher Marlowe.

Nor shall our cups make any guiltie men:
　　But, at our parting, we will be, as when
We innocently met. No simple word,
40　　　That shall be utter'd at our mirthfull boord,
Shall make us sad next morning: or affright
　　The libertie, that wee'll enjoy to night.

CII. TO WILLIAM EARLE OF PEMBROKE

I Doe but name thee *Pembroke*,[1] and I find
　　It is an *Epigramme*, on all man-kind;
Against the bad, but of, and to the good:
　　Both which are ask'd, to have thee understood.
5　Nor could the age have mist thee, in this strife
　　Of vice, and vertue; wherein all great life
Almost, is exercis'd: and scarse one knowes,
　　To which, yet, of the sides himselfe he owes.
They follow vertue, for reward, to day;
10　　To morrow vice, if shee give better pay:
And are so good, and bad, just at a price,
　　As nothing else discernes the vertue' or vice.
But thou, whose noblêsse keeps one stature still,
　　And one true posture, though besieg'd with ill
15　Of what ambition, faction, pride can raise;
　　Whose life, ev'n they, that envie it, must praise;
That art so reverenc'd, as[2] thy comming in,
　　But in the view, doth interrupt their sinne;
Thou must draw more: and they, that hope to see
20　　The common-wealth still safe, must studie thee.

CII:　[1] See the Dedication to the　　[2] that.
Epigrammes.

CIII. TO MARY LADY WROTH[1]

HOw well, faire crowne of your faire sexe, might hee,
    That but the twi-light[2] of your sprite did see,
And noted for what flesh such soules were fram'd,
    Know you to be a *Sydney*, though un-named?
5   And, being nam'd, how little doth that name
    Need any *Muses* praise to give it fame?
Which is, it selfe, the *imprese*[3] of the great,
    And glorie of them all, but to repeate!
Forgive me then, if mine but say you are
10 A *Sydney*: but in that extend as farre
As lowdest praisers, who perhaps would find
    For every part a character[4] assign'd.
My praise is plaine, and where so ere profest,
    Becomes none more then you, who need it least.

CIV. TO SUSAN COUNTESSE OF MONTGOMERY[1]

WEre they that nam'd you, prophets? Did they see,
    Even in the dew of grace, what you would bee?
Or did our times require it, to behold
    A new *Susanna*,[2] equall to that old?
5   Or, because some scarce thinke that storie true,
    To make those faithfull, did the *Fates* send you?
And to your *Scene* lent no lesse dignitie
    Of birth, of match, of forme, of chastitie?

CIII: [1] daughter of Sir Robert Sidney, who died when she was a child, and niece of Sir Philip. Jonson dedicated the *Alchemist* to her. See also *Epig.* 105.
  [2] early morning light.
  [3] emblem. "Mary" means "exalted" according to William Camden, *Remaines Concerning Britaine* (1637 ed.), p. 100.

[4] emblematic representation of moral qualities.
CIV: [1] Lady Susan de Vere (1587–1629), daughter of the Earl of Oxford. She married Sir Philip Herbert, who became Earl of Montgomery in 1605.
  [2] Her virtuous story is told in the book of Susanna in the Apocrypha.

Or, more then borne for the comparison
10   Of former age, or glorie of our one,
Were you advanced, past those times, to be
The light, and marke unto posteritie?
Judge they, that can: here I have rais'd to show
A picture, which the world for yours must know,
15   And like it too; if they looke equally:[3]
If not, 'tis fit for you, some should envy.

CV. TO MARY LADY WROTH

MA*dame*,[1] had all antiquitie beene lost,
All historie seal'd up, and fables crost;[2]
That we had left us, nor by time, nor place,
Least mention of a *Nymph*, a *Muse*, a *Grace*,
5   But even their names were to be made a-new,
Who could not but create them all, from you?
He, that but saw you weare the wheaten hat,[3]
Would call you more then *Ceres*, if not that:
And, drest in shepheards tyre, who would not say:
10   You were the bright *Oenone*, *Flora*, or *May?*
If dancing, all would cry th'*Idalian* Queene,[4]
Were leading forth the *Graces* on the greene:
And, armed to the chase, so bare her bow
Diana'alone, so hit, and hunted so.[5]
15   There's none so dull, that for your stile would aske,
That saw you put on *Pallas* plumed caske:
Or, keeping your due state, that would not cry,
There *Juno* sate, and yet no Peacock by.[6]
So are you *Natures Index*, and restore,
20   I' your selfe, all treasure lost of th'age before.

---

[3] justly.
CV: [1] See *Epig.* 103.
     [2] crossed out.
[3] As goddess of harvest, Ceres
is regularly represented as wearing
such a garland.

[4] Venus.
[5] Diana was goddess of hunting.
[6] The peacock was sacred to Juno.

CVI. TO SIR EDWARD HERBERT

IF men get name, for some one vertue: Then,
    What man art thou, that art so many men,
All-vertuous *Herbert!*[1] on whose every part
    Truth might spend all her voyce, *Fame* all her art.
5 Whether thy learning they would take, or wit,
    Or valour, or thy judgement seasoning it,
Thy standing upright to thy selfe, thy ends
    Like straight, thy pietie to God, and friends:
Their latter praise would still the greatest bee,
10   And yet, they, all together, lesse then thee.

CVII. TO CAPTAYNE HUNGRY

DOe what you come for, Captayne, with your newes;
    That's, sit, and eate: doe not my eares abuse.
I oft looke on false coyne, to know't from true:
    Not that I love it, more, then I will you.
5 Tell the grosse *Dutch* those grosser tales of yours,
    How great you were with their two Emperours;[1]
And yet are with their Princes: Fill them full
    Of your *Moravian* horse, *Venetian* bull.[2]
Tell them, what parts yo'have tane, whence run away,
10   What States yo'have gull'd, and which yet keepes
            [yo'in pay.
Give them your services, and embassies
    In *Ireland, Holland, Sweden,* pompous lies,
In *Hungary,* and *Poland, Turkie* too;
    What at *Ligorne, Rome, Florence* you did doe:

CVI: [1] philosopher (1583–1648) and poet, brother of George Herbert; later Lord Herbert of Cherbury.
CVII: [1] The Netherlands, lost to the Hapsburgs in 1579, had had two stadtholders, the Princes of Orange, William I (1579–84) and Maurice (1587–1625). H&S suggest instead the Germans Ferdinand I (1558–62) and Maximilian (1562–76).
[2] Moravian horses were fine Czech animals, but it is not clear what Venetian bulls were.

15   And, in some yeere, all these together heap'd,
         For which there must more sea, and land be
                                                [leap'd,
      If but to be beleev'd you have the hap,
         Then can a flea at twise[3] skip i'the Map.[4]
      Give your yong States-men, (that first make you
                                                [drunke,
20   And then lye with you, closer, then a punque,
      For newes) your *Ville-royes,* and *Silleries,*
         Janin's, your *Nuncio's,* and your *Tuilleries,*
      Your *Arch-Dukes* Agents, and your *Beringhams,*[5]
         That are your wordes of credit. Keepe your Names
25   Of *Hannow, Shieter-huissen, Popenheim,*
         Hans-spiegle, Rotteinberg, and *Boutersheim,*[6]
      For your next meale: this you are sure of. Why
         Will you part with them, here, unthriftely?
      Nay, now you puffe, tuske,[7] and draw up your chin,
30   Twirle the poore chaine you run a feasting in.
      Come, be not angrie, you are *Hungry*; eate;
         Doe what you come for, Captayne, There's your
                                                [meate.

---

[3] on two occasions.
[4] For a flea to "skip in the
Map" seems to be an unrecorded
proverb.
[5] various diplomatic names.
Ville-roy was a French Secretary
of State under Henry IV; Sillerie
was his chancellor; Janin was,
Newdigate suggests, Pierre
Jeannin, French statesman.
Nuncios are papal representatives;
the Tuilleries is part of the French
palace. Beringham is probably
Pierre de Beringhen (d. 1619),

Valet de Chambre and Commis-
saire des Guerres for Henry IV;
he later held high positions under
Louis XIII.
[6] Hannow is the modern city of
Hanou; Rotteinberg is Rothen-
burg. The other names are
coined: Shieter-huissen means
"privy"; Popenheim probably is
"puppet's home"; Hans-spiegle
"fool's mirror"; and Boutersheim
"butter home."
[7] show the teeth.

CVIII. TO TRUE SOULDIERS[1]

STrength of my Countrey, whilst I bring to view
    Such as are misse-call'd Captaynes, and wrong
                             [you;
And your high names: I doe desire, that thence
    Be nor put on you, nor you take offence.
5   I sweare by your true friend, my *Muse*, I love
    Your great profession; which I once,[2] did prove:
And did not shame it with my actions, then,
    No more, then I dare now doe, with my pen.
He that not trusts me, having vow'd thus much,
10   But's angry for the Captayne,[3] still: is such.

CIX. TO SIR HENRY NEVIL

WHo now calls on thee, *Nevil*,[1] is a *Muse*,
    That serves nor fame, nor titles; but doth chuse
Where vertue makes them both, and that's in thee:
    Where all is faire, beside thy pedigree.
5   Thou are not one, seek'st miseries with hope,
    Wrestlest with dignities, or fain'st a scope
Of service to the publique, when the end
    Is private gaine, which hath long guilt to friend.
Thou rather striv'st the matter to possesse,
10   And elements of honor, then the dresse;
To make thy lent life, good against the *Fates:*
    And first to know thine owne state, then the
                             [States.

CVIII: [1] also printed in "To the Reader," ll. 131–40, appended to *Poetaster*, which had offended some of the military.
  [2] in his youth, in Flanders.
  [3] Hungry, in the previous epigram.

CIX: [1] (c. 1564–1615) knighted in 1599 but imprisoned because of implication in the Essex plot. Nevil was not in James's favor because of his sympathy with the popular party.

To be the same in roote, thou art in height;
>And that thy soule should give thy flesh her
>[weight.

15 Goe on, and doubt not, what posteritie,
>Now I have sung thee thus, shall judge of thee.

Thy deedes, unto thy name, will prove new wombes,
Whil'st others toyle for titles to their tombes.

CX. TO CLEMENT EDMONDS, ON HIS
CAESARS *Commentaries observed, and translated*

NOt *Caesars*[1] deeds, nor all his honors wonne,
>In these west-parts, nor when that warre was done,

The name of *Pompey* for an enemie,
>*Cato's* to boote, *Rome*, and her libertie,

5 All yeelding to his fortune, nor, the while,
>To have engrav'd these acts, with his owne stile,[2]

And that so strong and deepe, as 't might be thought,
>He wrote, with the same spirit that he fought,

Nor that his worke liv'd in the hands of foes,
10 Un-argued then, and yet hath fame from those;

Not all these, *Edmonds*, or what else put too,
>Can so speake *Caesar*, as thy labours doe.

For, where his person liv'd scarce one just age,
>And that, midst envy, and parts;[3] then fell by
>[rage:

15 His deedes too dying, but in bookes (whose good
>How few have read! how fewer understood?)

Thy learned hand, and true *Promethean* art
>(As by a new creation) part by part,

In every counsell, stratageme, designe,
20 Action, or engine, worth a note of thine,

T'all future time, not onely doth restore
>His life, but makes, that he can dye no more.

CX: [1] Edmonds (c. 1564–
1622) published an analysis of
Caesar's *Gallic Wars* in 1600, re-
printed in 1604 and 1609; this
epigram and the next were pre-
fixed to the 1609 edition.
   [2] stylus.
   [3] part-fray, a conflict between
two parties (NED).

CXI. TO THE SAME; ON THE SAME

WHo *Edmonds*, reades thy booke, and doth not see
    What th'antique souldiers were, the moderne
         [bee?
Wherein thou shew'st, how much the latter are
    Beholding, to this master of the warre;
5   And that, in action, there is nothing new,
    More, then to varie what our elders knew:
Which all, but ignorant Captaynes will confesse:
    Nor to give *Caesar* this, makes ours the lesse.
Yet thou, perhaps, shalt meet some tongues will
         [grutch,
10   That to the world thou should'st reveale so much,
And thence, deprave thee, and thy worke. To those
    Caesar stands up, as from his urne late rose,
By thy great helpe: and doth proclaime by mee,
    They murder him againe, that envie thee.

CXII. TO A WEAKE GAMSTER IN POETRY

WIth thy small stocke, why art thou ventring still,
    At this so subtile sport: and play'st so ill?
Think'st thou it is meere fortune, that can win?
    Or thy ranke setting?[1] that thou dar'st put in
5   Thy all, at all: and what so ere I doe,
    Art still at that, and think'st to blow me'up too?
I cannot for the stage a *Drama* lay,
    Tragick, or *Comick*; but thou writ'st the play.
I leave thee there, and giving way, entend
10   An *Epick* poeme; thou hast the same end.
I modestly quit that, and thinke to write,
    Next morne, an *Ode:* Thou mak'st a song ere
         [night.

CXII: [1] excessive betting.

I passe to *Elegies;* Thou meet'st me there:
>   To *Satyres;* and thou dost pursue me. Where,
15 Where shall I scape thee? in an *Epigramme?*
>   O, (thou cry'st out) that is thy proper game.
Troth, if it be, I pitty thy ill lucke;
>   That both for wit, and sense, so oft dost plucke,[2]
And never art encounter'd, I confesse:
20   Nor scarce dost colour for it, which is lesse.
Pr'y thee, yet save thy rest; give ore in time:
>   There's no vexation, that can make thee prime.

CXIII. TO SIR THOMAS OVERBURY

SO *Phoebus* makes me worthy of his bayes,
>   As but to speake thee, *Overbury,*[1] is praise:
So, where thou liv'st, thou mak'st life understood!
>   Where, what makes others great, doth keepe thee
>   [good!
5   I thinke, the *Fate* of court thy comming crav'd,
>   That the wit there, and manners might be sav'd:
For since, what ignorance, what pride is fled!
>   And letters, and humanitie in the stead!
Repent thee not of thy faire precedent,
10   Could make such men, and such a place repent:
Nor may'any feare, to loose of their degree,
>   Who'in such ambition can but follow thee.

---

[2] Plucke (to draw a card), en-
countered, colour for it, rest (re-
maining stake), and make prime
(have a winning hand) are all
terms in the card game primero,
an ancestor of poker.
CXIII: [1] (1 5 8 1 – 1 6 1 3)
knighted in 1608; murdered by
poison in a sensational crime of
the day. Overbury tried to win
Miss Philip Sidney (see next
epigram) by writing his poem
The Wife to her (published
1614). Jonson says in the *Con-
versations with Drummond* that
he acted as intermediary (H&S
I.138).

CXIV. TO MRS. PHILIP SYDNEY[1]

I Must beleeve some miracles still bee
　　When *Sydnyes* name I heare, or face I see:
For *Cupid*, who (at first) tooke vaine delight,
　　In meere out-formes,[2] untill he lost his sight,
5　Hath chang'd his soule, and made his object you:
　　Where finding so much beautie met with vertue,
He hath not onely gain'd himselfe his eyes,
　　But, in your love, made all his servants wise.

CXV. ON THE TOWNES HONEST MAN

YOu wonder, who this is! and, why I name
　　Him not, aloud, that boasts so good a fame:
Naming so many, too! But, this is one,
　　Suffers no name, but a description:
5　Being no vitious person, but the vice[1]
　　About the towne; and knowne too, at that price.
A subtle thing, that doth affections win
　　By speaking well o' the company' it's[2] in.
Talkes loud, and baudy, has a gather'd deale
10　Of newes, and noyse, to sow[3] out a long meale.
Can come from *Tripoly*, leape stooles,[4] and winke,
　　Doe all, that longs to the *anarchy* of drinke,
Except the *duell*. Can sing songs, and catches;
　　Give every one his dose of mirth: and watches

CXIV: [1] daughter (1594–1620) of Sir Robert Sidney; married to Sir John Hobard. "Mrs." is equivalent to modern "Miss"; "Philip" is equivalent to "Philippa."
[2] outward forms.
CXV: [1] a stock character in the morality plays. Also, according to H&S, "vice" includes a pun on vice as iniquity—and iniquity involves the first name of Inigo Jones, Jonson's collaborator in producing masques and his enemy by this time. Thus H&S consider this epigram to be directed against Jones.
[2] Here and throughout the rest of the poem Jonson employs "it" instead of "he"—a contemptuous usage.
[3] perhaps, as H&S suggest, to be emended to "strow."
[4] some kinds of vigorous indoor sports.

15   Whose name's un-welcome to the present eare,
            And him it layes on; if he be not there.
        Tell's of him, all the tales, it selfe then makes;
            But, if it shall be question'd, undertakes,
        It will deny all; and forsweare it too:
20   Not that it feares, but will not have to doo
        With such a one. And therein keepes it's word.
            'Twill see it's sister naked, ere a sword.
        At every meale, where it doth dine, or sup,
            The cloth's no sooner gone, but it gets up
25   And, shifting of it's faces, doth play more
            Parts, then th'*Italian* could doe, with his dore.[5]
        Acts old *Iniquitie*, and in the fit
            Of miming, gets th'opinion of a wit.
        Executes men in picture. By defect,
30   From friendship, is it's owne fames architect.
        An inginer, in slanders, of all fashions,
            That seeming prayses, are, yet accusations.
        Describ'd, it's thus: Defin'd would you it have?
            Then, *The townes honest Man's* her errant'st
                                                    [knave.

CXVI. TO SIR WILLIAM JEPHSON

        JE*phson*,[1] thou man of men, to whose lov'd name
            All gentrie, yet, owe part of their best flame!
        So did thy vertue'enforme, thy wit sustaine
            That age, when thou stood'st up the master-
                                                    [braine:
5   Thou wert the first, mad'st merit know her strength,
            And those that lack'd it, to suspect at length,
        'Twas not entayl'd on title.[2] That some word
            Might be found out as good, and not *my Lord.*
        That *Nature* no such difference had imprest
10   In men, but every bravest was the best:

---

[5] What "th'Italian could doe,   CXVI: [1] knighted in 1603;
with his dore," is not known.   friend of Jonson.
                                         [2] dependent upon his title.

That bloud not mindes, but mindes did bloud adorne:
    And to live great, was better, then great borne.
These were thy knowing arts: which who doth now
    Vertuously practise must at least allow
15 Them in, if not, from thee; or must commit
    A desperate soloecisme in truth and wit.

CXVII. ON GROYNE

GR*oyne*, come of age, his state[1] sold out of hand
    For'his whore: *Groyne* doth still occupy[2] his land.

CXVIII. ON GUT

GU*t* eates all day, and lechers all the night,
    So all his meate he tasteth[1] over, twise:
And, striving so to double his delight,
    He makes himselfe a thorough-fare of vice.
5 Thus, in his belly, can he change a sin
    Lust it comes out, that gluttony went in.

CXIX. TO SIR RAPH SHELTON[1]

NOt he that flies the court for want of clothes,
    At hunting railes, having no guift in othes,
Cryes out 'gainst cocking, since he cannot bet,
    Shuns prease,[2] for two maine causes, poxe, and
                              [debt,
5 With me can merit more, then that good man,
    Whose dice not doing well, to'a pulpit ran.
No, *Shelton*, give me thee, canst want all these,
    But dost it out of judgement, not disease;
Dar'st breath in any ayre; and with safe skill,
10   Till thou canst finde the best, choose the least ill.

CXVII: [1] estate.
  [2] with a pun: to cohabit with.
CXVIII: [1] also meaning to
have carnal knowledge of.

CXIX: [1] knighted in 1607.
Shelton also appears humorously
in *Epig.* 133.
  [2] press, crowd.

That to the vulgar canst thy selfe apply,
    Treading a better path, not contrary;
And, in their errors maze, thine owne way know:
    Which is to live to conscience, not to show.
15 He, that, but living halfe his age, dyes such;
    Makes, the whole longer, then 'twas given him,
                                    [much.

CXX. EPITAPH ON S.P. A CHILD OF Q. EL. CHAPPEL[1]

WEepe with me all you that read
    This little storie:
And know, for whom a teare you shed,
    Death's selfe is sorry.
5   'Twas a child, that so did thrive
    In grace, and feature,
As *Heaven* and *Nature* seem'd to strive
    Which own'd the creature.
Yeeres he numbred scarse thirteene
10   When *Fates* turn'd cruell,
Yet three fill'd *Zodiackes* had he beene
    The stages jewell;
And did act (what now we mone)
    Old men so duely,
15 As, sooth, the *Parcae*[2] thought him one,
    He plai'd so truely.
So, by error, to his fate
    They all consented;
But viewing him since (alas, too late)
20   They have repented.
And have sought (to give new birth)
    In bathes to steepe him;
But, being so much too good for earth,
    Heaven vowes to keepe him.

CXX: [1] Salomon Pavy was a   Elizabeth's Chapel.
boy actor in plays which Jonson [2] the Fates.
wrote for the Children of Queen

CXXI. TO BENJAMIN RUDYERD

RU*dyerd*,[1] as lesser dames, to great ones use,
    My lighter comes, to kisse thy learned *Muse;*[2]
Whose better studies while shee emulates,
    Shee learnes to know long difference of their
                        [states.
5   Yet is the office not to be despis'd,
    If onely love should make the action pris'd:
Nor he, for friendship, to be thought unfit,
    That strives, his manners should procede his wit.

CXXII. TO THE SAME

IF I would wish, for truth, and not for show,
    The aged *Saturne's* age,[1] and rites to know;
If I would strive to bring backe times, and trie
    The world's pure gold, and wise simplicitie;
5   If I would vertue set, as shee was yong,
    And heare her speake with one, and her first
                        [tongue;
If holiest friend-ship, naked to the touch,
    I would restore, and keepe it ever such;
I need no other arts, but studie thee:
10   Who prov'st, all these were, and againe may bee.

CXXIII. TO THE SAME

WRiting thy selfe, or judging others writ,
    I know not which th'hast most, candor, or wit:
But both th'hast so, as who affects the state
    Of the best writer, and judge, should emulate.

CXXI: [1](1 5 7 2 – 1 6 5 8)   lished in 1660, after his death.
knighted 1618.   CXXII: [1] The Golden Age.
   [2] Rudyerd's poems were pub-

CXXIV. EPITAPH ON ELIZABETH, L.H.[1]

WOuld'st thou heare, what man can say
    In a little? Reader, stay.
Under-neath this stone doth lye
    As much beautie, as could dye:
5 Which in life did harbour give
    To more vertue, then doth live.
If, at all, shee had a fault,
    Leave it buryed in this vault.
One name was *Elizabeth*,
10   Th'other let it sleepe with death:
Fitter, where it dyed, to tell,
    Then that it liv'd at all. Farewell.

CXXV. TO SIR WILLIAM UVEDALE

UV'*dale*,[1] thou piece of the first times, a man
    Made for what *Nature* could, or *Vertue* can;
Both whose dimensions, lost, the world might finde
    Restored in thy body, and thy minde!
5 Who sees a soule, in such a body set,
    Might love the treasure for the cabinet.
But I, no child, no foole, respect the kinde,
    The full, the flowing graces there enshrin'd;
Which (would the world not mis-call't flatterie)
10   I could adore, almost t'idolatrie.

CXXIV: [1] "L.H." has not been identified.

CXXV: [1] knighted in November 1613; later appointed Treasurer of the Chamber and Treasurer of the Army of the North.

CXXVI. TO HIS LADY, THEN MRS. CARY[1]

REtyr'd, with purpose your faire worth to praise,
   'Mongst *Hampton* shades, and *Phoebus*[2] grove of
                         [bayes,
I pluck'd a branch; the jealous god did frowne,
   And bad me lay th'usurped laurell downe:
5 Said I wrong'd him, and (which was more) his love.
   I answer'd, *Daphne* now no paine can prove.[3]
Phoebus replyed. Bold head, it is not shee:
   Cary my love is, *Daphne* but my tree.[4]

CXXVII. TO ESME, LORD 'AUBIGNY

IS there a hope, that Man would thankefull bee,
   If I should faile, in gratitude, to thee
To whom I am so bound, lov'd *Aubigny*?[1]
   No, I doe, therefore, call *Posteritie*
5 Into the debt; and reckon on her head,
   How full of want, how swallow'd up, how dead
I, and this *Muse* had beene, if thou hadst not
   Lent timely succours, and new life begot:
So, all reward, or name, that growes to mee
10   By her attempt, shall still be owing thee.
And, than this same, I know no abler way
   To thanke thy benefits: which is, to pay.

CXXVI: [1] daughter of Sir Edward Carey. "Mrs." means "Miss."
   [2] Apollo, god of poetic inspiration.
   [3] experience.
   [4] Daphne was loved by Apollo. She fled him and, praying for help, was turned into a laurel tree.
CXXVII: [1] a patron (1574–1624) in whose house Jonson lived for several years and to whom he dedicated *Sejanus*.

CXXVIII. TO WILLIAM ROE

RO*e*[1] (and my joy to name) th'art now, to goe
    Countries, and climes, manners, and men to know,
T'extract, and choose the best of all these knowne,
    And those to turne to bloud, and make thine
                  [owne:
5   May windes as soft as breath of kissing friends,
    Attend thee hence; and there, may all thy ends,
As the beginnings here, prove purely sweet,
    And perfect in a circle alwayes meet.
So, when we, blest with thy returne, shall see
10   Thy selfe, with thy first thoughts, brought home
                  [by thee,
We each to other may this voyce enspire;
    This is that good *Aeneas*, past through fire,
Through seas, stormes, tempests: and imbarqu'd for
                  [hell,
    Came backe untouch'd. This man hath travail'd[2]
                  [well.

CXXIX. TO MIME[1]

THat, not a paire of friends each other see,
    But the first question is, when one saw thee?
That there's no journey set, or thought upon,
    To *Braynford, Hackney, Bow*,[2] but thou mak'st
                  [one;
5   That scarse the Towne designeth any feast
    To which thou'rt not a weeke, bespoke a guest;
That still th'art made the suppers flagge, the drum,
    The very call, to make all others come:
Think'st thou, *Mime*, this is great? or, that they strive
10   Whose noyse shall keepe thy miming most alive,

CXXVIII: [1] See *Epig.* 70.
  [2] in both senses: traveled and travailed (worked).

CXXIX: [1] H&S consider this to be another satire on Inigo Jones.
  [2] three English towns.

Whil'st thou dost rayse some Player, from the grave,
 Out-dance the *Babion*,[3] or out-boast the Brave;
Or (mounted on a stoole) thy face doth hit
 On some new gesture, that's imputed wit?
15 O, runne not proud of this. Yet, take thy due.
 Thou dost out-zany *Cokely, Pod*; nay, *Gue*:[4]
And thine owne *Coriat*[5] too. But (would'st thou see)
 Men love thee not for this: They laugh at thee.

CXXX. TO ALPHONSO FERRABOSCO,
on his Booke

TO urge, my lov'd *Alphonso*,[1] that bold fame,
 Of building townes, and making wilde beasts
         [tame,[2]
Which *Musick* had; or speake her knowne effects,
 That shee removeth cares, sadnesse ejects,
5 Declineth anger, perswades clemencie,
 Doth sweeten mirth, and heighten pietie,
And is t'a body, often, ill inclin'd,
 No lesse a sov'raigne cure, then to the mind;
T'alledge, that greatest men were not asham'd,
10 Of old, even by her practise to be fam'd;
To say, indeed, shee were the soule of heaven,
 That the eight spheare, no lesse, then planets
         [seaven,
Mov'd by her order, and the ninth more high,
 Including all, were thence call'd harmonie:

3 baboon.
4 Cokely was a jester who im-
provised at entertainments; Pod
was a puppet master; Gue was ap-
parently some stupid showman.
5 Thomas Coryate (1577–
1617), author of the *Crudities*.
CXXX: 1 Ferrabosco (d. 1628)
was a famous composer, per-
former, and teacher; among his
pupils was Prince Henry. He pub-
lished his *Ayres* in 1609, to which
this epigram was prefixed. The
volume includes a number of
Jonson's songs. *Epig.* 131 first ap-
peared in his *Lessons* of the same
year.
2 legendary powers attributed
to the music of Orpheus.

15   I, yet, had utter'd nothing on thy part,
     When these were but the praises of the Art.
    But when I have said, the proofes of all these bee
     Shed in thy Songs; 'tis true: but short of thee.

CXXXI. TO THE SAME

WHen we doe give, *Alphonso*, to the light,
    A worke of ours, we part with our owne right;
For, then, all mouthes will judge, and their owne way:
    The learn'd have no more priviledge, then the lay.
5   And though we could all men, all censures heare,
    We ought not give them taste, we had an eare.
For, if the hum'rous world will talke at large,
    They should be fooles, for me, at their owne
          [charge.
Say, this, or that man they to thee preferre;
10   Even those for whom they doe this, know they
          [erre:
And would (being ask'd the truth) ashamed say,
    They were not to be nam'd on the same day.
Then stand unto thy selfe, not seeke without
    For fame, with breath soone kindled, soone blowne
          [out.

CXXXII. TO MR. JOSUAH SYLVESTER[1]

IF to admire were to commend, my praise
    Might then both thee, thy worke and merit raise:
But, as it is (the Child of Ignorance,
    And utter stranger to all ayre of *France*)[2]
5   How can I speake of thy great paines, but erre?
    Since they can only judge, that can conferre.[3]

CXXXII: [1] translator (1563–1618), especially of Guillaume du Bartas' *Divine Weekes*. This epigram first appeared in the 1605 edition.

[2] that is, Jonson did not know French at this time.

[3] compare, so as to be able to translate.

Behold! the reverend shade of *Bartas* stands
    Before my thought, and (in thy right) commands
That to the world I publish, for him, this;
10   *Bartas doth wish thy* English *now were his.*
So well in that are his inventions wrought,
    As his will now be the *translation* thought,
Thine the *originall*; and *France* shall boast,
    No more, those mayden glories shee hath lost.

CXXXIII. ON THE FAMOUS VOYAGE

NO more let *Greece* her bolder fables tell
    Of *Hercules*, or *Theseus* going to *hell*,
Orpheus, *Ulysses*: or the *Latine Muse*,
    With tales of *Troyes* just knight,[1] our faiths abuse:
5   We have a *Shelton*, and a *Heyden*[2] got,
    Had power to act, what they to faine had not.
All, that they boast of *Styx*, of *Acheron*,
    Cocytus, *Phlegeton*,[3] our[4] have prov'd in one;[5]
The filth, stench, noyse: save only what was there
10   Subtly distinguish'd, was confused[6] here.
Their[7] wherry[8] had no saile, too; ours had none:
    And in it, two more horride knaves, then *Charon*.[9]
Arses were heard to croake, in stead of frogs;[10]
    And for one *Cerberus*,[11] the whole coast was dogs.
15 *Furies* there wanted not: each scold was ten.
    And, for the cryes of *Ghosts*, women, and men,

CXXXIII: [1] Virgil's story of Aeneas. The "Famous Voyage" is a mock epic of sorts.

[2] Shelton is mentioned in *Epig*. 119. Heyden has not been identified.

[3] four rivers of Hades.

[4] "Our" was still used in 1600 for "ours."

[5] the Fleet Ditch, running south into the Thames.

[6] so mixed together as to be impossible to separate.

[7] i.e., the Greek and Latin heroes already named.

[8] light rowing boat.

[9] god of Hades who ferried the souls of the dead across the rivers Styx and Acheron.

[10] as reported in Aristophanes' play of this name.

[11] three-headed watchdog of Hades.

Laden with plague-sores, and their sinnes, were heard,
Lash'd by their consciences, to die, affeard.
Then let the former age, with this content her,
20   Shee brought the *Poets* forth, but ours th'adven-
[ter.[12]

The Voyage It Selfe

I Sing the brave adventure of two wights,
And pitty 'tis, I cannot call 'hem knights:
One was; and he, for brawne, and braine, right able
To have beene stiled of King *Arthurs* table.
25   The other was a squire, of faire degree;
But, in the action, greater man then hee:
Who gave, to take at his returne from *Hell*,
His three for one.[13] Now, lordings, listen well.
        It was the day, what time the powerfull *Moone*
30   Makes the poore *Banck-side* creature wet it' shoone,[14]
In it' owne hall; when these (in worthy scorne
Of those, that put out moneyes, on returne
From *Venice, Paris,* or some in-land passage
Of sixe times to, and fro, without embassage,[15]
35   Or him that backward went to *Berwicke,*[16] or which
Did dance the famous Morrisse, unto *Norwich*)[17]
At *Bread-streets* Mermaid, having din'd, and merry,
Propos'd to goe to *Hol'borne*[18] in a wherry:
A harder tasque, then either his to *Bristo'*,
40   Or his to *Antwerpe.*[19] Therefore, once more, list ho'.
        A *Docke*[20] there is, that called is *Avernus,*
Of some *Bride-well,* and may, in time, concerne us
All, that are readers: but, me thinkes 'tis od,
That all this while I have forgot some *god,*

[12] adventure.
[13] a large profit from a voyage.
[14] i.e., at high tide. "It" in this line and the next is used contemptuously.
[15] being ambassadors.
[16] a publicity stunt of the day.
[17] Will Kemp, whose publicity for the feat was considerable.

[18] part of London north of the Thames.
[19] daring contemporary feats of rowing across the English Channel.
[20] Bridewell Dock, at the outlet of the Fleet Ditch; Jonson also refers to the prison located there.

45   Or *goddesse* to invoke, to stuffe my verse;
      And with both bombard-stile, and phrase, rehearse
      The many perills of this *Port*, and how
      Sans'helpe of *Sybil*, or a golden bough,[21]
      Or magick sacrifice, they past along!
50   *Alcides*,[22] be thou succouring to my song.
      Thou hast seene *hell*[23] (some say) and know'st all
                            [nookes there,
      Canst tell me best, how every *Furie* lookes there,
      And art a *god*, if *Fame* thee not abuses,
      Alwayes at hand, to aide the merry *Muses*.
55   Great *Club-fist*,[24] though thy backe, and bones be sore,
      Still, with thy former labours; yet, once more,
      Act a brave worke, call it thy last adventry:[25]
      But hold my torch, while I describe the entry
      To this dire passage. Say, thou stop thy nose:
60   'Tis but light paines: Indeede this *Dock's* no rose.
         In the first jawes appear'd that ugly monster,
      Ycleped *Mud*, which, when their oares did once stirre,
      Belch'd forth an ayre, as hot, as at the muster
      Of all your night-tubs, when the carts doe cluster,
65   Who shall discharge first his merd-urinous[26] load:
      Thorough her wombe they make their famous road,
      Betweene two walls; where, on one side, to scar men,
      Were seene your ugly *Centaures*, yee call Car-men,[27]
      Gorgonian scolds, and *Harpyes*: on the other
70   Hung stench, diseases, and old filth, their mother,
      With famine, wants, and sorrowes many a dosen,
      The least of which was to the plague a cosen.[28]
      But they unfrighted passe, though many a privie
      Spake to 'hem louder, then the oxe in *Livie*:[29]

[21] as Aeneas was assisted in *Aeneid* VI.

[22] Hercules.

[23] He went there to rescue Alcestis.

[24] Hercules once accidentally killed a man by striking him with his fist. He also is frequently pictured holding a great club.

[25] adventure.

[26] composed of excrement and urine.

[27] those who drive the dung carts.

[28] cousin.

[29] The Roman historian reports portents of oxen speaking.

75   And many a sinke[30] pour'd out her rage anenst[31] 'hem;
      But still their valour, and their vertue fenc't[32] 'hem,
      And, on they went, like *Castor* brave, and *Pollux*:
      Ploughing the mayne. When, see (the worst of all
                                              [lucks)
      They met the second Prodigie, would feare a
80   Man, that had never heard of a *Chimaera*.[33]
      One said, it was bold *Briareus*,[34] or the beadle,[35]
      (Who hath the hundred hands when he doth meddle)
      The other thought it *Hydra*, or the rock
      Made of the trull, that cut her fathers lock:[36]
85   But, comming neere,[37] they found it but a liter,[38]
      So huge, it seem'd, they could by no meanes quite[39]
                                              [her.
      Backe, cry'd their brace of *Charons*: they cry'd, no,
      No going backe; on still you rogues, and row.
      How hight the place? a voyce was heard, *Cocytus*.[40]
90   Row close then slaves. Alas, they will beshite us.
      No matter, stinkards, row. What croaking sound
      Is this we heare? of frogs? No, guts wind-bound,
      Over your heads: Well, row. At this a loud
      Crack did report it selfe, as if a cloud
95   Had burst with storme, and downe fell, *ab excelsis*,[41]
      Poore *Mercury*, crying out on *Paracelsus*,[42]
      And all his followers, that had so abus'd him:
      And, in so shitten sort, so long had us'd him:

[30] sewage drain.
[31] toward.
[32] protected.
[33] a fire-breathing monster with a lion's head, a goat's body, and a serpent's tail.
[34] a giant with a hundred heads.
[35] parish constable.
[36] "Jonson has copied the Roman poets in confusing the sea-monster Scylla with Scylla the daughter of Nisus of Megara, who, to win the love of Minos, cut off her father's hair on which his life depended." (H&S)
[37] nearer.
[38] lighter: barge.
[39] escape.
[40] the river of wailing in Hades.
[41] from above.
[42] some mercurial compound such as mercurous chloride (calomel). The Paracelsians had considered mercury to be one of the elements and had experimented with it in various medical and physical applications. It was much used in purges.

For (where[43] he[44] was the god of eloquence,
100 And subtiltie of mettalls) they dispense
His spirits, now, in pills, and eeke in potions,
Suppositories, cataplasmes,[45] and lotions.
But many Moones there shall not wane (quoth hee)
(In the meane time, let 'hem imprison mee)
105 But I will speake (and know I shall be heard)
Touching this cause, where they will be affeard
To answere me. And sure, it was th'intent
Of the grave fart, late let in parliament,[46]
Had it beene seconded, and not in fume
110 Vanish'd away: as you must all presume
Their *Mercury* did now. By this, the stemme
Of the hulke touch'd, and, as by *Polypheme*[47]
The slie *Ulysses* stole in a sheepes-skin,
The well-greas'd wherry now had got betweene,
115 And bad her *fare-well sough*,[48] unto the lurden:[49]
Never did bottom more betray her burden;
The meate-boate of Beares colledge, *Paris-garden*,[50]
Stunke not so ill; nor, when shee kist, *Kate Arden*.[51]
Yet, one day in the yeere, for sweet 'tis voyc't
120 And that is when it is the Lord *Maiors* foist.[52]
By this time had they reach'd the *Stygian* poole,
By which the *Masters* sweare, when, on the stoole
Of worship,[53] they their nodding chinnes doe hit
Against their breasts. Here, sev'rall ghosts did flit

[43] whereas.
[44] Mercury, as god of eloquence and metals.
[45] poultices.
[46] H&S identify the occasion as taking place in 1607, when there was a discussion in the House "on the peculiar manner in which Henry Ludlow said 'noe' to a message brought . . . from the Lords."
[47] the Cyclops past whom Odysseus escaped in the *Odyssey*.
[48] sigh.

[49] idleness; here apparently the slowness of the barge.
[50] Offal was carried by boat across the Thames to Paris Garden, near the Globe Theater, where bears and dogs were kept for baiting.
[51] the Moonbeam McSwine of early seventeenth-century London.
[52] the Mayor's barge, with a pun on the meaning *stink*.
[53] toilet.

125 About the shore, of farts, but late departed,
    White, black, blew, greene, and in more formes out-
                                        [started,
      Then all those *Atomi* ridiculous,
      Whereof old *Democrite,* and *Hill Nicholas,*[54]
      One said, the other swore, the world consists.
130 These be the cause of those thicke frequent mists
    Arising in that place, through which, who goes,
    Must trie the un-used valour[55] of a nose:
    And that ours did. For, yet, no nare[56] was tainted,
    Nor thumbe, nor finger to the stop acquainted,
135 But open, and un-armed encounter'd all:
    Whether it languishing stucke upon the wall,
    Or were precipitated downe the jakes,[57]
    And, after, swom abroad in ample flakes,
    Or, that it lay, heap'd like an usurers masse,
140 All was to them the same, they were to passe,
    And so they did, from *Stix,* to *Acheron:*
      The ever-boyling floud. Whose bankes upon
      Your *Fleet*-lane *Furies;*[58] and hot cookes doe dwell,
      That, with still-scalding steemes, make the place *hell.*
145 The sinkes[59] ran grease, and haire of meazled[60] hogs,
    The heads, houghs,[61] entrailes, and the hides of dogs:
    For, to say truth, what scullion is so nastie,
    To put the skins, and offall in a pastie?
      Cats there lay divers had beene flead,[62] and rosted,
150 And, after mouldie growne, againe were tosted,
    Then, selling not, a dish was tane to mince 'hem,
    But still, it seem'd, the ranknesse did convince[63] 'hem.
    For, here they were throwne in with'the melted pewter,
    Yet drown'd they not. They had five lives in future.

[54] Democritus was an epicu-
rean, founder of the Greek
atomic theory. Nicholas Hill was
a contemporary author of a work
on philosophy. See also Chaucer's
hende Nicholas, who had similar
difficulties in "The Miller's Tale."
[55] bravery.

[56] nostril.
[57] privy.
[58] cooks from Fleet Street.
[59] as above, n. 30.
[60] leprous.
[61] hocks.
[62] flayed.
[63] convict.

155   But 'mong'st these *Tiberts*,[64] who do'you thinke
                                        [there was?
        Old *Bankes*[65] the juggler,[66] our *Pythagoras*,
        Grave tutor to the learned horse. Both which,
        Being, beyond sea, burned for one witch:
        Their spirits transmigrated to a cat:
160   And, now, above the poole, a face right fat
        With great gray eyes, are lifted up, and mew'd;
        Thrise did it spit: thrise div'd. At last, it view'd
        Our brave *Heroes* with a milder glare,
        And, in a pittious tune, began. How dare
165   Your daintie nostrills (in so hot a season,
        When every clerke eates artichokes, and peason,[67]
        Laxative lettuce, and such windie meate[68])
        Tempte such a passage? when each privies seate
        Is fill'd with buttock? And the walls doe sweate
170   Urine, and plaisters?[69] when the noise doth beate
        Upon your eares, of discords so un-sweet?
        And out-cryes of the damned in the *Fleet*?[70]
        Cannot the *Plague*-bill keepe you backe? nor bells
        Of loud *Sepulchres*[71] with their hourely knells,
175   But you will visit grisly *Pluto's* hall?
        Behold where *Cerberus*, rear'd on the wall
        Of *Hol'borne* (three sergeants heads[72]) lookes ore,
        And stayes but till you come unto the dore!
        Tempt not his furie, *Pluto* is away:
180   And *Madame Caesar*, great *Proserpina*,[73]
        Is now from home. You lose your labours quite,
        Were you *Jove's* sonnes, or had *Alcides* might.
        They cry'd out *Pusse*. He told them he was *Bankes*,
        That had, so often, shew'd 'hem merry prankes.

---

[64] common word for cats.

[65] trainer of a famous performing horse. He was not dead, as Jonson implies. Pythagoras believed in the transmigration of souls.

[66] entertainer.

[67] the old plural of *pea*.

[68] food.

[69] daubings.

[70] prison.

[71] interments.

[72] named below in ll. 187–89.

[73] queen of Hades.

185   They laugh't, at his laugh-worthy fate. And past
      The tripple head without a sop.[74] At last,
      Calling for *Radamanthus*, that dwelt by,
      A sope-boyler; and *Æacus* him nigh,
      Who kept an ale-house; with my little *Minos*,[75]
190   An ancient pur-blinde fletcher,[76] with a high nose;
      They tooke 'hem all to witnesse of their action:
      And so went bravely backe, without protraction.[77]
            In memorie of which most liquid deed,
      The citie since hath rais'd a Pyramide.
195   And I could wish for their eterniz'd sakes,
      My *Muse* had plough'd with his, that sung *A-jax*.[78]

[74] Cerberus was bribed with food to permit one to go past him.

[75] the three judges of Hades: Rhadamanthus, Aeacus, and Minos.

[76] nearly or completely blind maker of arrows.

[77] delay.

[78] referring to Sir John Harrington's book, the *Metamorphosis of Ajax* (1596), with the current pronunciation of Ajax as *a jakes*.

THE FORREST

As Jonson explains "To the Reader" of *Under-wood, The Forrest* is a collection "of divers nature, and matter"—a miscellany. It is quite different from the *Epigrammes*, with which it was first published in the 1616 Folio.

In the first place, the poems here are almost all longer than Jonson's typical epigram and they are in general more serious. There are no caustic attacks upon individuals or types; otherwise the subject matter is more varied. Jonson seems to have been quite conscious of innovations which he was making in these poems but which have become so familiar today that one may miss their freshness. In the twelfth he writes to the Countess of Rutland of his "strange poems, which, as yet, Had not their forme touch'd by an English wit." Epistles like this one, deriving principally from those of Horace, were new to English poetry. The second poem, addressed to the Penshurst mansion and estate, home of the Sidney family, is the first example in English of its genre, the topographical poem, later imitated in Edmund Waller's "To Penshurst" and reaching its greatest popularity in "Cooper's Hill" of Sir John Denham.

Aside from content, the verse form is much more varied than that of the *Epigrammes*. Only four of these poems are in the near-universal couplet form of the other collection. The first sentence of the twelfth would be remarkable even for Milton, deliberately sustained as it is through nineteen lines. Another innovation appears in the fourteenth, an early attempt to introduce the complex form of the classical ode into English. Although not a very successful poem, it undoubtedly led to the fine Pindaric ode in *Under-wood* addressed to Sir Lucius Cary and Sir Henry Morison. Several songs are directed to Celia (Nos. 5, 6, and 9), the first used in *Volpone* and the second perhaps planned originally for the same play. The last is an independent production which today is Jonson's most famous poem. The fact that it is paraphrased or directly translated from several different prose passages in the *Epistles* of Philostratus does not obscure the fact that Jonson has brilliantly unified his source and has presented it with simplicity of diction and meter which Pope or Housman never excelled. The music to which it is sung today was written in the eighteenth century; if an earlier setting were made, it has not survived.

The Forrest, then, is both experimental and serious in its tone. It contains some of Jonson's finest work and in the last poem what is probably his best religious work in an area which he never learned to handle very well. In its diversification and high level of achievement the collection contrasts well with the larger collection of *Epigrammes*, to which it should not be considered as merely an appendage.

THE FORREST*

I. WHY I WRITE NOT OF LOVE

SOme act of *Love's* bound to reherse,[1]
I thought to binde him, in my verse:
Which when he felt, Away (quoth hee)
Can Poets hope to fetter mee?
5   It is enough, they once did get
Mars, and my *Mother,* in their net:[2]
I weare not these my wings in vaine.
With which he fled me: and againe,
Into my ri'mes could ne're be got
10   By any arte. Then wonder not,
That since, my numbers are so cold,
When *Love* is fled, and I grow old.

II. TO PENSHURST

THou art not, *Penshurst,*[1] built to envious show,
Of touch,[2] or marble; nor canst boast a row
Of polish'd pillars, or a roofe of gold:
Thou hast no lantherne,[3] whereof tales are told;

---

* translating *Silva,* a title which had been used for collections of occasional verse (especially by the Roman poet Statius).
I: [1] being required to relate some act of the god of love.
[2] referring to Vulcan's capture of his wife Venus (Cupid's mother) and her lover Mars in a net which he had made.
II: [1] the home of the Sidney family, in Kent. Sir Robert, brother of Sir Philip, was head of the household at this time.
[2] touchstone: fine black marble or basalt.
[3] lanthorn: a glassed-in room on the top of the house.

5   Or stayre, or courts; but stand'st an ancient pile,
            And these grudg'd at,[4] art reverenc'd the while.
     Thou joy'st in better markes, of soyle, of ayre,
            Of wood, of water: therein thou art faire.
     Thou hast thy walkes for health, as well as sport:
10   Thy *Mount*,[5] to which the *Dryads* doe resort,
     Where *Pan*, and *Bacchus* their high feasts have made,
            Beneath the broad beech, and the chest-nut shade;
     That taller tree, which of a nut was set,
            At his[6] great birth, where all the *Muses* met.
15   There, in the writhed barke, are cut the names
            Of many a *Sylvane*, taken with his flames.[7]
     And thence, the ruddy *Satyres* oft provoke
            The lighter *Faunes*, to reach thy *Ladies oke*.[8]
     Thy copp's, too, nam'd of *Gamage*,[9] thou hast there,
20   That never failes to serve thee season'd deere,
     When thou would'st feast, or exercise thy friends.
            The lower land, that to the river bends,
     Thy sheepe, thy bullocks, kine, and calves doe feed:
            The middle grounds thy mares, and horses breed.
25   Each banke doth yeeld thee coneyes;[10] and the topps
            Fertile of wood, *Ashore*, and *Sydney's* copp's,[11]
     To crowne thy open table, doth provide
            The purpled pheasant, with the speckled side:
     The painted partrich lyes in every field,
30   And, for thy messe, is willing to be kill'd.
     And if the high swolne *Medway*[12] faile thy dish,
            Thou hast thy ponds, that pay thee tribute fish,
     Fat, aged carps, that runne into thy net,
            And pikes, now weary their owne kinde to eat,

[4] envied: they are (generally) envied; you are admired.

[5] some elevated ground on the estate.

[6] Sir Philip's, November 30, 1554.

[7] of many country people overcome with love as was Sir Philip in the sonnet sequence *Astrophel and Stella.*

[8] Gifford reports a tradition that Lady Leicester began labor pains under a certain oak on the estate.

[9] a wooded area where Barbara Gamage, Sir Robert's wife, used to feed deer.

[10] rabbits.

[11] two thickets on the estate.

[12] a river bordering the estate.

35 As loth, the second draught,[13] or cast to stay,[14]
    Officiously,[15] at first, themselves betray.
Bright eeles, that emulate them, and leape on land,
    Before the fisher, or into his hand.
Then hath thy orchard fruit, thy garden flowers,
40   Fresh as the ayre, and new as are the houres.
The earely cherry, with the later plum,
    Fig, grape, and quince, each in his time doth
                    [come:
The blushing apricot, and woolly peach
    Hang on thy walls,[16] that every child may reach.
45 And though thy walls be of the countrey stone,
    They'are rear'd with no mans ruine, no mans
                    [grone,
There's none, that dwell about them, wish them
                    [downe;
    But all come in, the farmer, and the clowne:[17]
And no one empty-handed, to salute
50   Thy lord, and lady, though they have no sute.[18]
Some bring a capon, some a rurall cake,
    Some nuts, some apples; some that thinke they
                    [make
The better cheeses, bring 'hem; or else send
    By their ripe daughters, whom they would com-
                    [mend
55 This way to husbands; and whose baskets beare
    An embleme[19] of themselves, in plum, or peare.
But what can this (more then expresse their love)
    Adde to thy free provisions, farre above
The neede of such? whose liberall boord doth flow,
60   With all, that hospitalitie doth know!
Where comes no guest, but is allow'd to eate,
    Without his feare, and of thy lords owne meate:
Where the same beere, and bread, and selfe-same wine,
    That is his Lordships, shall be also mine.

---

[13] drawing in of a net.
[14] await.
[15] dutifully.
[16] espaliered fruit trees.
[17] peasant.
[18] request to make.
[19] symbolic representation.

65   And I not faine to sit (as some, this day,
            At great mens tables) and yet dine away.[20]
        Here no man tells my cups;[21] nor, standing by,
            A waiter, doth my gluttony envy:
        But gives me what I call, and lets me eate,
70   He knowes, below, he shall finde plentie of meate,
        Thy tables hoord not up for the next day,
            Nor, when I take my lodging, need I pray
        For fire, or lights, or livorie:[22] all is there;
            As if thou, then, wert mine, or I raign'd here:
75   There's nothing I can wish, for which I stay.
            That found King *James,* when hunting late, this
                                                    [way,
        With his brave sonne, the Prince,[23] they saw thy fires
            Shine bright on every harth as the desires
        Of thy *Penates*[24] had beene set on flame,
80   To entertayne them; or the countrey came,
        With all their zeale, to warme their welcome here.
            What (great, I will not say, but) sodayne[25] cheare
        Did'st thou, then, make 'hem! and what praise was
                                                    [heap'd
            On thy good lady, then! who, therein, reap'd
85   The just reward of her high huswifery;
            To have her linnen, plate, and all things nigh,
        When shee was farre: and not a roome, but drest,
            As if it had expected such a guest!
        These, *Penshurst,* are thy praise, and yet not all.
90   Thy lady's noble, fruitfull, chaste withall.
        His children thy great lord may call his owne:
            A fortune, in this age, but rarely knowne.
        They are, and have beene taught religion: Thence
            Their gentler spirits have suck'd innocence.
95   Each morne, and even, they are taught to pray,
            With the whole houshold, and may, every day,

---

[20] i.e., to sit at great men's
tables but, not being sufficiently
fed, to eat more elsewhere.

[21] counts how many glasses I
drink.

[22] provision.

[23] Prince Henry, who died in
November 1612.

[24] household gods.

[25] sudden: unpremeditated.

Reade, in their vertuous parents noble parts,
　　The mysteries of manners, armes, and arts.
Now, *Penshurst*, they that will proportion[26] thee
100　　With other edifices, when they see
Those proud, ambitious heaps, and nothing else,
　　May say, their lords have built, but thy lord dwells.

III. TO SIR ROBERT WROTH

HOw blest art thou, canst love the countrey, W*roth*,[1]
　　Whether by choice, or fate, or both;
And, though so neere the citie, and the court,
　　Art tane with neithers vice, nor sport:
5　　That at great times, art no ambitious guest
　　Of Sheriffes dinner, or Majors feast.
Nor com'st to view the better cloth of state;
　　The richer hangings, or crowne-plate;
Nor throng'st (when masquing is) to have a sight
10　　Of the short braverie[2] of the night;
To view the jewells, stuffes, the paines, the wit
　　There wasted, some not paid for yet!
But canst, at home, in thy securer[3] rest,
　　Live, with un-bought provision blest;
15　　Free from proud porches, or their guilded roofes,
　　'Mongst loughing[4] heards, and solide hoofes:
Along'st the curled woods, and painted meades,
　　Through which a serpent river leades
To some coole, courteous shade, which he calls his,
20　　And makes sleepe softer then it is!
Or, if thou list the night in watch to breake,
　　A-bed canst heare the loud stag speake,
In spring, oft roused for thy masters[5] sport,
　　Who, for it, makes thy house his court;

[26] compare.

III: [1] (1576–1614) son-in-law
of Sir Robert Sidney; in 1604
married Lady Mary Sidney (see
Epigs. 103 and 105). Knighted

1601.
[2] fine appearance.
[3] with less worry.
[4] lowing.
[5] i.e., the king's.

25   Or with thy friends; the heart of all the yeere,
         Divid'st, upon the lesser Deere;
     In autumne, at the Partrich makes a flight,
         And giv'st thy gladder guests the sight;
     And, in the winter, hunt'st the flying hare,
30   More for thy exercise, then fare;
     While all, that follow, their glad eares apply
         To the full greatnesse of the cry:
     Or hauking at the river, or the bush,
         Or shooting at the greedie thrush,
35   Thou dost with some delight the day out-weare,
         Although the coldest of the yeere!
     The whil'st, the severall seasons thou hast seene
         Of flowrie fields, of cop'ces greene,
     The mowed meddowes, with the fleeced sheepe,
40   And feasts, that either shearers[6] keepe;
     The ripened eares, yet humble in their height,
         And furrowes laden with their weight;
     The apple-harvest, that doth longer last;
         The hogs return'd home fat from mast;
45   The trees cut out in log; and those boughes made
         A fire now, that lent a shade!
     Thus *Pan*, and *Sylvane*, having had their rites,
         Comus[7] puts in, for new delights;
     And fills thy open hall with mirth, and cheere,
50   As if in *Saturnes* raigne[8] it were;
     Apollo's harpe, and *Hermes* lyre resound,
         Nor are the *Muses* strangers found:
     The rout of rurall folke come thronging in,
         (Their rudenesse then is thought no sinne)
55   Thy noblest spouse affords them welcome grace;
         And the great *Heroes*, of her race,
     Sit mixt with losse of state, or reverence.
         Freedome doth with degree dispense.
     The jolly wassall walkes the often round,[9]

---

[6] mowers of the meadows or shearers of the sheep.
[7] personified god of revelry.
[8] the Golden Age; cf. ll. 63–64 below.
[9] The drinking cup is often passed around.

60   And in their cups, their cares are drown'd:
They thinke not, then, which side the cause shall
               [leese,[10]
  Nor how to get the lawyer fees.
Such, and no other was that age, of old,
  Which boasts t'have had the head of gold.

65 And such since thou canst make thine owne content,
  Strive, *Wroth*, to live long innocent.
Let others watch in guiltie armes, and stand
  The furie of a rash command,
Goe enter breaches, meet the cannons rage,
70   That they may sleepe with scarres in age.
And shew their feathers shot, and cullors[11] torne,
  And brag, that they were therefore borne.
Let this man sweat, and wrangle at the barre,
  For every price, in every jarre,
75 And change possessions, oftner with his breath,
  Then either money, warre, or death:
Let him, then hardest sires, more disinherit,[12]
  And each where boast it as his merit,
To blow up orphanes, widdowes, and their states;
80   And thinke his power doth equall *Fates*.
Let that goe heape a masse of wretched wealth,
  Purchas'd by rapine, worse then stealth,
And brooding o're it sit, with broadest[13] eyes,
  Not doing good, scarce when he dyes.[14]
85 Let thousands more goe flatter vice, and winne,
  By being organes to great sinne,
Get place, and honor, and be glad to keepe
  The secrets, that shall breake their sleepe:
And, so they ride in purple, eate in plate,
90   Though poyson, thinke it a great fate.
But thou, my *Wroth*, if I can truth apply,
  Shalt neither that, nor this envy:

[10] lose.
[11] colors: flags.
[12] Let him disinherit more children than do the harshest fathers.

[13] ever-open.
[14] Cf. Malbecco in *Faerie Queene* III.ix and x, especially x. 54ff.

Thy peace is made; and, when man's state is well,
    'Tis better, if he there can dwell.
95   God wisheth, none should wracke on a strange shelfe:[15]
    To him, man's dearer, then t'himselfe.
And, howsoever we may thinke things sweet,
    He always gives what he knowes meet;
Which who can use is happy: Such be thou.
100   Thy morning's, and thy evening's vow
Be thankes to him, and earnest prayer, to finde
    A body sound, with sounder minde;
To doe thy countrey service, thy selfe right;
    That neither want doe thee affright,
105 Nor death; but when thy latest sand is spent,
    Thou maist thinke life, a thing but lent.

IV. TO THE WORLD

A Farewell for a Gentle-woman,[1] Vertuous and Noble

FAlse world, good-night: since thou hast brought
    That houre upon my morne of age,
Hence-forth I quit thee from my thought,
    My part is ended on thy stage.
5   Doe not once hope, that thou canst tempt
    A spirit so resolv'd to tread
Upon thy throate, and live exempt
    From all the nets that thou canst spread.
I know thy formes are studyed arts,
10   Thy subtle wayes, be narrow straits;
Thy curtesie but sodaine starts,
    And what thou call'st thy gifts are baits.
I know too, though thou strut, and paint,
    Yet art thou both shrunke up, and old,
15   That onely fooles make thee a saint,
    And all thy good is to be sold.

[15] No one should wreck on a foreign shore.

IV: [1] The lady who speaks this dramatic monologue has not been identified.

I know thou whole art but a shop
  Of toyes, and trifles, traps, and snares,
To take the weake, or make them stop:
20 Yet art thou falser then thy wares.
And, knowing this, should I yet stay,
  Like such as blow away their lives,
And never will redeeme a day,
  Enamor'd of their golden gyves?[2]
25 Or, having scap'd, shall I returne,
  And thrust my necke into the noose,
From whence, so lately, I did burne,
  With all my powers, my selfe to loose?
What bird, or beast, is knowne so dull,
30 That fled his cage, or broke his chaine,
And tasting ayre, and freedome, wull
  Render[3] his head in there againe?
If these, who have but sense,[4] can shun
  The engines,[5] that have them annoy'd;
35 Little, for me, had reason done,
  If I could not thy ginnes avoyd.
Yes, threaten, doe. Alas I feare
  As little, as I hope from thee:
I know thou canst nor shew, nor beare
40 More hatred, then thou hast to mee.
My tender, first, and simple yeeres
  Thou did'st abuse, and then betray;
Since stird'st up jealousies and feares,
  When all the causes were away.
45 Then, in a soile[6] hast planted me,
  Where breathe the basest of thy fooles;
Where envious arts professed be,
  And pride, and ignorance the schooles,
Where nothing is examin'd, weigh'd,
50 But, as 'tis rumor'd, so beleev'd:
Where every freedome is betray'd,
  And every goodnesse tax'd, or griev'd.

[2] fetters.
[3] put back.
[4] i.e., who lack the power of reason.

[5] snares; the same word appears as "ginnes" in l. 36.
[6] probably the court.

But, what we'are borne for, we must beare:
 Our fraile condition it is such,
55 That, what to all may happen here,
 If't chance to me, I must not grutch.[7]
Else, I my state should much mistake,
 To harbour a divided thought
From all my kinde: that, for my sake,
60 There should a miracle be wrought.
No, I doe know, that I was borne
 To age, misfortune, sicknesse, griefe:
But I will beare these, with that scorne,
 As shall not need thy false reliefe.
65 Nor for my peace will I goe farre,
 As wandrers doe, that still doe rome,
But make my strengths, such as they are,
 Here in my bosome, and at home.

V. SONG

To Celia[1]

COme my *Celia*, let us prove,
While we may, the sports of love;
Time will not be ours, for ever:
He, at length, our good will sever.
5 Spend not then his guifts in vaine.
Sunnes, that set, may rise againe:
But if once we loose this light,
'Tis, with us, perpetuall night.
Why should we deferre our joyes?
10 Fame, and rumor are but toyes.
Cannot we delude the eyes
Of a few poore houshold spyes?
Or his[2] easier eares beguile,
So removed by our wile?

---

[7] complain.
V: [1] This song appears in *Volpone* III.vii.166–83, where Volpone uses it to try to seduce the virtuous wife, Celia. It and the following song owe much to Catullus V and VII.
[2] the husband, Corvino.

15 'Tis no sinne, loves fruit to steale,
But the sweet theft to reveale:
To be taken, to be seene,
These have crimes accounted beene.

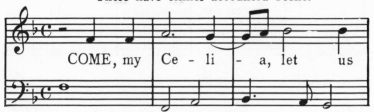

COME, my Ce - li - a, let us

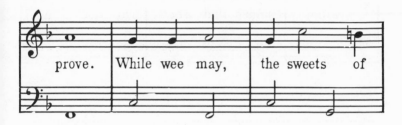

prove. While wee may, the sweets of

love. Time wil not be ours for-e-ver.

He at length our good will se-

Fig. 1 Song, "To Celia." From Alfonso Ferrabosco's *Ayres*, 1609.

FIG. 1 continued

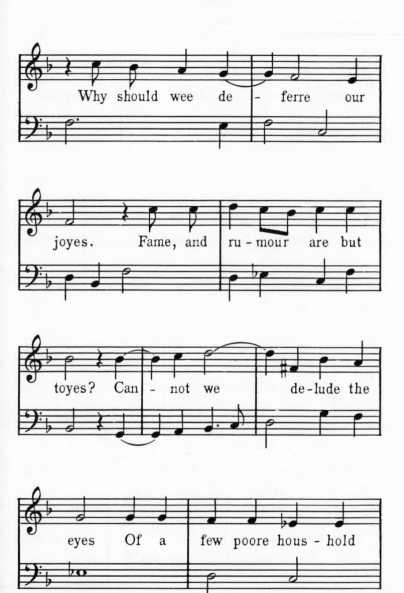

Fig. 1 continued

Fig. 1 continued

Fig. 1   continued

VI. TO THE SAME

KIsse me, sweet: The warie lover
Can your favours keepe, and cover,
When the common courting jay
All your bounties will betray.
5   Kisse againe: no creature comes.
Kisse, and score up wealthy summes
On my lips, thus hardly sundred,
While you breath. First give a hundred,
Then a thousand, then another
10   Hundred, then unto the tother[1]
Adde a thousand, and so more:
Till you equall with the store,
All the grasse that *Rumney*[2] yeelds,
Or the sands in *Chelsey*[3] fields,
15   Or the drops in silver *Thames,*
Or the starres, that guild his streames,
In the silent sommer-nights,
When youths ply their stolne delights.
That the curious may not know
20   How to tell'hem,[4] as they flow,
And the envious, when they find
What their number is, be pin'd.[5]

VI: [1] other.
   [2] a grassy marsh in Kent.
   [3] "Chelsea"   derives   from
"chesil," gravel.

[4] count them.
   [5] pained, distressed. Ll. 19–22
appear in *Volpone* III.vii. 236–
39.

VII. SONG

That Women Are But Mens Shaddowes[1]

FOllow a shaddow, it still flies you;
　　Seeme to flye it, it will pursue:
So court a mistris, shee denyes you;
Let her alone, shee will court you.
5　Say, are not women truely, then,
　　Stil'd but the shaddowes of us men?
At morne, and even, shades are longest;
　　At noone, they are or short, or none:
So men at weakest, they are strongest,
10　　But grant us perfect, they're not knowne.
Say, are not women truely, then,
　　Stil'd but the shaddowes of us men?

VIII. TO SICKNESSE

WHy, *Disease*, dost thou molest
Ladies? and of them the best?
Doe not men, ynow[1] of rites
To thy altars, by their nights
5　Spent in surfets: and their dayes,
And nights too, in worser wayes?
　　Take heed, *Sicknesse*, what you doe,
　　I shall feare, you'll surfet too.
Live not we, as, all thy stalls,
10　Spittles,[2] pest-house, hospitalls,
Scarce will take our present store?
　　And this age will build no more:

VII: [1] adapted from a Latin poem of Barthemi Aneau; see *N&Q* III.viii (1865), 187. Drummond reports in his *Conversations* that Jonson said, "Pembrok and his Lady discoursing, the Earl said, The woemen were mens shadowes, and she maintained them. Both appealing to Johnson, he affirmed it true; for which my Lady gave a pennance to prove it in verse, hence his epigrame."

VIII: [1] enough.
[2] hospitals for the poor.

'Pray thee, feed contented, then,
Sicknesse; onely on us men.
15   Or if needs thy lust will tast
Woman-kinde; devoure the wast
Livers, round about the towne.
But, forgive me, with thy crowne[3]
They maintayne the truest trade,
20   And have more diseases made.
What should, yet, thy pallat please?
Daintinesse, and softer ease,
Sleeked limmes, and finest blood?
If thy leanenesse love such food,
25   There are those, that, for thy sake,
Doe enough; and who would take
Any paines; yea, thinke it price,[4]
To become thy sacrifice.
That distill their husbands land
30   In decoctions;[5] and are mann'd
With ten Emp'ricks, in their chamber,
Lying for the spirit of amber.
That for th'oyle of *Talke*, dare spend
More then citizens dare lend
35   Them, and all their officers.
That, to make all pleasure theirs,
Will by coach, and water goe,
Every stew[6] in towne to know;
Dare entayle their loves on any,
40   Bald, or blinde, or nere so many:
And, for thee, at common game,
Play away, health, wealth, and fame.
These, *disease*, will thee deserve:
And will, long ere thou should'st starve[7]

---

[3] probably leadership.
[4] excellent, choice.
[5] This and the following are terms from alchemy: *decoctions* means reductions (chemical) and so here is the equivalent of liquidation (in a financial sense); *Emp'ricks* are quack experiment-ers; *spirit of amber* is an acid formed by dry distillation of amber; and *oyle of Talke* is a talcum preparation formerly used as a cosmetic (NED).
[6] brothel.
[7] die.

45   On their beds, most prostitute,[8]
     Move it, as their humblest sute,
     In thy justice to molest
     None but them, and leave the rest.

IX. SONG

To CELIA[1]

     DRinke to me, onely, with thine eyes,
        And I will pledge[2] with mine;
     Or leave a kisse but in the cup,
        And Ile not looke for wine.
5   The thirst, that from the soule doth rise,
        Doth aske a drinke divine:
     But might I of *Jove's Nectar* sup,
        I would not change[3] for thine.
     I sent thee, late, a rosie wreath,
10   Not so much honoring thee,
     As giving it a hope, that there
        It could not withered bee.
     But thou thereon did'st onely breath,
        And sent'st it backe to mee:
15   Since when it growes, and smells, I sweare,
        Not of it selfe, but thee.[4]

[8] with a punning confusion with "prostrate."

IX: [1] freely adapted from several of the *Epistles* of Philostratus.

[2] drink a toast.

[3] take it in exchange. (There is no textual support for reading "from" in place of "for.")

[4] An earlier version (Sloane MS. 1446, f. 54b. in the British Museum) reads:

Drinke to mee Coelia with thine eies
  And ile pledge thee with myne
Leave but a kisse within the cupp
  And Ile expect no wine
The thirst that from the Soule proceedes
  Doth aske a drinke Divine
But might I of loves Nectar Supp
I would not change for thine
I sent to thee a Rosie wreath
not so to honour thee
but beinge well assured that there
it would not withered bee
And thou there on didst onlie breath
  and sentst it back to mee
Since when it lives and smelles I sweare
  not of it selfe but thee

X[1]

ANd must I sing? what subject shall I chuse?
Or whose great name in *Poets* heaven use?
For the more countenance[2] to my active *Muse?*

Hercules? alas his bones are yet sore,
5 With his old earthly labours. T'exact more,
Of his dull god-head, were sinne. Ile implore

Phoebus. No? tend thy cart[3] still. Envious day
Shall not give out,[4] that I have made thee stay,[5]
And foundred thy hot teame, to tune my lay.

10 Nor will I beg of thee, *Lord of the vine,*[6]
To raise my spirits with thy conjuring wine,
In the greene circle of thy Ivy twine.

Pallas, nor thee I call on, mankinde[7] maid,
That, at thy birth, mad'st the poore Smith affraid,
15 Who, with his axe, thy fathers mid-wife plaid.[8]

Goe, crampe[9] dull *Mars,* light[10] *Venus,* when he
[snorts,[11]

X: [1] first printed, with the following poem, in an appendix to Robert Chester's *Love's Martyr* (1601), and headed *Praeludium.* There also are signed poems in the Appendix by Shakespeare, Marston, Chapman, and "Ignoto," all on the subject of the Phoenix and the Turtle(-dove), which are considered as Platonic ideals, the Phoenix as perfect woman and the Turtle as faithful man. See also *Uncol. P.* 9 and 10.
[2] for the better repute or appearance.

[3] chariot: the sun, of which Phoebus Apollo is god.
[4] report.
[5] stop.
[6] Bacchus, usually pictured as ivy-crowned.
[7] masculine.
[8] Pallas Athena was born from the head of Zeus when Vulcan cleft it.
[9] probably pinch, to awaken.
[10] of easy virtue.
[11] snores. Venus's extramarital affairs with Mars were notorious. She was married to Vulcan.

Or, with thy *Tribade* trine,[12] invent new sports,
Thou, nor thy loosenesse with my making[13] sorts.

Let the *old boy*,[14] your sonne, ply his old taske,
20   Turne the stale[15] prologue to some painted maske,
His absence in my verse, is all I aske.

Hermes, the cheater,[16] shall not mixe with us,
Though he would steale his sisters *Pegasus*,[17]
And riffle[18] him: or pawne his *Petasus*.[19]

25   Nor all the ladies of the *Thespian lake*,[20]
(Though they were crusht into one forme) could make
A beautie of that merit, that should take

My *Muse* up by *commission*:[21] No, I bring
My owne true fire. Now my thought takes wing,
30   And now an *Epode*[22] to deepe eares[23] I sing.

XI. EPODE[1]

NOt to know vice at all, and keepe true state,
    Is vertue, and not *Fate*:[2]
Next, to that vertue, is to know vice well,
    And her blacke spight expell.

[12] The three Graces, usually pictured as nude females embracing one another, comforted Venus in Paphos, according to Homer (*Odyssey* VIII. 364) after Vulcan had publicly revealed her unfaithfulness. A tribade is a female homosexual.

[13] poetry.

[14] Cupid, sometimes pictured as the oldest of the gods.

[15] out-of-date.

[16] Mercury, god of thieves and merchants.

[17] His sisters, the Muses, possessed the winged horse, Pegasus.

[18] raffle: gamble him away.

[19] his winged hat.

[20] the Muses, associated with the fountain Aganippe at the foot of Mount Helicon and near Thespia.

[21] order or command.

[22] a lyric form, generally on a grave subject, invented by Archilochus. In it a long line is followed by a shorter one.

[23] profound listeners.

XI: [1] For the subject see n. 1 of the previous poem.

[2] i.e., one's virtue, freely willed, determines one's morality.

5   Which to effect (since no brest is so sure,
            Or safe, but shee'll[3] procure
       Some way of entrance) we must plant a guard
            Of thoughts to watch, and ward
       At th'eye and eare (the ports unto the minde)[4]
10   That no strange, or unkinde[5]
       Object arrive there, but the heart (our spie)
            Give knowledge instantly,
       To wakefull reason, our affections king:
            Who (in th'examining)
15   Will quickly taste[6] the treason, and commit
            Close,[7] the close[8] cause of it.
       Tis the securest policie we have,
            To make our sense our slave.
       But this true course is not embrac'd by many:
20   By many? scarse by any.
       For either our affections doe rebell,
            Or else the sentinell
       (That should ring larum to the heart) doth sleepe,
            Or some great[9] thought doth keepe
25   Backe the intelligence, and falsely sweares,
            Th'are base, and idle feares
       Whereof the loyall conscience so complaines.
            Thus, by these subtle traines,

---

[3] vice.

[4] This passage is based on the Renaissance psychology of morality. Perceptions arise in the five senses (especially sight and hearing, l. 9); they are conveyed to the heart, center of one's emotions. The emotions (affections, l. 13) should be under the control of the reason, which decides on the proper (and moral) response to the stimulus. Thus sense is slave to reason in the moral person (l. 18). But most people do not follow this practice (ll. 19ff.): they are ruled by emotions (l. 21) or are not aware of the danger (l. 23); or the reason is deluded in its judgment (ll. 24ff.) so that it does not arrive at a proper response as it should, even though warned by conscience of the danger. Thus the stimuli arouse emotions or passions (l. 29) which rule instead of reason (l. 30). The emotion of love is especially likely to overthrow reason in this way (ll. 31ff.).

[5] unnatural.

[6] sense or apprehend.

[7] keep in custody; restrain.

[8] immediate or proximate.

[9] favorite.

Doe severall passions invade the minde,
30   And strike our reason blinde.
Of which usurping rancke, some have thought love
        The first; as prone to move
Most frequent tumults, horrors, and unrests,
        In our enflamed brests:
35   But this doth from the cloud of error grow,
        Which thus we over-blow.[10]
The thing, they here call Love, is blinde Desire,
        Arm'd with bow, shafts, and fire;
Inconstant, like the sea, of whence 'tis borne,
40   Rough, swelling, like a storme:
With whom who sailes, rides on a surge of feare,
        And boyles, as if he were
In a continuall tempest. Now, true Love
        No such effects doth prove;[11]
45   That is an essence, farre more gentle, fine,
        Pure, perfect, nay divine;
It is a golden chaine let downe from heaven,
        Whose linkes are bright, and even.[12]
That falls like sleepe on lovers, and combines
50   The soft,[13] and sweetest mindes
In equall knots: This beares no brands, nor darts,
        To murther different hearts,
But, in a calme, and god-like unitie,
        Preserves communitie.
55   O, who is he, that (in this peace) enjoyes
        The'*Elixir*[14] of all joyes?

---

[10] surmount (?)
[11] experience.
[12] In *Hymenaei*, l. 320, Jonson interprets the meaning of the golden chain in the *Iliad* (VIII. 19). He prefers Macrobius' interpretation: "since Mind emanates from the Supreme God and Soul from Mind, and Mind, indeed, forms and suffuses all below with life . . . , the close observer will find that from the Supreme God even to the bottommost dregs of the universe there is one tie, binding at every link and never broken. This is the golden chain of Homer." *Commentary on the Dream of Scipio*, trans. W. H. Stahl (New York, 1952), p. 145.
[13] i.e., softest.
[14] essence.

A forme more fresh, then are the *Eden* bowers
  And lasting, as her flowers:[15]
Richer then *Time*, and as *Time's* vertue,[16] rare.
60 Sober, as saddest[17] care:
A fixed thought, an eye un-taught to glance;
  Who (blest with such high chance)
Would, at suggestion of a steepe[18] desire,
  Cast himselfe from the spire[19]
65 Of all his happinesse? But soft: I heare
  Some vicious foole draw neare,
That cryes, we dreame, and sweares, there's no such
             [thing,
  As this chaste love we sing.
Peace Luxurie,[20] thou art like one of those
70 Who, being at sea, suppose,
Because they move, the continent doth so:
  No, vice, we let thee know
Though thy wild thoughts with sparrowes[21] wings doe
              [flye,
  Turtles[22] can chastly dye;[23]
75 And yet (in this t'expresse our selves more cleare)
  We doe not number, here,
Such spirits as are onely continent,
  Because lust's meanes are spent:
Or those, who doubt the common mouth of fame,[24]
80 And for their place, and name,
Cannot so safely sinne. Their chastitie
  Is meere necessitie.
Nor meane we those, whom vowes and conscience
  Have fill'd with abstinence:
85 Though we acknowledge, who can so abstayne,
  Makes a most blessed gayne.

---

[15] before death had entered the Garden.

[16] Truth, daughter of Time.

[17] most steadfast.

[18] headlong, impetuous.

[19] with a glance at Satan's temptation of Christ on the Temple pinnacle. Cf. Luke 4 and Matthew 4.

[20] Be quiet, lust.

[21] symbol of lechery.

[22] i.e., turtledoves.

[23] with the pun, to consummate sexual intercourse, probably intended.

[24] who are afraid of scandal.

He that for love of goodnesse hateth ill,
 Is more crowne-worthy still,
Then he, which for sinnes penaltie forbeares.
90 His heart sinnes, though he feares.
But we propose a person like our Dove,[25]
 Grac'd with a Phoenix love;
A beautie of that cleere, and sparkling light,
 Would make a day of night,
95 And turne the blackest sorrowes to bright joyes:
 Whose od'rous breath destroyes
All taste of bitternesse, and makes the ayre
 As sweet, as shee is fayre.
A body so harmoniously compos'd,
100 As if *Nature* disclos'd
All her best symmetrie in that one feature!
 O, so divine a creature
Who could be false to? chiefly, when he knowes
 How onely shee bestowes
105 The wealthy[26] treasure of her love on him;
 Making his fortunes swim
In the full floud of her admir'd perfection?
 What savage, brute affection,
Would not be fearefull to offend a dame
110 Of this excelling frame?[27]
Much more a noble, and right generous mind
 (To vertuous moods inclin'd)
That knowes the waight of guilt: He will refraine
 From thoughts of such a straine.
115 And to his sense object this sentence ever,[28]
 Man may securely[29] sinne, but safely never.

---

[25] i.e., the turtledove; cf. n. 1 to previous poem.
[26] copious.
[27] Cf. the Salvage Man of Spenser's *Faerie Queene* VI.ivff.

[28] He will always rule his senses with this maxim.
[29] with a pun: carelessly or safely.

XII. EPISTLE

To Elizabeth Countesse of Rutland[1]

Madame,
WHil'st that, for which, all vertue now is sold,
    And almost every vice, almightie gold,
That which, to boote with hell,[2] is thought worth
    [heaven,
    And, for it, life, conscience, yea, soules are given,
5   Toyles, by grave[3] custome, up and downe the court,
    To every squire, or groome, that will report
Well, or ill, onely, all the following yeere,
    Just to the waight their this dayes-presents beare;[4]
While it makes huishers[5] serviceable men,
10   And some one apteth to be trusted,[6] then,
Though never after; whiles it gaynes the voyce
    Of some grand peere, whose ayre[7] doth make re-
    [joyce
The foole that gave it; who will want, and weepe,
    When his proud patrons favours are asleepe;
15   While thus it buyes great grace, and hunts poore fame;
    Runs betweene man, and man; 'tweene dame, and
    [dame;
Solders crackt friendship; makes love last a day;
    Or perhaps lesse: whil'st gold beares all this sway,
I, that have none (to send you) send you verse.
20   A present, which (if elder writs reherse
The truth of times)[8] was once of more esteeme,
    Then this, our guilt,[9] nor golden age can deeme,

XII: [1] See *Epig.* 79; she married the Earl of Rutland in 1599.
[2] be of avail with hell.
[3] respected.
[4] to the extent that current bribery supports it.
[5] ushers, serving men.
[6] makes some one fit to be trusted.
[7] manner.
[8] if older writings reflect the truth of their days.
[9] gilded.

When gold was made no weapon to cut throtes,
    Or put to flight *Astrea*,[10] when her ingots

25 Were yet unfound,[11] and better plac'd in earth,
    Then, here, to give pride fame, and peasants
              [birth.[12]

But let this drosse carry what price it will
    With noble ignorants, and let them still,
Turne, upon scorned verse, their quarter-face:[13]

30   With you, I know, my offring will find grace.
For what a sinne 'gainst your great fathers[14] spirit,
    Were it to thinke, that you should not inherit
His love unto the *Muses*, when his skill
    Almost you have, or may have, when you will?

35 Wherein wise *Nature* you a dowrie gave,
    Worth an estate, treble to that you have.
Beautie, I know, is good, and bloud is more;
    Riches thought most: But, *Madame*, thinke what
             [store

The world hath seene, which all these had in trust,

40   And now lye lost in their forgotten dust.
It is the *Muse*, alone, can raise to heaven,
    And, at her strong armes end, hold up, and even,
The soules, shee loves. Those other glorious[15] notes,
    Inscrib'd in touch[16] or marble, or the cotes[17]

45 Painted, or carv'd upon our great-mens tombs,
    Or in their windowes; doe but prove the wombs,
That bred them, graves: when they were borne, they
             [di'd,

    That had no *Muse* to make their fame abide.
How many equall with the *Argive* Queene,[18]

50   Have beautie knowne, yet none so famous seene?

---

[10] Goddess of Justice during the Golden Age, who then became the constellation Virgo.

[11] unfounded: not yet cast or made. Apparently the stars in the constellation.

[12] than as now to give (unjustly) fame to pride and (high) birth to peasants.

[13] i.e., almost averted.

[14] Sir Philip Sidney.

[15] boastful.

[16] touchstone: fine marble.

[17] coats-of-arms.

[18] Helen of Troy.

Achilles was not first, that valiant was,
　　　Or, in an armies head, that, lockt in brasse,[19]
Gave killing strokes. There were brave men, before
　　　Ajax, or *Idomen*,[20] or all the store,
55　　That *Homer* brought to *Troy*; yet none so live:
　　　Because they lack'd the sacred pen, could give
Like life unto 'hem. Who heav'd *Hercules*[21]
　　　Unto the starres? or the *Tyndarides*?
Who placed *Jasons Argo* in the skie?
60　　　Or set bright *Ariadnes* crowne so high?
Who made a lampe of *Berenices* hayre?
　　　Or lifted *Cassiopea* in her chayre?
But onely *Poets*, rapt with rage divine?[22]
　　　And such, or my hopes faile, shall make you shine.
65　　You, and that other starre, that purest light,
　　　Of all *Lucina's*[23] traine; *Lucy*[24] the bright.
Then which, a nobler heaven it selfe knowes not.
　　　Who, though shee have a better verser[25] got,
(Or *Poet*, in the court account) then I,
70　　And, who doth me (though I not him) envy,
Yet, for the timely favours shee hath done,
　　　To my lesse sanguine *Muse*, wherein she'hath
　　　　　　　　　　　　　　　　　　　　　　[wonne
My gratefull soule, the subject of her powers,
　　　I have already us'd some happy houres,
75　　To her remembrance; which when time shall bring
　　　To curious light, to notes,[26] I then shall sing,

[19] leading an army, in armor.
[20] heroes of the *Iliad*.
[21] This and the following are all constellations. The Tyndarides are Castor and Pollux in the constellation Gemini; Jason's Argo is the Ptolemaic group Argo Navis; Ariadnes crowne is Corona Borealis; Berenices hayre is Coma Berenices; Cassiopea is known by the same title today.
[22] carried away by the divine madness of poetic inspiration.
[23] Queen Elizabeth's; derived from *lux*, bright.
[24] again derived from *lux*; Lucy Harrington, Countess of Bedford.
[25] disparagingly in contrast with "poet" in the next line. The other writer has sometimes been identified as Samuel Daniel, but Short argues that he is Michael Drayton in *RES*, XV (1939), 315–17.
[26] an unrealized plan of Jonson for a poem on the ladies of England.

Will prove old *Orpheus* act no tale to be:
  For I shall move stocks, stones,[27] no lesse then
               [he.
Then all, that have but done my *Muse* least grace,
80 Shall thronging come, and boast the happy place
They hold in my strange[28] *poems*, which, as yet
  Had not their forme touch'd by an English wit.[29]
There like a rich, and golden *pyramede*,
  Borne up by statues, shall I reare your head,
85 Above your under-carved ornaments,
  And show, how, to the life, my soule presents
Your forme imprest there: not with tickling rimes,
  Or common places,[30] filch'd, that take these
               [times,
But high, and noble matter, such as flies
90 From braines entranc'd, and fill'd with extasies;
Moodes, which the god-like *Sydney* oft did prove,[31]
  And your brave friend,[32] and mine so well did
               [love.
Who wheresoere he be . . . .

        The rest is lost.[33]

[27] Orpheus in the tradition could move stocks and stone; Jonson plays on the meaning "dull and stupid people."

[28] perhaps, alien or unfamiliar.

[29] Jonson apparently is admitting the origin of much of his writing in other literatures.

[30] clichés.

[31] experience.

[32] her husband, Earl of Rutland.

[33] Between the composition of this poem and its publication, the Earl was known to be impotent. Thus the following conclusion was canceled:

Who where so ere he be, on what
deare coast,
Now thincking on you though to England lost
For that firme grace he holdes in your regard
I that am gratefull for him have prepar'd,
This hastie sacrifice wherein I reare
A vow, as new and ominous as the yeare
Before his swift and circled race be run
My best of wishes; may you beare a sonne.
(Bodleian Rawlinson MS. 31, f. 20r–20v.)

XIII. EPISTLE

To Katherine, Lady Aubigny[1]

'TIs growne almost a danger to speake true
    Of any good minde, now: There are so few.
The bad, by number, are so fortified,
    As what th'have lost t'expect, they dare deride.
5 So both the prais'd, and praisers suffer: Yet,
    For others ill, ought none their good forget.
I, therefore, who professe my selfe in love
    With every vertue, wheresoere it move,
And howsoever; as I am at fewd
10   With sinne and vice, though with a throne en-
            [dew'd;
And, in this name, am given out dangerous
    By arts, and practise of the vicious,
Such as suspect them-selves, and thinke it fit
    For their owne cap'tall crimes, t'indite my wit;
15 I, that have suffer'd this; and, though forsooke
    Of *Fortune*, have not alter'd yet my looke,
Or so my selfe abandon'd, as because
    Men are not just, or keepe no holy lawes
Of nature, and societie, I should faint;
20   Or feare to draw true lines, 'cause others paint:
I, *Madame*, am become your praiser. Where,
    If it may stand with your soft blush to heare,
Your selfe but told unto your selfe, and see
    In my character, what your features bee,
25 You will not from the paper slightly[2] passe:
    No lady, but, at some time, loves her glasse.[3]
And this shall be no false one, but as much
    Remov'd, as you from need to have it such.
Looke then, and see your selfe. I will not say
30   Your beautie; for you see that every day:

XIII: [1] daughter (d. 1617) of   bigny (see *Epig.* 127).
Sir Gervase Clifton; married in   [2] indifferently.
1609 Lord Esmé, Seigneur d'Au-   [3] mirror.

And so doe many more. All which[4] can call
   It perfect, proper, pure, and naturall,
Not taken up o'th'doctors,[5] but as well
   As I, can say, and see it doth excell.
35 That[6] askes but to be censur'd[7] by the eyes:
   And, in those outward formes, all fooles are wise.
Nor that your beautie wanted not a dower,[8]
   Doe I reflect. Some alderman has power,
Or cos'ning farmer of the customes[9] so,
40   T'advance his doubtfull issue, and ore-flow
A Princes fortune: These are gifts of chance,
   And raise not vertue; they may vice enhance.
My mirror is more subtile, cleere, refin'd,
   And takes, and gives the beauties of the mind.
45 Though it reject not those of *Fortune:* such
   As bloud, and match.[10] Wherein, how more then
                      [much

Are you engaged to your happy fate,
   For such a lot![11] that mixt you with a state
Of so great title, birth, but vertue most,
50   Without which, all the rest were sounds, or lost.
'Tis onely that can time, and chance defeat:
   For he, that once is good, is ever great.
Wherewith, then, *Madame,* can you better pay
   This blessing of your starres, then by that way
55 Of vertue, which you tread? what if alone?
   Without companions? 'Tis safe to have none.
In single paths, dangers with ease are watch'd:
   Contagion in the prease is soonest catch'd.[12]
This makes, that wisely you decline[13] your life,
60   Farre from the maze of custome, error, strife,
And keepe an even, and unalter'd gaite;

---

[4] of whom.
[5] bought from physicians.
[6] i.e., her beauty.
[7] judged.
[8] a gift or talent.
[9] a tax collector who paid a fixed sum for the proceeds which

he was able to exact.
[10] marriage.
[11] destiny or fortune.
[12] Sickness is soonest caught in the crowd.
[13] in its etymological sense: turn aside.

Not looking by,[14] or back (like those, that waite
Times, and occasions, to start forth, and seeme[15])
   Which though the turning world may dis-esteeme,
65 Because that studies spectacles, and showes,
   And after varyed, as fresh objects goes,
Giddie with change, and therefore cannot see
   Right, the right way: yet must your comfort bee
Your conscience, and not wonder, if none askes
70   For truthes complexion, where they all weare
                                           [maskes.
Let who will follow fashions, and attyres,
   Maintayne their liedgers forth, for forraine
                                           [wyres,[16]
Melt downe their husbands land, to poure away
   On the close groome,[17] and page, on new-yeeres
                                           [day,
75 And almost, all dayes after, while they live;
   (They finde it both so wittie, and safe to give.)
Let 'hem on poulders, oyles, and paintings,[18] spend,
   Till that no usurer, nor his bawds[19] dare lend
Them, or their officers:[20] and no man know,
80   Whether it be a face they weare, or no.
Let 'hem waste body, and state; and after all,
   When their owne Parasites laugh at their fall,
May they have nothing left, whereof they can
   Boast, but how oft they have gone wrong[21] to
                                           [man:
85 And call it their brave[22] sinne. For such there be
   That doe sinne onely for the infamie:
And never thinke, how vice doth every houre,
   Eate on her clients, and some one devoure.
You, *Madame*, yong have learn'd to shunne these
                                           [shelves,[23]

[14] aside.
[15] come to view, appear.
[16] Support their agents else-
where, to report fashion changes.
[17] confidential male attendant.
[18] powders, cosmetic oils, and
make-ups.
[19] agents.
[20] subordinates.
[21] i.e., carnally, in sin.
[22] fine.
[23] shores.

90   Whereon the most of mankinde wracke them-
                                   [selves,
     And, keeping a just course, have earely put
       Into your harbor, and all passage shut
    'Gainst stormes, or pyrats, that might charge[24] your
                                 [peace;
       For which you worthy are the glad encrease
95   Of your blest wombe, made fruitfull from above,
        To pay your lord the pledges of chast love:
     And raise a noble stemme, to give the fame,
        To *Clifton's* bloud, that is deny'd their name.[25]
     Grow, grow, faire tree, and as thy branches shoote,
100   Heare, what the *Muses* sing about thy roote,
     By me, their priest (if they can ought divine)
        Before the moones have fill'd their tripple trine,[26]
     To crowne the burthen which you goe withall,
       It shall a ripe and timely issue fall,
105   T"expect the honors of great *'Aubigny:*
        And greater rites, yet writ in mysterie,
     But which the *Fates* forbid me to reveale.
        Onely, thus much, out of a ravish'd[27] zeale,
     Unto your name, and goodnesse of your life,
110   They speake; since you are truly that rare wife,
     Other great wives may blush at: when they see
        What your try'd manners are, what theirs should
                                 [bee.
     How you love one, and him you should; how still
       You are depending on his word, and will;
115   Not fashion'd for the court, or strangers eyes;
        But to please him, who is the dearer prise
     Unto himselfe, by being so deare to you.
        This makes, that your affections still be new,
     And that your soules conspire, as they were gone
120   Each into other, and had now made one.[28]

---

[24] burden.
[25] Sir Gervase had no sons.
[26] nine months.
[27] enraptured.

[28] an image frequently used by Donne to describe the union of two people.

Live that one, still; and as long yeeres doe passe,
    Madame, be bold to use this truest glasse:
Wherein, your forme, you still the same shall finde;
    Because nor it can change, nor such a minde.

XIV. ODE

To Sir William Sydney,[1] on His Birth-day

NOw that the harth is crown'd with smiling fire,
    And some doe drinke, and some doe dance.
        Some ring,
        Some sing,
5   And all doe strive t'advance
The gladnesse higher:
        Wherefore should I
        Stand silent by.
        Who not the least,
10   Both love the cause, and authors of the
                     [feast?

Give me my cup, but from the *Thespian*[2] well,
    That I may tell to *Sydney*, what
        This day
        Doth say,
15   And he may thinke on that
Which I doe tell:
        When all the noyse
        Of these forc'd joyes,
        Are fled and gone,
20   And he, with his best *Genius*[3] left alone.

This day sayes, then, the number of glad yeeres
    Are justly summ'd, that make you man;
        Your vow
        Must now
25   Strive all right wayes it can,
T'out-strip your peeres:

XIV: [1] son (1590–1612) of Sir
Robert Sidney. Knighted in Janu-
ary 1611.
  [2] pertaining to the Muses.
  [3] guide or guardian spirit.

Since he doth lacke
Of going backe
Little, whose will
30   Doth urge him to runne wrong, or to stand
[still.

Nor can a little of the common store,
Of nobles vertue, shew in you;
Your blood
So good
35   And great, must seeke for new,
And studie more:
Not weary, rest
On what's deceast.
For they, that swell
40   With dust of ancestors, in graves but
[dwell.

'T will be exacted of your name, whose sonne,
Whose nephew, whose grand-child you are;[4]
And men
Will, then,
45   Say you have follow'd farre,
When well begunne:
Which must be now,
They teach you, how.
And he that stayes
50   To live untill to morrow' hath lost **two**
[dayes.

So may you live in honor, as in name,
If with this truth you be inspir'd,
So may
This day
55   Be more, and long desir'd:
And with the flame
Of love be bright,
As with the light
Of bone-fires.[5] Then
60   The Birth-day shines, when logs not burne,
[but men.

[4] Sir William was nephew of   Henry Sidney.
Sir Philip and grandson of Sir   [5] the etymology of "bonfires."

XV. TO HEAVEN

GOod, and great *God*, can I not thinke of thee,
    But it must, straight, my melancholy bee?
Is it interpreted in me disease,
    That, laden with my sinnes, I seeke for ease?
5   O, be thou witnesse, that the reynes[1] dost know,
    And hearts of all, if I be sad for show,
And judge me after: if I dare pretend
    To ought but grace, or ayme at other end.
As thou art all, so be thou all to mee,
10   First, midst, and last, converted[2] one, and three;
My faith, my hope, my love: and in this state,
    My judge, my witnesse, and my advocate.
Where have I beene this while exil'd from thee?
    And whither rap'd,[3] now thou but stoup'st to
                           [mee?
15   Dwell, dwell here still: O, being every-where,
    How can I doubt to finde thee ever, here?
I know my state, both full of shame, and scorne,
    Conceiv'd in sinne, and unto labour borne,
Standing with feare, and must with horror fall,
20   And destin'd unto judgement, after all.
I feele my griefes too, and there scarce is ground,
    Upon my flesh t'inflict another wound.
Yet dare I not complaine, or wish for death
    With holy *Paul*,[4] lest it be thought the breath
25   Of discontent; or that these prayers bee
    For wearinesse of life, not love of thee.

XV: [1] thought of as the seat of the feelings or affections.
[2] changed to, or perhaps appearing as.
[3] taken.
[4] as he does in Romans 7:24.

UNDER-WOOD

Jonson seems to have planned about 1631 to publish a collection of his writings which would bring up to date the *Works* of 1616. For the lyrics which he had composed since about 1613, when he had completed the text for the 1616 folio, he chose as title *Under-wood*, wrote a brief preface, and probably arranged much of the contents. But nothing came of the venture except the publication of several plays. After Jonson's death in 1637, the manuscripts passed to his friend Sir Kenelm Digby, who included the poems in the second volume of the folio *Works* of 1640–41. *Under-wood* is Jonson's finest collection of verse, evidence of the fact that as he turned away in his forties from writing for the stage his poetic powers showed no decline. Rather, they increased in that these poems show for the most part a greater variety and force than had the two earlier collections of 1616, the *Epigrammes* and *The Forrest*.

He deliberately began his new volume with three religious poems in meters which he did not use elsewhere. Like his other pious efforts, they are not very successful, though they are honestly devout. They certainly do not compare in intensity with the religious poetry of Donne or in artistry with that of Crashaw, Herrick, Herbert, or Milton. Next is a collection of love songs, beginning with the longest, a group addressed to Charis. This group, probably composed at various times in Jonson's life, he unified about 1623 when he was fifty. In the series Jonson sustains the traditional praise of women for much longer than he usually does; he is at his best in describing their still unidentified subject as one

> Of whose beauty it was sung
> She shall make the old man young.

More often Jonson displays toward women a morose or hostile manner, which appears here in the final poem of the group. Generally, indeed, he is not very profound when writing about love; the ninth poem of *Under-wood*, for example, merely debates whether the girl should reveal her affair and is witty without being profound. On the other hand, the sixth has been widely admired.

Although Jonson praised Donne in two of his *Epigrammes*, the earlier poems do not show much influence of this powerful contemporary. In *Under-wood*, however, many evidences of indebtedness appear, as in such lyrics as Nos. 7, 8, 10, 12, and 13. The problem of the relationship between the two men becomes acute in the group of elegies beginning with No. 40, for they write in such a similar manner that critics are perplexed about the authorship of the series. Some have concluded that Jonson wrote them all and others that they are all from Donne's hand. No. 41 is almost certainly Donne's, since it appears in his manuscripts and in his *Poems* of 1633; but there is no evidence to connect him with the others. On the other hand, the sequence presents a certain unity of subject and style. Although the problem of authorship will probably remain baffling, its presence shows the real similarities which exist between the two writers.

Distinctively in Jonson's style are his vigorous attacks upon social corruption and upon individuals, deriving from Roman satire. Thus in No. 17, he urges a friend to go to war in order to escape his decadent surroundings, which he paints with gusto. The same qualities mark his epistle to Sir Edward Sacvile and the "Speach according to Horace." He can excoriate individuals as well: the attack on the "Little Shrub" in No. 23 equals in its caustic rhetoric the bitterness of E. A. Robinson; that on the Court Whore, No. 51, is a scathing picture of a woman.

Under-wood also includes several funeral poems of varying power. The Elegy on the Marchioness of Winchester suffers in comparison with Milton's to the same lady, for Jonson confuses exclamations with emotions; the same banality marks his obsequies for Lady Venetia Digby. Much better

are the shorter poems for an old friend, Vincent Corbet, for
the otherwise unknown Philip Gray, and for a child (No.
38). Undoubtedly the finest is his Pindaric Ode to Sir
Lucius Cary and Sir Henry Morison, a noble work, the first
of its kind in English and still one of the best after Jonson
passes beyond its unfortunate opening image of a newborn
child crawling back into the womb.

In many ways his most interesting poems are those which
Jonson wrote about himself. Like Donne and unlike Shake-
speare, Jonson utilized the lyric for personal confession; un-
like Donne he dwells more on his relations with others and
less upon his mental or spiritual problems. His most out-
standing work in this vein is the "Execration upon Vulcan,"
for the lame god of fire had burned Jonson's house and all of
its contents late in 1623. He observes that the fire would not
have been so bad if it had destroyed only romances—he never
had any use for that kind of unrealistic writing—or the works
of some of his contemporaries. But it wiped out several of
his most prized compositions: his translations of Horace
with a commentary derived from Aristotle, his English gram-
mar (perhaps rewritten since one appears in the 1640
Works), some kind of poetic history of his walking trip to
Scotland, a history of Henry V, and so on. The whole poem
conveys a stoical good humor over the catastrophe.

In the same tone of masculine gusto are such poems as his
Ode on Himself, his Fit of Rime against Rime, and the re-
ply to someone who "asked to be sealed of the Tribe of Ben"
—with Inigo Jones, his old rival, led again to the pillory.
Often Jonson describes himself in unflattering terms: he
weighs about 280 pounds and mentions "My mountaine
belly, and my rockie face"; he compares himself to "one great
blot" (Nos. 11, 54, and 58). But after 1630 the aging poet
fell upon hard times. Among his most pathetic works are his
requests for financial assistance (Nos. 64ff.), written when
he had been cut down by a stroke, had lost his standing at
the court of Charles I, and had turned in desperation back
to the stage with *The New Inn*, so bad a failure that the
audience would not permit its first performance to be com-

pleted. In these pitiful poems of his last years Jonson for the first time compromises his principles and is forced in humiliation to beg. The former pride and self-confidence are gone, leaving a hungry, sick, and broken old man.

UNDER-WOODS

CONSISTING OF
DIVERS
POEMS

Martial—*Cineri, gloria sera venit.**

TO THE READER

WIth the same leave the Ancients call'd
that kind of body *Sylva,* or ὕλη, in
which there were workes of divers nature,
and matter congested; as the multitude
call Timber-trees, promiscuously growing,
a *Wood,* or *Forrest:* so am I bold to entitle
these lesser Poems, of later growth, by
this of *Under-wood,* out of the Analogie
they hold to the *Forrest,* in my former
booke, and no otherwise.

BEN. JOHNSON.

* *Epigrams* I.xxv.8: Glory
comes too late to the ashes of the
dead.

UNDER-WOOD*

POEMS OF DEVOTION

THE SINNERS SACRIFICE

1. To the Holy Trinitie

1. O Holy, blessed, glorious *Trinitie*
Of persons, still one God, in *Unitie*.
The faithfull mans beleeved Mysterie,[1]
    Helpe, helpe to lift

5   2. My selfe up to thee, harrow'd, torne, and bruis'd
By sinne, and Sathan, and my flesh misus'd,
As my heart lies in peeces, all confus'd,
    O take my gift.

3. All-gracious God, the *Sinners Sacrifice*.

10 A broken heart thou wert not wont despise,[2]
But 'bove the fat of rammes, or bulls,[3] to prize
    An offring meet,

4. For thy acceptance. O, behold me right,
And take compassion on my grievous plight.

15 What odour[4] can be, then a heart contrite,
    To thee more sweet?

5. *Eternall Father*, God, who did'st create
This All of nothing, gavest it forme, and fate,
And breath'st into it, life, and light, with state[5]

20   To worship thee.

---

* 1640 Title Under-woods; running titles either Under-woods or Under-wood; Under-wood in To the Reader (previous page). See B. H. Newdigate's edition of the *Poems* (Oxford, 1936), p. 355, and the review by W. W. Greg in *RES*, XVIII (1942), 160 n.

1: [1] The Trinity and the Incarnation have been traditionally recognized by Christians as major "mysteries" to be accepted on faith.
[2] Cf. Ps. 51:17.
[3] Cf. 1 Sam. 15:22.
[4] of sacrifice.
[5] in a natural condition.

6. *Eternall God the Sonne,* who not denyd'st
To take our nature; becam'st man, and dyd'st,
To pay our debts, upon thy Crosse, and cryd'st
   All's done in me.[6]

25 7. *Eternall Spirit,* God from both proceeding,
Father and Sonne; the Comforter, in breeding
Pure thoughts in man: with fiery zeale them feeding
   For acts of grace.

8. Increase those acts, ô glorious *Trinitie*
30 Of persons, still one God in *Unitie;*
Till I attaine the long'd-for mysterie
   of seeing your face.[7]

9. Beholding one in three, and three in one,
A *Trinitie,* to shine in *Union;*
35 The gladdest light, darke man can think upon;
   O grant it me!

10. Father, and Sonne, and Holy Ghost, you three
All coeternall in your Majestie,
Distinct in persons, yet in Unitie
40   One God to see.

11. My Maker, Saviour, and my Sanctifier.
To heare, to meditate, sweeten my desire,
With grace, with love, with cherishing intire,
   O, then how blest;

45 12. Among thy Saints elected to abide,
And with thy Angels, placed side, by side,
But in thy presence, truly glorified
   Shall I there rest!

2. A HYMNE TO GOD THE FATHER

  HEare mee, O God!
   A broken heart,
   Is my best part:
  Use still thy rod,
5   That I may prove[1]
   Therein, thy Love.

---

[6] It is finished. John 19:30. 2: [1] know by experience.
[7] I Cor. 13:12.

           If thou hadst not
               Beene sterne to mee,
               But left me free,
10   I had forgot
               My selfe and thee.

           For, sin's so sweet,
               As[2] minds ill bent
               Rarely repent,
15   Until they meet
               Their punishment.

           Who more can crave
               Then thou hast done:
               That gav'st a Sonne,
20   To free a slave?
               First made of nought,
               Withall since bought.[3]

           Sinne, Death, and Hell,
               His glorious Name
25   Quite overcame,
           Yet I rebell,
               And slight the same.

           But, I'le come in,
               Before my losse,
30   Me farther tosse,
           As sure to win
               Under his Crosse.

           3. A Hymne on the Nativitie of My Saviour

           I Sing the birth, was borne to night,
           The Author both of Life, and light;
               The Angels so did sound it,
           And like[1] the ravish'd Sheep'erds said,
5   Who saw the light, and were afraid,
               Yet search'd, and true they found it.[2]

---

² that.   3:   ¹ said similar things to.
³ i.e., ransomed from sin.   ² See Luke 2:8ff.

The Sonne of God, th' Eternall King,
That did us all salvation bring,
 And freed the soule from danger;
10 Hee whom the whole world could not take,[3]
The Word, which heaven, and earth did make,[4]
 Was now laid in a Manger.

The Fathers wisedome will'd it so,
The Sonnes obedience knew no No,
15 Both wills were in one stature;[5]
And as that wisedome had decreed,
The Word was now made Flesh indeed,[6]
 And tooke on him our Nature.

What comfort by him doe wee winne?
20 Who made him selfe the prince[7] of sinne,
 To make us heires of glory?[8]
To see this Babe, all innocence;
A Martyr borne in our defence;
 Can man forget this Storie?

4. A Celebration of CHARIS[1] in Ten Lyrick Peeces

1. *His Excuse for loving*

LEt it not your wonder move,
Lesse your laughter; that I love.
Though I now write fiftie yeares,
I have had, and have my Peeres;

[3] contain.
[4] See John 1:3.
[5] The Persons of Father and Son have the same will.
[6] See John 1:14.
[7] ruler.

[8] a Biblical phrase found at several places in the New Testament, e.g., Rom. 8:17 and James 2:5.
4: [1] The lady has not been identified. The group of poems was not composed as a unit.

5   Poëts, though devine[2] are men:
       Some have lov'd as old agen.
       And it is not always face,
       Clothes, or Fortune gives the grace;
       Or the feature,[3] or the youth:
10   But the Language, and the Truth,
       With the Ardor, and the Passion,
       Gives the Lover weight, and fashion.
       If you will then read the Storie,
       First, prepare you to be sorie,
15   That you never knew till now,
       Either whom to love, or how:
       But be glad, as soone with me,
       When you know, that this is she,
       Of whose Beautie it was sung,
20   She shall make the old man young.
       Keepe the middle age at stay,
       And let nothing high decay.
       Till she be the reason why,
       All the world for love may die.

2. *How he saw her*

       I Beheld her, on a Day,
       When her looke out-flourisht[4] May:
       And her dressing did out-brave[5]
       All the Pride the fields than have:
5   Farre I was from being stupid,
       For I ran and call'd on *Cupid*;
       Love if thou wilt ever see
       Marke of glorie, come with me;
       Where's thy Quiver? bend thy Bow:
10   Here's a shaft, thou art to[6] slow!
       And (withall) I did untie
       Every Cloud about his eye;[7]

---

[2] a commonplace of literary criticism. See, e.g., the conclusion of Sidney's *Defense of Poetry*: poets "are so beloved of the gods that whatsoever they write proceeds of a divine fury."

[3] comeliness.
[4] excelled in adornment.
[5] surpass in finery.
[6] too.
[7] Cupid is traditionally blind.

But, he had not gain'd his sight
Sooner, then he lost his might,
Or his courage; for away
Strait hee ran, and durst not stay,
Letting Bow and Arrow fall,
Nor for any threat, or Call,
Could be brought once back to looke.
I foole-hardie, there up tooke
Both the Arrow he had quit,
And the Bow: with thought to hit
This my object. But she threw
Such a Lightning (as I drew)
At my face, that tooke my sight,
And my motion from me quite;
So that there, I stood a stone,
Mock'd of all: and call'd of one
(Which with griefe and wrath I heard)
Cupids Statue with a Beard,
Or else one that plaid his Ape,
In a *Hercules*-his shape.

3. *What hee suffered*

AFter many scornes like these,
Which the prouder Beauties please,
She content was to restore
Eyes and limbes; to hurt me more
And would on Conditions, be
Reconcil'd to Love, and me.
First, that I must kneeling yeeld
Both the Bow, and shaft I held
Unto her; which love[8] might take
At her hand, with oath, to make
Mee, the scope[9] of his next draught.[10]
Armed, with that selfe-same shaft
He no sooner heard the Law,
But the Arrow home did draw

[8] Cupid.
[9] aim.
[10] shot.

15   And (to gaine her by his Art)
            Left it sticking in my heart:
            Which when she beheld to bleed,
            She repented of the deed,
            And would faine have chang'd the fate,
20   But the Pittie comes too late.
            Looser-like,[11] now, all my wreake[12]
            Is, that I have leave to speake,
            And in either Prose, or Song,
            To revenge me with my Tongue,
25   Which how Dexterously I doe,
            Heare and make Example[13] too.

4. Her Triumph

SEe the Chariot at hand here of Love
     Wherein my Lady rideth!
Each that drawes, is a Swan, or a Dove
     And well the Carre Love guideth.
5   As she goes, all hearts doe duty
               Unto her beauty;
And enamour'd, doe wish, so they might
               But enjoy such a sight,
     That they still were, to run[14] by her side,
10   Through[15] Swords, through Seas, whether[16] she would
                                                  [ride.

Doe but looke on her eyes, they doe light
     All that Loves world compriseth!
Doe but looke on her Haire, it is bright
     As Loves starre[17] when it riseth!
15   Doe but marke her forhead's smoother
               Then words that sooth her!
And from her arched browes, such a grace
               Sheds it selfe through the face,

[11] Like a loser.   to run.
[12] revenge.   [15] pronounced in two syllables.
[13] take as an example.   [16] whithersoever.
[14] that they were to continue   [17] Venus.

As alone there triumphs to the life
20   All the Gaine, all the Good, of the Elements strife.[18]

Have you seene but a bright Lillie grow,
    Before rude hands have touch'd it?
Ha' you mark'd but the fall o' the Snow
    Before the soyle hath smutch'd it?
25   Ha' you felt the wooll of Bever?
        Or Swans Downe ever?
Or have smelt o' the bud o' the Brier?
        Or the Nard[19] in the fire?
Or have tasted the bag of the Bee?
30   O so white! O so soft! O so sweet is she!

5. *His discourse with Cupid*

NOblest *Charis*, you that are
Both my fortune, and my Starre!
And doe governe more my blood
Then the various[20] Moone the flood!
5   Heare, what late Discourse of you,
Love, and I have had; and true.
'Mongst my Muses finding me,
Where he chanc't your name to see
Set, and to this softer straine;
10   Sure, said he, if I have Braine,
This here sung, can be no other
By description, but my Mother![21]
So hath *Homer* prais'd her haire;
So, *Anacreon* drawne the Ayre[22]
15   Of her face, and made to rise
Just about[23] her sparkling eyes,
Both her Browes, bent like my Bow.
By her lookes I doe her know,
Which you call my Shafts. And see!
20   Such my Mothers blushes be,

---

[18] The four elements, earth, water, air, and fire, were thought to be constantly at war.
[19] an aromatic plant.
[20] changing.
[21] Venus.
[22] expression or look.
[23] above.

As the Bath your verse discloses
In her cheekes, of Milke, and Roses;
Such as oft I wanton in.
And, above her even chin,
25   Have you plac'd the banke of kisses,
Where you say, men gather blisses,
Rip'ned with a breath more sweet,
Then when flowers, and West-winds meet,
Nay her white and polished neck,
30   With the Lace that doth it deck,
Is my Mothers! Hearts of slaine
Lovers, made into a Chaine!
And betweene each rising breast,
Lyes the Valley, cal'd my nest,[24]
35   Where I sit and proyn[25] my wings
After flight; and put new stings
To my shafts! Her very Name,
With my Mothers is the same.[26]
I confesse all, I replide,
40   And the Glasse hangs by her side,
And the Girdle 'bout her waste,
All is *Venus:* save unchaste.
But alas, thou seest the least
Of her good, who is the best
45   Of her Sex; But could'st thou *Love*,
Call to mind the formes, that strove
For the Apple,[27] and those three
Make in one, the same were shee.
For this Beauty yet doth hide,
50   Something more then thou hast spi'd.
Outward Grace weake love beguiles:
Shee is *Venus*, when she smiles,

[24] probably referring to the story of Cupid and Psyche; Cupid took Psyche to a retired place.

[25] preen.

[26] Because Vulcan's wife in the *Odyssey* (VIII. 364) is Venus and in the *Iliad* (XVIII. 382) is Charis, some students of mythology identified the two goddesses.

[27] a contest, judged by Paris, of the beauty of Venus, Minerva, and Juno; the prize was a golden apple offered by Eris, goddess of discord.

But shee's *Juno*, when she walkes,
And *Minerva*, when she talkes.

6. *Clayming a second kisse by Desert*

CH*aris* guesse, and doe not misse,
Since I drew a Morning kisse
From your lips, and suck'd an ayre
Thence, as sweet, as you are faire,
5   What my Muse and I have done:
Whether we have lost, or wonne,
If by us, the oddes were laid,
That the Bride (allow'd a Maid)
Look'd not halfe so fresh, and faire,
10   With th' advantage of her haire,
And her Jewels, to the view
Of th' Assembly, as did you!
    Or, that did you sit, or walke,[28]
You were more the eye, and talke
15   Of the Court, to day, then all
Else that glister'd in *White-hall*;
So, as those that had your sight,[29]
Wisht the Bride were chang'd to night,
And did think, such Rites were due
20   To no other Grace but you!
    Or, if you did move to night
In the Daunces, with what spight[30]
Of your Peeres, you were beheld,
That at every motion sweld
25   So to see a Lady tread,
As might all the Graces lead,
And was worthy (being so seene)
To be envi'd of the Queene.
Or if you would yet have stay'd,
30   Whether any would up-braid
To himself his losse of Time;
Or have charg'd[31] his sight of Crime,

---

[28] Or that (parallel to line 8)
if you sat or walked.
[29] i.e., saw you.
[30] jealousy.
[31] accused.

> To have left all sight for you:
>> Guesse of these, which is the true;
35   And, if such a verse as this,
>> May not claime another kisse.

7. *Begging another, on colour[32] of mending the former*

FOr *Loves*-sake, kisse me once againe,
>> I long, and should not beg in vaine,
>> Here's none to spie, or see;
>>> Why doe you doubt, or stay?
5   I'le taste as lightly as the Bee,
That doth but touch his flower, and flies away.
>> Once more, and (faith) I will be gone:
>> Can he that loves, aske lesse then one?
>>> Nay, you may erre in this,
10   And all your bountie wrong:
>> This could be call'd but halfe a kisse.
What w'are but once to doe, we should doe long:
>> I will but mend the last, and tell
>> Where, how it would have relish'd well;
15   Joyne lip to lip, and try:
>>> Each suck others breath.
>> And whilst our tongues perplexed lie,
Let who will thinke us dead, or wish our death.

8. *Urging her of a promise*

> CHaris one day in discourse
> Had of Love, and of his force,
> Lightly promis'd, she would tell
> What a man she could love well:
5   And that promise set on fire
> All that heard her, with desire.
> With the rest, I long expected,[33]
> When the worke would be effected:
> But we find that cold delay,
10   And excuse spun every day,

---

[32] pretense.   [33] looked forward to.

As, untill she tell her one,
We all feare, she loveth none.
Therefore, *Charis*, you must do't,
For I will so urge you to't
15 You shall neither eat nor sleepe,
No, nor forth your window peepe,
With your emissarie[34] eye,
To fetch in the Formes goe by:[35]
And pronounce, which band or lace,
20 Better fits him, then his face;
Nay I will not let you sit
'Fore your Idoll Glasse a whit,
To say over every purle[36]
There; or to reforme a curle;
25 Or with Secretarie[37] *Sis*[38]
To consult, if *Fucus*[39] this
Be as good, as was the last:
All your sweet of life is past,
Make accompt unlesse you can,
30 (And that quickly) speake[40] your Man.

9. *Her man described by her owne Dictamen*[41]

OF your Trouble, *Ben*, to ease me,
I will tell what Man would please me.
I would have him if I could,
Noble; or of greater[42] Blood:
5 Titles, I confesse, doe take me;
And a woman God did make me,
French[43] to boote, at least in fashion,
And his Manners of that Nation.
Young Il'd have him to, and faire,
10 Yet a man;[44] with crisped[45] haire

34 news gathering.
35 To see the (masculine) shapes passing by.
36 loop of lace.
37 confidential maid.
38 original name (Cis) of the chambermaid Prudence in *The New Inn.*
39 cosmetic.
40 make known.
41 pronouncement.
42 i.e., royal.
43 (He should be) French.
44 i.e., adult.
45 curly.

Cast in thousand snares, and rings
For *Loves* fingers, and his wings:
Chestnut colour, or more slack[46]
Gold, upon a ground[47] of black.

15   *Venus*, and *Minervd's* eyes[48]
For he must looke wanton-wise.
Eye-brows bent like *Cupids* bow,
Front,[49] an ample field of snow;
Even nose, and cheeke (withall)

20   Smooth as is the Billiard Ball:
Chin, as woolly as the Peach;
And his lip should kissing teach,
Till he cherish'd too much beard,
And make *Love* or me afeard.

25   He would have a hand as soft
As the Downe, and shew it oft;
Skin as smooth as any rush,
And so thin to see a blush
Rising through it e're it came;

30   All his blood should be a flame
Quickly fir'd as in beginners
In loves schoole, and yet no sinners.
'Twere to long to speake of all,
What we harmonie doe call

35   In a body should be there.
Well he should his clothes to weare;
Yet no Taylor help to make him
Drest,[50] you still for man should take him;
And not thinke h'had eat a stake,

40   Or were set up in a Brake.[51]
Valiant he should be as fire,
Shewing danger[52] more then ire.

---

[46] perhaps drossy, not a pure color.

[47] prevailing color.

[48] i.e., blue and gleaming.

[49] forehead.

[50] Yet even if no tailor help dress him. Cf. the proverb, "Clothes make the man."

[51] be stiffly upright or assume an immovable countenance. A brake is a framework intended to hold anything steady.

[52] bravery.

Bounteous as the clouds to earth;
And as honest as his Birth.
45   All his actions to be such,
As to doe nothing too much.
Nor o're-praise, nor yet condemne;
Nor out-valew, nor contemne;
Nor doe wrongs, nor wrongs receave;
50   Nor tie knots, nor knots unweave;
And from basenesse to be free,
As he durst love Truth and me.
    Such a man, with every part,
I could give my very heart;
55   But of one, if short he came,[53]
I can rest me where I am.

10. *Another Ladyes exception present at the hearing*

FOr his Mind, I doe not care,
That's a Toy, that I could spare:
Let his Title be but great,
His Clothes rich, and band[54] sit neat,
5   Himselfe young, and face be good,
All I wish is understood.
What you please, you parts may call,
'Tis one good part I'ld lie withall.

5. THE MUSICALL STRIFE; IN A PASTORALL DIALOGUE

Shee:
COme with our Voyces, let us warre,
    And challenge all the Spheares,[1]
Till each of us be made a Starre,
    And all the world turne Eares.

Hee:
5   At such a Call, what beast or fowle,
    Of reason emptie is!
What Tree or stone doth want a soule?
    What man but must lose his?

---

[53] if he comes short in one part.   5: [1] contest with the music of
[54] collar or ruff.   the spheres.

Shee:

Mixe[2] then your Notes, that we may prove[3]
10　　　　To stay the running floods?
To make the Mountaine Quarries move?
　　　　And call the walking woods?[4]

Hee:

What need of mee? doe you but sing
　　　　Sleepe, and the Grave will wake,
15　　No tunes are sweet, nor words have sting,
　　　　But what those lips doe make.

Shee:

They say the Angells marke each deed,
　　　　And exercise[5] below,
And out of inward pleasure feed
20　　　　On what they viewing know.

Hee:

O sing not you then, lest the best
　　　　Of Angels should be driven
To fall againe; at such a feast,
　　　　Mistaking earth for heaven.

Shee:

25　　Nay, rather both our soules bee strayn'd
　　　　To meet their high desire;
So they in state of Grace retain'd,
　　　　May wish us of their Quire.

6. A Song

OH doe not wanton with those eyes,
　　　　Lest I be sick with seeing;
Nor cast them downe, but let them rise,
　　　　Lest shame destroy their being:
5　　O, be not angry with those fires,
　　　　For then their threats will kill me;
Nor looke too kind on my desires,
　　　　For then my hopes will spill[1] me;

---

[2] harmonize.　　　　　　　　[5] activity.
[3] attempt.　　　　　　　　　6:　[1] destroy.
[4] as Orpheus did.

O, doe not steepe them in thy Teares,
10   For so will sorrow slay me;
Nor spread[2] them as distract with feares,
      Mine owne enough betray me.

7. In the Person of Woman Kind

A *Song Apologetique*

MEn if you love us, play no more
      The fooles, or Tyrants with your friends,
To make us still sing o're, and o're,
      Our owne false praises, for your ends:
5   Wee have both wits, and fancies too,
            And if wee must, let's sing of you.

Nor doe we doubt, but that we can,
      If wee would search with care, and paine,
Find some one good, in some one man;
10   So going thorow[1] all your straine:[2]
            Wee shall at last, of parcells[3] make
            One good enough for a songs sake.

And as a cunning Painter takes
      In any curious[4] peece you see
15 More pleasure while the thing he makes
      Then when 'tis made, why so will wee.
            And having pleas'd our art, wee'll try
            To make a new, and hang that by.[5]

8. Another
In Defence of Their Inconstancie

A *Song*

HAng up those dull, and envious fooles
      That talke abroad of Womans change,
We were not bred to sit on stooles,
      Our proper vertue is to range:[1]

2 open wide.
7:   1 through.
   2 race: all men.

3 parts from various individuals.
4 skillfully done; excellent.
5 put the first one aside.
8:   1 Our nature is to get about.

5   Take that[2] away, you take our lives,
            We are no women then, but wives.

       Such as in valour would excell
           Doe change,[3] though man, and often fight
       Which we in love must doe aswell,
10   If ever we will love aright.
            The frequent varying of the deed,
            Is that which doth perfection breed.

       Nor is't inconstancie to change
           For what is better, or to make
15   (By searching) what before was strange,
           Familiar, for the uses sake;
            The good, from bad, is not describe,
            But as 'tis often vext[4] and tri'd.

       And this profession of a store[5]
20   In love, doth not alone help forth[6]
       Our pleasure; but preserves us more
           From being forsaken, then doth worth,
            For were the worthiest woman curst
            To love one man, hee'd leave her first.

9. A Nymphs Passion

       I Love, and he loves me againe,
           Yet dare I not tell who;
       For if the Nymphs[1] should know my Swaine,
           I feare they'd love him too;
5   Yet if it be not knowne,
            The pleasure is as good as none,
       For that's a narrow joy is but our owne.[2]

       I'le tell, that if they be not glad,
           They yet may envie me:
10   But then if I grow jealous madde,
           And of them pittied be,

[2] the power of ranging.
[3] i.e., their methods.
[4] examined closely.
[5] plenty, abundance.

[6] assist.
9: [1] other girls.
[2] that is a constricted joy which we cannot share.

It were a plague 'bove scorne
And yet it cannot be foreborne,[3]
Unlesse my heart would as my thought be torne.

15　He is if they can find him, faire,
　　And fresh and fragrant too,
As Summers sky, or purged[4] Ayre,
　　And lookes as Lillies doe,
　　　That are this morning blowne,
20　　　Yet, yet I doubt he is not knowne,
And feare much more, that more of him be showne.

But he hath eyes so round, and bright,
　　As make away my doubt,
Where Love may all his Torches light
25　　Though hate had put them out;
　　　But then t'increase my feares,
　　　What Nymph so e're his voyce but heares
Will be my Rivall, though she have but eares.

I'le tell no more, and yet I love,
30　　And he loves me; yet no
One un-becomming thought doth move
　　From either heart, I know,
　　　But so exempt from blame,
　　　As it would be to each a fame:
35　If Love, or feare, would let me tell his name.

10. The Houre-glasse

DOe but consider this small[1] dust,
　　Here running in the Glasse,
　　　By Atomes mov'd;
　　Could you beleeve, that this,
5　　　The body was
　　　　Of one that lov'd?
And in his Mrs.[2] flame, playing like a flye,
　　Turn'd to cinders by her eye?

---

[3] shunned.　　　　　　　10:　[1] fine; not coarse.
[4] purified.　　　　　　　　　　[2] mistress's.

Yes; and in death, as life unblest,

10   To have't exprest,[3]

Even ashes of lovers find no rest.

11. MY PICTURE LEFT IN SCOTLAND

I Now thinke, Love is rather deafe, then blind,

    For else it could not be,

        That she,

Whom I adore so much, should so slight me,

5   And cast my love behind:

I'm sure my language to her, was as sweet,

        And every close[1] did meet

      In sentence,[2] of as subtile feet,

        As hath the youngest Hee,

10   That sits in shadow of *Apollo's*[3] tree.

Oh, but my conscious feares,

      That flie my thoughts betweene,

      Tell me that she hath seene

    My hundreds of gray haires,

15   Told seven and fortie yeares.

Read so much wast,[4] as she cannot imbrace

My mountaine belly, and my rockie face,

And all these through her eyes, have stopt her eares.

12. AGAINST JEALOUSIE

WRetched and foolish Jealousie,

How cam'st thou thus to enter me?

    I n're was of thy kind;

Nor have I yet the narrow mind

5   To vent that poore desire,

That others should not warme them at my fire:

    I wish the Sun should shine

On all mens Fruit, and flowers, as well as mine.

But under the Disguise of love

10   Thou sai'st, thou only cam'st to prove[1]

---

[3] represented.   [3] as god of poetic inspiration.

11: [1] conclusion of a (musical)   [4] waist, with pun on waste.

phrase.   12: [1] test.

  [2] substance, meaning.

What my affections were.
Think'st thou that love is help'd by feare?
Goe, get thee quickly forth:
Loves sicknesse, and his noted want of worth
15   Seeke doubting Men to please,
I ne're will owe my health to a disease.

13. THE DREAME

OR Scorne, or pittie on me take,
I must the true Relation make,
        I am undone to Night;
    Love in a subtile Dreame disguis'd,
5   Hath both my heart and me surpriz'd,
Whom never yet he durst attempt t'awake;
Nor will he tell me for whose sake
            He did me the Delight,
                Or Spight,
10   But leaves me to inquire,
        In all my wild desire
    Of sleepe againe, who was his Aid;[1]
    And sleepe so guiltie and afraid,
As[2] since he dares not come within my sight.

14. AN EPITAPH ON MASTER VINCENT CORBET[1]

I Have my Pietie too, which could
It vent it selfe, but as it would,
        Would say as much, as both have done
        Before me here, the Friend and Sonne;[2]
5   For I both lost a friend and Father,
Of[3] him whose bones this Grave doth gather:
        Deare *Vincent Corbet* who so long
        Had wrestled with Diseases strong,
    That though they did possesse each limbe,
10   Yet he broke them, e're they could him,

13: [1] Love leaves me to find out, by going back to sleep and dreaming again, who his aide, the girl, was.
    [2] that.
14: [1] father (d. 1619) of the bishop and poet Richard Corbet.
    [2] Richard wrote an elegy on his father's death. The friend has not been identified (and may be Richard himself).
    [3] in.

With the just Canon[4] of his life,
    A life that knew nor noise, or strife:
But was by sweetning so his will,
All order, and Disposure,[5] still.
15   His Mind as pure, and neatly kept,
    As were his Nourceries;[6] and swept
So of uncleannesse, or offence,
That never came ill odour thence:
    And adde his Actions unto these,
20   They were as specious[7] as his Trees.
'Tis true, he could not reprehend;
His very Manners taught t' amend,[8]
    They were so even, grave, and holy;
    No stubbornnesse so stiffe, nor folly
25   To license ever was so light,[9]
As twice to trespasse in his sight,
    His lookes would so correct it, when
    It chid the vice, yet not the Men.
Much from him I professe I wonne,
30   And more, and more, I should have done,
    But that I understood him scant;
    Now I conceive him by my want,
And pray who shall my sorrowes read,
That they for me their teares will shed;
35   For truly, since he left to be,
    I feele, I'm rather dead then he!

Reader, whose life, and name, did e're become
    An *Epitaph*, deserv'd a *Tombe*:
Nor wants it here through penurie, or sloth,
40   Who makes the *one*, so't be first makes *both*.[10]

---

[4] rule.
[5] orderly arrangement.
[6] Vincent was a gardener.
[7] pleasing, lovely.
[8] taught (one) to amend (his own).
[9] indifferent.
[10] Reader, anyone whose life and name were suitable for an epitaph also deserved a tomb; the latter is not lacking here because of my penury or sloth: whoever makes an epitaph makes a tomb if the epitaph is first (-rate in execution). It is not clear whether these four lines are part of the preceding poem.

15. An Epistle to Sir Edward Sacvile, Now Earle of Dorset

IF *Sackvile*,[1] all that have the power to doe
Great and good turns, as wel could time them too,
And knew their how, and where: we should have, then
Lesse[2] list of proud, hard, or ingratefull men.

5   For benefits are ow'd[3] with the same mind
As they are done, and such returnes they find:
You then whose will not only, but desire[4]
To succour my necessities tooke fire,
Not at my prayers, but your sense;[5] which laid

10   The way to meet,[6] what others would upbraid;
And in the Act did so my blush prevent,[7]
As I did feele it done, as soone as meant:
You cannot doubt, but I who freely know
This Good from you, as freely will it owe;

15   And though my fortune humble me, to take
The smallest courtesies with thankes, I make
Yet choyce from whom I take them; and would shame
To have such doe me good, I durst not name:
They are the Noblest benefits, and sinke

20   Deepest in Man of which when he doth thinke,
The memorie delights him more, from whom
Then what he hath receiv'd. Gifts stinke from some,
They are so long a comming, and so hard;
Where any Deed is forc't, the Grace is mard.

25   Can I owe thankes, for Curtesies receiv'd
Against his will that doe's 'hem? that hath weav'd
Excuses, or Delayes? or done 'hem scant,
That they have more opprest me, then my want?
Or if he did it not to succour me,

30   But by meere Chance? for interest? or to free

15: [1] (1591–1652). Much of the poem is a more or less close paraphrase of Seneca's *De Beneficiis.*

[2] a shorter.
[3] acknowledged.

[4] not only your will but also your desire.
[5] perception (of them).
[6] sc. my needs.
[7] anticipate.

Himselfe of farther trouble, or the weight
Of pressure, like one taken in a streight?[8]
All this corrupts the thankes, lesse hath he wonne,
That puts it in his Debt-booke e're't be done;
35   Or that doth sound a Trumpet, and doth call
His Groomes to witnesse; or else lets it fall
In that proud manner: as a good so gain'd,
Must make me sad for what I have obtained.
      No! Gifts and thankes should have one cheerefull
                                              [face,
40   So each, that's done, and tane,[9] becomes a Brace.[10]
He neither gives, or do's, that doth delay
A Benefit or that doth throw't away,
No more then he doth thanke, that will receive
Nought but in corners; and is loath to leave,
45   Lest[11] Ayre, or Print, but flies it: Such men would
Run from the Conscience of it if they could.
As I have seene some Infants of the Sword
Well knowne, and practiz'd borrowers on their word,
Give thankes by stealth, and whispering in the eare,
50   For what they streight would to the world forsweare;
And speaking worst of those, from whom they went
But[12] then, fist fill'd[13] to put me off the sent.[14]
Now dam'mee, Sir, if you shall not command
My Sword ('tis but a poore Sword understand)
55   As farre as any poore Sword i' the Land;
Then turning unto him is[15] next at hand,
Dam's whom he damn'd to, as the veriest Gull,
H'as Feathers, and will serve a man to pull.[16]
      Are they[17] not worthy to be answer'd so,
60   That to such Natures let their full hands flow,

---

[8] difficulty.
[9] taken.
[10] pair.
[11] perhaps least: the recipient is loath to leave the least spoken (Ayre) or written (Print) thanks.
[12] just, only.
[13] i.e., with money.

[14] scent.
[15] who is.
[16] damns the one (to whom he has just damned himself) as the truest gull who has feathers that will serve to be plucked.
[17] the benefactors.

And seeke not wants to succour:[18] but enquire
Like Money-brokers, after Names, and hire
Their bounties forth, to him that last was made,[19]
Or stands to be'n Commission o' the blade?
65 Still, still, the hunters of false fame[20] apply
Their thoughts and meanes to making loude the cry;
But one is bitten by the Dog he fed,
And hurt seeks Cure, the Surgeon bids take bread,
And spunge-like with it dry up the blood quite:
70 Then give it to the Hound that did him bite;[21]
Pardon, sayes he, that were a way to see
All the Towne-curs take each their snatch[22] at me.
O, is it so? knowes he so much? and will
Feed those, at whom the Table points at still?[23]
75 I not deny it, but to helpe the need
Of any, is a Great and generous Deed:
Yea, of th'ingratefull: and he forth must tell[24]
Many a pound, and piece; will place one well;[25]
But these men ever want: their very trade
80 Is borrowing; that but stopt they doe invade
All as their prize, turne Pyrats here at Land,
Ha' their *Bermudas*, and their streights[26] i'th'*Strand*:
Man out of their Boates to th' Temple,[27] and not
                                                    [shift[28]
Now, but command; make tribute, what was gift;
85 And it is paid 'hem with a trembling zeale,
And superstition I dare scarce reveale
If it were cleare, but being so in cloud
Carryed and wrapt, I only am aloud[29]
My wonder, why the taking a Clownes[30] purse,

[18] do not try to help those with genuine needs.
[19] him who was last knighted or is about to be.
[20] the benefactors.
[21] from one of Aesop's fables.
[22] bite.
[23] "At still" means "nevertheless" (Newdigate).
[24] count.
[25] will give one where it should go.
[26] The Bermudas and various narrows were places of piracy.
[27] Leave their boats to attack the Inns of Court.
[28] support themselves precariously.
[29] allowed.
[30] peasant's.

90 Or robbing the poore Market-folkes should nurse
 Such a religious horrour in the brests
 Of our Towne Gallantry! or why there rests
 Such worship due to kicking of a Punck![31]
 Or swaggering with the Watch, or Drawer[32] drunke;
95 Or feats of darknesse acted in Mid-Sun,
 And told of with more License then th' were done!
 Sure there is Misterie in it, I not know[33]
 That men such reverence to such actions show!
 And almost deifie the Authors! make
100 Lowd sacrifice of drinke, for their health-sake
 Reare Suppers[34] in their Names! and spend whole
              [nights
 Unto their praise, in certaine swearing rites;
 Cannot a man be reck'ned in the State
 Of Valour, but at this Idolatrous rate?
105 I thought that Fortitude had beene a meane
 'Twixt feare and rashnesse:[35] not a lust obscene,
 Or appetite[36] of offending, but a skill,
 Or Science of discerning Good and Ill.
 And you Sir know it well to whom I write,
110 That with these mixtures we put out her[37] light.
 Her ends are honestie, and publike good!
 And where they want,[38] she is not understood.
 No more are these of us, let them then goe,
 I have the lyst of mine owne faults to know,
115 Looke too[39] and cure; Hee's not a man hath none,
 But like to be, that every day mends one,[40]
 And feels it, Else he tarries by the Beast:[41]
 Can I discerne how shadowes are decreast,
 Or growne; by height or lowenesse of the Sunne?

[31] prostitute.

[32] the police or a waiter in an inn.

[33] I do not know.

[34] Reare suppers were sumptuous repasts eaten late in the evening.

[35] Cf. Aristotle's discussion of virtue in the *Nicomachean Ethics*.

[36] desire.

[37] Fortitude's: she was considered one of the cardinal virtues.

[38] are lacking.

[39] to.

[40] But would like to be such a man as every day cures one of his faults.

[41] remains at a bestial, subhuman level.

120 And can I lesse of substance?[42] when I runne,
Ride, saile, am coach'd,[43] know I how farre I have
[gone,
And my minds motion not?[44] or have I none:
No! he must feele and know, that will advance.
Men have beene great, but never good by chance,
125 Or on the sudden. It were strange[45] that he
Who was this Morning such a one, should be
Sydney[46] e're night? or that did goe to bed
Coriat,[47] should rise the most sufficient head
Of Christendome? And neither of these know
130 Were the Rack offer'd them how they came so;
'Tis by degrees that men arrive at glad
Profit in ought: each day some little adde,
In time 'twill be a heape; This is not true
Alone in money, but in manners too.
135 Yet we must more then move still, or goe on,
We must accomplish; 'Tis the last Key-stone
That makes the Arch, The rest that there were put
Are nothing till that[48] comes to bind and shut.
Then stands it a triumphall marke! then Men
140 Observe the strength, the height, the why, and when,
It was erected; and still walking under
Meet some new matter[49] to looke up and wonder!
Such Notes are vertuous men! they live as fast[50]
As they are high; are rooted and will last.
145 They need no stilts, nor rise upon their toes,
As if they would belie their stature; those[51]
Are Dwarfes of Honour, and have neither weight
Nor fashion; if they chance aspire to height,
'Tis like light Canes, that first rise big and brave,
150 Shoot forth in smooth and comely spaces; have

[42] And can I judge less of the substance (of morality)?
[43] driven by coach.
[44] And not know the movement or development of my mind?
[45] Would it not be strange.
[46] Sir Philip.

[47] Thomas Coryate, author of the *Crudities;* here taken as the type of stupid, irresponsible author.
[48] the keystone.
[49] reason.
[50] steadfast.
[51] other men.

But few and faire Devisions: but being got
Aloft, grow lesse and streightned;[52] full of knot.
And last, goe out in nothing: You that see
Their difference, cannot choose which you will be.
155 You know (without my flatt'ring you) too much
For me to be your Indice.[53] Keep you such,
That I may love your Person (as I doe)
Without your gift, though I can rate[54] that too,
By thanking thus the curtesie[55] to life,
160 Which you will bury, but therein,[56] the strife
May grow so great to be example, when
(As their true rule or lesson) either[57] men
Donnor's or *Donnee's*[58] to their practise shall
Find you to reckon[59] nothing, me owe all.

16. An Epistle to Master John Selden[1]

I Know to whom I write: Here, I am sure,
Though I am short,[2] I cannot be obscure:
Lesse shall I for the Art or dressing care,
Truth, and the Graces best, when naked are.
5   Your Booke, my *Selden*, I have read, and much
Was trusted, that you thought my judgement such
To aske it: though in most of workes it be
A pennance, where a man may not be free,
Rather then Office, when it doth or may
10   Chance that the Friends affection proves Allay
Unto the Censure.[3] Yours all need doth flie
Of this so vitious[4] Humanitie:

[52] narrowed.
[53] indicator.
[54] appreciate.
[55] benevolence.
[56] perhaps thereafter.
[57] perhaps to be emended to "other."
[58] donors or recipients.
[59] owe.
16: [1] jurist (1584–1654), author of many books, including *Titles of Honour* (1614), to which this poem is prefixed. Selden mentions Jonson with praise in the Preface.
[2] brief.
[3] When one undergoes penance, he has no choice of what he will do; when he performs an ecclesiastical office (such as giving penance) he has freedom but the affection for a friend may allay the censure.
[4] reprehensible.

Then which there is not unto Studie, a more
Pernitious enemie. We see before

15 A many[5] of bookes, even good judgements wound
Themselves through favouring what is there not found:
But I on yours farre otherwise shall doe,
Not flie the Crime, but the Suspition too:
Though I confesse (as every Muse hath err'd,

20 And mine not least) I have too oft preferr'd
Men, past their termes,[6] and prais'd some names too
                                                    [much,
But 'twas with purpose to have made them such.
Since being deceiv'd, I turne a sharper eye
Upon my selfe, and aske to whom? and why?

25 And what I write? And vexe[7] it many dayes
Before men get a verse: much lesse a Praise;
So that my Reader is assur'd, I now
Meane what I speake: and still will keepe that Vow.
Stand forth my Object, then you that have beene

30 Ever at home:[8] yet, have all Countries seene:
And like a Compasse keeping one foot still
Upon your Center, doe your Circle fill
Of generall knowledge; watch'd men, manners too,
Heard what times past have said, seene what ours doe:

35 Which Grace shall I make love too first? your skill,
Or faith in things?[9] or is't your wealth and will
T' instruct and teach? or your unweary'd paine
Of Gathering? Bountie in pouring out againe?
What fables have you vext![10] what truth redeem'd!

40 Antiquities search'd! Opinions dis-esteem'd!
Impostures branded! And Authorities urg'd!
What blots and errours, have you watch'd and purg'd
Records, and Authors of! how rectified,[11]
Times, manners, customes! Innovations spide!

[5] a number (confused with "meinie").
[6] more than is warranted.
[7] examine closely.
[8] Selden was not a traveler. Cf. the different application of the compass image in Donne's "Valediction Forbidding Mourning."
[9] facts or events.
[10] See n. 7 opposite.
[11] reformed.

45 Sought out the Fountaines, Sources, Creekes, paths,
                                                    [wayes,
    And noted the beginnings and decayes!
    Where is that nominall marke, or reall rite,[12]
    Forme Act or Ensigne,[13] that hath scap'd your sight.
    How are Traditions there examined: how
50 Conjectures retriv'd![14] And a Storie now
    And then of times (besides the bare Conduct
    Of what it tells us) weav'd in to instruct.
    I wonder'd at the richnesse, but am lost,
    To see the workmanship so'xceed the cost!
55 To marke the excellent seas'ning of your Stile!
    And manly elocution, not one while
    With horrour rough, then rioting with wit!
    But to the Subject, still the Colours[15] fit
    In sharpnesse of all Search, wisdome of Choise,
60 Newnesse of Sense, Antiquitie of voyce!
        I yeeld, I yeeld, the matter of your praise
    Flowes in upon me, and I cannot raise
    A banke against it. Nothing but the round
    Large claspe of Nature,[16] such a wit can bound.
65 Monarch in Letters! 'Mongst thy Titles[17] showne
    Of other honours, thus, enjoy thine owne.
    I first salute thee so; and gratulate[18]
    With that thy Stile, thy keeping of thy State;
    In offering this thy worke to no great Name,[19]
70 That would, perhaps, have prais'd, and thank'd the
                                                    [same,
    But nought beyond. He thou hast given it to,
    Thy learned Chamber-fellow, knowes to doe
    It true respects. He will not only love

[12] token sign or true ceremony.
[13] conception, actuality, or symbol.
[14] restored to knowledge.
[15] of rhetoric: ornaments of style or diction.
[16] the whole creation.
[17] Cf. Selden's work, *Titles of Honour.*
[18] hail, greet.
[19] *Titles of Honour* was not dedicated to a patron but, as l. 72 says, to Selden's "learned Chamber-fellow," Edward Hayward (d. 1658), member of the Inner Temple and a minor poet.

Embrace, and cherish; but he can approve[20]
75   And estimate thy Paines; as having wrought
In the same Mines of knowledge; and thence brought
Humanitie enough to be a friend,
And strength to be a Champion, and defend
Thy gift 'gainst envie. O how I doe count
80   Among my commings in,[21] and see it mount,
The gaine of your two friendships! *Hayward* and
Selden! two Names that so much understand![22]
On whom I could take up,[23] and ne're abuse
The Credit, what would furnish a tenth Muse!
85   But here's no time, nor place, my wealth to tell,
You both are modest. So am I. Farewell.

17. An Epistle to a Friend, to Perswade Him to the Warres

WAke, friend[1] from forth thy Lethargie: the Drum
Beates brave, and loude in *Europe*, and bids come
All that dare rowse:[2] or are not loth to quit
Their vitious[3] ease, and be o'rewhelm'd with it.
5   It is a call to keepe the spirits alive
That gaspe for action, and would yet revive
Mans buried honour, in his sleepie life:
Quickning dead Nature,[4] to her noblest strife.
All other Acts of Worldlings, are but toyle
10   In dreames, begun in hope, and end[5] in spoile.[6]
Looke on th' ambitious man, and see him nurse,
His unjust hopes, with praises begg'd, or (worse)
Bought Flatteries, the issue of his purse,
Till he becomes both their, and his owne curse!
15   Looke on the false, and cunning man, that loves

[20] confirm.
[21] income.
[22] support.
[23] get.
17: [1] The friend is named Colby in l. 176 but is not otherwise identified.
[2] H&S suggest a date about 1620, when English volunteers went to support Frederick of the Palatinate.
[3] reprehensible.
[4] Man's nature is to struggle for the good and honorable.
[5] ended.
[6] failure.

No person, nor is lov'd: what wayes he proves[7]
To gaine[8] upon his belly; and at last
Crush'd in the snakie brakes,[9] that he had past!
See, the grave, sower,[10] and supercilious Sir
20 In outward face, but inward, light as Furre,
Or Feathers: lay his fortune out to show
Till envie wound, or maime it at a blow!
See him, that's call'd, and thought the happiest man,
Honour'd at once,[11] and envi'd (if it can
25 Be honour is so mixt) by such as would
For all their spight be like him if they could:
No part or corner man can looke upon,
But there are objects,[12] bid him to be gone
As farre as he can flie, or follow Day,[13]
30 Rather then here so bogg'd in vices stay:
The whole world here leaven'd with madnesse swells.
And being[14] a thing, blowne[15] out of nought, rebells
Against his Maker; high alone with weeds,
And impious ranknesse of all Sects and seeds:
35 Not to be checkt, or frighted now with fate,
But more licentious made, and desperate!
Our Delicacies are growne capitall,[16]
And even our sports are dangers! what we call
Friendship is now mask'd Hatred! Justice fled,
40 And shamefastnesse together![17] All lawes dead
That kept man living! Pleasures only sought!
Honour and honestie, as poore things thought
As they are made! Pride, and stiffe Clownage[18] mixt
To make up Greatnesse! and mans whole good fix't
45 In bravery,[19] or gluttony, or coyne,
All which he makes the servants of the Groine,

[7] attempts.
[8] get ahead, or prosper.
[9] thicket: having succeeded by obsequious means, he later is destroyed by his past.
[10] sour.
[11] at the same time.
[12] objects which bid.
[13] avoid darkness.
[14] And he (the man of l. 27) being.
[15] created.
[16] deadly, fatal.
[17] Justice and modesty have fled together.
[18] probably unbending stupidity.
[19] fine clothes.

Thither[20] it flowes. How much did *Stallion* spend
To have his Court-bred-fillie there commend
His Lace and Starch; And fall[21] upon her back
50 In admiration, stretch'd upon the rack
Of lust, to his rich Suit and Title, Lord?[22]
I, that's a Charme and halfe![23] She must afford
That all respect; She must lie downe: Nay more
'Tis there civilitie to be a whore;
55 Hee's one of blood, and fashion! and with these
The bravery makes, she can no honour leese:[24]
To do't with Cloth, or Stuffes, lusts name might merit;
With Velvet, Plush, and Tissues, it is spirit.[25]
   O, these so ignorant Monsters! light, as proud,
60 Who can behold their Manners, and not clowd-
Like upon them lighten?[26] If nature could
Not make a verse; Anger; or laughter would
To see 'hem aye discoursing with their Glasse,
How they may make some one that day an Asse
65 Planting their Purles,[27] and Curles spread forth like
[Net;
And every Dressing for a Pitfall set
To catch the flesh in, and to pound a Prick[28]
Be at their Visits, see 'hem squemish, sick,
Ready to cast,[29] at one, whose band[30] sits ill,
70 And then, leape mad on a neat Pickardill;[31]
As if a Brize[32] were gotten i' their tayle,
And firke,[33] and jerke, and for the Coach-man raile,[34]
And jealous each of other, yet thinke long
To be abroad chanting some baudie song,

---

[20] whither.
[21] And to have her fall.
[22] title of Lord.
[23] Ay, the title of Lord is more than sufficient.
[24] lose.
[25] To be an adultress for cheap goods (Cloth, or Stuffes) might merit the name of lust; to do so for expensive materials (Velvet, Plush, and Tissues—a rich cloth) is spirit.
[26] perhaps fulminate.
[27] laces.
[28] excite sexually.
[29] criticize.
[30] collar or ruff.
[31] one who wore a large, fashionable collar.
[32] gadfly.
[33] flounce.
[34] utter abusive language.

75   And laugh, and measure thighes, then squeake, spring,
                                                    [itch,
        Doe all the tricks of a saut[35] Lady Bitch;
        For t' other pound of sweet-meats, he shall feele
        That payes, or what he will.[36] The Dame is steele,
        For these[37] with her young Companie shee'll enter,
80   Where *Pittes*, or *Wright*, or *Modet*[38] would not venter,
        And comes by these Degrees, the Stile t' inherit
        Of woman of fashion, and a Lady of spirit:
        Nor is the title question'd with our proud,
        Great, brave,[39] and fashion'd folke, these are allow'd
85   Adulteries now, are not so hid, or strange,
        They're growne Commoditie upon Exchange;
        He that will follow but anothers wife,
        Is lov'd, though he let out his owne for life:
        The Husband now's call'd churlish, or a poore
90   Nature, that will not let his Wife be a whore;
        Or use all arts, or haunt all Companies
        That may corrupt her, even in his eyes.[40]
        The brother trades a sister; and the friend
        Lives to the Lord, but to the Ladies end.[41]
95   Lesse must not be thought on then Mistresse: or
        If it be thought kild like her Embrions;[42] for,
        Whom no great[43] Mistresse, hath as yet infam'd[44]
        A fellow of course Letcherie is nam'd,
        The Servant of the Serving-woman in scorne,
100   Ne're[45] came to taste the plentous Mariage-horne.
            Thus they doe talke. And are these objects fit
        For man to spend his money on? his wit?

[35] salt: in heat.

[36] probably, He who pays or does as he will shall enjoy the rest of her pleasures.

[37] i.e., places of ill repute.

[38] evidently infamous contemporary women.

[39] fine.

[40] before his face.

[41] probably, Lives for the lord but with the goal of his lady.

[42] probably, One must not consider relations with less than the mistress of the house; or, if one does consider less, the thought must be aborted (as she literally does).

[43] important—or pregnant.

[44] defamed.

[45] Who never.

His time? health? soule? will he for these goe throw[46]
Those thousands on his back,[47] shall after blow
105 His body to the Counters,[48] or the Fleete?[49]
Is it for these that fine man meets the street[50]
Coach'd, or on foot cloth,[51] thrice chang'd every day,
To teach each suit,[52] he has the ready way
From *Hide-Parke* to the Stage, where[53] at the last
110 His deare and borrow'd Bravery[54] he must cast?[55]
When not his Combes, his Curling-irons, his Glasse,
Sweet bags,[56] sweet Powders, nor sweet words will
[passe
For lesse Securitie? O   [57] for these
Is it that man pulls on himselfe Disease?
115 Surfet? and Quarrell? drinkes the tother health?[58]
Or by Damnation voids it?[59] or by stealth?
What furie of late is crept into our Feasts?
What honour given to the drunkennest Guests?
What reputation to beare[60] one Glasse more?
120 When oft the Bearer, is borne out of dore?
This hath our ill-us'd freedome, and soft peace
Brought on us, and will every hour increase
Our vices, doe[61] not tarry in a place,
But being in Motion still (or rather in race)
125 Tilt[62] one upon another, and now beare
This way, now that, as if their number were
More then themselves, or then our lives could take,
But both[63] fell[64] prest under the load they make.
   I'le bid thee looke no more, but flee, flee friend,
130 This *Praecipice*, and Rocks that have no end,

[46] spend.
[47] on clothes to wear.
[48] prisons for debtors.
[49] another prison.
[50] travels in town.
[51] riding in a coach or on a horse, the latter covered with a large, richly ornamented cloth.
[52] probably, follower.
[53] whereas.
[54] finery.
[55] take off.
[56] bags of perfumes affected by gallants.
[57] probably God or Heaven or Friend.
[58] drinks just one more toast.
[59] abstains, with criticism from his companions.
[60] take.
[61] Our vices, which do.
[62] contend.
[63] probably, we and our vices.
[64] emend to "fall"?

Or side, but threatens Ruine. The whole Day
Is not enough now, but the Nights to play:
And whilst our states, strength, body, and mind we
[waste,

Goe make our selves the Usurers at a cast.[65]

135   He that no more for Age, Cramps, Palsies, can
Now use the bones,[66] we see doth hire a man
To take the box up for him; and pursues
The Dice with glassen[67] eyes, to the glad viewers
Of what he throwes: Like letchers growne content

140   To be beholders, when their powers are spent.
            Can we not leave this worme? or will we not?
Is that the truer excuse? or have we got
In this, and like,[68] an itch of Vanitie,
That scratching now's our best Felicitie?

145   Well, let it goe. Yet this is better, then
To lose the formes, and dignities of men;
To flatter my good Lord, and cry his Bowle
Runs sweetly, as[69] it had his Lordships Soule;
Although, perhaps it has, what's that to me,

150   That may stand by, and hold my peace? will he
When I am hoarse, with praising his each cast,[70]
Give me but that againe,[71] that I must wast[72]
In Sugar Candide, or in butter'd beere,
For the recovery of my voyce? No, there

155   Pardon his Lordship. Flattry's growne so cheape
With him, for he is followed with that heape
That watch, and catch, at what they may applaud
As[73] a poore single flatterer, without Baud
Is nothing, such scarce meat and drinke he'le give,

160   But he that's both,[74] and slave to both,[75] shall live,
And be belov'd, while the Whores last. O times,
Friend flie from hence; and let these kindled rimes

---

[65] i.e., of dice.
[66] dice.
[67] glassy.
[68] and the like.
[69] as though.
[70] roll of the ball.
[71] only in return.

[72] waste away; lose strength.
[73] That.
[74] flatterer and baud.
[75] meat and drinke. H&S emend to "boote" with MS. support.

Light thee from hell on earth: where flatterers,[76]
[spies,
    Informers, Masters both of Arts and lies;
165 Lewd slanderers, soft whisperers that let blood
    The life,[77] and fame-vaynes[78] (yet not understood[79]
    Of the poore sufferers); where the envious, proud,
    Ambitious, factious, superstitious, lowd
    Boasters, and perjur'd, with the infinite more
170 Praevaricators swarme. Of which the store,
    (Because th' are everywhere amongst Man-kind
    Spread through the World) is easier farre to find,
    Then once to number, or bring forth to hand,
    Though thou wert Muster-master[80] of the Land.
175   Goe quit[81] 'hem all. And take along with thee,
    Thy true friends wishes, *Colby* which shall be,
    That thine[82] be just, and honest, that thy Deeds
    Not wound thy conscience, when thy body bleeds;
    That thou dost all things more for truth, then glory,
180 And never but for doing wrong be sory;
    That by commanding first thy selfe, thou mak'st
    Thy person fit for any charge thou tak'st;
    That fortune never make thee to complaine,
    But what she gives, thou dar'st give her again;
185 That whatsoever face thy fate puts on,
    Thou shrinke or start not; but be alwayes one;
    That thou thinke nothing great, but what is good,
    And from that thought strive to be understood.
    So, 'live or dead, thou wilt preserve a fame
190 Still pretious, with the odour of thy name.
    And last, blaspheme not, we did never heare
    Man thought the valianter, 'cause he durst sweare,
    No more, then we should think a Lord had had
    More honour in him, 'cause we'ave knowne him mad:
195 These take, and now goe seeke thy peace in Warre,
    Who falls for love of God, shall rise a Starre.

---

[76] where swarme (l. 170) flat-
terers, etc.

[77] probably, let out the life
blood.

[78] those proud of their fame.

[79] realized.

[80] with the right to muster out
everyone.

[81] leave.

[82] thy wishes.

18. An Epitaph on Master Philip Gray

Reader stay,
And if I had no more to say,
But here doth lie till the last Day,
All that is left of *Philip Gray*.[1]
5   It might thy patience richly pay:
For, if such men as he could die,
What suretie of life have thou, and I.

19. Epistle To a Friend[1]

THey are not, Sir, worst Owers, that doe pay
Debts when they can: good men may breake their
[day.[2]
And yet the noble Nature never grudge,[3]
'Tis then a crime, when the Usurer is Judge,
5   And he is not in friendship. Nothing there[4]
Is done for gaine: If't be 'tis not sincere.
Nor should I at this time protested be,[5]
But that some greater names have broke[6] with me,
And their words too; where I but breake my Band.[7]
10   I adde that (but)[8] because I understand
That as the lesser breach: for he that takes
Simply my Band, his trust in me forsakes,
And lookes unto the forfeit. If you be
Now so much friend, as you would trust in me,
15   Venter[9] a longer time, and willingly:
All is not barren land, doth fallow lie.
Some grounds are made the richer, for the Rest;[10]
And I will bring a Crop, if not the best.

18:   [1] not identified.
19:   [1] not identified.
[2] fail to pay on time.
[3] never vex the noble nature (of the good lender).
[4] with the good lender.
[5] be formally charged for non-payment.
[6] both their agreements and their connections.
[7] bond.
[8] I add the word *but* (only).
[9] Venture.
[10] lying fallow.

20. An Elegie

CAn Beautie that did prompt me first to write,
>Now threaten, with those meanes she did invite:
Did her perfections call me on to gaze!
>Then like, then love;[1] and now would they
>>[amaze!][2]

5 Or was she gracious a-farre off? but neere
>A terror? or is all this but my feare?
That as the water makes things, put in't, streight,
>Crooked appeare; so that doth my conceipt:
I can helpe that with boldnesse; And love sware,
10 >And fortune once,[3] t'assist the spirits that dare.
But which shall lead me on? both these are blind:
>Such Guides men use not, who their way would
>>[find.

Except[4] the way be errour[5] to those ends:
>And then the best are still, the blindest friends!
15 Oh how a Lover may mistake! to thinke,
>Or love, or fortune blind, when they but winke[6]
To see men feare: or else for truth, and State,
>Because they would free Justice imitate,[7]
Vaile their owne eyes, and would impartially
20 >Be brought by us to meet our Destinie.
If it be thus, Come love, and fortune goe,[8]
>I'le lead you on, or if my fate will so,
That I must send one first, my Choyce assignes,
>Love to my heart, and fortune to my lines.

20: [1] Then to like her, then to love her.
>[2] bewilder, perplex.
>[3] love and fortune once swore.
>[4] Unless.
>[5] a devious or wandering one.

[6] shut their eyes.
[7] Both Love and Fortune are traditionally pictured as blind; Justice is blindfolded.
[8] Let us—Love, Fortune, and me—go together.

21. AN ELEGIE

BY those bright Eyes, at whose immortall fires
    Love lights his torches to inflame desires;
By that faire Stand,[1] your forehead, whence he bends
    His double Bow, and round his Arrowes sends;
5   By that tall Grove, your haire; whose globy[2] rings
    He flying curles, and crispeth,[3] with his wings.
By those pure bathes your either cheeke discloses,
    Where he doth steepe himselfe in Milke and
                    [Roses;
And lastly by your lips, the banke of kisses,
10   Where men at once may plant, and gather blisses:
Tell me (my lov'd Friend)[4] doe you love or no?
    So well as I may tell in verse, 'tis so?
You blush, but doe not: friends are either none,
    (Though they may number bodyes) or but one.[5]
15   I'le therefore aske no more, but bid you love;
    And so that either may example prove
Unto the other; and live patternes,[6] how
    Others, in time may love, as we doe now.
Slip[7] no occasion; As time stands not still,
20   I knowe no beautie, nor no youth that will.[8]
To use the present, then, is not abuse;
    You have a Husband is[9] the just excuse
Of all that can be done him; Such a one
    As would make shift, to make himself alone,[10]
25   That which we can, who both in you, his Wife,
    His Issue, and all Circumstance of life
As in his place, because he would not varie,
    Is constant to be extraordinarie.

21:   [1] station.
    [2] spherical.
    [3] curls.
    [4] the girl.
    [5] Friendship (i.e., love) does not exist unless the two participants are a single entity. Donne frequently develops this idea—e.g., "The Good Morrow."

[6] "Live" is apparently a verb: live as patterns. See a similar statement in Donne, "The Relique."
    [7] Let slip.
    [8] will (stand still).
    [9] who is.
    [10] Such a one as would attempt to do, all by himself.

22. A Satyricall Shrub[1]

A Womans friendship! God whom I trust in,
  Forgive me this one foolish deadly sin[2]
Amongst my many other, that I may
  No more, I am sorry for so fond[3] cause, say
5 At fifty yeares, almost, to value it,
  That ne're was knowne to last above a fit![4]
Or have the least of Good, but what it must
  Put on for fashion, and take up on trust:
Knew I all this afore? had I perceiv'd,
10 That their whole life was wickednesse, though
  [weav'd
Of many colours; outward fresh, from spots,
  But their whole inside full of ends, and knots?
Knew I, that all their Dialogues, and discourse,
  were such as I will now relate, or worse.

Here, something is wanting.

15 Knew I this Woman? yes; And you doe see,
  How penitent I am, or I should be?
Doe not you aske to know her, she is worse
  Then all Ingredients made into one curse,
And that pour'd out upon Man-kind can be![5]
20 Thinke but the Sin of all her sex, 'tis she!
I could forgive her being proud! a whore!
  Perjur'd! and painted! if she were no more—,
But she is such, as she might yet forestall[6]
  The Divell; and be the damning of us all.

22: [1] Cf. the general title *Under-wood*.
  [2] of love for a woman.
  [3] foolish.
  [4] short period (of madness).
  [5] alluding to Pandora's box.
  [6] apparently, to stand in place of.

23. A LITTLE SHRUB GROWING BY

ASke not to know this Man. If fame should speake[1]
　　His name in any mettall, it would breake.
Two letters[2] were enough the plague[3] to teare
　　Out of his Grave, and poyson every eare.
5　A parcell of Court-durt, a heape, and masse
　　Of all vice hurld together, there he was,
Proud, false, and trecherous, vindictive, all
　　That thought can adde, unthankfull, the lay-stall[4]
Of putrid flesh alive! of blood, the sinke![5]
10　　And so I leave to stirre him, lest he stinke.

24. AN ELEGIE

THough Beautie be the Marke of praise,
　　And yours of whom I sing be such
　　As not the World can praise too much,
Yet is't your vertue now I raise.

5　A vertue, like Allay,[1] so gone
　　Throughout your forme; as[2] though that[3] move,
　　And draw, and conquer all mens love,
This[4] subjects you to love of one.

Wherein you triumph yet: because
10　　'Tis of your selfe, and that you use
　　The noblest freedome, not to chuse
Against or Faith, or honours lawes.

But who should lesse expect from you,
　　In whom alone love lives agen?
15　　By whom he is restor'd to men:
And kept, and bred,[5] and brought up true?

23:　[1] reveal.
　　[2] He has not been identified.
　　[3] perhaps, of gossip or talk.
　　[4] a place to put garbage and dung.
　　[5] cesspool.

24:　[1] alloy.
　　[2] that.
　　[3] your beauty.
　　[4] your virtue.
　　[5] educated, trained.

His falling Temples you have rear'd,
    The withered Garlands tane[6] away;
    His Altars kept from the Decay,
20 That envie wish'd, and Nature fear'd.

And on them, burne so chaste a flame,
    With so much Loyalties expence
    As[7] Love t'aquit[8] such excellence,
Is gone himselfe into your Name.[9]

25 And you are he: the Dietie
    To whom all Lovers are design'd;
    That would their betters object find:
Among which faithfull troope am I.

Who as an off-spring[10] at your shrine,
30   Have sung this Hymne, and here intreat
    One sparke of your Diviner heat
To light upon a Love[11] of mine.

Which if it kindle not, but scant
    Appeare, and that to shortest view,
35   Yet give me leave t'adore in you
What I, in her, am grievd to want.

25. An Ode. To Himselfe

WHere do'st thou carelesse lie
    Buried in ease and sloth?
    Knowledge, that sleepes, doth die;
    And this Securitie,
5   It is the common Moath,
That eats on wits, and Arts, and destroyes[1] them both.

---

[6] taken.
[7] that.
[8] reward (requite).
[9] That is, the letters l, o, v, e make an anagram in part with her name. Fleay suggested possibly Lady Covell (see *Under*. 58).
[10] Whalley emended to "of-fering."
[11] another girl, repeated as "her" in l. 36.
25: [1] Various emendations have been suggested before "destroyes" to complete the meter: oft, quite, so, yet, or soon. MSS. support *oft*.

Are all th'*Aonian*[2] springs
   Dri'd up? lyes *Thespia*[3] wast?
Doth *Clarius*[4] Harp want strings,
10   That not a Nymph now sings!
   Or droop they as disgrac't,
To see their Seats and Bowers by chattring Pies[5] de-
                    [fac't?

If hence thy silence be,
   As 'tis too just a cause;
15   Let this thought quicken thee,
Minds that are great and free,
   Should not on fortune pause,
'Tis crowne enough to vertue still, her owne applause.

What though the greedie Frie
20   Be taken with false Baytes
Of worded[6] Balladrie,
   And thinke it Poësie?
   They die with their conceits,
And only pitious scorne, upon their folly waites.

25   Then take in hand thy Lyre,
   Strike in thy proper straine,
With *Japhets* lyne,[7] aspire[8]
Sols Chariot for new fire,
   To give the world againe:
30 Who aided him, will thee, the issue of *Joves* braine.[9]

And since our Daintie age,
   Cannot indure reproofe.
Make not thy selfe a Page,
   To that strumpet the Stage,
35   But sing high and aloofe,
Safe from the wolves black jaw, and the dull Asses
                    [hoofe.

---

[2] region sacred to the Muses.
[3] at the foot of Mount Helicon, sacred to the Muses.
[4] Apollo.
[5] magpies.
[6] wordy.
[7] i.e., Prometheus (H&S).
[8] aspire to.
[9] Minerva.

26. THE MIND OF THE FRONTISPICE TO A BOOKE[1]

FRom Death, and darke oblivion, neere the same,
    The Mistresse of Mans life, grave Historie,
Raising the World to good or evill fame,
    Doth vindicate it to eternitie.
5   Wise Providence would so; that nor the good
    Might be defrauded, nor the great secur'd,[2]
But both might know their wayes were understood,
    When Vice alike in time with vertue dur'd.[3]
Which makes that (lighted by the beamie hand
10   Of Truth that searcheth the most hidden Springs
And guided by experience, whose straite wand
    Doth meet, whose lyne doth sound the depth of
                    [things:)
Shee[4] chearfully supporteth what she reares,
    Assisted by no strengths, but art[5] her owne,
15   Some note of which each varied Pillar beares,
    By which as proper titles, she is knowne
Times witnesse, herald of Antiquitie,
    The light of Truth, and life of Memorie.[6]

27. AN ODE TO JAMES EARLE OF DESMOND,[1] WRIT IN QUEENE ELIZABETHS TIME, *since lost, and recovered*

WHere art thou *Genius?* I should use
    Thy present Aide: Arise Invention,
Wake, and put on the wings of *Pindars*[2] Muse,
    To towre[3] with my intention

26: [1] printed facing the frontispiece of Sir Walter Raleigh's *History of the World* (1614). (See Plate I, facing p. 222.) The poem accurately describes the picture; for its symbolism see Gilbert.
   [2] made overconfident.
   [3] existed.
   [4] Historie (of l. 2).
   [5] except those which are.
   [6] H&S point out that the last two lines are translated from Cic-ero's definition of history in *De Oratore* 2.36.

27: [1] James Fitzgerald, the Earl (d. 1601), sent to Ireland in 1579 but jailed there and kept in prison until released in 1600 to combat the pretensions to his title raised by a cousin.
   [2] Greek writer of odes (518–438 B.C.).
   [3] soar (as a hawk) above the prey.

5   High, as his mind, that doth advance
Her[4] upright head, above the reach of Chance,
                    Or the times envie:
                    Cynthius,[5] I applie
My bolder numbers to thy golden *Lyre:*
10   O, then inspire
Thy Priest in this strange rapture; heat my braine
                    With *Delphick*[6] fire:
That I may sing my thoughts, in some unvulgar straine.

      Rich beame of honour, shed your light
15   On these darke rymes; that my affection
May shine (through every chincke) to every sight
                    graced by your Reflection!
Then shall my Verses, like strong Charmes
Breake the knit Circle of her[7] Stonie Armes,
20   That hold your spirit:
                    And keepes your merit
Lock't in her cold embraces, from the view
                    Of eyes more true,
Who would with judgement search, searching con-
                                        [clude,
25   (As prov'd in you)
True noblêsse Palme[8] growes straight, though handled
                                        [ne're so rude.

      Nor thinke your selfe unfortunate,
      If subject to the jealous errors
Of politique pretext, that wryes[9] a State,
30   Sinke not beneath these terrors:
                    But whisper; O glad Innocence
Where only a mans birth is his offence;[10]
                    Or the dis-favour,
                    Of such as savour

----

[4] Invention's: poetic composition is not the result of chance.

[5] Apollo.

[6] Greek oracle.

[7] probably the prison's.

[8] the palm of true nobility.

[9] perverts; deflects from its course.

[10] perhaps referring to the fact that Sir James's father had been executed in 1582 as rebel to the Crown.

35 Nothing, but practise upon honours thrall.
　　　　　O vertues fall,[11]
When her dead essence (like the Anatomie
　　　　in Surgeons hall)
Is but a Statists[12] theame, to read[13] Phlebotomie.[14]

40 　　　　　Let *Brontes*, and black *Steropes*,
　　　　　　Sweat at the forge, their hammers beating;
Pyracmon's[15] houre will come to give them ease,
　　　　　　Though but while mettal's heating:
　　　　　And, after all the *Ætnean* Ire,
45 Gold, that is perfect, will out-live the fire.
　　　　　　For fury wasteth,
　　　　　　As patience lasteth.
No Armour to the mind! he is shot free[16]
　　　　　From injurie,
50 That is not hurt; not he, that is not hit;
　　　　　So fooles we see,
Oft scape an Imputation, more through luck, then wit.

But to your selfe most loyall Lord,
　　　　　(Whose heart in that bright Sphere flames clearest,
55 Though many Gems be in your bosome stor'd,
　　　　　　Unknowne which is the Dearest.)
　　　　　If I auspitiously devine,
(As my hope tells) that our faire *Phœbes*[17] shine,
　　　　　Shall light those places,
60 　　　　　With lustrous Graces,
Where darknesse with her glomie[18]-Sceptred hand,
　　　　　Doth now command.
O then (my best-best lov'd) let me importune,
　　　　　That you will stand,
65 As farre from all revolt, as you are now from Fortune.

[11] perish.
[12] politicians.
[13] lecture on.
[14] the medical practice of bleeding.
[15] Brontes, Steropes, and Pyr-acmon are the Cyclopes working under Etna who make Aeneas' shield (*Aeneid* VIII, 424–45).
[16] safe from shot.
[17] i.e., Elizabeth's.
[18] gloomy-.

28. An Ode

HIgh spirited friend,[1]
I send nor Balmes, nor Cor'sives[2] to your wound:
Your fate hath found,
A gentler, and more agile hand, to tend
5   The Cure of that, which is but corporall,
And doubtfull Dayes (which were nam'd *Criticall*,)[3]
Have made their fairest flight,
And now are out of sight.
Yet doth some wholsome Physick[4] for the mind,
10   Wrapt in this paper lie,
Which in the taking if you mis-apply,
You are unkind.[5]

Your covetous hand,
Happy in that faire honour it hath gain'd,
15   Must now be rayn'd.[6]
True valour doth her owne renowne command
In one full Action; nor have you now more
To doe, then be a husband of that store.
Thinke but how deare you bought,
20   This same[7] which you have caught,
Such thoughts wil make you more in love with Truth:
'Tis wisdome and that high,
For men to use their fortune reverently,
Even in youth.

29. An Ode

HE*llen*, did *Homer* never see
Thy beauties, yet could write of thee?
Did *Sappho* on her seven-tongu'd Lute,
So speake (as yet it is not mute)

28:    [1] not identified.
[2] corrosives: strong medicines.
[3] Critical days occur at the turning point of a disease.
[4] medicine.

[5] unnatural, as well as the modern meaning.
[6] reined, governed.
[7] Newdigate emends to "fame."

5   Of *Phaos*[1] forme? or doth the Boy[2]
In whom *Anacreon* once did joy,
Lie drawne to life, in his soft Verse,
As he[3] whom *Maro* did rehearse?
Was *Lesbia* sung by learn'd *Catullus?*
10   Or *Delia's* Graces, by *Tibullus?*
Doth *Cynthia*, in *Propertius*[4] song
Shine more, then she the Stars among?
Is *Horace* his each love so high
Rap't from the Earth, as not to die?
15   With bright *Lycoris*, *Gallus*[5] choice,
Whose fame hath an eternall voice.
Or hath *Corynna*, by the name
Her *Ovid* gave her,[6] dimn'd[7] the fame
Of *Cæsars* Daughter, and the line
20   Which all the world then styl'd devine?
Hath *Petrarch* since his *Laura* rais'd
Equall with her? or *Ronsart*[8] prais'd
His new *Cassandra*, 'bove the old,
Which all the Fate of *Troy* foretold?
25   Hath our great *Sidney*, *Stella* set,[9]
Where never Star shone brighter yet?
Or *Constables* Ambrosiack Muse,[10]
Made *Dian*, not his notes refuse?
Have all these done (and yet I misse
30   The Swan that so relish'd *Pancharis*)[11]
And shall not I my *Celia* bring,
Where men may see whom I doe sing?

29: [1] Sappho's Sicilian love, Phaon.

[2] Bathyllus (Anacreon, 17).

[3] In Eclogue 4 Virgil prophesied the birth of a child who would become great.

[4] Catullus, Tibullus, and Propertius, Roman poets, wrote love songs to these women.

[5] said to have written elegies to her, but they do not survive.

[6] in the *Tristia*; Jonson takes her to be Caesar's daughter Julia.

[7] dimmed.

[8] Pierre Ronsard (1524–85). His lady's name comes from the princess in Greek legend who could foresee the future but was not believed.

[9] Sir Philip's *Astrophel and Stella*. Stella means star.

[10] Constable's sonnets to Diana were first printed in 1592.

[11] Hugh Holland published this poem in 1603. In it the lover is allegorized as a swan.

Though I, in working of my song
Come short of all this learned throng,
35   Yet sure my tunes will be the best,
So much my Subject drownes the rest.

30. A Sonnet, to the Noble Lady, the Lady Mary Wroth[1]

I That have beene a lover, and could shew it,
        Though not in these, in rithmes not wholly
                                                    [dumbe,
        Since I exscribe[2] your Sonnets, am become
A better lover, and much better Poët.
5   Nor is my Muse, or I asham'd to owe it
        To those true numerous Graces; whereof some,
        But charme the Senses, others over-come
Both braines and hearts; and mine now best doe know
                                                    [it:
        For in your verse all *Cupids* Armorie,
10   His flames, his shafts, his Quiver, and his Bow,
        His very eyes are yours to overthrow.
But then his Mothers[3] sweets you so apply,
        Her joyes, her smiles, her loves, as[4] readers take
For *Venus Ceston*,[5] every line you make.

31. A Fit of Rime against Rime

RIme the rack of finest wits,
That expresseth but by fits,[1]
                        True Conceipt.
Spoyling Senses of their Treasure,

30: [1] Mary, Lady Wroth, daughter of Robert Sidney and his wife Barbara Gamage (see *The Forrest*, 2). She married Sir Robert Wroth in 1604. See *Epigs*. 103 and 105 and *The Forrest*, 3. Jonson dedicated the *Alchemist* to her.
  [2] copy out. The sonnets were first printed in *The Countesse of Montgomeries Urania Written by the Right Honorable the Lady Mary Wroath*, 1621.
  [3] Venus.
  [4] that.
  [5] girdle.
31: [1] fitfully, with pun.

5   Cosening[2] Judgement with a measure,[3]
      But false weight.
    Wresting words, from their true calling;
    Propping Verse, for feare of falling
      To the ground.
10   Joynting[4] Syllabes, drowning Letters,
    Fastning Vowells, as with fetters
      They were bound!
    Soone as lazie thou wert knowne,
    All good Poëtrie[5] hence was flowne,
15   And Art banish'd.
    For a thousand yeares together,
    All *Pernassus*[6] Greene did wither,
      And wit vanish'd.
    Pegasus[7] did flie away,
20   At the Wells[8] no Muse did stay,
      But bewail'd,
    So to see the Fountaine drie,
    And *Apollo's* Musique die,
      All light failed!
25   Starveling rimes did fill the Stage,
    Not a Poët in an Age,
      Worth crowning.
    Not a worke deserving Baies,[9]
    Nor a lyne deserving praise,
30   *Pallas* frowning;
    Greeke was free from Rimes infection,
    Happy Greeke by this protection!
      Was not spoyled.
    Whilst the Latin, Queene of Tongues,
35   Is not yet free from Rimes wrongs,[10]
      But rests foiled.

[2] cheating.
[3] rhythm, with pun.
[4] disjointing.
[5] Greek and Roman classics did not use rime.
[6] mountain sacred to Phoebus Apollo and the Muses.
[7] winged horse of the Muses.
[8] Hippocrene: fountain on Mount Helicon sacred to the Muses.
[9] bays: poetic award.
[10] medieval and Renaissance Latin included rime.

Scarce the hill[11] againe doth flourish,
Scarce the world a Wit doth nourish,
　　　　To restore,
40 *Phœbus* to his Crowne againe;
And the Muses to their braine;
　　　　As before.
Vulgar[12] Languages that want
Words, and sweetnesse, and be scant
45 　　　　Of true measure,[13]
Tyran[14] Rime hath so abused,
That they long since have refused,
　　　　Other ceasure;[15]
He that first invented thee,
50 May his joynts tormented bee,
　　　　Cramp'd for ever;
Still may Syllabes jarre with time,
Stil may reason warre with rime,
　　　　Resting never.
55 May his Sense when it would meet,
The cold tumor in his feet,[16]
　　　　Grow unsounder.
And his Title be long foole,[17]
That in rearing such a Schoole,
60 　　　　Was the founder.

32. An Epigram on William Lord Burl:[1] Lo: High Treasurer of England

Presented upon a plate of Gold to his son Rob. E. *of* Salisbury, *when he was also Treasurer*

IF thou wouldst know the vertues of Man-kind,
　Read here in one, what thou in all canst find,

---

[11] Parnassus.
[12] nonclassical.
[13] quantitative as opposed to other kinds of scansion.
[14] tyrant.
[15] caesura: division of a classical foot of poetry between two words.
[16] with pun on poetic feet.

[17] with pun on *ars* (i.e., English ass or fool) *longa, vita breve*: art is long, life short.
32: [1] Burleigh (1521–98) was Elizabeth's leading minister. His son Robert Cecil became Lord High Treasurer in 1608. Cf. *Epig.* 64.

And goe no farther: let this Circle be
    Thy Universe, though his[2] *Epitome.*
5   *Cecill,* the grave, the wise, the great, the good,
    What is there more that can ennoble blood?
The *Orphans* Pillar, the true Subjects shield,
    The poores full Store-house, and just servants field.[3]
The only faithfull Watchman for the Realme,
10   That in all tempests, never quit the helme,
But stood unshaken in his Deeds, and Name,
    And labour'd in the worke; not with the fame:
That still was good for goodnesse sake, nor thought
    Upon reward, till the reward him sought.
15   Whose Offices, and honours did surprize,
    Rather than meet him: And, before his eyes
Clos'd to their peace, he saw his branches shoot,[4]
    And in the noblest Families tooke root
Of all the Land. Who now at such a Rate,[5]
20   Of divine blessing, would not serve a State?

33. An Epigram.[1] To Thomas Lo: Elsmere,[2] *the last Terme[3] he sate Chancellor*

SO justest Lord, may all your Judgements be
    Lawes; and no change e're come to one decree:
So, may the King proclaime your Conscience is
    Law, to his Law; and thinke your enemies his:
5   So, from all sicknesse, may you rise to health,
    The Care, and wish still of the publike wealth,
So may the gentler Muses, and good fame
    Still flie about the Odour[4] of your Name;
As with the safetie, and honour of the Lawes,
10   You favour Truth, and me, in this mans Cause.

---

[2] its: the Universe's. Or the epigram may be Burleigh's "Epitome," presented on the "Circle"—the golden plate.

[3] area of service.

[4] he had several grandchildren.

[5] such esteem.

33: [1] For a poore Man (Jonson's note).

[2] See *Epig.* 74.

[3] Elsmere was last active as judge in early 1617.

[4] good repute.

34. ANOTHER TO HIM[1]

THe Judge his favour timely then extends,
    When a good Cause is destitute of friends,
Without the pompe of Counsell; or more Aide,
    Then to make falshood blush, and fraud afraid:
5   When those good few, that her Defenders be,
    Are there for Charitie, and not for fee.
Such shall you heare to Day, and find great foes
    Both arm'd with wealth, and slander to oppose,
Who thus long safe, would gaine upon the times
10 A right by the prosperitie of their Crimes;
Who, though their guilt, and perjurie they know,
    Thinke, yea and boast, that they have done it so
As though the Court pursues them on the sent,[2]
    They will come of,[3] and scape the Punishment.
15 When this appeares, just Lord, to your sharp sight,
    He do's you wrong, that craves you to doe right.

35. AN EPIGRAM TO THE COUNCELLOUR THAT PLEADED, AND CARRIED THE CAUSE

THat I hereafter, doe not thinke the Barre,
    The Seat made of a more then civill warre;
Or the great Hall at *Westminster*, the field
    Where mutuall frauds are fought, and no side yeild;
5   That henceforth, I beleeve nor bookes, nor men,
    Who'gainst the Law, weave Calumnies my ——;[1]
But when I read or heare the names so rife
    Of hirelings, wranglers, stitchers-to[2] of strife,
Hook-handed *Harpies*,[3] gowned Vultures, put
10   Upon the reverend Pleaders; doe now shut

34: [1] For the same (Jonson's note).
  [2] scent.
  [3] come off; succeed.
35: [1] Whalley conjectures Benn: Sir Anthony Benn (d. 1618), lawyer and Recorder of London.
  [2] tailors.
  [3] a monster with a woman's face and body and a bird's wings and claws; hence a rapacious person.

All mouthes, that dare entitle them (from hence)
  To the Wolves studie, or Dogs eloquence;
Thou art my Cause: whose manners since I knew,
  Have made me to conceive a Lawyer new.[4]
15 So dost thou studie matter, men, and times,
  Mak'st it religion[5] to grow rich by Crimes!
Dar'st[6] not abuse thy wisdome, in the Lawes,
  Or skill[7] to carry out an evill cause!
But first dost vexe,[8] and search it! If not sound,
20 Thou prov'st[9] the gentler wayes, to clense the
    [wound,
And make the Scarre faire; If that will not be,
  Thou hast the brave scorne, to put back[10] the fee!
But in a businesse, that will bide the Touch,[11]
  What use, what strength of reason! and how much
25 Of Bookes, of Presidents,[12] hast thou at hand?
  As if the generall store thou didst command
Of Argument, still drawing forth the best,
  And not being borrowed by thee, but possest.
So comm'st thou like a Chiefe into the Court
30 Arm'd at all peeces,[13] as to keepe a Fort
Against a multitude; and (with thy Stile[14]
  So brightly brandish'd) wound'st, defend'st! the
    [while
Thy Adversaries fall, as not a word
  They had, but were a Reed unto thy Sword.
35 Then com'st thou off with Victorie and Palme,
  Thy Hearers Nectar, and thy Clients Balme,
The Courts just honour, and thy Judges love.
  And (which doth all Atchievements get above)[15]

---

[4] Have made me think of law-
yers in a new light.

[5] matter, men, and times (who)
make it their belief: paralleling
"Mak'st" to "Dar'st," both of
which perhaps should be emended
to "Make" and "Dare."

[6] (They) dare.

[7] Or (exercise their) skill. H&S
add a comma after "skill," paral-
leling it with "wisdome."

[8] examine. The subject is prob-
ably "thou."

[9] triest.

[10] return.

[11] close examination.

[12] precedents.

[13] points.

[14] stylus, pen.

[15] surpass.

Thy sincere practise, breeds not thee a fame
40   Alone, but all thy ranke[16] a reverend Name.

36. An Epigram. To the Small Poxe

ENvious and foule Disease, could there not be
One beautie in an Age, and free from thee?
What did she worth thy spight? were there not store
Of those that set by their false faces more
5   Then this did by her true? she never sought
Quarrell with Nature, or in ballance brought
Art[1] her false servant; Nor, for Sir *Hugh Plot*,[2]
Was drawne to practise other hue, then that
Her owne bloud gave her: Shee ne're had, nor hath
10   Any beliefe, in Madam Baud-bees bath,[3]
Or Turners[4] oyle of Talck.[5] Nor ever got
Spanish receipt,[6] to make her teeth to rot.
What was the cause then? Thought'st thou in disgrace
Of Beautie, so to nullifie a face,
15   That heaven should make no more; or should amisse,
Make all hereafter, had'st thou ruin'd this?[7]
I,[8] that thy Ayme was; but her fate prevail'd:
And scorn'd,[9] thou'ast showne thy malice, but hast
[fail'd.

37. An Epitaph[1]

WHat Beautie would have lovely stilde,
What manners prettie, Nature milde,

[16] colleagues.
36:    [1] make-up.
[2] Sir Hugh Platt, author of a very popular work on cosmetics: *Delights for Ladies to Adorne Their Persons . . .* (1602).
[3] not identified.
[4] H&S consider to be Mrs. Turner, agent of Lady Frances Howard in the poisoning of Sir Thomas Overbury.
[5] a cosmetic.

[6] What it was is not known.
[7] since thou hast ruined this.
[8] Ay.
[9] (thou being) scorned.
37:    [1] H&S identify as Elizabeth Chute, daughter of Sir George Chute, who died aged 3½ years on May 18, 1627. A tablet in her memory, with Jonson's epitaph, is in the Sonning Church, Berkshire.

What wonder perfect, all were fil'd,
Upon record[2] in this blest child.
5 And, till the comming of the Soule
To fetch the flesh, we keepe the Rowle.[3]

38. A SONG

LOVER

COme, let us here enjoy the shade;
For Love in shadow best is made.
Though Envie oft his shadow be,
None brookes the Sun-light worse then he.

MISTRES

5 Where love doth shine, there needs no Sunne,
All lights into his one doth run;
Without which all the world were darke;
Yet he himselfe is but a sparke.

ARBITER

A Sparke to set whole worlds a-fire,
10 Who more they burne, they more desire,
And have their being, their waste[1] to see;
And waste still, that they still might bee.

CHORUS

Such are his powers, whom time hath stil'd,
Now swift, now slow, now tame, now wild;
15 Now hot, now cold, now fierce, now mild.
The eldest God,[2] yet still a Child.

39. AN EPISTLE TO A FRIEND

SIr,[1] I am thankfull, first, to heaven, for you;
Next to your selfe, for making your love true:
Then to your love, and gift. And all's but due.

---

[2] set down.
[3] the "record" of line 4.
38: [1] as a fire owes its existence to its self-destruction.

[2] Cupid was often described as the oldest god.
39: [1] not identified.

You have unto my Store added a booke,
5   On which with profit, I shall never looke,
       But must confesse[2] from whom what[3] gift I tooke.

Not like your Countrie-neighbours, that commit
    Their vice of loving for a Christmasse fit;[4]
    Which is indeed but friendship of the spit:[5]

10 But, as a friend, which name your selfe receave,
       And which you (being the worthier) gave me leave
       In letters, that mixe spirits,[6] thus to weave.

Which, how most sacred I will ever keepe,
    So may the fruitfull Vine my temples steepe,[7]
15   And Fame wake for me, when I yeeld to sleepe.

Though you sometimes proclaime me too severe,
    Rigid, and harsh, which is a Drug austere
    In friendship, I confesse: But deare friend, heare.

Little know they, that professe Amitie,
20   And seeke to scant[8] her comelie libertie,
       How much they lame her in her propertie.

And lesse they know, who being free to use
       That friendship which no chance but love did
                                                    [chuse,
       Will unto Licence that faire leave abuse.

25 It is an Act of tyrannie, not love
       In practiz'd[9] friendship wholly to reprove,
       As flatt'ry[10] with friends humours still to move.[11]

From each of which I labour to be free,
    Yet if with eithers vice I teynted be,
30   Forgive it, as my frailtie, and not me.

For no man lives so out of passions sway,
    But shall sometimes be tempted to obey
    Her furie, yet no friendship to betray.

---

2 without confessing.   7 perhaps, So may I get drunk.
3 that.   8 limit.
4 limited to the holiday season. 9 exercised, active.
5 feasting time.   10 As it is flattery.
6 communicate between us.   11 agree.

40. An Elegie[1]

'TIs true, I'm broke! Vowes, Oathes, and all I had
    Of Credit lost. And I am now run madde,
Or doe upon my selfe some desperate ill;
    This sadnesse makes no approaches, but to kill.
5   It is a Darknesse hath blockt up my sense,
    And drives it in to eat on my offence,
Or there to sterve[2] it. Helpe O you that may
    Alone lend succours, and this furie stay,
Offended Mistris; you are yet so faire,
10   As light breakes from you, that affrights despaire,
And fills my powers with perswading joy,
    That you should be too noble to destroy.
There may some face or menace of a storme
    Looke forth, but cannot last in such a forme.
15 If there be nothing worthy you can see
    Of Graces, or your mercie here in me,
Spare your owne goodnesse yet; and be not great
    In will and power, only to defeat.
God, and the good, know to forgive, and save.
20   The ignorant, and fooles, no pittie have.
I will not stand to justifie my fault,
    Or lay the excuse upon the Vintners vault;[3]
Or in confessing of the Crime be nice,[4]
    Or goe about to countenance the vice,
25 By naming in what companie 'twas in,
    As[5] I would urge Authoritie for sinne.
No, I will stand arraign'd, and cast,[6] to be
    The Subject of your Grace in pardoning me,
And (Stil'd your mercies Creature) will live more
30   Your honour now, then your disgrace before.
Thinke it was frailtie, Mistris, thinke me man;
    Thinke that your selfe like heaven forgive me can;

40: [1] On the authenticity of this poem, see n. 1 to *Under.* 41.

  [2] starve: destroy.

  [3] Jonson has betrayed a confidence of hers, evidently under the influence of wine.

[4] reluctant.

[5] As if.

[6] found guilty.

Where weaknesse doth offend, and vertue grieve,
There greatnesse takes a glorie to relieve.
35 Thinke that I once was yours, or may be now;
Nothing is vile, that is a part of you:
Errour and folly in me may have crost
Your just commands; yet those, not I be lost.
I am regenerate now, become the child
40 Of your compassion; Parents should be mild:
There is no Father that for one demerit,
Or two, or three, a Sonne will dis-inherit:
That as the last of punishments is meant;
No man inflicts that paine, till hope be spent:
45 An ill-affected limbe (what e're it aile)
We cut not off, till all Cures else doe faile:
And then with pause; for sever'd once, that's gone,
Would[7] live his glory that could keepe it on:
Doe not despaire my mending; to distrust
50 Before you prove[8] a medicine, is unjust.
You may so place me, and in such an ayre
As not alone the Cure, but scarre be faire.[9]
That is, if still your Favours you apply,
And not the bounties you ha'done, deny.
55 Could you demand the gifts you gave, againe!
Why was't? did e're the Cloudes aske back their
[raine?
The Sunne his heat, and light, the ayre his dew?
Or winds the Spirit, by which the flower so grew?
That were to wither all, and make a Grave
60 Of that wise[10] Nature would a Cradle have.
Her order is to cherish, and preserve,
Consumptions nature to destroy, and sterve.[11]
But to exact againe what once is given,
Is natures meere obliquitie![12] as[13] Heaven
65 Should aske the blood, and spirits he[14] hath infus'd
In man, because man hath the flesh abus'd.

---

[7] which would.
[8] try.
[9] even the scar may look good.
[10] Of that which wise.
[11] The nature of consumption
is to destroy and kill.
[12] aberration, fault.
[13] as though.
[14] God.

O may your wisdome take example hence,
    God lightens[15] not at mans each fraile offence,
He pardons slips, goes by a world of ills,
70   And then his thunder frights more, then it kills.
He cannot angrie be, but all must quake,
    It shakes even him, that all things else doth shake.
And how more faire, and lovely lookes the world
    In a calme skie; then when the heaven is horl'd[16]
75 About in Cloudes, and wrapt in raging weather,
    As[17] all with storme and tempest ran together.
O imitate that sweet Serenitie
    That makes us live, not that which calls to die.
In darke, and sullen mornes, doe we not say
80   This looketh like an Execution day?
And with the vulgar doth it not obtaine
    The name of Cruell weather, storme, and raine?
Be not affected with these markes too much
    Of crueltie, lest they doe make you such.
85 But view the mildnesse of your Makers state,
    As I the penitents here emulate:
He when he sees a sorrow such as this,
    Streight puts off all his Anger, and doth kisse
The contrite Soule, who hath no thought to win
90   Upon the hope to have another sin
Forgiven him; And in that lyne stand I,
    Rather then once displease you more, to die,
To suffer tortures, scorne, and Infamie,
    What Fooles, and all their Parasites can apply;
95 The wit of Ale, and *Genius* of the Malt
    Can pumpe for;[18] or a Libell without salt[19]
Produce; though threatning with a coale, or chalke
    On every wall, and sung where e're I walke.
I number these as being of the Chore[20]
100   Of Contumelie, and urge a good man more
Then sword, or fire, or what is of the race[21]
    To carry[22] noble danger in the face:

---

15 fulminates.
16 hurled.
17 as though.
18 work for.

19 wit.
20 chorus: company.
21 similar.
22 meet.

There is not any punishment, or paine,
    A man should flie from, as he would disdaine.[23]
105 Then Mistress here, here let your rigour end,
    And let your mercie make me asham'd t'offend.
I will no more abuse my vowes to you,
    Then I will studie falshood, to be true.
O, that you could but by dissection see
110   How much you are the better part of me;
How all my Fibres by your Spirit doe move,
    And that there is no life in me, but love.
You would be then most confident, that tho
    Publike affaires command me now to goe
115 Out of your eyes, and be awhile away,
    Absence, or Distance, shall not breed decay.[24]
Your forme shines here, here fixed in my heart;
    I may dilate[25] my selfe, but not depart.
Others by common Stars their courses run:[26]
120   When I see you, then I doe see my Sun;
Till then 'tis all but darknesse, that I have;
    Rather then want[27] your light, I wish a grave.

41. An Elegie[1]

TO make the Doubt cleare that no Woman's true,
    Was it my fate to prove it full in you?

---

[23] would (from) disdain.

[24] This idea, frequent in Donne because of his travels, is seldom if ever found in Jonson, though he would of course travel with his company of players. On the other hand, the utter subserviency of the rest of the poem is not typical of Donne; nor did he write of drinking to excess.

[25] extend.

[26] direct.

[27] lack, with a pun.

41: [1] by John Donne; printed as an Elegy, "The Expostulation," in his *Poems* of 1633 and surviving in several collections of his MSS. Although claimed for Jonson by some (e.g., M. L. Wilder, *MLR*, XXI [1926], 431–35), the evidence clearly points to Donne as author (see Evelyn Simpson in *RES*, XV [1939], 274–82, and H&S XI. 66–68). The elegies in the *Under-wood* preceding and following this one have also been claimed for Donne (e.g., by Swinburne, Castelain, and C. H. Herford [H&S II. 383f.]), but there is no MS. or other attestation, and internal evidence is inconclusive. See H&S XI. 68–70.

Thought I but one had breath'd the purer Ayre,
　　And must she needs be false, because she's faire?
5　It is your beauties Marke, or of your youth,
　　Or your perfection not to studie truth;
Or thinke you heaven is deafe? or hath no eyes?
　　Or those it has, winke[2] at your perjuries?
Are vowes so cheape with women? or the matter
10　Whereof they are made, that they are writ in water;
And blowne away with wind? or doth their breath
　　Both hot and cold at once, threat life and death?
Who could have thought so many accents sweet
　　Tun'd to our words, so many sighes should meet
15　Blowne from our hearts, so many oathes and teares
　　Sprinkled among? All sweeter by our feares,
And the Devine Impression of stolne kisses,
　　That seal'd the rest, could now prove emptie blisses?
Did you draw bonds to forfeit? Signe, to breake?[3]
20　Or must we read[4] you quite from what you speake,
And find the truth out the wrong way? or must
　　He first desire you false, would wish you just?
O, I prophane! though most of women be,
　　The common Monster, Love shall except thee
25　My dearest Love, how ever jealousie,[5]
　　With Circumstance might urge the contrarie.
Sooner I'le thinke the Sunne would cease to cheare
　　The teeming Earth, and that[6] forget to beare;
Sooner that Rivers would run back, or Thames
30　With ribs of Ice in June would bind his streames:
Or Nature, by whose strength the world indures,
　　Would change her course, before you alter yours:
But, O, that trecherous breast,[7] to whom, weake you
　　Did trust our counsells, and we both may rue,

[2] shut the eyes.
[3] Sign (them, only) to break (them)?
[4] understand.
[5] however much jealousy.
[6] the Earth.
[7] Who was the traitor is not known. The potential connection with the betrayed confidence of the previous elegy may explain the fact that they are printed here together: Jonson may be the traitor and author of No. 40.

35   Having his falshood found too late! 'twas he
        That made me cast[8] you Guiltie, and you me.
    Whilst he black wretch, betray'd each simple word
        We spake unto the comming of a third!
    Curst may he be that so our love hath slaine,
40   And wander wretched on the earth, as *Cain*.
    Wretched as he, and not deserve least pittie;
        In plaguing him let miserie be wittie.
    Let all eyes shun him, and he shun each eye,
        Till he be noysome as his infamie;
45   May he without remorse deny God thrice,
        And not be trusted more on his soules price;
    And after all selfe-torment, when he dyes
        May Wolves teare out his heart, Vultures his eyes,
    Swyne eat his Bowels, and his falser Tongue,
50   That utter'd all, be to some Raven flung,
    And let his carrion corse be a longer feast
        To the Kings Dogs, then any other beast.
    Now I have curst, let us our love revive;
        In me the flame was never more alive.
55   I could begin againe to court and praise,
        And in that pleasure lengthen the short dayes
    Of my lifes lease; like Painters that doe take
        Delight, not in made workes, but whilst they make.[9]
    I could renew those times, when first I saw
60   Love in your eyes, that gave my tongue the Law
    To like what you lik'd, and at Masques, or Playes,
        Commend the selfe-same Actors, the same wayes;
    Aske how you did? and often with intent
        Of being officious, grow impertinent;
65   All which were such soft pastimes, as in these
        Love was as subtly catch'd as a Disease.
    But, being got, it is a treasure, sweet,
        Which to defend, is harder then to get;
    And ought not be prophan'd on either part,
70   For though 'tis got by chance, 'tis kept by art.

[8] judge.
[9] Cf. *Under.* 7, ll. 13–16 for the same idea. It derives from Seneca, *Epistles* IX.7.

42. An Elegie[1]

THat Love's a bitter sweet, I ne're conceive
    Till the sower Minute comes of taking leave,
And then I taste it. But as men drinke up
    In hast the bottome of a med'cin'd Cup,
5   And take some sirrup after; so doe I
    To put all relish from my memorie
Of parting, drowne it in the hope to meet
    Shortly againe: and make our absence sweet.
This makes me, M[rs.], that sometime by stealth
10   Under another Name, I take your health;
And turne the Ceremonies of those Nights
    I give, or owe my friends, into your Rites,
But ever without blazon,[2] or least shade[3]
    Of vowes so sacred, and in silence made;
15   For though Love thrive, and may grow up with cheare,
    And free societie, hee's borne else-where,
And must be bred, so to conceale his birth,
    As neither wine doe rack it out, or mirth.
Yet should the Lover still be ayrie and light,
20   In all his Actions rarified to spright;
Not like a *Midas* shut up in himselfe,
    And turning all he toucheth into pelfe,
Keepe in reserv'd in his Dark-lanterne[4] face,
    As if that ex'lent[5] Dulnesse were Loves grace;
25   No Mistress no, the open merrie Man
    Moves like a sprightly River, and yet can
Keepe secret in his Channels what he breedes[6]
    'Bove[7] all your standing waters, choak'd with weedes.
They looke at best like Creame-bowles, and you soone
30   Shall find their depth: they're sounded with a
                                        [spoone.

42: [1] For authenticity see n. 1   which its light could be concealed.
to previous poem.   [5] excellent.
    [2] show.   [6] is doing.
    [3] shadow.   [7] more than.
    [4] a lantern with a slide by

They may say Grace, and for Loves Chaplaines passe;
    But the grave Lover ever was an Asse;
Is fix'd upon one leg, and dares not come
    Out[8] with the other, for hee's still at home;
35   Like the dull wearied Crane that (come on land)
    Doth while he keepes his watch, betray his stand.
Where[9] he that knowes will like a Lapwing flie
    Farre from the Nest, and so himselfe belie
To others as he will deserve the Trust
40   Due to that one, that doth believe him just.
And such your Servant is, who vowes to keepe
    The Jewell of your name, as close as sleepe
Can lock the Sense up, or the heart a thought,
    And never be by time, or folly brought,
45   Weaknesse of braine, or any charme of Wine,
    The sinne of Boast, or other countermine
(Made to blow up loves secrets) to discover
    That Article, may[10] not become our lover:
Which in assurance to your brest I tell,
50   If I had writ no word, but Deare, farewell.

43. AN ELEGIE[1]

SInce you must goe, and I must bid farewell,
    Heare, Mistress, your departing servant tell
What it is like: And doe not thinke they can
    Be idle words, though of a parting[2] Man;
5   It is as if a night should shade noone-day,
    Or that the Sun was here, but forc't away;
And we were left under that Hemisphere,
    Where we must feele it Darke for halfe a yeare.
What fate is this to change mens dayes and houres,
10   To shift their seasons, and destroy their powers!
Alas I ha' lost my heat, my blood, my prime,
    Winter is come a Quarter e're his Time,
My health will leave me; and when you depart,
    How shall I doe sweet Mistris for my heart?

---

[8] step ahead.
[9] whereas.
[10] Article which may.

43: [1] For authenticity see n. 1 to No. 41 above.
[2] departing.

15   You would restore it? No, that's worth a feare,
         As if it were not worthy to be there:
      O, keepe it still; for it had rather be
      Your sacrifice, then here remaine with me.
      And so I spare it: Come what can become
20   Of me, I'le softly tread unto my Tombe;
      Or like a Ghost walke silent amongst men,
         Till I may see both it and you agen.

44. An Elegie

LEt me be what I am, as *Virgil* cold,
   As *Horace* fat; or as *Anacreon* old;[1]
No Poets verses yet did ever move,
   Whose Readers did not thinke he was in love.
5 Who shall forbid me then in Rithme to bee
   As light, and Active as the youngest hee
That from the Muses fountaines doth indorse[2]
   His lynes, and hourely sits[3] the Poets horse?[4]
Put on my Ivy Garland, let me see
10   Who frownes, who jealous is, who taxeth me.
Fathers, and Husbands, I doe claime a right
   In all that is call'd lovely: take my sight
Sooner then my affection from the faire.
   No face, no hand, proportion, line, or Ayre
15 Of beautie; but the Muse hath interest in:
   There is not worne that lace, purle,[5] knot or pin,
But is the Poëts matter: And he must
   When he is furious love, although not lust.
But then consent, your Daughters and your Wives,
20   (If they be faire and worth it) have their lives
Made longer by our praises. Or, if not,
   Wish, you had fowle ones, and deformed got;
Curst in their Cradles, or there chang'd by Elves,
   So to be sure you doe injoy your selves.

44: [1] These three classical poets are so described in Suetonius and Lucian.

[2] be on the back of and to certify.

[3] sits on.

[4] Pegasus.

[5] ornamental loop of fabric.

25   Yet keepe those up in sackcloth too, or lether,
  For Silke will draw some sneaking Songster thither.
It is a ryming Age, and Verses swarme
  At every stall; The Cittie Cap's a charme.[6]
But I who live, and have liv'd[7] twentie yeare
30   Where I may handle Silke, as free, and neere,
As any Mercer; or the whale-bone man
  That quilts those bodies, I have leave to span;[8]
Have eaten with the Beauties, and the wits,
  And braveries[9] of Court, and felt their fits
35   Of love, and hate: and came so nigh to know
  Whether their faces were their owne, or no.
It is not likely I should now looke downe
  Upon a Velvet Petticote, or a Gowne,
Whose like I have knowne the Taylors Wife put on
40   To doe her Husbands rites in, e're 'twere gone
Home to the Customer: his Letcherie
  Being, the best clothes still to præoccupie.[10]
Put a Coach-mare in Tissue,[11] must I horse[12]
  Her presently?[13] Or leape thy Wife of force,
45   When by thy sordid bountie she hath on,
  A Gowne of that, was the Caparison?[14]
So[15] I might dote upon thy Chaires and Stooles
  That are like cloath'd, must I be of those fooles
Of race accompted, that no passion have
50   But when thy Wife (as thou conceiv'st) is brave?[16]
Then ope thy wardrobe, thinke me that poore Groome
  that from the Foot-man, when he was become
An Officer there, did make most solemne love,
  To ev'ry Petticote he brush'd, and Glove
55   He did lay up, and would adore the shooe,
  Or slipper was[17] left off, and kisse it too,

---

[6] i.e., living in the city, one naturally writes verse.

[7] i.e., in court.

[8] perhaps, have permission to put my arm about.

[9] fine ones.

[10] occupy in advance of delivery; "occupy" also means to deal with sexually.

[11] fine cloth.

[12] mount.

[13] immediately.

[14] dress; also cloth covering of a horse.

[15] just because.

[16] well dressed.

[17] slipper that was.

Court every hanging Gowne, and after that,
    Lift up some one, and doe, I tell not what.
Thou didst tell me; and wert o're-joy'd to peepe
60   In at a hole, and see these Actions creepe
From the poore wretch, which though he play'd in
                                     [prose,
He would have done in verse, with any of those
Wrung on the Withers,[18] by Lord Loves despight,
    Had he had the facultie to reade, and write!
65 Such Songsters there are store of; witnesse he
    That chanc'd the lace, laid on a Smock, to see,
And straight-way spent[19] a Sonnet; with that other
    That (in pure Madrigall) unto his Mother
Commended the French-hood,[20] and Scarlet gowne
70   The Lady Mayresse[21] pass'd in through the Towne,
Unto the Spittle Sermon.[22] O, what strange
    Varietie of Silkes were on th'Exchange!
Or in Moore-fields![23] this other night, sings one:[24]
    Another answers, 'Lasse[25] those Silkes are none,
75 In smiling *L'envoye*,[26] as[27] he would deride
    Any Comparison had with his Cheap-side.
And vouches[28] both the Pageant, and the Day,
    When not the Shops, but windowes doe display
The Stuffes, the Velvets, Plushes, Fringes, Lace,
80   And all the originall riots of the place:
Let the poore fooles enjoy their follies, love
    A Goat[29] in Velvet; or some block[30] could move
Under that cover; an old Mid-wives hat!
    Or a Close-stoole[31] so cas'd; or any fat
85 Bawd, in a Velvet scabberd![32] I envy
    None of their pleasures! nor will aske thee, why

[18] spurred on.
[19] expended; uttered.
[20] fashionable clothes.
[21] wife of the mayor.
[22] Socially prominent sermons were preached during Lent near the Hospital of St. Mary, Bishops-gate.
[23] a park outside the London wall.
[24] a man.
[25] Alas.
[26] conclusion.
[27] as though.
[28] attests to.
[29] symbol of lechery.
[30] opposite of the goatish person.
[31] chamber pot.
[32] covering: velvet-covered scabbards were popular.

Thou art jealous of thy Wifes, or Daughters Case:[33]
More then of eithers manners, wit, or face!

45. An Execration upon Vulcan

ANd why to me this,[1] thou lame Lord of fire,
    What had I done that might call on thine ire?
Or urge thy Greedie flame, thus to devoure
    So many my Yeares-labours in an houre?
5   I ne're attempted, *Vulcan*, 'gainst thy life;
        Nor made least line of love to thy loose Wife;[2]
Or in remembrance of thy afront, and scorne[3]
    With Clownes, and Tradesmen, kept thee clos'd in
                        [home.[4]
'Twas *Jupiter* that hurl'd thee headlong downe,
10   And *Mars*, that gave thee a Lanthorne[5] for a Crowne:
Was it because thou wert of old denied
    By *Jove* to have *Minerva* for thy Bride,[6]
That since thou tak'st all envious care and paine,
    To ruine any issue of the braine?
15   Had I wrote treason there, or heresie,
        Imposture, witchcraft, charmes, or blasphemie,
I had deserv'd then, thy consuming lookes,
    Perhaps, to have beene burned with my bookes.
But, on thy malice, tell me, didst thou spie
20   Any, least loose, or scurrile paper, lie
Conceal'd, or kept there, that was fit to be,
    By thy owne vote, a sacrifice to thee?
Did I there wound the honours of the Crowne?
    Or taxe the Glories of the Church, and Gowne?[7]
25   Itch to defame the State? or brand the Times?
    And my selfe most, in some selfe-boasting Rimes?

---

[33] dress, and situation.

45: [1] Jonson's house and possessions burned in November 1623. He half-humorously blames Vulcan, god of fire, lamed by having been thrown from heaven by Jupiter.

[2] Venus.

[3] In heaven Vulcan was scorned by the other gods.

[4] cuckolded (by Mars), and in horn lanterns.

[5] punning on "horn"; see n. 4.

[6] Neptune urged such a union, but at Jupiter's suggestion she refused.

[7] legal and clerical.

If none of these, then why this fire? Or find
  A cause before; or leave me one behind.
Had I compil'd from *Amadis de Gaule*,[8]
30 Th'*Esplandians*,[9] *Arthur's*, *Palmerins*,[10] and all
The learned Librarie of *Don Quixote*,[11]
  And so some goodlier monster had begot,
Or spun out Riddles, and weav'd fiftie tomes
  Of *Logogriphes*,[12] and curious *Palindromes*,[13]
35 Or pomp'd for[14] those hard trifles *Anagrams*,[15]
Or *Eteostichs*,[16] or those finer flammes[17]
Of Egges, and Halberds, Cradles, and a Herse,
A paire of Scisars, and a Combe in verse;[18]
Acrostichs,[19] and *Telestichs*,[20] on jumpe[21] names,
40 Thou then hadst had some colour[22] for thy flames,
On such my serious follies; But, thou'lt say,
  There were some pieces of as base allay,[23]
And as false stampe there; parcels of a Play,[24]
  Fitter to see the fire-light, then the day;
45 Adulterate[25] moneys, such as might not goe:[26]
  Thou should'st have stay'd,[27] till publike fame said
                                                    [so.

[8] romance by Montalvo, 1510, translated by Antony Munday, 1590 *et seq.*

[9] son of Amadis de Gaul.

[10] See Munday's translations of *Palmerin d'Oliva* (1588 *et seq.*) and *Palmerin of England* (1596 *et seq.*). Both are romances.

[11] described in Cervantes' novel, I. vi; it included many romances.

[12] "A kind of enigma, in which a certain word, and other words that can be formed out of all or any of its letters, are to be guessed from synonyms of them introduced into a set of verses." (NED)

[13] a word or sentence which reads the same backwards and forwards: Madam, I'm Adam.

[14] pumped for: worked for.

[15] transposition of letters in a word so as to spell a new one.

[16] chronogram: a group of words "in which certain letters . . . express by their numerical values a date or epoch." (NED)

[17] conceits.

[18] poems in which such objects as these are pictured in the printed shape of the poetic lines. A famous one is George Herbert's "Easter Wings."

[19] For an example see *Epig.* 40.

[20] Like an acrostic, but with the final letters of each line spelling the name.

[21] exactly corresponding.

[22] reason (with pun).

[23] alloy.

[24] G. B. Johnstone (*MLN*, XLVI [1931], 150–53) argues for *The Staple of News*.

[25] counterfeit.

[26] pass in payment.

[27] waited.

Shee is the Judge, Thou Executioner,[28]
   Or if thou needs would'st trench[29] upon her power,
Thou mightst have yet enjoy'd thy crueltie
50   With some more thrift, and more varietie:
Thou mightst have had me perish, piece by piece,
   To light Tobacco, or save roasted Geese,
Sindge Capons, or poore Pigges, dropping their eyes;[30]
   Condemn'd me to the Ovens with the pies;
55 And so, have kept me dying a whole age,
   Not ravish'd all hence in a minutes rage.
But that's a marke, wherof thy Rites doe boast,
   To make consumption, ever where thou go'st;
Had I fore-knowne of this thy least desire
60   T'have held a Triumph, or a feast of fire,
Especially in paper; that, that steame[31]
   Had tickled your large Nosthrill: many a Reame
To redeeme mine, I had sent in; enough,
   Thou should'st have cry'd, and all beene proper
                         [stuffe.
65 The *Talmud*,[32] and the *Alcoran*[33] had come,
   With pieces of the *Legend*;[34] The whole summe
Of errant Knight-hood, with the Dames, and
                         [Dwarfes;[35]
The charmed Boates,[36] and the inchanted Wharfes;
   The *Tristram's*, *Lanc'lots*,[37] *Turpins*,[38] and the
                         [Peer's,[39]

---

[28] Or, as punctuated in QD, a colon after "Executioner," meaning, "She is the Judge; Thou art the Executioner."

[29] encroach.

[30] uses to which scrap paper was put.

[31] fume.

[32] traditional Jewish civil and ceremonial law.

[33] The Koran.

[34] the *Legenda Aurea*: a medieval collection of saints' lives.

[35] e.g., Una and her dwarf in *Faerie Queene* I.

[36] e.g., Wades boat in Chaucer's "The Merchant's Tale," l. 1424, or the one in *Faerie Queene* II.xif.

[37] associated with the Arthurian legends.

[38] supposed author of one of the Charlemagne stories and one of the last to die in their climactic battle at Roncesvalles.

[39] twelve Paladins who accompany Charlemagne in the romances.

70   All the madde *Rolands*,[40] and sweet *Oliveer's*;[41]
    To *Merlins*[42] Marvailes, and his *Caballs* losse,
    With the Chimæra of the *Rosie-Crosse*,[43]
    Their Seales, their Characters, Hermetique rings,
    Their Jemme of Riches, and bright Stone, that brings
75   Invisibilitie, and strength, and tongues:[44]
    The art of kindling the true Coale, by lungs,[45]
    With *Nicholas Pasquill's*,[46] Meddle with your match,[47]
    And the strong lines, that so the times doe catch,
    Or Captaine *Pamplets*[48] horse, and foot; that sallie
80   Upon th'Exchange, still out of Popes-head-Alley.[49]
    The weekly Corrants,[50] with *Pauls* Seale; and all
    Th'admir'd discourses of the Prophet *Ball*:[51]
    These, had'st thou pleas'd either to dine, or sup,
    Had made a meale for *Vulcan* to lick up.

[40] In some of the Charlemagne material Roland (the hero) goes mad for a time. Or Jonson may be translating the title of Ariosto's *Orlando Furioso*, a book treating of the same legendary materials.

[41] Roland's best friend in the romances.

[42] He appears in both Arthurian and Charlemagnian material.

[43] the Rosicrucians, a secret society formed about 1420. In 1614 its *Fama Fraternitatis* appeared, telling of its founder (Christian Rosenkreuz) and his trip through the Near East and Egypt, where he learned many secrets. The leading contemporary Englishman in the movement was Robert Fludd (1574–1637), followed at his death by Sir Kenelm Digby, Jonson's close friend in later years.

[44] various objects with magical powers. *Tongues* is knowledge of various languages.

[45] the blower of the alchemists' fires.

[46] Nicholas Breton, who published several pamphlets, e.g., *Pasquils Madcap* (1600).

[47] perhaps the title of a lost pamphlet.

[48] H&S (II. 173n.) identify as Thomas Gainsford, earlier a fighter in Ireland but by 1620 a pamphleteer associated with the publisher Nathaniel Butter and others.

[49] a street where some publishers were located.

[50] forerunners of newspapers, published in St. Paul's Courtyard. G. B. Johnston (*MLN*, XLVI [1931], 152f.) argues that Nathaniel Butter's *Currant of News* is meant.

[51] Gifford suggested a tailor named Ball, and H&S accept the attribution. Newdigate argues for John Ball (1585–1640) or Thomas Ball (1590–1659), prominent Puritan preachers. But there is no surviving publication of any of them.

85 But in my Deske, what was there to accite[52]
    So ravenous, and vast an appetite?
    I dare not say a body, but some parts
    There were of search, and mastry in the Arts.
    All the old *Venusine*,[53] in *Poëtrie*,
90   and lighted by the *Stagerite*,[54] could spie,
    Was there made English: with the Grammar[55] too,
    To teach some that, their Nurses could not doe,
    The puritie of Language; and among
    The rest, my journey into *Scotland*[56] song,
95 With all th'adventures; Three bookes not afraid
    To speake the Fate of the *Sicilian* Maid[57]
    To our owne Ladyes; and in storie[58] there
    Of our fift *Henry*, eight of his nine yeare;
    Wherein was oyle, beside the succour spent,
100   Which noble *Carew, Cotton, Selden* lent:[59]
    And twice-twelve-yeares stor'd up humanitie,[60]
    With humble Gleanings in Divinitie,[61]
    After the Fathers, and those wiser Guides[62]
    Whom Faction had not drawne to studie sides.
105 How in these ruines *Vulcan*, thou dost lurke,
    All soote, and embers! odious, as thy worke!

[52] excite.
[53] Horace, born in Venusia.
[54] with commentaries drawn from Aristotle's *Poetics*. Even if one translation of Horace's *Ars Poetica* burned, two versions were published in 1640.
[55] Jonson's *English Grammar* is printed in the 1640 folio.
[56] Jonson had made this trip on foot in mid-1618 to early 1619. Its most noteworthy record is his *Conversations* with William Drummond at Hawthornden in January.
[57] identified from MS. variants by W. D. Briggs (*Anglia*, XXXVII [1913], 488f.) as a Latin romance of Princess Argenis by John Barclay. James I asked Jonson to translate it in 1622.
[58] history. Henry V was much admired as king.
[59] Richard Carew (1555–1620) was a poet and antiquary. Sir Robert Cotton (1571–1631) was a famous antiquarian. For Selden see *Under.* 16. Evidently all three had loaned Jonson books which perished in the fire. We know the titles of two of Cotton's (H&S XI. 78).
[60] a commonplace book; perhaps some survives in Jonson's *Discoveries.*
[61] Nothing of this has survived.
[62] pre-Reformation commentators.

I now begin to doubt, if ever Grace,
 Or Goddesse, could be patient of thy face.
Thou woo *Minerva!* or to wit aspire!
110 'Cause thou canst halt, with us in Arts,[63] and Fire!
Sonne of the Wind! for so thy mother gone
 With lust conceiv'd thee;[64] Father thou hadst none.
When thou wert borne, and that[65] thou look'st at best,
 She durst not kisse, but flung thee from her brest.[66]
115 And so did *Jove*, who ne're meant thee his Cup:[67]
 No mar'le the Clownes of *Lemnos* tooke thee up.[68]
For none but Smiths would have made thee a God.
 Some Alchimist there may be yet, or odde
Squire of the Squibs,[69] against the Pageant day,
120 May to thy name a *Vulcanale*[70] say;
And for it lose his eyes with Gun-powder,
 As th'other may his braines with Quicksilver.
Well-fare the Wise-men yet, on the *Banckside*,[71]
 My friends, the Watermen![72] They could provide
125 Against thy furie, when to serve their needs,
 They made a *Vulcan*[73] of a sheafe of Reedes,
Whom they durst handle in their holy-day coates,
 And safely trust to dresse, not burne their Boates.
But, O those Reeds! thy meere disdaine of them,
130 Made thee beget that cruell Stratagem,
 (Which, some are pleas'd to stile but thy madde
            [pranck)
 Against the *Globe*,[74] the Glory of the *Banke*.

[63] of metal, work.

[64] According to Hesiod, *Theogony* 927, Juno was the sole parent.

[65] perhaps, then.

[66] Again according to Hesiod, Juno was so disgusted with the child that she flung him away.

[67] In *Iliad* I. 571ff. Vulcan is cupbearer to the gods.

[68] The peasants of Lemnos picked up Vulcan after Jupiter had thrown him down there from heaven.

[69] Fleay refers this to John Squire's *The Triumphs of Peace*, written for the Lord Mayor's fireworks show of October 1620.

[70] hymn to Vulcan.

[71] in London, the south shore of the Thames.

[72] who ferried people across.

[73] a torch.

[74] the famous theater, burned June 29, 1613, during a performance of *Henry VIII*. Rebuilt in 1614.

Which, though it were the Fort of the whole Parish,
    Flanck'd with a Ditch, and forc'd out of a Marish,
135 I saw with two poore Chambers[75] taken in
    And raz'd; e're thought could urge, this might have
                  [been!
See the Worlds[76] Ruines! nothing but the piles
    Left! and wit since to cover it with Tiles.[77]
The Brethren,[78] they streight nois'd it out for Newes,
140 'Twas verily some Relique of the Stewes.[79]
And this a Sparkle of that fire let loose
    That was lock'd up in the *Winchestrian* Goose[80]
Bred on the *Banck*, in time of Poperie,
    When *Venus* there maintain'd the Misterie.[81]
145 But, others fell, with that conceipt by the eares,[82]
    And cry'd, it was a threatning to the beares;[83]
And that accursed ground, the *Parish-Garden*:[84]
    Nay, sigh'd, ah Sister 'twas the Nun, *Kate Arden*[85]
Kindled the fire! But, then did one returne,[86]
150 No Foole would his owne harvest spoile, or burne!
If that were so, thou rather would'st advance
    The place, that was thy Wives inheritance.
O no, cry'd all. *Fortune*,[87] for being a whore,
    Scap'd not his Justice any jot the more.
155 He burnt that Idoll of the *Revels*[88] too:
    Nay, let *White-Hall*[89] with Revels have to doe,
Though but in daunces, it shall know his power;
    There was a Judgement shew'n too in an houre.

---

[75] ordnance used to fire salutes; burning wadding from them set the roof on fire.

[76] i.e., the Globe's.

[77] rather than thatch, the old roofing.

[78] publishers, who promptly brought out reports and ballads about the fire.

[79] brothels.

[80] venereal disease. The brothels in this area were part of the property of the Bishop of Winchester.

[81] calling, occupation.

[82] at variance with.

[83] the Bear Garden was nearby.

[84] also known as Paris Garden; same as Bear Garden.

[85] See *Epig.* 133, n. 51.

[86] answer.

[87] another theater, burned in December 1621.

[88] i.e., the playhouse.

[89] The banqueting house at Whitehall burned in January 1618 (H&S).

Hee is true *Vulcan* still! He did not spare
160   *Troy*, though it were so much his *Venus* care.[90]
Foole, wilt thou let that in example come?
    Did not she save from thence, to build a *Rome?*[91]
And what hast thou done in these pettie spights,
    More then advanc'd the houses, and their rites?[92]
165 I will not argue thee, from those of guilt,
    For they were burnt, but to be better built.
'Tis true, that in thy wish they were destroy'd,
    Which thou hast only vented,[93] not enjoy'd.
So would'st th'have run upon the *Rolls*[94] by stealth,
170   And didst invade part of the Common-wealth,
In those Records, which were all Chroniclers gone,
    Will be remembred by *Six Clerkes*, to one.
But, say all sixe, Good Men, what answer yee?
    Lyes there no Writ, out of the *Chancerie*
175 Against this *Vulcan?* No Injunction?
    No Order? No Decree? Though we be gone
At *Common-Law:* Me thinkes in his despight
    A Court of *Equitie*[95] should doe us right.
But to confine him to the Brew-houses,
180   The Glasse-house, Dye-fats,[96] and their Fornaces;
To live in Sea-coale,[97] and goe forth in smoake;
    Or lest that vapour might the Citie choake,
Condemne him to the Brick-kills,[98] or some Hill-
    foot (out in *Sussex*) to an iron Mill;
185 Or in small Fagots have him blaze about
    Vile Tavernes, and the Drunkards pisse him out;
Or in the *Bell*-Mans[99] Lanthorne like a spie,
    Burne to a snuffe, and then stinke out, and die:

[90] Venus, his wife, helped the Trojans in the *Iliad* and the *Aeneid*.
[91] Aeneas, who escaped from Troy at its destruction, founded Rome.
[92] honors.
[93] uttered (thy wish).
[94] The "Six Clerkes" recording office was burned in 1621 (H&S).
[95] a body of law supplementary to the common law.
[96] vats.
[97] coal (as opposed to charcoal; hence smoky).
[98] kilns.
[99] night watchman's.

I could invent a sentence, yet were worse;
190   But I'le conclude all in a civill curse.
Pox on your flameship, *Vulcan;* if it be
        To all as fatall as't hath beene to me,
And to *Pauls-Steeple;*[1] which was unto us
        'Bove all your Fire-workes, had at *Ephesus,*[2]
195   Or *Alexandria;*[3] and though a Divine
        Losse remaines yet, as unrepair'd as mine.
Would you had kept your Forge at *Ætna* still,
        And there made Swords, Bills, Glaves,[4] and Armes
                                                                [your fill.
Maintain'd the trade at *Bilbo;* or else-where;
200   Strooke in at *Millan*[5] with the Cutlers there;
Or stay'd but where the Fryar,[6] and you first met,
        Who from the Divels-Arse did Guns beget;
Or fixt in the *Low-Countrey's,*[7] where you might
        On both sides doe your mischiefes with delight;
205   Blow up, and ruine, myne, and countermyne,
        Make your Petards,[8] and Granats,[9] all your fine
Engines of Murder, and receive the praise
        Of massacring Man-kind so many wayes.
We aske your absence here, we all love peace,
210   And pray the fruites thereof, and the increase;
So doth the *King,* and most of the *Kings men*
        That have good places: therefore once agen,
Pox on thee *Vulcan,* thy *Pandora's* pox,[10]
        And all the Evils that flew out of her box

---

[1] The spire and roof burned in June 1561.

[2] Herostratus burned the temple of Diana there in 356 B.C.

[3] the Library, burned in A.D. 640.

[4] a kind of sword or halbert.

[5] Fine swords were made at Milan.

[6] Roger Bacon (H&S) or Berthold Schwartz (Newdigate), noted as magicians. For both as inventors of guns see William Camden, *Remaines Concerning Britaine* (1637 ed.), pp. 202–3.

[7] in their continuing struggle against Spain.

[8] a kind of artillery to batter down doors or walls.

[9] grenades.

[10] Vulcan created Pandora ("All-gifts") at Jupiter's command. She had a box which contained all evils, and she emptied it on mankind. *Pox* (either imprecation or disease) is smallpox or great pox (syphilis).

215 Light on thee: Or if those plagues will not doo,
    Thy Wives pox on thee, and *B.B.'s*[11] too.

46. A Speach According to[1] Horace

WHy yet my noble hearts they cannot say,
    But we have Powder still for the Kings Day,[2]
And Ord'nance too: so much as from the Tower
    T'have wak'd, if sleeping, *Spaines* Ambassadour,
5 Old *Æsope*[3] *Gundomar:*[4] the French can tell,
    For they did see it the last tilting well,
That we have Trumpets, Armour, and great Horse,
    Launces, and men, and some a breaking force.
They saw too store of feathers,[5] and more may,
10   If they stay here, but till Saint *Georges* Day.[6]
All Ensignes of a Warre, are not yet dead,
    Nor markes of wealth so from our Nation fled,
But they may see Gold-Chaines, and Pearle worne
                          [then,
    Lent by the *London* Dames, to the Lords men;
15 Withall, the dirtie[7] paines those Citizens take,
    To see the Pride at Court, their Wives doe make:
And the returne those thankfull Courtiers yeeld
    To have their Husbands drawne forth to the field,
And comming home, to tell what acts were done
20   Under the Auspice of young *Swynnerton*.[8]
What a strong Fort old *Pimblicoe*[9] had beene!
    How it held out! how (last) 'twas taken in!
Well, I say thrive, thrive brave Artillerie yard,[10]
    Thou Seed-plot of the warre, that hast not spar'd

---

[11] Bess Broughton, famous London courtesan.

46: [1] in the spirit of. Horace had attacked Roman degeneracy.

[2] a public tilt in the King's honor, held on his coronation day or birthday.

[3] teller of fables: liar.

[4] Spanish ambassador to England, 1613–18 and 1620–22.

[5] red ostrich feathers worn by members of the Royal Artillery Company as a badge (Newdigate).

[6] April 23, when the group had a parade or public showing.

[7] repulsive.

[8] a captain in the Company (Newdigate).

[9] an old fort near London.

[10] where the Company practiced maneuvers.

25   Powder, or paper, to bring up the youth
            Of *London,* in the Militarie truth,
        These ten yeares day;[11] As all may sweare that looke
            But on thy practise, and the Posture booke:[12]
        He that but saw thy curious[13] Captaines drill,
30   Would thinke no more of *Vlushing,* or the *Brill:*[14]
        But give them over to the common eare
            For that unnecessarie Charge[15] they were.
        Well did thy craftie Clerke, and Knight, Sir *Hugh*[16]
            Supplant bold *Panton;* and brought there to view
35   Translated *Ælian* tactickes[17] to be read,
            And the Greeke Discipline (with the moderne) shed
        So, in that ground, as soone it grew to be
            The Cittie-Question, whether *Tilly,*[18] or he,
        Were now the greater Captaine? for they saw
40   The *Berghen* siege, and taking in *Breda,*[19]
        So acted to the life, as *Maurice*[20] might,
            And *Spinola* have blushed at the sight.
        O happy Art! and wise Epitome
            Of bearing Armes! most civill Soldierie!
45   Thou canst draw forth thy forces, and fight drie[21]
            The Battells of thy Aldermanitie;[22]

[11] The Company was begun again in 1611, after a lapse of a year. In 1616 its *Orders* were printed. H&S suggest that Jonson is thinking of the latter date and thus is writing about 1626.

[12] some text on military bearing.

[13] careful, expert.

[14] towns in the Netherlands captured from the Spanish in 1572 by followers of William of Orange.

[15] effort at capture.

[16] Hugh Hamersley, president of the Company at this time. Actually Edward Panton had been succeeded by John Bingham (Newdigate).

[17] Bingham had translated the *Tactiks of Aelian or Art of Embattailing an Army* (1616). Bingham urged that the Greek phalanx was not obsolete for the English.

[18] Johann Tzerclaes, Count of Tilly (1559–1632), general of the Army of the Catholic League in the Thirty Years War (H&S).

[19] Bergen, Holland, was unsuccessfully besieged by Spinola, the Spanish general, in 1622; he was successful in reducing Breda in 1625.

[20] Prince of Orange (1567–1625).

[21] without bloodshed.

[22] office of alderman.

Without the hazard of a drop of blood:
> More then the surfets, in thee, that day stood.
Goe on, increast in vertue; and in fame:
50   And keepe the Glorie of the English name,
Up among Nations. In the stead of bold
> *Beauchamps,* and *Nevills, Cliffords, Audley's* old;[23]
Insert thy *Hodges,* and those newer men,[24]
> As *Stiles, Dike, Ditchfield, Millar, Crips,* and *Fen:*
55   That keepe the warre, though now't be growne more
                                                    [tame,
> Alive yet, in the noise; and still the same;
And could (if our great men would let their Sonnes
> Come to their Schooles,) show'hem the use of
                                                  [Guns,[25]
And there instruct the noble English heires
60   In Politique, and Militar Affaires;
But he that should perswade, to have this done
> For education of our Lordings;[26] Soone
Should he heare of billow, wind, and storme,
> From the Tempestuous Grandlings,[27] who'll in-
                                                    [forme
65 Us, in our bearing,[28] that are thus, and thus,
> Borne, bred, allied? what's he dare tutor us?[29]
Are we by Booke-wormes to be awde? must we
> Live by their Scale, that dare doe nothing free?
Why are we rich, or great, except to show
70   All licence in our lives? What need we know?
More then to praise a Dog? or Horse? or speake
> The Hawking language? or our Day to breake[30]
With Citizens? let Clownes,[31] and Tradesmen breed
> Their Sonnes to studie Arts, the Lawes, the Creed:
75 We will beleeve like men of our owne Ranke,
> In so much land a yeare, or such a Banke,

[23] famous old English families.
[24] members of the Company
(Newdigate). In the margin was
added yet another name, *Waller.*
[25] Aristocrats shied away from
this innovation.

[26] little lords.
[27] little grand ones.
[28] sc. arms.
[29] the Grandlings.
[30] interrupt.
[31] ordinary folk.

That turnes[32] us so much moneys, at which rate
   Our Ancestors impos'd on Prince and State.
Let poore Nobilitie be vertuous: Wee,
80   Descended in a rope of Titles, be
From *Guy,* or *Bevis,*[33] *Arthur,* or from whom
   The Herald[34] will. Our blood is now become[35]
Past any need of vertue. Let them care,
   That in the Cradle of their Gentrie are;[36]
85 To serve the State by Councels, and by Armes:
   We neither love the Troubles, nor the harmes.
What love you[37] then? your whore? what study?
                              [gate,[38]
   Carriage, and dressing? There is up of late
The Academie,[39] where the Gallants meet—
90   What, to make legs? yes, and to smell most sweet,
All that they doe at Playes. O, but first here[40]
   They learne and studie; and then practise there.
But why are all these Irons i'the fire
   Of severall makings? helps, helps, t'attire
95 His Lordship. That is for his Band,[41] his haire
   This, and that box his Beautie to repaire;
This other for his eye-browes; hence, away,
   I may no longer on these pictures stay,
These Carkasses of honour; Taylors blocks,[42]
100   Cover'd with Tissue,[43] whose prosperitie mocks
The fate of things: whilst totter'd[44] vertue holds
   Her broken Armes up, to their emptie moulds.[45]

[32] returns.
[33] medieval romance heroes: Guy of Warwick and Bevis of Hampton.
[34] the officer who recorded armorial bearings and pedigrees.
[35] come.
[36] are just beginning to be gentlemen.
[37] the Grandlings.
[38] gait.
[39] some social group instructing in social decorum.
[40] at the "Academy."
[41] ruff.
[42] dummies.
[43] fine cloth.
[44] tottering.
[45] patterns or fashions.

47. An Epistle to Master Arth: Squib

WHat I am not, and what I faine would be,
    Whilst I informe my selfe, I would teach thee,
My gentle *Arthur;*[1] that it might be said
    One lesson we have both learn'd, and well read;[2]
5   I neither am, nor art thou one of those
    That harkens to a Jacks-pulse,[3] when it goes;
Nor ever trusted to that friendship yet
    Was issue of the Taverne, or the Spit:[4]
Much lesse a name would we bring up, or nurse,
10   That could but claime a kindred from the purse.
Those are poore Ties, depend on those false ends,
    'Tis vertue alone, or nothing that knits friends:
And as within your Office, you doe take
    No piece of money, but you know, or make
15   Inquirie of the worth: So must we doe,
    First weigh a friend, then touch,[5] and trie him too:
For there are many slips, and Counterfeits.
    Deceit is fruitfull. Men have Masques and nets,
But these with wearing will themselves unfold:
20   They cannot last. No lie grew ever old.
Turne him, and see his Threds: looke, if he be
    Friend to himselfe, that would be friend to thee.
For that is first requir'd, A man be his owne.
    But he that's too-much that, is friend of none.
25   Then rest, and a friends value understand:
    It is a richer Purchase then of land.

48. An Epigram on Sir Edward Coke,[1] When He Was Lord Chiefe Justice of England

HE that should search all Glories of the Gowne,[2]
    And steps of all rais'd servants of the Crowne,

47: [1] Arthur Squib was an officer of the Exchequer (H&S).
  [2] understood.
  [3] Jack was a metal figure which struck the hour on clocks; hence a time-server (H&S).

[4] dining together.
[5] test.
48: [1] (1552–1634), legal writer and Chief Justice of the King's Bench.
  [2] i.e., legal profession.

He could not find, then thee of all that store
　　Whom[3] Fortune aided lesse, or vertue more.
5　　Such, *Coke,* were thy beginnings, when thy good
　　　In others evill best was understood:
　　When, being the Strangers helpe, the poore mans aide,
　　　Thy just defences made th' oppressor afraid.
　　Such was thy Processe,[4] when Integritie,
10　　And skill in thee, now, grew Authoritie;
　　That Clients strove, in Question of the Lawes,
　　　More for thy Patronage, then for their Cause,
　　And that thy strong and manly Eloquence
　　　Stood up thy Nations fame, her Crownes defence,
15　　And now such is thy stand; while thou dost deale
　　　Desired Justice to the publique Weale
　　Like *Solons*[5] selfe; explat'st[6] the knottie Lawes
　　　With endlesse labours, whilst thy learning drawes
　　No lesse of praise, then readers in all kinds
20　　Of worthiest knowledge, that can take mens minds.
　　Such is thy All; that (as I sung before)
　　　None Fortune aided lesse, or Vertue more.
　　Or if Chance must, to each man that doth rise
　　　Needs lend an aide, to thine she had[7] her eyes.

49. AN EPISTLE ANSWERING TO ONE THAT ASKED TO BE SEALED OF THE TRIBE OF BEN[1]

MEn that are safe, and sure, in all they doe,
　　Care not what trials they are put unto;
　　They meet the fire, the Test, as Martyrs would;
　　　And though Opinion stampe them not, are gold.
5　　I could say more of such, but that I flie[2]
　　　To speake my selfe out too ambitiously,
　　And shewing so weake an Act to vulgar eyes,
　　　Put conscience and my right to comprimise.[3]

---

[3] one whom.
[4] progress.
[5] famous ancient Greek law-giver.
[6] unravelest.
[7] had given.

49:　[1] "Of the tribe of Benjamin were sealed twelve thousand": Rev. 7:8. Sealed: assured.
　　[2] avoid.
　　[3] in a compromising position.

Let those that meerely talke, and never thinke,
10   That live in the wild Anarchie of Drinke,
Subject to quarrell only; or else such
      As make it their proficiencie, how much
They'ave glutted in, and letcher'd out that weeke,
      That never yet did friend, or friendship seeke
15   But for a Sealing: let these men protest.
      Or th'other on their borders,[4] that will jeast
On all Soules that are absent; even the dead
      Like flies, or wormes, with mans corrupt parts fed:
That to speake well, thinke it above all sinne,
20   Of any Companie but that they are in,
Call every night to Supper in these fitts,
      And are receiv'd for[5] the Covey of Witts;
That censure all the Towne, and all th'affaires,
      And know whose ignorance is more then theirs;
25   Let these men have their wayes, and take their times
      To vent their Libels, and to issue rimes,
I have no portion in them, nor their deale
      Of newes they get, to strew out the long meale,
I studie other friendships, and more one,
30   Then these can ever be; or else wish none.
What is't to me whether the French Designe
      Be, or be not, to get the V*al-telline*?[6]
Or the States[7] Ships sent forth belike to meet
      Some hopes of *Spaine* in their West-Indian Fleet?
35   Whether the Dispensation[8] yet be sent,
      Or that the Match from *Spaine* was ever meant?
I wish all well, and pray high heaven conspire
      My Princes safetie, and my Kings desire.
But if for honour, we must draw the Sword,
40   And force back that,[9] which will not be restor'd,

4 like them.
5 accepted as.
6 a valley stretching from Lake
Como to the Tyrol; controlled by
Spain after 1620 until France
took it over in 1624 (H&S).
7 Dutch.

8 for Charles to marry the In-
fanta of Spain. How serious
Charles was in the match is not
certain.
9 probably, the forces of Catho-
lic Spain.

    I have a body, yet, that spirit drawes
        To live, or fall, a Carkasse in the cause.
    So farre without inquirie what the States,
        Brunsfield,[10] and *Mansfield*[11] doe this yeare, my
                              [fates
45   Shall carry me at Call; and I'le be well,
        Though I doe neither heare these newes, nor tell
    Of *Spaine* or *France*; or were not prick'd down[12] one
        Of the late Mysterie of reception; [13]
    Although my Fame, to his, not under-heares,[14]
50   That guides the Motions,[15] and directs the beares.[16]
    But that's a blow, by which in time I may
        Lose all my credit with my Christmas Clay,[17]
    And animated *Porc'lane* of the Court,
        I,[18] and for this neglect, the courser sort
55   Of earthen Jarres, there may molest me too:
        Well, with mine owne fraile Pitcher, what to doe
    I have decreed; keepe it from waves, and presse;[19]
        Lest it be justled, crack'd, made nought, or lesse:
    Live to that point[20] I will; for which I am man,
60   And dwell as[21] in my Center, as I can,
    Still looking too,[22] and ever loving heaven;
        With reverence using all the gifts thence given.
    'Mongst which, if I have any friendships sent
        Such as are square, wel-tagde,[23] and permanent,
65   Not built with Canvasse, paper, and false lights[24]
        As are the Glorious Scenes, at the great sights;

[10] probably Christian of Brunswick, in the service of Frederick, Elector Palatine; defeated by Tilly in the battles of Höchst (1622) and Stadtlohn (1623).

[11] commanding the army of Bohemia and the Palatine.

[12] listed.

[13] Inigo Jones among others (Mysterie, i.e., ministry) arranged for a reception of the Infanta at Southampton in 1624. Jonson was left out.

[14] is not inferior.

[15] puppets.

[16] apparently some kind of bear baiting devised by Inigo Jones.

[17] perhaps his entertainments offered at court during the Christmas season. Jonson is afraid of losing his standing there.

[18] Ay.

[19] crowds.

[20] probably, direction of the compass.

[21] as much in; as near to.

[22] to.

[23] well built.

[24] lighting and shadows painted on the scenery of the masques.

And that there be no fev'ry heats, nor colds,
　Oylie Expansions,[25] or shrunke durtie folds,
But all so cleare, and led by reasons flame,
70　　As but to stumble in her sight were shame;
These I will honour, love, embrace, and serve:
　And free it[26] from all question to preserve.
So short[27] you read my Character, and theirs
　I would call mine, to which not many Staires
75　Are asked to climbe. First give me faith, who[28] know
　My selfe a little. I will take you so,
As you have writ your selfe. Now stand, and then,
　Sir, you are Sealed of the Tribe of *Ben*.

50. THE DEDICATION OF THE KINGS NEW CELLAR[1] TO BACCHUS

SInce, *Bacchus*, thou art father
Of Wines, to thee the rather
We dedicate this Cellar,
Where new, thou art made Dweller;
5　And seale thee thy Commission:
But 'tis with a condition,
That thou remaine here taster
Of all to the great Master.
And looke unto their faces,
10　Their Qualities, and races,
That both, their odour[2] take him,
And relish merry make him.
　For *Bacchus* thou art freer
Of cares, and over-seer,
15　Of feast, and merry meeting,
And still begin'st the greeting:
See then thou dost attend him,
Lyæus,[3] and defend him,
By all the Arts of Gladnesse
20　From any thought like sadnesse.

[25] apparently the stretching of the cloth after it has been painted.
[26] friendship.
[27] in brief.
[28] (I) who.

50: [1] in Whitehall, designed by Inigo Jones.
[2] appearance.
[3] surname for Bacchus: deliverer from care.

So mayst thou still be younger
Then *Phœbus*;[4] and much stronger
To give mankind their eases,
And cure the Worlds diseases:
25   So may the Muses follow
Thee still, and leave *Apollo*
And thinke thy streame more quicker
Then *Hippocrenes*[5] liquor:
And thou make many a poet,
30   Before his braine doe know it;
So may there never Quarrell
Have issue from the Barrell;
But *Venus* and the Graces
Pursue thee in all places,
35   And not a Song be other
Then *Cupid*, and his Mother.
        That when King *James*, above here
Shall feast it, thou maist love there
The causes and the Guests too,
40   And have thy tales and jests too,
Thy Circuits, and thy Rounds free
As shall the feasts faire grounds be.
        Be it he hold Communion
In great Saint *Georges* Union;[6]
45   Or gratulates[7] the passage
Of some wel-wrought Embassage:
Whereby he may knit sure up
The wished Peace of *Europe*:
Or else a health advances,
50   To put his Court in dances,
And set us all on skipping,[8]
When with his royall shipping
The narrow Seas are shadie,
And *Charles* brings home the Ladie.[9]
Accessit fervor Capiti, Numerusque Lucernis.[10]

[4] Apollo, inspirer of poetry.
[5] fountain sacred to the Muses.
[6] of the Knights of the Garter on St. George's Day, April 23.
[7] celebrates.
[8] a-skipping.
[9] Charles was expected to bring home the Spanish Infanta as his bride in 1623.

[10] Horace, *Satires* 2.i.25: The heat has mounted to his (drunken) head and the lamps are double.

51. An Epigram on the Court Pucell[1]

 DO's the Court-Pucell then so censure me,
  And thinkes I dare not her? let the world see.
 What though her Chamber be the very pit
  Where fight the prime Cocks of the Game, for wit?
5 And that as any are strooke, her breath creates
  New in their stead, out of the Candidates?
 What though with Tribade[2] lust she force a Muse,
  And in an Epicæne[3] fury can write newes
 Equall with that, which for the best newes goes
10 As aërie light, and as like wit as those?
 What though she talke, and cannot once with them,
  Make State, Religion, Bawdrie, all a theame.
 And as lip-thirstie, in each words expence,
  Doth labour with the Phrase more then the sense?
15 What though she ride two mile on Holy-dayes
  To Church, as others doe to Feasts and Playes,
 To shew their Tires?[4] to view, and to be view'd?
  What though she be with Velvet gownes indu'd,[5]
 And spangled Petticotes brought forth to eye,
20 As new rewards of her old secrecie!
 What though she hath won on Trust, as many doe,
  And that her truster feares her? Must I too?
 I never stood for any place:[6] my wit
  Thinkes it selfe nought, though she should valew it.
25 I am no States-man, and much lesse Divine;
  For bawdry, 'tis her language, and not mine.
 Farthest I am from the Idolatrie
  To stuffes and Laces, those my Man can buy.

51: [1] Pucelle: slut. Usually identified, from two passages in Jonson's *Conversations with Drummond*, as Cecily Bulstrode (1584–1609), friend of Lucy, Countess of Bedford. But Donne wrote her an Elegy of high praise, and Jonson praised her (and her virginity) highly after her death (*Uncol. P.* 26).
 [2] female homosexual.
 [3] partaking of the characteristics of both sexes.
 [4] dresses.
 [5] clothed (L. *induere*).
 [6] tried to get a position at court.

And trust her I would least, that hath forswore
30   In Contract twice,[7] what can shee perjure more?
Indeed, her Dressing some man might delight,
    Her face there's none can like by Candle light.
Not he, that should the body have, for Case[8]
    To his poore Instrument, now out of grace.
35   Shall I advise thee *Pucell?* steale away
    From Court, while yet thy fame hath some small
                             [day;
The wits will leave you, if they once perceive
    You cling to Lords, and Lords, if them you leave
For Sermoneeres: of which now one, now other,
40   They say you weekly invite with fits o' th'Mother,[9]
And practise for a Miracle;[10] take heed,
    This Age would lend no faith to *Dorrels*[11] Deed;
Or if it would, the Court is the worst place,
    Both for the Mothers, and the Babes of grace,[12]
45   For there the wicked in the Chaire of scorne,
    Will cal't a Bastard, when a Prophet's borne.

52. AN EPIGRAM. TO THE HONOUR'D ———— COUNTESSE OF ————[1]

THe Wisdome Madam of your private Life,
    Where with this while[2] you live a widowed wife,[3]
And the right wayes you take unto the right,
    To conquer rumour, and triumph on[4] spight;
5   Not only shunning by your act, to doe
    Ought that is ill, but the suspition too,
Is of so brave[5] example, as[6] he were
    No friend to vertue, could[7] be silent here.

[7] The circumstances are not known.

[8] covering.

[9] hysteria, with pun.

[10] virgin birth.

[11] John Darrel, Puritan preacher and religious quack, exposed by investigation in 1599 (H&S X. 251, with list of contemporary books about him).

[12] probably, miracles.

52: [1] Elizabeth, Countess of Rutland (Cunningham). See *The Forrest* 12. She died in 1612.

[2] during this time.

[3] the Count was impotent.

[4] over.

[5] fine.

[6] that.

[7] who could.

The rather when the vices of the Time
10   Are growne so fruitfull, and false pleasures climbe
By all oblique Degrees, that killing height
    From whence they fall, cast downe with their owne
                                [weight.
And though all praise bring nothing to your name,
    Who (herein studying conscience, and not fame)
15   Are in your selfe rewarded; yet 't will be
A cheerefull worke to all good eyes, to see
Among the daily Ruines that fall foule,
    Of State, of fame, of body, and of soule,
So great a Vertue stand upright to view,
20   As makes *Penelopes* old fable true,
Whilst your *Ulisses* hath ta'ne leave to goe,[8]
    Countries, and Climes, manners and men to know.
Only your time you better entertaine,
    Then the great *Homers* wit, for her, could faine;
25   For you admit no companie, but good,
    And when you want[9] those friends, or neere in
                                  [blood,
Or your Allies, you make your bookes your friends,
    And studie them unto the noblest ends,
Searching for knowledge, and to keepe your mind
30   The same it was inspir'd, rich, and refin'd.
These Graces, when the rest of Ladyes view
    Not boasted in your life, but practis'd true,
As they are hard, for them to make their owne,
    So are they profitable to be knowne:
35   For when they find so many meet in one,
    It will be shame for them, if they have none.

53. Lord Bacons Birth-day[1]

HAile happy *Genius* of this antient pile![2]
How comes it all things so about thee smile?

---

[8] In the *Odyssey* Penelope faithfully awaited her husband during his long absence abroad. Rutland traveled abroad several times.

[9] lack.

53: [1] Sir Francis, born January 22, 1561; created Baron Verulam July 1618.

[2] York House.

The fire, the wine, the men! and in the midst,
Thou stand'st as if some Mysterie[3] thou did'st!
5   Pardon, I read it in thy face, the day
For whose returnes, and many, all these pray:
And so doe I. This is the sixtieth yeare[4]
Since *Bacon*, and thy Lord was borne, and here;
Sonne to the grave wise Keeper of the Seale,[5]
10   Fame, and foundation of the English Weale.
What then his Father was, that since is hee,[6]
Now with a Title more to the Degree;
Englands high Chancellor:[7] the destin'd heire
In his soft Cradle to his Fathers Chaire,
15   Whose even Thred the Fates spinne round, and full,
Out of their Choysest, and their whitest[8] wooll.
   'Tis a brave[9] cause of joy, let it be knowne,
For 't were a narrow gladnesse, kept thine owne.
Give me a deep-crown'd-Bowle, that I may sing
20   In raysing him the wisdome of my King.

54. A Poëme Sent Me by Sir William Burlase[1]

The Painter to the Poet

TO paint thy Worth, if rightly I did know it,
And were but Painter halfe like thee, a Poët;[2]
         Ben, I would show it:
But in this skill, m'unskilfull pen will tire,
5   Thou, and thy worth, will still be found farre higher;
         And I a Lier.
Then, what a Painter's here! or what an eater
Of great attempts! when as his skil's no greater,
         And he a Cheater!

[3] religious ordinance, or secret of state.
   [4] i.e., 1621.
   [5] Sir Nicholas Bacon (1509–79).
   [6] on March 7, 1617.
   [7] on January 7, 1618.
   [8] On January 27, 1621, he became Viscount St. Albans. Albans: white.
   [9] fine.
54: [1] (d. 1629), sheriff of Buckinghamshire; no standing to-day as a painter.
   [2] half as good a painter as you are a poet.

10   Then what a Poet's here! whom, by Confession
Of all with[3] me, to paint without Digression
           There's no Expression.

My Answer. The Poet to the Painter

WHy? though I seeme of a prodigious wast,[4]
I am not so voluminous, and vast,
   But there are lines, wherewith I might b'embrac'd.

'Tis true, as my wombe swells, so my backe stoupes,
5   And the whole lumpe growes round, deform'd, and
                           [droupes,
   But yet the Tun at *Heidelberg*[5] had houpes.

You were not tied, by any Painters Law
To square my Circle, I confesse; but draw
   My Superficies: that was all you saw.

10   Which if in compasse of no Art it came
To be described by a *Monogram*,[6]
   With one great blot, yo'had form'd me as I am.

But whilst you curious were to have it be
An *Archetipe*, for all the world to see,
15   You made it a brave[7] piece, but not like me.

O, had I now your manner, maistry, might,
Your Power of handling shadow, ayre, and spright,
   How I would draw, and take hold and delight.

But, you are he can paint; I can but write:
20   A Poet hath no more but black and white,
   Ne knowes he flatt'ring Colours, or false light.

Yet when of friendship I would draw the face,
A letter'd mind, and a large heart would place
   To all posteritie; I will write *Burlase*.

---

[3] of everyone along with.
[4] Jonson several times (e.g., in No. 58) mentions his great weight in his later years.
[5] a great cask described by Coryate in the *Crudities* (1611).
[6] unshaded and uncolored outline.
[7] fine.

55. AN EPIGRAM.
TO, WILLIAM, EARLE OF NEWCASTLE[1]

WHen first my Lord, I saw you backe your horse,
Provoke his mettall, and command his force
To all the uses of the field, and race,
Me thought I read[2] the ancient Art[3] of *Thrace*,
5   And saw a Centaure, past those tales of *Greece*,
    So seem'd your horse and you, both of a peece!
You shew'd like *Perseus*[4] upon *Pegasus*;
    Or *Castor* mounted on his *Cyllarus:*[5]
Or what we heare our home-borne Legend tell,
10   Of bold Sir *Bevis*, and his *Arundell:*[6]
Nay, so your Seate his beauties did endorse,[7]
    As I began to wish my selfe a horse:
And surely had I but your Stable seene
    Before: I thinke my wish absolv'd[8] had beene.
15   For never saw I yet the Muses dwell,
    Nor any of their houshold halfe so well.
So well! as[9] when I saw the floore, and Roome
    I look'd for *Hercules* to be the Groome:[10]
And cri'd, away, with the *Cæsarian* bread,
20   At these Immortall Mangers *Virgil* fed.[11]

55: [1] William Cavendish (1592–1676); see also No. 71. Created Earl March 7, 1628. Great horseman, cavalier; subject of the *Memoirs* of his wife. See also No. 61 and *Uncol. P.* 39.

[2] understood.

[3] of raising horses.

[4] rather, Bellerophon, who rode Pegasus to fight the Chimera. But in Jonson's time and earlier Perseus frequently took his place. Cf. T. W. Baldwin, "Perseus Purloins Pegasus," *PQ*, XX (1941), 361–70, and the notes by J. D. Reeves and G. B. Johnston in *RES*, VI (n.s.) (1955), 65–67 and 397–99.

[5] Castor's (or Pollux's) horse.

[6] Sir Bevis of Hampton and his horse, from medieval romance.

[7] sit on the back of, with pun.

[8] resolved, granted.

[9] that.

[10] Jonson compares William's great stable with the Augean after it had been cleansed by Hercules.

[11] A tradition of Virgil's life was that he judged dogs and horses for Caesar and was rewarded with a groom's pay. See A. C. Taylor, "Virgil and the Bread," *TLS*, Aug. 28, 1937.

56. Epistle to Mr. Arthur Squib[1]

I Am to dine, Friend, where I must be weigh'd
    For a just wager, and that wager paid
If I doe lose it: And, without a Tale[2]
    A Merchants Wife is Regent of the Scale.
5   Who when shee heard the match,[3] concluded streight,
    An ill commoditie! 'T must make good weight.
So that upon[4] the point, my corporall feare
    Is, she will play Dame Justice,[5] too severe;
And hold me to it close; to stand upright
10   Within the ballance; and not want a mite;
But rather with advantage to be found
    Full twentie stone;[6] of which I lack two pound:
That's six in silver; now within the Socket[7]
    Stinketh my credit, if into the Pocket
15   It doe not come: One piece I have in store,
    Lend me, deare *Arthur*, for a weeke five more,
And you shall make me good, in weight, and fashion,
    And then to be[8] return'd; on protestation
To goe out after—till when take this letter
20   For your securitie. I can no better.

57. To Mr. John Burges

WOuld God my *Burges*,[1] I could thinke
    Thoughts worthy of thy gift, this Inke,
Then would I promise here to give
    Verse, that should thee, and me out-live.
5   But since the Wine hath steep'd my braine,
    I only can the Paper staine;
Yet with a Dye,[2] that feares no Moth,
    But Scarlet-like out-lasts the Cloth.

56: [1] See No. 47.
  [2] story, lie.
  [3] wager.
  [4] to get to.
  [5] Blindfolded Justice is pictured holding scales.
  [6] A stone usually equals 14 pounds.

[7] as a candle burns low.
[8] the loan will be.
57: [1] a clerk of the Exchequer (H&S). Newdigate suggests that he may have been a member of the Artillery Company (see No. 46).
[2] "deathless" ink.

58. Epistle. To My Lady Covell[1]

YOu won not Verses, Madam, you won mee,
　　When you would play so nobly, and so free.
A booke to[2] a few lynes: but, it was fit
　　You won them too, your oddes did merit it.
5　So have you gain'd a Servant, and a Muse:
　　The first of which I fear, you will refuse;
And you may justly, being a tardie, cold,
　　Unprofitable Chattell, fat and old,
Laden with Bellie, and doth hardly approach
10　　His friends, but to breake Chairs, or cracke a Coach.
His weight is twenty Stone within two pound;[3]
　　And that's made up[4] as doth the purse abound.
Marrie the Muse is one, can tread the Aire,
　　And stroke the water, nimble, chast, and faire,
15　Sleepe in a Virgins bosome without feare,
　　Run all the Rounds in a soft Ladyes eare,
Widow or Wife, without the jealousie
　　Of either Suitor, or a Servant by.
Such, (if her manners like you) I doe send:
20　　And can for other Graces her commend,
To make you merry on the Dressing stoole
　　A mornings, and at afternoones to foole
Away ill company, and helpe in rime
　　Your *Joane*[5] to passe her melancholie time.
25　By this, although you fancie not the man,
　　Accept his Muse; and tell, I know you can:
How many verses, Madam, are your Due!
　　I can lose none in tendring these to you.
I gaine, in having leave to keepe my Day,[6]
30　　And should grow rich, had I much more to pay.

58:　[1] See No. 24, n. 9. The
lady is otherwise unidentified.
　[2] in comparison to.
　[3] See No. 56, n. 6.

[4] supported.
[5] not identified.
[6] agreement.

59. To Master John Burges

FAther *John Burges*,[1]
Necessitie urges
My wofull crie,
To Sir *Robert Pie:*[2]
5 And that he will venter
To send my *Debentur.*[3]
Tell him his *Ben*
Knew the time, when
He lov'd the Muses;
10 Though now he refuses,
To take Apprehension[4]
Of a yeares Pension,
And more is behind:
Put him in mind
15 Christmas is neere;
And neither good Cheare,
Mirth, fooling, nor wit,
Nor any least fit
Of gambol, or sport
20 Will come at the Court,
If there be no money,
No Plover, or Coney
Will come to the Table,
Or Wine to enable
25 The Muse, or the Poet,
The Parish will know it.
Nor any quick-warming-pan helpe him to bed,
If the 'Chequer be emptie, so will be his Head.

59: [1] See No. 57, n. 1.
[2] (1585–1662), knighted
1621: the person in the Ex-
chequer who sent Jonson his
pension granted by James in 1610.
[3] what sums are owing to me.
[4] care.

60. Epigram, to My Book-seller[1]

THou, Friend, wilt heare all censures; unto thee
    All mouthes are open, and all stomacks[2] free:
Bee thou my Bookes intelligencer, note
    What each man sayes of it, and of what coat[3]
5   His judgement is; If he be wise, and praise,
    Thanke him: if other, hee can give no Bayes.[4]
If his wit reach no higher, but to spring
    Thy Wife a fit of laughter; a Cramp-ring[5]
Will be reward enough: to weare like those,
10   That hang their richest jewells i'their nose;
Like a rung[6] Beare, or Swine: grunting out wit
    As if that part lay for a [   ][7] most fit!
If they goe on, and that[8] thou lov'st a-life[9]
    Their perfum'd judgements, let them kisse thy Wife.

61. An Epigram. To William Earle of Newcastle[1]

THey talke of Fencing, and the use of Armes,
    The art of urging,[2] and avoyding harmes,
The noble Science, and the maistring skill
    Of making just approaches how to kill:
5   To hit in angles, and to clash with[3] time:
    As[4] all defence, or offence were a chime!
I hate such measur'd, give me mettall'd fire
    That trembles in the blaze, but (then) mounts
                                                    [higher!

60: [1] Fleay suggested Thomas Alchorne, who published *The New Inn* in 1631. Newdigate and H&S add that it might be Robert Allot, who published *Bartholomew Fair*, *The Devil is an Ass*, and *The Staple of News* in the same year.
    [2] secret thoughts.
    [3] class.
    [4] poetic award.
    [5] a hallowed ring held to be efficacious against some diseases and worn on the finger by nobles. Jonson connects it with the nose ring, fixed in an animal's nose as a lead.
    [6] with a ring in its nose.
    [7] some profane word omitted.
    [8] if.
    [9] dearly.
61: [1] See No. 55 on the Earl's horsemanship.
    [2] doing.
    [3] in.
    [4] as if.

A quick, and dazeling motion! when a paire
10   Of bodies, meet like rarified ayre![5]
Their weapons shot out, with that flame, and force,
    As they out-did the lightning in the course;
This were a spectacle! A sight to draw
    Wonder to Valour! No, it is the Law
15 Of daring, not to doe a wrong, is[6] true
    Valour! to sleight[7] it, being done to you!
To know the heads of danger! where 'tis fit
    To bend, to breake, provoke, or suffer it!
All this (my Lord) is Valour! This is yours!
20   And was your Fathers! All your Ancestours!
Who durst live great, 'mongst all the colds, and heates,
    Of humane life! as all the frosts, and sweates
Of fortune! when, or death appear'd, or bands![8]
    And valiant were, with, or without their hands.

62. An Epitaph, on Henry L. La-ware.
To the Passer-by

IF, Passenger,[1] thou canst but reade:
Stay, drop a teare for him that's dead,
Henry, the brave young Lord *La-ware*,[2]
Minerva's and the *Muses* care!
5   What could their care doe 'gainst the spight
Of a Disease, that lov'd no light
Of honour, nor no ayre of good?
But crept like darknesse[3] through his blood?
Offended with the dazeling flame
10   Of Vertue, got above his name?
No noble furniture of parts,
No love of action, and high Arts,
No aime at glorie, or in warre,
Ambition to become a Starre,

---

[5] so as to move rapidly.
[6] that is.
[7] ignore.
[8] bonds.
62:   [1] passer-by.
[2] Henry West (1603–28). His father was a leader in the founding of Delaware and was a colonial governor of the Virginia Colony.
[3] some form of melancholy.

15   Could stop the malice of this ill,
            That spread his body o're, to kill:
            And only, his great Soule envy'd,[4]
            Because it durst have noblier dy'd.

63. An Epigram

THat you[1] have seene the pride, beheld the sport,
        And all the games of Fortune, plaid at Court;
    View'd there the mercat,[2] read the wretched rate[3]
        At which there are, would[4] sell the Prince, and
                                                    [State:
5   That scarce you heare a publike voyce alive,
        But whisper'd Counsells, and those only thrive;
    Yet are got off thence, with cleare mind, and hands
        To lift to heaven: who is't not understands
    Your happinesse, and doth not speake[5] you blest,
10   To see you set apart, thus, from the rest,
        T'obtaine of God, what all the Land should aske?
    A Nations sinne got pardon'd! 'twere a taske
        Fit for a Bishops knees! O bow them oft,
        My Lord, till felt griefe make our stone hearts soft,
15   And wee doe weepe, to water, for our sinne.
        He, that in such a flood, as we are in
    Of riot, and consumption knowes the way
        To teach the people, how to fast, and pray,
    And doe their penance, to avert Gods rod,
20   He is the Man, and Favorite of God.

64. An Epigram. To K. Charles for a 100. Pounds He Sent Me in My Sicknesse[1]
1629

GReat *Charles*, among the holy gifts of grace
    Annexed to thy Person, and thy place,

---

[4] regretted.
63: [1] Gifford identifies as John Williams (1582–1650), Bishop of Lincoln and Lord Keeper of the Privy Seal (1621–28). The poem may relate to his removal from the latter office.

[2] market.
[3] price.
[4] who would.
[5] term.
64: [1] *The New Inn* had failed in 1629; Jonson had been paralyzed by a stroke the year before.

'T is not enough (thy pietie is such)
 To cure the call'd *Kings Evill*[2] with thy touch;
5 But thou wilt yet a Kinglier mastrie trie,
 To cure the *Poëts Evill,* Povertie:
And, in these Cures, do'st so thy selfe enlarge,
 As thou dost cure our *Evill,* at thy charge.
Nay, and in this, thou show'st to value more
10 One *Poët,* then of other folke ten score.[3]
O pietie! so to weigh the poores estates!
 O bountie! so to difference the rates![4]
What can the *Poët* wish his *King* may doe,
 But, that he cure the Peoples Evill too?[5]

65. To K. Charles, and Q. Mary. For the Losse of Their First-borne[1]

An Epigram Consolatorie
1629

WHo dares denie, that all first fruits are due
 To God,[2] denies the God-head to be true:
Who doubts, those fruits God can with gaine restore,
 Doth by his doubt, distrust his promise more.
5 Hee can, he will, and with large int'rest pay,
 What (at his liking) he will take away.
Then Royall *Charles,* and *Mary,* doe not grutch
 That the Almighties will to you is such:
But thanke his greatnesse, and his goodnesse too;
10 And thinke all still the best, that he will doe.
That thought shall make, he will this losse supply
 With a long, large, and blest posteritie!
For God, whose essence is so infinite,
 Cannot but heape that grace, he will requite.

[2] scrofula, supposedly cured by the touch of royalty. Formerly there was an office for this ceremony in the Prayer Book.

[3] Each person whom the King treated received an "angel"—a coin worth half a pound.

[4] distinguish the awards.

[5] The King was at odds with Parliament, which he had dissolved in March.

65: [1] The baby, named Charles, died at birth May 12, 1629.

[2] Part of Old Testament law; e.g., Deut. 26:2.

66. An Epigram. To Our Great and Good
K. Charles on His Anniversary Day[1]
1629

HOw happy were the Subject! if he knew
    Most pious King, but his owne good in you!
How many times, live long, *Charles,* would he say,
    If he but weigh'd the blessings of this day?
5   And as it turnes our joyfull yeare about,
        For safetie of such Majestie, cry out?
Indeed, when had great *Brittaine* greater cause
        Then now, to love the Soveraigne, and the Lawes?
When you that raigne, are her Example growne,
10   And what are bounds to her, you make your owne?[2]
When your assiduous practise doth secure
        That Faith,[3] which she professeth to be pure?
When all your life's a president[4] of dayes,
        And murmure cannot quarrell at your wayes?
15   How is she barren growne of love! or broke![5]
        That nothing can her gratitude provoke!
O Times! O Manners![6] Surfet bred of ease,
        The truly Epidemicall disease!
'T is not alone the Merchant, but the Clowne,[7]
20   Is Banke-rupt turn'd! the Cassock, Cloake, and
                            [Gowne,
Are lost upon accompt![8] And none will know
        How much to heaven for thee, great *Charles* they
                            [owe!

66: [1] of the King's ascension,
March 27. For Charles's troubles,
see No. 64, n. 5.
  [2] the English principle of law
that the sovereign is bound by it
as is the subject.
  [3] of the Church of England.

[4] precedent.
[5] enfeebled.
[6] Cicero's famous phrase
against Catiline: *O tempora! O
mores!*
[7] ordinary person.
[8] in the reckoning or trade.

67. AN EPIGRAM ON THE PRINCES BIRTH
1630

ANd art thou borne, brave Babe?[1] Blest be thy birth,
   That so hath crown'd our hopes, our spring, and
                        [earth,
The bed of the chast *Lilly*,[2] and the *Rose!*[3]
   What Month then *May*, was fitter to disclose,
5   This Prince of flowers? Soone shoot thou up, and grow
   The same that thou art promis'd, but be slow,
And long in changing. Let our Nephewes[4] see
   Thee, quickly come the gardens[5] eye to bee,
And there to stand so. Hast,[6] now envious Moone,
10   And interpose thy selfe, ('care not how soone.)
And threat' the great Eclipse.[7] Two houres but runne,
   Sol will re-shine. If not, *Charles* hath a Sonne.[8]

————*Non displicuisse meretur*
Festinat Cæsar qui placuisse tibi.[9]

68. AN EPIGRAM TO THE QUEENE, THEN
LYING IN[1]
1630

HAile *Mary*, full of grace,[2] it once was said,
   And by an Angell, to the blessed'st Maid
The Mother of our Lord: why may not I
   (Without prophanenesse) yet, a Poët, cry

67: [1] Charles II, born May 29,
1630. See also *Uncol. P.* 53.
  [2] the fleur-de-lis of France:
Charles's wife Henrietta Marie
was daughter of Henry IV of
France and sister to Louis XIII.
  [3] the English (father's) side;
cf. Henry VIII as uniting in his
person the white and red roses
of the two warring parties of the
War of the Roses.
  [4] descendants.
  [5] i.e., of England.

[6] Haste.
  [7] The sun was eclipsed two days
later, according to Fuller,
Worthies (1840 ed.), II, 416.
  [8] with pun on son and sun.
  [9] He deserves not to displease
you, Caesar, who hastes to please
you: Martial, "On the Specta-
cles," *Epig.* 31.
68: [1] See No. 67, n. 1.
  [2] the Service words, Ave Maria;
Luke 1:28.

5   Haile *Mary*, full of honours, to my Queene,
        The Mother of our Prince? When was there seene
     (Except the joy that the first *Mary* brought,
        Whereby the safetie of Man-kind was wrought)
     So generall a gladnesse to an Isle,
10   To make the hearts of a whole Nation smile,
     As in this Prince? Let it be lawfull, so
        To compare small with great, as still we owe
     Glorie to God. Then, Haile to *Mary!* spring
     Of so much safetie to the Realme, and King.

69. An Ode, or Song, by All the Muses. In Celebration of Her Majesties Birth-day[1]
1630

1. Clio.[2]   UP publike joy, remember
              This sixteenth of *November*,
                 Some brave un-common way:
              And though the Parish-steeple
5   Be silent,[3] to the people
                 Ring thou it Holy-day.

2. Mel.   What, though the thriftie Tower
              And Gunnes there, spare to poure
                 Their noises forth in Thunder:
10   As fearfull to awake
              This Citie, or to shake
                 Their guarded gates asunder?

3. Thal.   Yet, let our Trumpets sound;
              And cleave both ayre and ground,
15   With beating of our Drum's:
              Let every Lyre be strung,
              Harpe, Lute, Theorbo[4] sprung,
                 With touch of daintie thum's!

69: [1] November 16.
     [2] The singers of the stanzas are the nine Muses: Clio, Melpomene, Thalia, Euterpe, Terpsichore, Erato, Calliope, Urania, and Polyhymnia. Jonson does not seem to have tried to fit their stanzas to the kind of writing which each is supposed to inspire.
     [3] The silence of the church bells and guns (ll. 7–9) in the Tower may reveal her unpopularity.
     [4] a kind of lute.

20	4. Eut.	That when the Quire is full, The Harmony may pull The Angels from their Spheares:[5] And each intelligence May wish it selfe a sense; Whilst it the Dittie heares.
25	5. Terp.	Behold the royall *Mary*,[6] The Daughter of great *Harry*! And Sister to just *Lewis*! Comes in the pompe, and glorie Of all her Brothers storie,
30		And of her Fathers prowesse!
	6. Erat.	Shee showes so farre above The fained Queene of Love, This sea-girt Isle upon: As[7] here no *Venus* were;
35		But, that shee raigning here, Had got the *Ceston*[8] on!
	7. Calli.	See, see our active *King* Hath taken twice the Ring Upon his pointed Lance:[9]
40		Whilst all the ravish'd rout Doe mingle in a shout, Hay! for the flowre of *France*!
	8. Ura.	This day the Court doth measure Her joy in state, and pleasure;
45		And with a reverend feare, The Revells, and the Play,[10] Summe up this crowned day, Her two and twenti'th yeare!
	9. Poly.	Sweet! happy *Mary*! All
50		The People her doe call!

[5] Angels (intelligences in Aristotelian terminology, l. 22) were thought to rule each of the heavenly spheres, which produced a harmony of their own (the music of the spheres).

[6] See No. 67, n. 2.

[7] That.

[8] Venus' girdle.

[9] by riding and thrusting his spear through a suspended ring. Also, the fact that Mary had been pregnant twice (see Nos. 65 and 67).

[10] Thomas Randolph's *Amyntas* (H&S from Malone).

And this the wombe divine!
So fruitfull, and so faire,
Hath brought the Land an Heire!
And *Charles* a *Caroline*.[11]

70. An Epigram, to the House-hold[1]
1630

WHat can the cause be, when the *K.* hath given
His *Poët* Sack,[2] the *House-hold* will not pay?
Are they so scanted[3] in their store? or driven
For want of knowing the *Poët,* to say him nay?
5   Well, they should know him, would the *K.* but grant
His *Poët* leave to sing his *House-hold* true;
Hee'ld frame such ditties of their store, and want,
      Would make the very *Greene-cloth*[4] to looke blew:
And rather wish, in their expence of Sack,
10   So, the allowance from the King to use,
As the old *Bard,* should no Canary lack:
      'T were better spare a Butt, then spill[5] his *Muse.*
For in the *Genius* of a *Poëts* Verse
      The Kings fame lives. Go now, denie his *Teirce*.[6]

71. Epigram. To a Friend, and Sonne[1]

SOnne, and my Friend, I had not call'd you so
To mee; or beene the same to you; if show,
Profit, or Chance had made us: But I know
What, by that name, wee each to other owe,
5   Freedome, and Truth; with love from those begot.
      Wise-crafts, on which the flatterer ventures not.

[11] both adjective: pertaining to Charles, and noun: a line (successor) to Charles.

70: [1] of the King.

[2] ordered given yearly to Jonson, March 26, 1630. See H&S I.247. Chaucer had had a similar grant.

[3] diminished.

[4] the Board of Green Cloth, part of the royal household assigned control of the royal domestic expenditures.

[5] with pun on both Butt and spill (spoil). Cf. the adage, "Spare the rod and spoil the child."

[6] 42 gallons.

71: [1] Fleay suggests Cary (see No. 72).

[1] The engraved title-page of Raleigh's
History of the World, 1614

[2] Frontispiece of *Coryats Crudities*, 1611

His is more safe commoditie, or none:
  Nor dares he come in the comparison.
But as the wretched Painter,[2] who so ill
10   Painted a Dog, that now his subtler skill
Was, t'have a Boy stand with a Club, and fright
  All live dogs from the lane, and his shops sight,
Till he had sold his Piece, drawne so unlike:
  So doth the flatt'rer with faire cunning strike
15   At a Friends freedome, proves[3] all circling meanes
  To keepe him off; and how-so-e're he gleanes
Some of his formes, he lets him not come neere
  Where he would fixe, for the distinctions feare.
For as at distance, few have facultie
20   To judge; So all men comming neere can spie,
Though now of flattery, as of picture are
  More subtle workes, and finer pieces farre,
Then knew the former ages: yet to life,
  All is but web, and painting; be the strife
25   Never so great to get them: and the ends,
  Rather to boast rich hangings, then rare friends.

72. To the Immortall Memorie, and Friendship of That Noble Paire, Sir Lucius Cary,[1] and Sir H. Morison[2]

The Turne

BRave Infant of *Saguntum*,[3] cleare
Thy comming forth in that great yeare,
When the Prodigious[4] *Hannibal* did crowne
His rage, with razing your immortall Towne.

2 from Plutarch, "How to Tell a Flatterer from a Friend," xxiv, in *Moralia* (Loeb ed., I.347), where the painter paints cocks.

3 tries.

72: 1 Viscount Falkland (1610?–43), son of Sir Henry Cary (*Epig.* 66). Brought up and educated in Ireland, he died fighting for Charles in the battle of Newbury.

2 Henry Morison (1608?–29), eldest son of Sir Richard Morison and nephew of the traveler Fynes Morison. Knighted October 1627. Cary married his sister.

3 Hannibal, who captured Saguntum in 219 B.C. to start the second Punic War.

4 like a prodigy: ominous or amazing.

5   Thou, looking then about,
       E're thou wert halfe got out,
       Wise child,[5] did'st hastily returne,
       And mad'st thy Mothers wombe thine urne.
       How summ'd a circle didst thou leave man-kind
10   Of deepest lore, could we the Center find!

The Counter-turne

       Did wiser Nature draw thee back,
       From out the horrour of that sack,
       Where shame, faith, honour, and regard of right
       Lay trampled on; the deeds of death, and night,
15   Urg'd, hurried forth, and horld
       Upon th'affrighted world:
       Sword, fire, and famine, with fell fury met;
       And all on utmost ruine set;
       As, could they but lifes miseries fore-see,
20   No doubt all Infants would returne like thee?

The Stand

       For, what is life, if measur'd by the space,[6]
       Not by the act?[7]
       Or masked man, if valu'd by his face,
       Above his fact?[8]
25   Here's one out-liv'd his Peeres,[9]
       And told forth fourescore yeares;
       He vexed time, and busied the whole State;
       Troubled both foes, and friends;
       But ever to no ends:
30   What did this Stirrer, but die late?
       How well at twentie had he falne, or stood!
       For three of his foure-score, he did no good.

---

[5] Pliny reports (*Nat. Hist.* VII.3) that a child being born saw the city being destroyed and returned to the womb (H&S).

[6] time.

[7] deed.

[8] deed.

[9] Newdigate suggests that Sir Edward Coke, the lawyer, is meant.

The Turne

Hee entred well, by vertuous parts,
Got up and thriv'd with honest arts:
35 He purchas'd friends, and fame, and honours then,
And had his noble name advanc'd with men:
But weary of that flight,
Hee stoop'd in all mens sight
To sordid flatteries, acts of strife,
40 And sunke in that dead sea of life
So deep, as he did then death's waters sup;
But that the Corke of Title boy'd him up.

The Counter-turne

Alas, but *Morison* fell young:
Hee never fell, thou fall'st, my tongue.
45 Hee stood, a Souldier to the last right end,
A perfect Patriot, and a noble friend,
But most a vertuous Sonne.
All Offices were done
By him, so ample, full, and round,
50 In weight, in measure, number, sound,
As though his age imperfect might appeare,
His life was of Humanitie the Spheare.[10]

The Stand

Goe now, and tell out dayes summ'd up with feares,
And make them yeares;
55 Produce thy masse of miseries on the Stage,
To swell thine age;
Repeat of things a throng,
To shew thou hast beene long,
Not liv'd; for life doth her great actions spell,[11]
60 By what was done and wrought
In season, and so brought
To light: her measures are, how well
Each syllab'e[12] answer'd, and was form'd, how faire;
These make the lines of life, and that's her ayre.[13]

---

[10] i.e., completion.
[11] declare.

[12] i.e., detail.
[13] probably, manner.

The Turne

65 It is not growing like a tree
    In bulke, doth make man better bee;
    Or standing long an Oake, three hundred yeare,
    To fall a logge, at last, dry, bald, and seare:
    A Lillie of a Day,
70 Is fairer farre, in May,
    Although it fall, and die that night;
    It was the Plant, and flowre of light.
    In small proportions, we just beauties see:
    And in short measures, life may perfect bee.

The Counter-turne

75 Call, noble *Lucius*, then for Wine,
    And let thy lookes with gladnesse shine:
    Accept this garland, plant it on thy head,
    And thinke, nay know, thy *Morison*'s not dead.
    Hee leap'd the present age,
80 Possest with holy rage,
    To see that bright eternall Day:
    Of which we *Priests*, and *Poëts* say
    Such truths, as we expect for happy men,
    And there he lives with memorie; and *Ben*

The Stand

85 *Johnson*, who sung this of him, e're he went
    Himselfe to rest,
    Or taste a part of that full joy he meant
    To have exprest,
    In this bright *Asterisme*:[14]
90 Where it were friendships schisme,
    (Were not his *Lucius* long with us to tarry)
    To separate these twi-
    Lights, the *Dioscuri*;[15]
    And keepe the one halfe from his *Harry*.
95 But fate doth so alternate the designe,
    Whilst that in heav'n, this light on earth must shine.

---

[14] constellation.   [15] the twins Castor and Pollux.

The Turne

And shine as you exalted are;
Two names of friendship, but one Starre:
Of hearts the union. And those not by chance
100 Made, or indentur'd, or leas'd out t'advance
The profits for a time.
No pleasures vaine did chime,
Of rimes, or ryots, at your feasts,
Orgies of drinke, or fain'd protests:
105 But simple love of greatnesse, and of good;
That knits brave minds, and manners, more then blood.

The Counter-turne

This made you first to know the Why
You lik'd, then after, to apply
That liking; and approach so one the tother,[16]
110 Till either grew a portion of the other:
Each stiled by his end,
The Copie of his friend.
You liv'd to be the great surnames,
And titles, by which all made claimes
115 Unto the Vertue. Nothing perfect done,
But as a *Cary*, or a *Morison*.

The Stand

And such a force the faire example had,
As they that saw
The good, and durst not practise it, were glad
120 That such a Law
Was left yet to Man-kind;
Where they might read, and find
Friendship, in deed, was written, not in words:
And with the heart, not pen,
125 Of two so early[17] men,
Whose lines her rowles were, and records.
Who, e're the first downe bloomed on the chin,
Had sow'd these fruits, and got the harvest in.

---

[16] other.   [17] such young.

73. To the Right Honourable, the Lord High Treasurer of England.[1] An Epistle Mendicant
1631

My Lord;
POore wretched states, prest by extremities,
Are faine to seeke for succours, and supplies
Of *Princes* aides, or *good mens* Charities.

Disease,[2] the Enemie, and his Ingineeres,[3]
5   *Want*, with the rest of his conceal'd compeeres,
Have cast a trench about mee, now five yeares.

And made those strong approaches, by *False braies*,[4]
Reduicts,[5] *Halfe-moones*,[6] *Horne-workes*,[7] and such
[close[8] wayes,
The *Muse* not peepes out, one of hundred dayes.

10   But lyes block'd up, and straightned, narrow'd in,
Fix'd to the bed, and boords, unlike to win
Health, or scarce breath, as[9] she had never bin.

Unlesse some saving-*Honour* of the *Crowne*,
Dare thinke it, to relieve, no lesse renowne,
15   A *Bed-rid* Wit, then a *besieged* Towne.

74. To the King. On His Birth-day
An Epigram Anniversarie

Novemb. 19. 1632

THis is King *Charles* his Day. Speake it[1] thou *Towre*
Unto the *Ships*, and they from *tier*, to *tier*,[2]

73: [1] Richard, Lord Weston (1577–1635), Chancellor and Under-Treasurer of the Exchequer; Lord High Treasurer beginning in 1628 and in the eyes of Parliament one of its major enemies. See also Nos. 75, 76, 77, and 79.
[2] Jonson had been paralyzed from a stroke in 1628.
[3] assistants or workers.
[4] faussebraies: artificial defensive walls in front of the main rampart.
[5] strongholds within the walls for defense after the fall of the outer defenses.
[6] works fanned out in this shape to protect a major position.
[7] outworks protecting ground not in the original protection of the walls of a garrison.
[8] hidden.
[9] as though.
74: [1] i.e., by firing cannon.
[2] row of guns.

Discharge it 'bout the *Iland*, in an houre,
   As lowd as Thunder, and as swift as fire.
5 Let *Ireland* meet it out at Sea, halfe way,
   Repeating all Great *Brittain*'s joy, and more,
Adding her owne glad accents, to this *Day*,
   Like *Eccho* playing from the other shore.
What *Drum*'s or *Trumpets*, or great *Ord'nance* can,
10 The *Poëtrie* of *Steeples*, with the *Bells*,
Three Kingdomes Mirth, in light, and aërie man,
   Made lighter with the Wine. All noises else,
At *Bonefires*, *Rockets*, *Fire-workes*, with the *Shoutes*
   That cry that gladnesse, which their hearts would
                    [pray,
15 Had they but grace, of thinking, at these routes,
   On th'often comming of this *Holy-day*:
And ever close the burden of the Song,
   Still to have such a *Charles*, but this *Charles* long.

    The wish is great; but where the Prince is such,
20   What prayers (*People*) can you thinke too
                    [much!

75. ON THE RIGHT HONOURABLE, AND VERTUOUS
LORD WESTON, L. HIGH TREASURER OF ENGLAND,
UPON THE DAY, HEE WAS MADE EARLE OF
PORTLAND[1]
17. *Febr.* 1632

TO THE ENVIOUS

LOoke up thou seed of envie, and still bring
   Thy faint, and narrow eyes, to reade[2] the *King*
In his great Actions: view whom his large hand,
   Hath rais'd to be the *Port* unto his *Land!*
5 *Weston!* That waking man! that Eye of State![3]
   Who seldome sleepes! whom bad men only hate!
Why doe I irritate, or stirre up thee,[4]
   Thou sluggish spawne, that canst, but wilt not see!

75: [1] See No. 73.
    [2] learn from.
  [3] See the interpretation of the
Eye in No. 26.
    [4] In his position Weston had
many enemies as the split between
Charles and Parliament continued
to widen after the dissolution of
Parliament in 1629.

Feed on thy selfe for spight, and shew thy *Kind:*[5]
10   To vertue, and true worth, be ever blind.
Dreame thou could'st hurt it, but before thou wake,
T'effect it; Feele, thou'ast made thine owne heart
[ake.

76. To the Right Hon'ble Hierome, L. Weston.[1] An Ode Gratulatorie.[2] For His Returne from His Embassie. 1632

SUch pleasure as the teeming *Earth*,
Doth take in easie *Natures* birth,
When shee puts forth the life of ev'ry thing:
And in a dew of sweetest Raine,
5   Shee lies deliver'd without paine,
Of the prime beautie of the yeare, the *Spring*.
The Rivers in their shores doe run,
The Clowdes rack[3] cleare before the Sun,
The rudest Winds obey the calmest Ayre:
10   Rare[4] Plants from ev'ry banke doe rise,
And ev'ry Plant the sense surprize,
Because the order of the *whole* is faire!
The very verdure of her nest,
Wherein she sits so richly drest,
15   As[5] all the wealth of *Season*, there was spread;
Doth show, the *Graces*, and the *Houres*
Have multipli'd their arts, and powers,
In making soft her aromatique bed.
Such joyes, such sweet's doth your *Returne*
20   Bring all your friends, (faire Lord) that burne
With love, to heare your modestie relate,
The bus'nesse of your blooming wit,
With all the fruit shall follow it,
Both to the honour of the *King* and *State*.
25   O how will then our Court be pleas'd,
To see great *Charles* of Travaile[6] eas'd,

---

[5] nature.
76: [1] son of the Earl of the previous poem. See also No. 77. He had been in Paris and Turin for diplomatic negotiations.

[2] expressing gratitude.
[3] blow.
[4] fine.
[5] as though.
[6] travail (work) and travel.

When he beholds a graft of his owne hand,
Shoot up an *Olive* fruitfull, faire,
To be a shadow to his *Heire*,
30   And both a strength, and Beautie to his Land!

77. EPITHALAMION; OR, A SONG: CELEBRATING
THE NUPTIALS OF THAT NOBLE GENTLEMAN,
MR. HIEROME WESTON,[1] SON, AND HEIRE, OF
THE LORD WESTON, LORD HIGH TREASURER OF
ENGLAND, WITH THE LADY FRANCES STUART,
DAUGHTER OF ESME D. OF LENOX DECEASED, AND
SISTER OF THE SURVIVING DUKE OF THE SAME
NAME[2]

EPITHALAMION

THough thou hast past thy Summer standing,[3] stay
    A-while with us bright Sun, and helpe our light;
Thou can'st not meet more Glory, on the way,
    Betweene thy Tropicks,[4] to arrest thy sight,
5   Then thou shalt see to day:
        We wooe thee, stay,
        And see, what can be seene,
The bountie of a King, and beautie of his Queene!
See, the Procession! what a Holy day
10   (Bearing the promise of some better fate)
Hath filled, with *Caroches*,[5] all the way,
    From *Greenwich*, hither, to *Row-hampton*[6] gate!
        When look'd the yeare, at best,
        So like a feast?

77: [1] See the previous poem.
  [2] The Lennox family were close friends and kinsmen of James I (cf. Shakespeare's character in *Macbeth*). The family name was Stuart. Ludovick, eldest son of Esmé (see *Epig.* 127), died without issue and was succeeded by his brother Esmé (1579–1624), third Duke of Lennox and Seigneur of Aubigny. He was father of the bride here celebrated, but died before the marriage, which took place on June 25, 1632. The mother was Katherine Clifton, only daughter to Sir Gervase Clifton. Their oldest son James became the fourth duke.
  [3] i.e., solstice. The poem is addressed to the sun.
  [4] of Cancer and Capricorn.
  [5] fine carriages.
  [6] Roehampton Chapel, where the service took place.

15   Or were Affaires in tune,
          By all the Spheares consent,[7] so in the heart of June?

          What Beavie of beauties, and bright youth's at charge[8]
              Of Summers Liveries, and gladding[9] greene;
          Doe boast their Loves, and Brav'ries[10] so at large,
20   As they came all to see, and to be seene!
                  When look'd the Earth so fine,
                      Or so did shine,
                  In all her bloome, and flower;
          To welcome home a Paire, and deck the nuptiall bower?

25   It is the kindly Season of the time,
              The Month of youth, which calls all Creatures forth
          To doe their Offices in Natures Chime,
              And celebrate (perfection at the worth)
                  Mariage, the end of life,
30   That holy strife,
                  And the allowed warre:
          Through which not only we, but all our *Species* are.

          Harke how the Bells upon the waters play
              Their Sister-tunes, from *Thames* his either side,
35   As[11] they had learn'd new changes,[12] for the day,
              And all did ring th'approches of the Bride;
                  The Lady *Frances*, drest
                      Above the rest
                  Of all the Maidens faire;
40   In gracefull Ornament of Garland, Gemmes, and Haire.

          See, how she paceth forth in Virgin-white,
              Like what she is, the Daughter of a Duke,
          And Sister: darting forth a dazling light
              On all that come her Simplêsse[13] to rebuke!
45   Her tresses trim her back,
                      As she did lack

---

[7] the heavens as affecting the weather.

[8] have the expense or responsibility.

[9] making glad.

[10] fine clothes.

[11] as though.

[12] the different orders in which a peal of bells may be rung.

[13] simplicity of dress.

Nought of a Maiden Queene,
With Modestie so crown'd, and Adoration seene.

Stay, thou wilt see what rites the Virgins doe!
50   The choisest Virgin-troup of all the Land!
Porting[14] the Ensignes of united Two,[15]
      Both Crownes, and Kingdomes in their either hand;
            Whose Majesties appeare,
            To make more cleare[16]
55   This Feast, then can the Day,
Although that thou, O Sun, at our intreaty stay![17]

See, how with Roses,[18] and with Lillies[19] shine,
      (Lillies and Roses, Flowers of either Sexe)
The bright Brides paths, embelish'd more then thine[20]
60   With light of love, this Paire doth intertexe![21]
            Stay, see the Virgins sow,
            (Where she shall goe)[22]
            The Emblemes of their way.
O, now thou smil'st, faire Sun, and shin'st, as thou
                              [wouldst stay!

65   With what full hands, and in how plenteous showers
      Have they bedew'd the Earth, where she doth tread,
As if her ayrie steps did spring the flowers,
      And all the Ground, were Garden, where she led!
            See, at another doore,
70   On the same floore,
            The Bridegroome meets the Bride
With all the pompe of Youth, and all our Court beside.

Our Court, and all the Grandees;[23] now, Sun, looke,
      And looking with thy best Inquirie, tell,
75   In all thy age of Journals[24] thou hast tooke,
      Saw'st thou that Paire, became these Rites so well,

[14] carrying.
[15] England and France: Charles I and his French wife Henrietta Maria.
[16] bright.
[17] i.e., not be eclipsed, a bad omen.
[18] representing England.
[19] the fleur-de-lis of France.
[20] the sun's.
[21] interweave (L. *intertexo*).
[22] like Flora, goddess of flowers: wherever she walked, flowers grew.
[23] eminent people.
[24] daily travels.

Save the preceding Two?
Who, in all they doe,
Search, Sun, and thou wilt find
80   They are th'exampled[25] Paire, and mirrour of their
[kind.

Force from the Phœnix[26] then, no raritie
Of Sex, to rob the Creature; but from Man
The king of Creatures; take his paritie
With Angels, Muse, to speake these: Nothing can
85   Illustrate these, but they
Themselves to day,
Who the whole Act expresse;
All else we see beside, are Shadowes, and goe lesse.[27]

It is their Grace, and favour, that makes seene,
90   And wonder'd at the bounties of this day:
All is a story of the King and Queene!
And what of Dignitie, and Honour may
Be duly done to those
Whom they have chose,
95   And set the marke upon
To give a greater Name, and Title to! Their owne!

Weston, their Treasure, as their Treasurer,
That Mine of Wisdome, and of Counsells deep,
Great Say-Master[28] of State, who cannot erre,
100   But doth his Carract,[29] and just Standard keepe
In all the prov'd assayes,
And legall wayes
Of Tryals, to worke downe[30]
Mens Loves unto the Lawes, and Lawes to love the
[Crowne.

105   And this well mov'd the Judgement of the King
To pay with honours, to his noble Sonne
To day, the Fathers service; who could bring
Him up, to doe the same himselfe had done.

---

[25] made an example or ideal.
[26] See *The Forrest* 10, n. 1.
[27] are worth less.
[28] assay-master.

[29] carat: worth, value (confused with *character*).
[30] influence or lead.

That farre-all-seeing Eye
110   Could soone espie
What kind of waking Man
He had so highly set; and, in what *Barbican*.[31]

Stand there; for when a noble Nature's rais'd,
    It brings Friends Joy, Foes Griefe, Posteritie Fame;
115 In him the times, no lesse then Prince, are prais'd,
    And by his Rise, in active men, his Name
        Doth Emulation stirre;
        To th'dull, a Spur
    It is: to th'envious meant,[32]
120 A meere upbraiding Griefe, and tort'ring punishment.

See, now the Chappell opens; where the King
    And Bishop[33] stay, to consummate the Rites:
The holy Prelate prayes, then takes the Ring,
    Askes first, Who gives her (I *Charles*)[34] then he
                                        [plights
125   One in the others hand,
            Whilst they both stand
        Hearing their charge, and then
The Solemne Quire cryes, Joy; and they returne, Amen.

O happy bands! and thou more happy place,
130   Which to this use, wer't built and consecrate!
To have thy God to blesse, thy King to grace,
    And this their chosen Bishop celebrate;
        And knit the Nuptiall knot,
        Which Time shall not,
135   Or canker'd Jealousie,
With all corroding Arts, be able to untie!

The Chappell empties, and thou may'st be gone
    Now, Sun, and post away the rest of day:
These two, now holy Church hath made them one,
140   Doe long to make themselves, so, another way:

[31] watch tower.
[32] thought of as.
[33] Laud, then Bishop of London (H&S).

[34] Since Frances' father was dead, Charles gives away the bride.

There is a Feast behind,[35]
　　To them of kind,
　　Which their glad Parents taught
One to the other, long e're these to light were brought.

145　Haste, haste, officious Sun, and send them Night
　　Some houres before it should, that these may know
All that their Fathers, and their Mothers might
　　Of Nuptiall Sweets, at such a season, owe,
　　　　To propagate their Names,
150　　　　And keepe their Fames
　　　Alive, which else would die,
For Fame keepes Vertue up, and it Posteritie.

Th'ïgnoble never liv'd, they were a-while
　　Like Swine, or other Cattell here on earth:
155　Their names are not recorded on the File
　　Of Life, that fall[36] so; Christians know their birth
　　　　Alone, and such a race,
　　　　We pray may grace
　　　Your fruitfull spreading Vine,
160　But dare not aske our wish in Language *fescennine:*[37]

Yet, as we may, we will,[38] with chast desires,
　　(The holy perfumes of the Mariage bed.)
Be kept alive, those Sweet, and Sacred fires
　　Of Love betweene you, and your Lovely-head:
165　　　　That when you both are old,
　　　　You find no cold
　　　There; but, renewed, say,
(After the last child borne;) This is our wedding day.

Till you behold a race to fill your Hall,
170　A *Richard*, and a *Hierome*, by their names
　　Upon a *Thomas*, or a *Francis* call;
　　　A *Kate*, a *Frank*,[39] to honour their Grand-dames,

---

[35] yet to come.
[36] perish.
[37] licentious.
[38] will or wish that.
[39] from Richard Weston, the groom's father; Hierome (Jerome) Weston, the groom; Thomas Weston, one of his brothers; Francis Weston (not identified); Katherine Clifton, the bride's mother; and Frances Clifton, the bride. Actually, a son Charles was born.

And 'tweene their Grandsires thighes,
Like pretty Spies,
175   Peepe forth a Gemme; to see
How each one playes his part, of the large Pedigree.

And never may there want one of the Stem,[40]
To be a watchfull Servant for this State;
But like an Arme of Eminence 'mongst them,
180   Extend a reaching vertue, early and late:
Whilst the maine tree still found
Upright and sound,
By this Sun's Noone sted's[41] made
So great; his Body now alone projects the shade.

185 They both are slip'd to Bed; Shut fast the Doore,
And let him freely gather Loves First-fruits:
Hee's Master of the Office; yet no more
Exacts then she is pleas'd to pay: no suits,
Strifes, murmures, or delay,
190   Will last till day;
Night, and the sheetes will show,
The longing Couple, all that elder Lovers know.[42]

78. The Humble Petition of Poore Ben.
To th'best of Monarchs, Masters, Men,
King Charles

—Doth most humbly show it,
To your Majestie your Poët:

5   THat whereas your royall *Father*
James the blessed, pleas'd the rather,
Of his speciall grace to *Letters,*
To make all the *Muses* debters
To his bountie; by extension
10   Of a free Poëtique Pension,[1]

[40] trunk (of the family and pedigree).
[41] place is.
[42] from *Hero and Leander:* "Which taught him all that elder lovers know" (H&S).

78: [1] The pension had been granted by James in 1616 (see H&S I.231–32).

>   A large hundred Markes annuitie,
>   To be given me in gratuitie
>   For done service, and to come:
>   And that this so accepted summe,
> 15   Or dispenc'd in bookes, or bread,
>   (For with both the *Muse* was fed)
>   Hath drawne on me, from the times,
>   All the envie of the *Rymes*,
>   And the ratling pit-pat-noyse,
> 20   Of the lesse-*Poëtique* boyes;[2]
>   When their pot-guns ayme to hit,
>   With their pellets of small wit,
>   Parts of me (they judg'd) decay'd,
>   But we last out, still unlay'd.[3]
> 25   Please your Majestie to make
>   Of your grace, for goodnesse sake,
>   Those your *Fathers Markes*,[4] your *Pounds*;
>   Let their[5] spite (which now abounds)
>   Then goe on, and doe its worst;
> 30   This would all their envie burst:
>   And so warme the *Poëts* tongue
>   You'ld reade a Snake,[6] in his next Song.

79. TO THE RIGHT HONOURABLE, THE LORD TREASURER OF ENGLAND

AN EPIGRAM

> IF to my mind, great Lord,[1] I had a state,
>   I would present you now with curious plate
> Of *Noremberg*,[2] or *Turkie*;[3] hang your roomes
>   Not with the Arras,[4] but the *Persian*[5] Loomes.

[2] Inigo Jones, according to H&S.

[3] not laid in the grave (NED).

[4] a mark is two-thirds of a pound.

[5] the rival poets'.

[6] from Aesop's story about a farmer who carried home a frozen snake. He thawed it out and it bit him. Jonson's petition for renewal of the pension at a higher figure was granted on March 26, 1630 (H&S I.245–48).

79: [1] See Nos. 73 and 75.

[2] Nuremburg, seat of a famous group of silversmiths (H&S).

[3] probably Byzantine.

[4] ordinary wall hangings.

[5] representing fine weaving.

5 I would, if price, or prayer could them get,
  Send in, what or *Romano*,[6] *Tintaret*,
 Titian, or *Raphael*, *Michael Angelo*
  Have left in fame to equall, or out-goe
 The old Greek-hands in picture, or in stone.
10 This I would doe, could I know *Weston*, one
  Catch'd with these Arts, wherein the Judge is wise
 As farre as sense, and onely by the eyes.
  But you I know, my Lord; and know you can
 Discerne betweene a Statue, and a Man;
15 Can doe the things that Statues doe deserve,
  And act the businesse, which they paint, or carve.
 What you have studied are the arts of life;
  To compose men, and manners; stint the strife
 Of murmuring Subjects; make the Nations know
20 What worlds of blessings to good Kings they owe:
  And mightiest Monarchs feele what large increase
 Of sweets, and safeties, they possesse by Peace.[7]
  These I looke up at, with a reverent eye,
 And strike[8] Religion in the standers-by;
25 Which, though I cannot as an Architect[9]
  In glorious Piles, or Pyramids erect
 Unto your honour: I can tune in song
  Aloud; and (happ'ly) it may last as long.

80. AN EPIGRAM
TO MY MUSE, THE LADY DIGBY, ON HER HUSBAND, SIR KENELME DIGBY[1]

THo', happy *Muse*, thou know my *Digby* well;
  Yet read him in these lines: He doth excell

---

[6] Romanino (1485–1565), painter in the school of Giorgione.

[7] Weston's policies attempted a peaceful solution of the difficulties in England.

[8] imprint on the mind; cf. "strike fear."

[9] i.e., Inigo Jones, Jonson's former collaborator and now enemy.

80: [1] (1603–65), traveler and diplomat but best known today as an early commentator on Sir Thomas Browne's *Religio Medici* and as an early scientist, member of the Royal Society and author of *Two Treatises* upon science. He supplied the text to the printer for the Jonson 1640 Folio. After an irregular courtship, in 1626 he married Lady Venetia, daughter of Sir Edward Stanley of Shropshire. She died in 1633; see No. 86.

In honour, courtesie, and all the parts
    Court can call hers, or Man could call his Arts.
5   Hee's prudent, valiant, just, and temperate;
    In him all vertue is beheld in State:
And he is built like some imperiall roome
    For that to dwell in, and be still at home.
His brest is a brave Palace, a broad Street
10   Where all heroique ample thoughts doe meet:
Where Nature such a large survey hath ta'en,
    As other soules to his dwelt in a Lane:
Witnesse his Action done at *Scanderone*; [2]
    Upon my Birth-day the eleventh of *June*;[3]
15   When the Apostle *Barnabee* the bright[4]
    Unto our yeare doth give the longest light,
In signe the Subject, and the Song will live
    Which I have vow'd posteritie to give.
Goe, *Muse*, in, and salute him. Say he be
20   Busie, or frowne at first; when he sees thee,
He will cleare up his forehead: thinke thou bring'st
    Good *Omen* to him, in the note thou sing'st,
For he doth love my Verses, and will looke
    Upon them, (next to *Spenser's* noble booke.)[5]
25   And praise them too. O! what a fame 't will be?
    What reputation to my lines, and me,
When hee shall read them at the Treasurers[6] bord?
    The knowing *Weston*, and that learned Lord[7]
Allowes them? Then, what copies shall be had,
30   What transcripts begg'd? how cry'd up, and how
                   [glad,
Wilt thou be, *Muse*, when this shall them befall?
    Being sent to one, they will be read of all.

---

[2] near Aleppo, in Turkey, where on June 11, 1628, Digby led a group of privateers to victory over some French and Venetian ships.

[3] That this is Jonson's birthday see W. D. Briggs, *MLN*, XXXIII (1918), 137.

[4] St. Barnabas's Day, longest in the year by the old calendar.

See Spenser, *Epithalamion*, ll. 265f.: "This day the sunne is in his chiefest hight, / With Barnaby the bright."

[5] In 1644 Digby published a commentary on *Fairie Queene* II.ix.22.

[6] For Richard Weston see Nos. 73 *et seq.*

[7] probably Digby.

81

NEw yeares, expect *new* gifts:[1] Sister, your Harpe,
  Lute, Lyre, Theorbo,[2] all are call'd to day.
Your change of Notes, the *flat*, the *meane*,[3] the
                    [*sharpe,*
  To shew the rites, and t'usher forth the way
5 Of the *New Yeare*, in a new silken warpe[4]
    To fit the softnesse of our *Yeares-gift:* When
    We sing the best of *Monarchs, Masters, Men;*
For, had we here said lesse, we had sung nothing then.

A NEW-YEARES-GIFT SUNG TO KING CHARLES,
1635

Rector   TO day old *Janus*[6] opens the new yeare,
10 *Chori.*[5]   And shuts the old. Haste, haste, all loyall
                          [Swaines,
        That know the times, and seasons when t'ap-
                          [peare,
        And offer your just service on these
                          [plaines;
        Best Kings expect first-fruits of your glad
                          [gaines.

      1. *Pan*[7] is the great Preserver of our bounds.
15   2. To him we owe all profits of our grounds.

81: [1] Gifts were given at New Year's rather than at Christmas.
  [2] a kind of lute.
  [3] natural.
  [4] weaving.
  [5] leader of the chorus.
  [6] god of the new year (January).

[7] representing Charles I. Much of the poem is a reworking of Jonson's masque *Pan's Anniversary* (1620), addressed to James I. See Simpson, *RES*, XIV (1938), 175–78. Newdigate takes Pan to be Charles's brother-in-law Louis XIII.

		3. Our milke. 4. Our fells.[8] 5. Our fleeces.
		[6. and first Lambs.
		7. Our teeming Ewes, 8. and lustie-mount-
		[ing Rammes.
		9. See where he walkes with *Mira*[9] by his
		[side.
	Chor.	Sound, sound his praises loud, and with his,
		[hers divide.
20	*Shep.*	Of *Pan* wee sing, the best of Hunters, *Pan*,
		That drives the Hart to seeke unused
		[wayes,
		And in the chase, more then *Sylvanus*[10] can,
	Chor.	Heare, ô you Groves, and, Hills, resound
		[his praise.
	Nymp.	Of brightest *Mira*, doe we raise our Song,
25		Sister[11] of *Pan*, and glory of the Spring:
		Who walkes on earth as[12] *May* still went
		[along,
	Chor.	Rivers, and Vallies, *Eccho* what wee
		[sing.
	Shep.	Of *Pan* wee sing, the Chiefe of Leaders,
		[*Pan*,
		That leades our flocks and us, and calls
		[both forth
30		To better Pastures then great *Pales*[13] can:
	Chor.	Heare, O you Groves, and, Hills, resound
		[his worth.
	Nymp.	Of brightest *Mira*, is our Song; the grace
		Of all that Nature, yet, to life did bring;
		And were shee lost, could[14] best supply her
		[place,
35	*Chor.*	Rivers, and Valleys *Eccho* what wee sing.

[8] hides.
[9] Queen Henrietta-Maria.
[10] rural deity, half man and half goat.
[11] rather than wife: Pan's mythological love-making was not suitable for that of a husband.
[12] as though.
[13] a shepherd-goddess: Virgil, *Georgics* III.1.
[14] if Nature were lost, Mira could.

1. Where ere they tread th'enamour'd
[ground,
The Fairest flowers are always found;
2. As if the beauties of the yeare,
Still waited on 'hem where they were.
40 1. Hee is the Father of our peace;
2. Shee to the Crowne, hath brought en-
[crease.
1. Wee know no other power then his,
Pan only our great Shep'ard is,
Chorus. Our great, our good. Where one's so drest
45 In truth of colours,[15] both are best.

Haste, haste, you hither, all you gentler
[Swaines,[16]
That have a Flock, or Herd, upon these
[plaines;
This is the great Preserver of our bounds,[17]
To whom you owe all duties of your grounds;
50 Your Milkes, your Fells, your Fleeces, and
[first Lambes.
Your teeming Ewes, as well as mounting
[Rammes.
Whose praises let's report unto the Woods,
That they may take it eccho'd by the Floods.
'Tis hee, 'tis hee, in singing hee,
55 And hunting, *Pan*, exceedeth thee.[18]
Hee gives all plentie, and encrease,
Hee is the author of our peace.

Where e're he goes upon the ground,
The better grasse, and flowers are found.
60 To sweeter Pastures lead hee can,
Then ever *Pales* could, or *Pan*;

[15] probably, in one's true colors.

[16] H&S suggest that ll. 46–66 were originally a separate poem, since they are not consistent with the previous allegory or verse pat-tern.

[17] Silvanus, god of boundaries, with whom the object of praise (Charles?) is now identified.

[18] He (Silvanus-Charles) ex-ceedeth thee (Pan).

Hee drives diseases from our Folds,
The theefe from spoyle, his presence holds.
Pan knowes no other power then his,
65　　This only the great Shep'ard is.
'Tis hee, 'tis hee, *&c.*

82

FAire Friend,[1] 'tis true, your beauties move
　　My heart to a respect:
Too little to bee paid with love,
　　Too great for your neglect.

5　　I neither love, nor yet am free,
　　For though the flame I find
Be not intense in the degree,
　　'Tis of the purest kind.

It little wants[2] of love, but paine,
10　　Your beautie takes my sense,
And lest you should that price disdaine,
　　My thoughts, too, feele the influence.

'Tis not a passions first accesse
　　Readie to multiply,
15　But like Loves calmest State it is
　　Possest with victorie.

It is like Love to Truth reduc'd,
　　All the false values gone,
Which were created, and induc'd
20　　By fond imagination.

'Tis either Fancie, or 'tis Fate,
　　To love you more then I;
I love you at your beauties rate,
　　Lesse were an Injurie.

82: [1] no title; printed as a continuation of No. 81 but obviously not connected with it. H&S observe that in one MS. it is attributed to Sidney Godolphin (d. 1643), minor poet and Cavalier.
[2] lacks.

25   Like unstamp'd Gold, I weigh each grace,
          So that you may collect,
      Th' intrinsique value of your face,
          Safely from my respect.

      And this respect would merit love,
30   Were not so faire a sight
      Payment enough; for, who dare move
          Reward for his delight?

83. ON THE KINGS BIRTH-DAY[1]

      ROwse up thy selfe, my gentle Muse,
          Though now our greene conceits be gray,
      And yet once more doe not refuse
          To take thy Phrygian[2] Harp, and play
5   In honour of this cheerefull Day:
              Long may they both[3] contend to prove,
              That best of Crownes is such a love.

      Make first a Song of Joy, and Love,
          Which chastly flames in royall eyes,
10   Then tune it to the Spheares above,
              When the benignest Stars doe rise,
          And sweet Conjunctions[4] grace the skies.
              Long may, &c.

      To this let all good hearts resound,
15   Whilst Diadems invest[5] his head;
      Long may he live, whose life doth bound
          More then his Lawes, and better lead
          By high Example, then by dread.
              Long may, &c.

83: [1] November 19. Accepted
by H&S as by Sir Henry Wotton
(1568–1639), diplomatist, poet,
provost of Eton College from
1624, friend of Donne and Mil-
ton. The poem is attributed to Sir
Henry in two MSS. as having
been written to the king after
his return from his coronation in
Scotland (in 1633) and is
printed in the *Reliquiae Wot-
tonianae* (1651), p. 521. W. D.
Briggs argued for Jonson's author-
ship in *Anglia*, XXXIX (1915),
213–15.
    [2] a musical mode or scale.
    [3] the Muse and her harp(?).
    [4] good astrological influences.
    [5] adorn.

20   Long may he round about him see
    His Roses, and his Lillies[6] blowne:
Long may his only Deare, and Hee
    Joy in Idæas of their owne,
    And Kingdomes hopes so timely sowne.
25   Long may they both contend to prove,
    That best of Crownes is such a love.

84. To My L. the King, on the Christning His Second Sonne James[1]

THat thou art lov'd of God, this worke is done,
    Great King, thy having of a second Sonne:
And by thy blessing, may thy *People* see
    How much they are belov'd of God, in thee;
5   Would they would understand it![2] Princes are
    Great aides to Empire, as they are great care
To pious Parents, who would have their blood
    Should take first Seisin[3] of the publique good,
As hath thy *James*; cleans'd from originall drosse,
10   This day, by Baptisme, and his Saviours crosse:
Grow up, sweet Babe, as blessed, in thy Name,
    As in renewing thy good Grandsires[4] fame;
Me thought, *Great Brittaine* in her Sea, before,
    Sate safe enough, but now secured more,
15   At land she triumphs in the triple shade,[5]
    Her Rose, and Lilly,[6] intertwind, have made.

Oceano secura meo, securior umbris.[7]

[6] See No. 77, notes 18 and 19.
84: [1] the future James II, born October 14, 1633, and christened by Laud on November 24.
[2] Cf. Charles's troubles in Nos. 64 and 66.
[3] primer seisin: the right of the Crown to receive from an heir the profits of his estate for the first year.
[4] James I's.
[5] Charles II, James II, and Mary (born November 4, 1631).
[6] See No. 77, notes 18 and 19.
[7] "Safe in my ocean, safer in my shades"; the source is not identified.

85. An Elegie on the Lady Jane Pawlet Marchion: of Winton[1]

WHat gentle Ghost, besprent[2] with *April* deaw,
    Hayles me, so solemnly, to yonder Yewgh?[3]
And beckning wooes me, from the fatall tree
    To pluck a Garland, for her selfe, or mee?
5   I doe obey you, Beauty! for in death,
    You seeme a faire one! O that you had breath,
To give your shade a name! Stay, stay, I feele
    A horrour in mee! all my blood is steele!
Stiffe! starke! my joynts 'gainst one another knock!
10   Whose Daughter? ha? Great *Savage* of the Rock?[4]
Hee's good, as great. I am almost a stone!
    And e're I can aske more of her shee's gone!
Alas, I am all Marble! write the rest
    Thou wouldst have written, Fame, upon my brest:
15   It is a large faire table, and a true,
    And the disposure[5] will be something new,
When I, who would her Poët have become,
    At least may beare th'inscription to her Tombe.
Shee was the Lady *Jane*, and *Marchionisse*
20   Of *Winchester*; the Heralds[6] can tell this.
Earle *Rivers*[7] Grand-Child—serve not formes, good
                     [Fame,
    Sound thou her Vertues, give her soule a Name.
Had I a thousand Mouthes, as many Tongues,
    And voyce to raise them from my brazen Lungs,
25   I durst not aime at that: The dotes[8] were such
    Thereof, no notion can expresse how much

85: [1] Lady Jane, Marchioness of Winchester (1607–April 15, 1631), daughter of Thomas, Viscount Savage. She married John Paulet, Marquis of Winchester, in 1622 and died in giving birth to her second son. See Milton's "Epitaph" on her.
[2] sprinkled.

[3] the yew as symbol of sadness.
[4] her father, of Rock Savage in Cheshire.
[5] arrangement.
[6] recorders of family arms and pedigrees.
[7] Thomas Darcy, her maternal grandfather.
[8] natural gifts or endowments.

Their Carract⁹ was! I, or my trump¹⁰ must breake,
    But rather I, should I of that part speake!
It is too neere of kin to Heaven, the Soule,
30   To be describ'd! Fames fingers are too foule
To touch these Mysteries! We may admire
    The blaze, and splendor, but not handle fire!
What she did here, by great example, well,
    T' inlive¹¹ posteritie, her Fame may tell!
35   And, calling truth to witnesse, make that good
    From the inherent Graces in her blood!
Else, who doth praise a person by a new,
    But a fain'd way, doth rob it of the true.
Her Sweetnesse, Softnesse, her faire Courtesie,
40   Her wary guardes, her wise simplicitie,
Were like a ring of Vertues, 'bout her set,
    And pietie the Center, where all met.
A reverend State she had, an awfull Eye,
    A dazling, yet inviting, Majestie:
45   What Nature, Fortune, Institution, Fact¹²
    Could summe to a perfection, was her Act!
How did she leave the world? with what contempt?
    Just as she in it liv'd! and so exempt
From all affection! when they urg'd the Cure
50   Of her disease, how did her soule assure¹³
Her suffrings, as¹⁴ the body had beene away!
    And to the Torturers (her Doctors) say,
Stick on your Cupping-glasses,¹⁵ fear not, put
    Your hottest Causticks to, burne, lance, or cut:
55   'Tis but a body which you can torment,
    And I, into the world, all Soule, was sent!
Then comforted her Lord! and blest her Sonne!¹⁶
    Chear'd her faire Sisters¹⁷ in her race to runne!
With gladnesse temper'd her sad Parents teares!
60   Made her friends joyes, to get above their feares!

⁹ carat: worth; confused with "character."
¹⁰ trumpet (of fame).
¹¹ give life to.
¹² deed.
¹³ reassure.

¹⁴ as though.
¹⁵ for bleeding.
¹⁶ Charles, born about 1625.
¹⁷ Elizabeth and Dorothy, who took part in Jonson's masque *Chloridia* (H&S).

And, in her last act, taught the Standers-by,
  With admiration, and applause to die!
Let Angels sing her glories, who did call
  Her spirit home, to her originall!
65 Who saw the way was made it! and were sent
  To carry, and conduct the Complement[18]
'Twixt death and life! Where her mortalitie
  Became her Birth-day to Eternitie!
And now, through circumfused light, she lookes
70   On Natures secrets, there, as her owne bookes:
Speakes Heavens Language! and discourseth free
  To every *Order*,[19] ev'ry *Hierarchie!*
Beholds her Maker! and, in him, doth see
  What the beginnings of all beauties be;
75 And all beatitudes, that thence doe flow:
  Which they that have the Crowne[20] are sure to
                              [know!

Goe now, her happy Parents, and be sad
  If you not understand, what child you had.
If you dare grudge at Heaven, and repent
80   T' have paid againe a blessing was[21] but lent,
And trusted so, as it deposited lay
  At pleasure, to be call'd for, every day!
If you can envie your owne Daughters blisse,
  And wish her state lesse happie then it is!
85 If you can cast about your either eye,
  And see all dead here, or about to dye!
The Starres, that are the Jewels of the Night,
  And Day, deceasing! with the Prince of light,
The Sunne! Great Kings! and mightiest Kingdomes
                              [fall!
90   Whole Nations! nay Mankind! the World, with all
That ever had beginning there, to'ave end!
  With what injustice should one soule pretend
T'escape this common knowne necessitie,
  When we were all borne, we began to die;

---

[18] union which makes a whole.   [20] of Life.
[19] of angels.   [21] that was.

95 And, but for that Contention, and brave strife
　　The Christian hath t'enjoy the future life,
　Hee were the wretched'st of the race of men:
　　But as he soares at that, he bruiseth then
　The Serpents head: Gets above Death, and Sinne
100 　And, sure of Heaven, rides triumphing in.

86. EUPHEME;[1] OR, THE FAIRE FAME. LEFT TO POSTERITIE

Of that truly-noble Lady, the Lady *Venetia Digby*,[2]
　　late Wife of Sir *Kenelme Digby*, Knight:
　A Gentleman absolute[3] in all numbers;[4]
　　Consisting of these Ten Pieces.

The Dedication of her CRADLE.
The Song of her DESCENT.
The Picture of her BODY.
Her MIND.
Her being chosen a MUSE.
Her faire OFFICES.
Her happie MATCH.
Her hopefull ISSUE.
Her ΑΠΟΘΕΩΣΙΣ,[5] *or Relation to the Saints.*
Her Inscription, or CROWNE.

Vivam amare voluptas, defunctam Religio.[6]
　　　　　　　　　　　　　　　　Stat.

1. *The Dedication of her Cradle*

FAire *Fame*, who art ordain'd to crowne
With ever-greene, and great renowne,
Their Heads, that *Envy* would hold downe
　　With her, in shade

86: [1] of good omen or good fame.
　[2] See No. 80, n. 1.
　[3] perfect.
　[4] parts.

[5] apotheosis: glorification.
[6] "The Voluptuous loves life; the Religious death." Statius, *Silvae* V, Preface.

5   Of Death, and Darknesse; and deprive
      Their names of being kept alive,
      By *Thee*, and *Conscience*, both who thrive
           By the just trade

      Of Goodnesse still: Vouchsafe to take
10   This *Cradle*, and for Goodnesse sake,
      A dedicated Ensigne[1] make
           Thereof, to *Time*.

      That all Posteritie, as wee,
      Who read what the *Crepundia*[2] bee,
15   May something by that twilight[3] see
           'Bove rattling Rime.

      For, though that Rattles, Timbrels, Toyes,
      Take little Infants with their noyse,
      As prop'rest gifts, to Girles, and Boyes
20   Of light expence;

      Their Corrals,[4] Whistles, and prime Coates,[5]
      Their painted Maskes, their paper Boates,
      With Sayles of silke, as the first notes
           Surprize their sense:

25   Yet, here are no such Trifles brought,
      No cobweb Call's;[6] no Surcoates[7] wrought
      With Gold, or Claspes, which might be bought
           On every Stall.

      But, here's a Song of her *Descent*;
30   And Call to the high Parliament
      Of Heaven; where *Seraphim* take tent[8]
           Of ord'ring all.

86–1: [1] emblem.
  [2] child's rattle.
  [3] dawn.
  [4] toy made of coral to aid in cutting teeth.

[5] first clothes.
[6] cauls: netted caps.
[7] decorated outer coats.
[8] attention.

This, utter'd by an antient *Bard*,
Who claimes (of reverence) to be heard,
35   As comming with his Harpe, prepar'd
To chant her 'gree,[9]

Is sung: as als' her getting up
By *Jacobs* Ladder,[10] to the top
Of that eternall Port kept ope'
40   For such as *Shee*.

2. *The Song of her Descent*

I Sing the just, and uncontrol'd[1] Descent[2]
Of Dame *Venetia Digby*, styl'd The Faire:
For Mind, and Body, the most excellent
That ever Nature, or the later Ayre
5   Gave two such Houses as *Northumberland*,[3]
And *Stanley*,[4] to the which shee was Co-heire.
Speake it, you bold *Penates*,[5] you that stand
At either Stemme,[6] and know the veines of good
Run from your rootes; Tell, testifie the grand
10   Meeting of Graces, that so swell'd the flood
Of vertues in her, as, in short, shee grew
The wonder of her Sexe, and of your Blood.
And tell thou, *Alde-Legh*,[7] None can tell more true
Thy Neeces[8] line, then thou that gav'st thy Name
15   Into the Kindred, whence thy *Adam* drew
Meschines honour with the *Cestrian* fame
Of the first *Lupus*,[9] to the Familie
By *Ranulph*———

The rest of this Song is lost.

[9] pedigree.
[10] Gen. 28:10ff., interpreted as the way to heaven.
86–2:   [1] undisputed.
[2] ancestry.
[3] her mother was a Percy.
[4] her father's side: the Derbys.
[5] household gods.
[6] of the family tree.
[7] Adam Aldelegh was father of the first Stanley (H&S from Camden, *Remaines Concerning Britaine*).

[8] granddaughters or further descendants.
[9] Hugh de Avranche (d. 1101), who supported William the Conqueror and was nicknamed Wolf (Lupus) for fighting the Welsh. Ranulf, called "le Meschin" (d. 1129?), succeeded his kinsmen, the Avranches, when that line became extinct. Both were earls of Chester (Cestrian). See H&S XI.106.

3. *The Picture of the Body*

SItting, and ready to be drawne,
 What makes[1] these Velvets, Silkes, and Lawne,
 Embroderies, Feathers, Fringes, Lace,
 Where every lim[2] takes[3] like a face?

5 Send these suspected helpes, to aide
 Some Forme defective, or decay'd;
 This beautie without falshood fayre,
 Needs nought to cloath it but the ayre.

Yet something, to the Painters[4] view,
10 Were fitly interpos'd; so new:
 Hee shall, if he can understand,
 Worke with[5] my fancie, his owne hand.

Draw first a Cloud:[6] all save her neck;
 And, out of that, make Day to breake;
15 Till, like her face, it doe appeare,
 And Men may thinke, all light rose there.

Then let the beames of that, disperse
 The Cloud, and show the Universe;
 But at such distance, as the eye
20 May rather yet adore, then spy.

The Heaven design'd, draw next a Spring,
 With all that Youth, or it can bring:
 Foure Rivers[7] branching forth like Seas,
 And Paradise confining[8] these.

25 Last, draw the circles of this Globe,
 And let there be a starry Robe
 Of Constellations 'bout her horld;[9]
 And thou hast painted beauties world.

86–3: [1] What are they producing, or doing?

[2] limb: detail, possibly with a pun on limn: paint.

[3] attracts.

[4] a painting of Lady Venetia by Van Dyke survives. This poem and the next were written before her death.

[5] direct.

[6] In lines 13–24 Jonson loosely follows the story of the creation of the universe as related in Genesis.

[7] Genesis 2:11–14.

[8] adjacent to.

[9] hurled.

But, Painter, see thou doe not sell
30   A Copie of this peece; nor tell
            Whose 'tis: but if it favour find,
            Next sitting we will draw her mind.

4. *The Mind*

PAinter yo' are come, but may be gone,
            Now I have better thought thereon,
            This worke I can performe alone;
            And give you reasons more then one.

5   Not, that your Art I doe refuse:
            But here I may no colours[1] use.
            Beside, your hand will never hit,
            To draw a thing that cannot sit.[2]

You could make shift to paint an Eye,
10   An Eagle towring in the skye,
            The Sunne, a Sea, or soundlesse Pit;
            But these are like a Mind, not it.

No, to expresse Mind to sense,
            Would aske a Heavens Intelligence;
15   Since nothing can report that flame,
            But what's of kinne to whence it came.

Sweet Mind, then speake your selfe, and say,
            As you goe on, by what brave[3] way
            Our sense you doe with knowledge fill,
20   And yet remaine our wonder still.

I call you *Muse*;[4] now make it true:
            Hence-forth may every line be you;
            That all may say, that see the frame,
            This is no Picture, but the same.

25   A Mind so pure, so perfect fine,
            As 'tis not radiant, but divine:
            And so disdaining any tryer;[5]
            'Tis got where it can try the fire.

86–4:   [1] of the painter and of   [3] fine, excellent.
rhetoric such as metaphors.   [4] Cf. No. 8o, title.
     [2] be still, or sit for a painting.   [5] tester.

There, high exalted in the Spheare,
30   As[6] it another Nature were,
        It moveth all;[7] and makes a flight
        As circular, as infinite.

Whose Notions when it will expresse
        In speech; it is with that excesse
35   Of grace, and Musique to the eare,
        As[8] what it spoke, it planted there.

The Voyce so sweet, the words so faire,
        As some soft chime had stroak'd the ayre;
        And, though the sound were parted thence,
40   Still left an Eccho in the sense.

But, that a Mind so rapt, so high,
        So swift, so pure, should yet apply
        It selfe to us, and come so nigh
        Earths grossnesse; There's the how, and why.

45   Is it because it sees us dull,
        And stuck in clay here, it would pull
        Us forth, by some Celestiall flight
        Up to her owne sublimed[9] hight?

Or hath she here, upon the ground,
50   Some Paradise, or Palace found
        In all the bounds of beautie fit
        For her t'inhabit? There is it.

Thrice happy house, that hast receipt
        For this so loftie forme, so streight,
55   So polisht, perfect, round, and even,
        As it slid moulded off from Heaven.

Not swelling like the Ocean proud,
        But stooping gently, as a Cloud,
        As smooth as Oyle pour'd forth, and calme
60   As showers; and sweet as drops of Balme.

[6] as though.
[7] as *primum mobile*, the first mover of the universe. Circular motion (in the heavens) was thought to be perfect.
[8] as if.
[9] exalted.

Smooth, soft, and sweet, in all a floud
Where it may run to any good;
And where it stayes, it there becomes
A nest of odorous spice, and gummes.

65   In action, winged as the wind,
In rest, like spirits left behind
Upon a banke, or field of flowers,
Begotten by that wind, and showers.

In thee, faire Mansion, let it rest,
70   Yet know, with what thou art possest,
Thou entertaining in thy brest,
But such a Mind, mak'st God thy Guest.

A *whole quaternion*[10] *in the middest of this Poem is lost,
containing entirely the three next pieces of it, and all of the
fourth* (*which in the order of the whole, is the eighth*) *ex-
cepting the very end: which at the top of the next quaternion
goeth on thus:*

BUt, for you (growing Gentlemen)[11] the happy branches of
two so illustrious Houses as these, where from your honour'd
Mother, is in both lines descended; let me leave you this last
Legacie of Counsell; which so soone as you arrive at yeares of
mature Understanding, open you (Sir) that are the eldest,
and read it to your Brethren, for it will concerne you all alike.
Vowed by a faithfull Servant, and Client of your Familie,
with his latest breath expiring it.

B.J.

To Kenelme, John, George

BOast not these Titles of your Ancestors;
(Brave Youths) th'are their possessions, none of
[yours:
When your owne Vertues, equall'd have their Names,
'T will be but faire, to leane upon their *Fames;*

---

[10] a sheet of paper folded
twice to make four leaves.
[11] Kenelm (b. 1625), John
(b. 1627), and George (b. 1632).
Another son, Everard, had died in
1629.

5   For they are strong Supporters: But, till then,
      The greatest are but growing Gentlemen.
   It is a wretched thing to trust to reedes;
      Which all men doe, that urge[12] not their owne
                                  [deeds
   Up to their Ancestors; the rivers side,
10   By which yo'are planted, shew's your fruit shall bide:
   Hang all your roomes, with one large Pedigree:
      'Tis Vertue alone, is true Nobilitie.
   Which Vertue from your Father, ripe, will fall;
      Study illustrious Him, and you have all.

9. *Elegie on my Muse*[1]

THe truly honoured Lady, the Lady V*enetia*
D*igby;* who living, gave me leave to call her so.
Being
Her ΑΠΟΘΕΩΣΙΣ, *or Relation to the Saints.*

Sera quidem tanto struitur medicina dolori.[2]

An Elegie on my Muse

'TWere time that I dy'd too, now shee is dead,
   Who was my *Muse,* and life of all I sey'd.[3]
The Spirit that I wrote with, and conceiv'd,
   All that was good, or great in me she weav'd,
5   And set it forth; the rest were Cobwebs fine,
   Spun out in name of some of the old *Nine!*[4]
To hang a window, or make darke the roome,
   Till swept away, th'were cancell'd with a broome!
Nothing, that could remaine, or yet can stirre
10   A sorrow in me, fit to wait to her!
O! had I seene her laid out a faire Corse,
   By *Death,* on Earth, I should have had remorse[5]

---

[12] push forward.

86–9: [1] See No. 80, title.

  [2] Statius, *Silvae* V.i.16 (written to console a friend whose wife had died): "Late indeed is the balm composed for so great a sorrow."

[3] assayed: tried.

[4] Muses.

[5] pity; or perhaps a biting back (L. *remorsus*).

On *Nature*, for her: who did let her lie,
  And saw that portion of her selfe to die.
15 Sleepie, or stupid Nature, couldst thou part
  With such a *Raritie*, and not rowse *Art*
  With all her aydes, to save her from the seize
  Of *Vulture death*, and those relentlesse cleies?[6]
  Thou wouldst have lost the *Phœnix*, had the kind[7]
20   Beene trusted to thee: not to't selfe assign'd.
  Looke on thy sloth, and give[8] thy selfe undone,
  (For so thou art with me) now shee is gone.
  My wounded mind cannot sustaine this stroke,
  It rages, runs, flies, stands, and would provoke[9]
25 The world to ruine with it; in her *Fall*,
  I summe up mine owne breaking, and wish all.[10]
  Thou hast no more blowes, *Fate*, to drive at one:
  What's left a *Poët*, when his *Muse* is gone?
  Sure, I am dead, and know it not! I feele
30   Nothing I doe; but, like a heavie wheele,
  Am turned with an others powers. My Passion
  Whoorles me about, and to blaspheme in fashion,
  I murmure against *God*, for having ta'en
  Her blessed Soule, hence, forth this valley vane
35 Of teares, and dungeon of calamitie!
  I envie it the Angels amitie![11]
  The joy of Saints! the *Crowne* for which it lives,
  The glorie, and gaine of rest, which the place gives!
  Dare I prophane, so irreligious bee
40 To 'greet,[12] or grieve her soft Euthanasee![13]
  So sweetly taken to the Court of blisse,
  As[14] spirits had stolne her *Spirit*, in a kisse,
  From off her pillow, and deluded bed;
  And left her lovely body unthought dead!
45 Indeed, she is not dead! but laid to sleepe
  In earth, till the last *Trumpe*[15] awake the *Sheepe*

---

6 claws.
7 species: there was only one
of this fabulous bird.
8 admit.
9 invite.
10 sc. to break or fall.

11 friendship, association.
12 regret, weep for.
13 gentle or easy death.
14 as though.
15 Matt. 25:32–33.

And *Goates* together, whither they must come
   To heare their Judge, and his eternall doome;
   To have that finall retribution,
50   Expected with the fleshes restitution.
For, as there are three *Natures*,[16] *Schoolemen* call
   One *corporall*, only; th'other *spirituall*,
Like single; so, there is a third, commixt,
   Of *Body* and *Spirit* together, plac'd betwixt
55 Those other two; which must be judg'd, or crown'd:
   This[17] as it guilty is, or guiltlesse found,
Must come to take a sentence, by the sense
   Of that great Evidence, the *Conscience!*
Who will be there, against that day prepar'd,
60   T'accuse, or quit all *Parties* to be heard!
O *Day* of joy, and suretie to the just!
   Who in that feast of *Resurrection* trust!
That great eternall *Holy-day* of rest,
   To Body, and Soule! where *Love* is all the guest!
65 And the whole *Banquet* is full sight of *God!*
   Of joy the *Circle*, and sole *Period!*
All other gladnesse, with the thought is barr'd;
   Hope, hath her end! and *Faith* hath her reward!
This being thus: why should my tongue, or pen
70   Presume to interpell[18] that fulnesse, when
Nothing can more adorne it, then the seat
   That she is in, or, make it more compleat?
Better be dumbe, then superstitious!
   Who violates the God-head, is most vitious
75 Against the Nature he would worship. *Hee*
   Will honour'd be in all simplicitie!
Have all his actions, wondred at, and view'd
   With silence, and amazement! not with rude,
Dull, and prophane, weake, and imperfect eyes,
80   Have busie search made in his mysteries![19]

---

[16] Medieval theology distinguished the corporeal nature (of bodies), the spiritual nature (of souls), and their combination in the living being, to be achieved again at the Resurrection.

[17] the resurrected union.

[18] break in upon, interrupt (L. *interpellere*).

[19] the hidden things of God; e.g., Matt. 13:11.

Hee knowes, what worke h'hath done, to call this
[*Guest*,
   Out of her noble body, to this *Feast:*
And give her place, according to her blood
   Amongst her *Peeres*, those Princes of all good!
85   *Saints, Martyrs, Prophets*, with those *Hierarchies*,[20]
   Angels, Arch-angels, Principalities,
The *Dominations, Vertues*, and the *Powers*,
   The *Thrones*, the *Cherube*, and *Seraphick* bowers,[21]
That, planted round, there sing before the *Lamb*,
90   A new Song to his praise, and great *I AM*:[22]
And she doth know, out of the shade of Death,
   What 't is t'enjoy, an everlasting breath!
To have her captiv'd spirit freed from flesh,
   And on her Innocence, a garment fresh
95   And white, as that, put on: and in her hand
   With boughs of Palme,[23] a crowned *Victrice* stand!
And will you, worthy Sonne, Sir, knowing this,
   Put black, and mourning on? and say you misse
A *Wife*, a *Friend*, a *Lady*, or a *Love*;
100   Whom her *Redeemer*, honour'd hath above
Her fellowes, with the oyle of gladnesse, bright
   In heaven *Empyre*,[24] and with a robe of light?
Thither, you[25] hope to come; and there to find
   That pure, that pretious, and exalted mind
105   You once enjoy'd: A short space severs yee,
   Compar'd unto that long eternitie,
That shall re-joyne yee. Was she, then, so deare,
   When shee departed? you will meet her there,
Much more desir'd, and dearer then before,
110   By all the wealth of blessings, and the store
Accumulated on her, by the *Lord*
   Of life, and light, the Sonne of *God*, the *Word!*

---

[20] the familiar nine orders of angels, which follow in ascending order.

[21] abodes.

[22] God: Exod. 3:14.

[23] with boughs of Palme in her hand.

[24] the Empyrean Heaven, abode of God, angels, and saints.

[25] Sir Kenelm.

There, all the happy soules, that ever were,
 Shall meet with gladnesse in one *Theatre*;[26]
115 And each shall know, there, one anothers face:
 By beatifick vertue of the Place.
There shall the Brother, with the Sister walke,
 And Sons, and Daughters, with their Parents talke;
But all of *God*; They still shall have to say,
120 But make him *All in All*,[27] their *Theme*, that *Day*:
That happy *Day*, that never shall see night!
 Where *Hee* will be, all Beautie to the *Sight*;
Wine, or delicious fruits, unto the *Taste*;
 A Musique in the *Eares*, will ever last;
125 Unto the *Sent*,[28] a Spicerie, or Balme;
 And to the *Touch*, a Flower, like soft as Palme.
Hee will all Glory, all Perfection be,
 God, in the *Union*, and the *Trinitie!*
That holy, great, and glorious Mysterie,
130 Will there revealed be in Majestie!
By light, and comfort of spirituall *Grace*;
 The vision of our *Saviour*, face, to face[29]
In his humanitie![30] To heare him preach
 The price of our *Redemption*, and to teach
135 Through his inherent righteousnesse, in death,
 The safetie of our soules, and forfeit breath![31]
What fulnesse of beatitude is here?
 What love with mercy mixed doth appeare?
To style us Friends, who were, by Nature, Foes?[32]
140 Adopt us Heires,[33] by grace, who were of those
Had lost our selves? and prodigally spent
 Our native portions, and possessed rent;[34]
Yet have all debts forgiven us, and advance
 B'imputed right to an inheritance

[26] the etymological meaning from Greek: a place for viewing.
[27] 1 Cor. 15:28.
[28] scent.
[29] 1 Cor. 13:12.
[30] The divine union of God and man in Christ continues after the Resurrection.
[31] perhaps, even in death (the forfeiture of breath).
[32] e.g., Phil. 3:18.
[33] Rom. 8:15–17.
[34] tribute which we have which is owed God.

145 In his eternall Kingdome, where we sit
    Equall with Angels, and Co-heires of it.
    Nor dare we under blasphemy conceive
    He that shall be our supreme Judge, should leave
    Himselfe so un-inform'd of his elect
150   Who knowes the hearts of all, and can dissect
    The smallest Fibre of our flesh; he can
    Find all our Atomes from a point t' a span!³⁵
    Our closest Creekes,³⁶ and Corners, and can trace
    Each line, as it were graphick,³⁷ in the face.
155 And best he knew her noble Character,
    For't was himselfe who form'd, and gave it her.
    And to that forme, lent two such veines of blood³⁸
    As nature could not more increase the flood
    Of title in her! All nobilitie
160   (But pride, that schisme of incivilitie)
    She had, and it became her! she was fit
    T' have knowne no envy, but by suffring it!³⁹
    She had a mind as calme, as she was faire;
    Not tost or troubled with light Lady-aire;
165 But, kept an even gate, as some streight tree
    Mov'd by the wind, so comely moved she.
    And by the awfull manage⁴⁰ of her Eye
    She swaid all bus'nesse in the Familie!
    To one she said, Doe this, he did it; So
170   To another, Move; he went; To a third, Go,
    He run; and all did strive with diligence
    T'obey, and serve her sweet Commandements.
    She was in one, a many⁴¹ parts of life;
    A tender *Mother,* a discreeter *Wife,*
175 A solemne *Mistresse,*⁴² and so good a *Friend,*

---

³⁵ from a moment to an entire life ("Man's life is but a span"); or from a point to the entire universe, spanned by God's hands (Ps. 38:6 or Isa. 40:12).
³⁶ secret nooks or crannies.
³⁷ drawn with pencil or pen.
³⁸ her noble descent from the Stanleys and Northumberlands.
³⁹ but by having others envy her.
⁴⁰ management, rule.
⁴¹ a great number of the. See NED *Many* B.1.
⁴² head of the household.

So charitable, to religious end
In all her petite[43] actions, so devote,
    As[44] her whole life was now become one note
Of Pietie, and private holinesse.
180 She spent more time in teares her selfe to dresse
For her devotions, and those sad essayes
    Of sorrow, then all pompe of gaudy[45] daies:
And came forth ever cheered, with the rod[46]
    Of divine Comfort, when sh' had talk'd with *God*.
185 Her broken sighes did never misse whole sense:
    Nor can the bruised heart want eloquence:
For, Prayer is the Incense[47] most perfumes
    The holy Altars, when it least presumes.
And hers were all Humilitie! they beat
190   The doore of *Grace*, and found the *Mercy-Seat*.
In frequent speaking by the pious Psalmes
    Her solemne houres she spent, or giving Almes,
Or doing other deeds of Charitie,
    To cloath the naked, feed the hungry. Shee
195 Would sit in an Infirmery, whole dayes
    Poring, as on a Map, to find the wayes
To that eternall Rest, where now sh'hath place
    By sure Election, and predestin'd grace!
Shee saw her Saviour, by an early light,
200   Incarnate in the Manger, shining bright
On all the world! Shee saw him on the Crosse
    Suffring, and dying to redeeme our losse!
Shee saw him rise, triumphing over Death
    To justifie,[48] and quicken us in breath!
205 Shee saw him too, in glory to ascend
    For his designed worke the perfect end
Of raising, judging, and rewarding all
    The kind[49] of Man, on whom his doome should fall!
All this by *Faith* she saw, and fram'd a Plea,
210   In manner of a daily *Apostrophe*,[50]

43 minor.
44 that.
45 festival.
46 Ps. 23:4.

47 Rev. 8:3–4.
48 e.g., Rom. 3:24.
49 race.
50 exclamatory prayer.

To him should[51] be her Judge, true *God*, true *Man*,
    Jesus, the onely gotten[52] *Christ!* who can
As being Redeemer, and Repairer too
    (Of lapsed Nature) best know what to doe,
215 In that great Act of judgement: which the *Father*
    Hath given wholly to the Sonne (the rather
As being the Sonne of *Man*) to shew his *Power*,
    His *Wisdome*, and his *Justice*, in that houre,
The last of houres, and shutter up of all;
220 Where first his *Power* will appeare, by call
Of all are[53] dead to life! His *Wisdome* show
    In the discerning of each conscience, so!
And most his *Justice*, in the fitting parts,
    And giving dues to all Mankinds deserts!
225 In this sweet *Extasie*, she was rapt hence.
    Who reades, will pardon my Intelligence,
That thus have ventur'd these true straines upon;
    To publish her a *Saint*. My *Muse* is gone.

In pietatis memoriam
quam præstas
Venetiæ *tuæ illustrissim:*
Marit: dign: Digbeie
Hanc ΑΠΟθΕΩΣ ΙΝ, *tibi, tuisque sacro.*[54]

The Tenth, being her Inscription, or CROWNE, *is lost.*

87. THE PRAISES OF A COUNTRIE LIFE[1]

HAppie is he, that from all Businesse cleere,
    As the old race of Mankind were,
With his owne Oxen tills his Sires left lands,
    And is not in the Usurers bands:[2]
5 Nor Souldier-like started with rough alarmes,
    Nor dreads the Seas inraged harmes:

---

[51] who should.
[52] begotten.
[53] who are.
[54] adapted from Statius, *Silvae* V, Preface: "In memory of the devotion which you show to your most illustrious Venetia, worthy Digby, [I offer] this apotheosis —to you and to your honor."
87: [1] translated from Horace, *Epode* II.
  [2] bonds, toils.

But flees the Barre and Courts, with the proud bords,[3]
    And waiting Chambers of great Lords.
The Poplar tall, he then doth marrying twine
10   With the growne issue of the Vine;
And with his hooke lops off the fruitlesse race,
    And sets more happy in the place:
Or in the bending Vale beholds a-farre
    The lowing herds there grazing are:
15 Or the prest honey in pure pots doth keepe
    Of Earth, and sheares the tender Sheepe:
Or when that Autumne, through the fields lifts round
    His head, with mellow Apples crown'd,
How plucking Peares, his owne hand grafted had,
20   And purple-matching[4] Grapes, hee's glad!
With which, *Priapus*,[5] he may thanke thy hands,
    And, *Sylvane*,[6] thine that keptst his Lands!
Then now beneath some ancient Oke he may,
    Now in the rooted Grasse, him lay,
25 Whilst from the higher Bankes doe slide the floods,
    The soft birds quarrell in the Woods,
The Fountaines murmure as the streames doe creepe,
    And all invite to easie sleepe.
Then when the thundring *Jove*, his[7] Snow and showres
30   Are gathering by the Wintry houres;
Or hence, or thence, he drives with many a Hound
    Wild Bores into his toyles[8] pitch'd round:
Or straines on his small forke his subtill nets
    For th'eating Thrush, or Pit-falls sets:
35 And snares the fearfull Hare, and new-come[9] Crane,
    And 'counts them sweet rewards so ta'en:
Who (amongst these delights) would not forget
    Loves cares so evill, and so great?
But if, to boot[10] with these, a chaste Wife meet[11]
40   For houshold aid, and Children sweet;

---

3 dining tables.
4 equaling purple dyes.
5 here, the god of gardens.
6 god of the boundaries of fields.
7 Jove's.

8 traps.
9 in Horace's Italy, a summer visitor (H&S).
10 to the good: in addition.
11 suited.

Such as the *Sabines*,[12] or a Sun-burnt-blowse,[13]
   Some lustie quick *Apulians*[14] spouse,
To deck the hallow'd Harth with old wood fir'd
   Against[15] the Husband comes home tir'd;
45   That penning the glad flock in hurdles[16] by
      Their swelling udders doth draw dry:
And from the sweet Tub Wine of this yeare takes,
   And unbought viands ready makes:
Not Lucrine[17] Oysters I could then more prize,
50   Nor Turbot,[18] nor bright Golden eyes:[19]
If with East floods, the Winter troubled much,
   Into our Seas send any such:
Th'Ionian God-wit,[20] nor the Ginny[21] hen
   Could not goe downe my belly then
55   More sweet then Olives, that new gather'd be
      From fattest branches of the Tree:
Or the herb Sorrell, that loves Meadows still,
   Or Mallowes[22] loosing bodyes ill:
Or at the Feast of Bounds,[23] the Lambe then slaine,
60   Or Kid forc't from the Wolfe againe.
Among these Cates[24] how glad the sight doth come
   Of the fed flocks approaching home!
To view the weary Oxen draw, with bare
   And fainting necks, the turned Share![25]
65   The wealthy houshold swarme of bondmen met,
      And 'bout the steeming Chimney set!
These thoughts when Usurer *Alphius*, now about
   To turne mere farmer, had spoke out,
'Gainst th'Ides,[26] his moneys he gets in with paine,
70   At th'Calends, puts all out againe.

[12] the type of ancient virtuous women.

[13] blowsy woman.

[14] Italian district famous for its wools.

[15] sc. the time when.

[16] temporary pen.

[17] near Baiae; its oysters were highly prized.

[18] a large flat fish.

[19] another fish.

[20] a marsh bird.

[21] guinea.

[22] herb sometimes used as medicine.

[23] March festival of the god Terminus. The countryman eats meat only when it is killed for a sacrifice or by an accident.

[24] viands.

[25] plowshare.

[26] a time of month to settle debts in Rome. The Calends began the next month.

88. ODE THE FIRST. THE FOURTH BOOKE.
To VENUS[1]

VE*nus* againe thou mov'st a warre
     Long intermitted, pray thee, pray thee spare:
  I am not such, as in the Reigne
Of the good *Cynara*[2] I was: Refraine,
5   Sower Mother of sweet Loves, forbeare
To bend a man now at his fiftieth yeare
     Too stubborne for Commands, so slack:
Goe where Youths soft intreaties call thee back.
     More timely hie thee to the house,
10 With thy bright Swans,[3] of *Paulus Maximus:*[4]
     There jest, and feast, make him thine host,
If a fit livor[5] thou dost seeke to toast;
     For he's both noble, lovely, young,
And for the troubled Clyent fyl's his tongue,
15   Child of a hundred Arts, and farre
Will he display the Ensignes of thy warre.
     And when he smiling finds his Grace
With thee 'bove all his Rivals gifts take place,
     He will thee a Marble Statue make
20 Beneath a Sweet-wood[6] Roofe, neere *Alba Lake:*
     There shall thy dainty Nostrill take
In many a Gumme, and for thy soft eares sake
     Shall Verse be set to Harpe and Lute,
And *Phrygian* Hau'boy,[7] not without the Flute.
25   There twice a day in sacred Laies,
The Youths and tender Maids shall sing thy praise:
     And in the *Salian*[8] manner meet
Thrice 'bout thy Altar with their Ivory feet.

88: [1] translated from Horace's *Odes.*
[2] one of Horace's female friends.
[3] Swans traditionally accompanied Venus.
[4] Consul in 11 B.C.; friend of Ovid and Augustus.
[5] The liver was thought to be the seat of love.
[6] a sweet-smelling African cedar.
[7] oboe: a pipe used to worship Cybele, mother of the gods, in Phrygia.
[8] dancing like the Salii, priests of Mars.

Me now, nor Wench, nor wanton Boy,
30   Delights, nor credulous hope of mutuall Joy,
       Nor care I now healths to propound;[9]
       Or with fresh flowers to girt my Temple round.
          But, why, oh why, my *Ligurine,*[10]
       Flow my thin teares, downe these pale cheeks of mine?
35   Or why, my well-grac'd words among,
       With an uncomely silence failes my tongue?
          Hard-hearted, I dreame every Night
       I hold thee fast! but fled hence, with the Light,
          Whether in *Mars* his field[11] thou bee,
40   Or *Tybers* winding streames, I follow thee.

89. Ode IX. 3 Booke, to Lydia. Dialogue of Horace, and Lydia[1]

Hor.   WHilst, *Lydia,* I was lov'd of thee,
             And ('bout thy Ivory neck,) no youth did
                                                      [fling,
                His armes more acceptable free,
             I thought me richer then the Persian King.
5   Lyd.   Whilst *Horace* lov'd no Mistres more,
             Nor after *Chloë* did his *Lydia* sound;[2]
                In name, I went all names before,
             The Roman *Ilia*[3] was not more renown'd.
     Hor.   'T is true, I'am *Thracian Chloes,* I,
10   Who sings so sweet, and with such cunning
                                                      [plaies,
                As, for her, I'l'd not feare to die,
             So Fate would give her life, and longer daies.

[9] propose.
[10] a handsome boy (see *Ode* IV.10).
[11] the Campus Martius in Rome.
89: [1] translated from Horace's *Odes.*
[2] nor did he rate Lydia after Chloe.
[3] mother of Romulus and Remus, legendary founders of Rome.

LYD.   And, I am mutually on fire
          With gentle *Calais, Thurine*[4] *Orniths* Sonne;
15   For whom I doubly would expire,
          So[5] Fates would let the Boy a long thred run.[6]

HOR.   But, say old Love returne should make,
          And us dis-joyn'd force to her brazen yoke,
              That I bright *Chloë* off should shake;
20   And to left-*Lydia*, now the gate stood ope.

LYD.   Though he be fairer then a Starre;
          Thou lighter then the barke of any tree,
              And then rough *Adria*, angrier, farre;
          Yet would I wish to love, live, die with thee.

90

DOing,[1] a filthy pleasure is, and short;
And done, we straight repent us of the sport:
Let us not then rush blindly on unto it,
Like lustfull beasts, that onely know to doe it:
5 For lust will languish, and that heat decay,
But thus, thus, keeping endlesse Holy-day,
Let us together closely lie, and kisse,
There is no labour, nor no shame in this;
This hath pleas'd, doth please, and long will please;
                              [never
10 Can this decay, but is beginning ever.

91

LIber,[1] of all thy friends, thou sweetest care,
      Thou worthy in eternall Flower to fare,

[4] of Thureus, a town in southern Italy.
[5] If.
[6] i.e., live a long life.
90: [1] copulation. The poem is translated from a text supposed to be by Petronius and included in the Paris 1585 edition.
91: [1] the name of a friend. Translated from Martial, *Epig.* VIII.77.

If thou be'st wise, with *'Syrian* Oyle let shine
  Thy locks, and rosie garlands crowne thy head;
5 Darke thy cleare glasse with old *Falernian* Wine;
  And heat, with softest love, thy softer bed.
Hee, that but living halfe his dayes, dies such,
  Makes his life longer then 't was given him, much.

THE ART OF POETRIE

Along with Martial, Horace interested and influenced Jonson more than did any other classical author. In the "Execration upon Vulcan" he complains that he lost in the fire of 1623, which destroyed his home, "some parts . . . of search, and mastry in the arts." Heading the list which follows is the translation of "All the old Venusine [Horace], in Poetrie," interpreted in the light of Aristotle's *Poetics*. Although the Aristotelian commentary is gone, two versions of Jonson's translation of Horace's *Art of Poetry* have somehow survived. In them Jonson clearly shows his limitations as a translator. When he talked with William Drummond in Scotland, he damned Sylvester's translation of the *Divine Weekes* of du Bartas, Fairfax's of Tasso, and Harrington's of Ariosto (the last, he said, "under all translations was the worst"). These judgments and his own work show that Jonson was primarily interested in literal translation, a characteristic lacking for him in Sylvester, Fairfax, and Harrington. The two translations of *The Art of Poetry*—or rather the original translation and its revision—exhibit this strength and weakness. They are accurate but pedestrian. The wittiness of the original has almost completely disappeared.

But there are compensations. The revision shows the care with which Jonson reconsidered much of his work. For instance, in advising the writer to stay within his natural capabilities, he first translated,

> Take therefore, you that write, a subject fit
> Unto your strength, and long be turning it:
> Prove what your shoulders will, or will not beare.

After revision these lines become,

> Take, therefore, you that write, still, matter fit
> Unto your strength, and long examine it,
> Upon your shoulders. Prove what they will beare,
> And what they will not. (ll. 53–56)

"Matter" is for Jonson now better than "subject" (the Latin reads *materiam*); "examine" is preferred to "turning" (Latin *versate*). The changed sentence division reflects a break in the rhythm of the line in the original. But the second version is not a new translation: it is only a revision of the first. Horace's original 476 lines are expanded to 680 in both versions. The variation tends mainly to be in exact choice of words rather than in a recasting of the meaning.

The same qualities of his *Art of Poetry* appear in Jonson's other translations, whether they be passages in his plays or the translations which conclude *Under-wood*. He is able to convey the impact of his original best when he is para-phrasing, as when he imitated Horace in *Under-wood* 46 or Philostratus in "Drink to me only." The literal translations show in their lack of force only the scholarship which lay back of all of Jonson's writing. When it was not touched by his personal feelings, his learning stood in the way of his creative abilities.

HORACE HIS ART OF POETRY

HORACE, OF THE ART OF POETRIE

Quintus Horatius Flaccus
his book of the Art of
Poetry to the
PISO'S[1]

IF to a womans head, a painter would
A horse neck joyn, & sundry plumes ore-fold
On every limb, ta'ne from a several[3] creature,
Presenting upwards a fair female feature,
5   Which in a blacke foule fish uncomely ends:
Admitted to the sight, although his friends,[4]
Could you containe your laughter? credit me,
That Book, my *Piso's*, and this piece agree,
Whose shapes like sick mens dreams are form'd so vain,

10   As[5] neither head, nor foot, one forme[6] retain:
But equall power to Painter, and to Poet,
Of daring ought, hath still bin given; we know it:
And both doe crave, and give again this leave:
Yet not as therefore cruell things should cleave
15   To gentle; not that we should Serpents see
With Doves; or Lambs with Tigres coupled be.
In grave beginnings, and great things profest,
You have oft-times, that[7] may out-shine the rest,
A purple piece,[8] or two stitch'd in: when either
20   *Diana's* Grove, and Altar, with the nether[9]

[1] The version printed in the 1640 Duodecimo. H&S consider it to have been made about 1605. The family of the Pisos, to whom the work is addressed, were friends of Horace. The father was Consul in A.D. 23 as were his two sons later.

[3] different.

[4] although the viewers are his friends.

[5] that.

[6] a unity.

[7] what.

[8] patch. The following examples are apparently taken from works contemporary with Horace.

[9] apparently, underground.

HORACE,
OF
THE ART
OF POETRIE[2]

IF to a Womans head a Painter would
Set a Horse-neck, and divers feathers fold
On every limbe, ta'en from a severall creature,
Presenting upwards, a faire female feature,
5 Which in some swarthie fish uncomely ends:
Admitted to the sight, although his friends
Could you containe your laughter? Credit mee,
This peece, my *Piso's*, and that booke agree,
Whose shapes, like sick-mens dreames, are fain'd so
[vaine,
10 As neither head, nor foot, one forme retaine.
But equall power, to Painter, and to Poët,
Of daring all, hath still beene given; we know it:
And both doe crave, and give againe, this leave.
Yet, not as therefore wild, and tame should cleave
15 Together: not that we should Serpents see
With Doves; or Lambes, with Tygres coupled be.
   In grave beginnings, and great things profest,
Ye have oft-times, that may ore-shine the rest,
A Scarlet peece, or two, stitch'd in: when or
20 *Diana's* Grove, or Altar, with the bor-

---

[2] The version printed in the 1640 Folio. Jonson revised it from the earlier Duodecimo, in accordance with Heinsius' Latin text of 1610. Heinsius rearranged some passages; his changes are not ac-cepted by modern editors and accordingly the line order of the Duodecimo is followed here, the Folio text being reordered to ac-cord with it.

Bouts of fleet waters, that doe intertwine
The pleasant grounds, or when the River *Rhine*,
Or Rain-bow is describ'd; but here was now
No place for these: And, Painter, haply thou
25   Knowst well alone to paint a *Cypresse*[10] Tree;
What's this, if he whose mony hireth thee
To paint him, hath by swimming, hopelesse, scap'd,
The whole Fleet wrack'd? a great jarre to be shap'd
Was meant at first, why, forcing still about
30   Thy labouring wheel, comes scarce a pitcher out?
Heare me conclude; let what thou workst upon
Be simple quite throughout, and alwayes one.

      The greater part, that boast the Muses fire,
Father, and sons[11] right worthy of your Sire,
35   Are with the likeness of the truth beguil'd:
My selfe for shortnesse labour, and am stil'd
Obscure. Another striving smooth to runne,
Wants strength, and sinewes, as[12] his spirits were
                                                      [done;
His[14] Muse professing height, and greatnesse, swells;
40   Downe close by shore, this other creeping steales,
Being over-safe, and fearing of the flaw:
So he that varying still affects to draw
One thing prodigiously, paints in the woods
A Dolphin and a Boare amidst the floods.
45   The shunning vice, to greater vice doth lead,
If in th'escape an artlesse path we tread.
      The worst of statuaries, here about
Th'*Æmilian* Schoole, in Brasse can figure out
The nailes, and every gentle haire disclose;
50   Yet in the main work haplesse: since he knowes
Not to designe the whole. Should I aspire
To frame a worke, I would no more desire
To be that fellow, then to be markt out
With faire black eyes, and hair, and some vile snout.

----

10 i.e., he paints the cypress
tree into a picture where it does
not belong.

11 the Pisos.
12 as though.
14 another's.

Dring Circles of swift waters that intwine
The pleasant grounds, or when the River *Rhine*,
Or Rainbow is describ'd. But here was now
No place for these. And, Painter, hap'ly, thou
25 Know'st only well to paint a Cipresse tree.
What's this? if he whose money hireth thee
To paint him, hath by swimming hopelesse scap'd,
The whole fleet wreck'd? a great jarre to be shap'd,
Was meant at first. Why forcing still about
30 Thy labouring wheele, comes scarce a Pitcher out?
In short; I bid, Let what thou work'st upon,
Be simple quite throughout, and wholly one.
    Most Writers, noble Sire, and either Sonne,
Are, with the likenesse of the truth, undone.
35 My selfe for shortnesse labour; and I grow
Obscure. This striving to run smooth, and flow,
Hath neither soule, nor sinewes. Loftie he
Professing greatnesse, swells: That low by lee[13]

Creepes on the ground; too safe, too afraid of storme.
40 This seeking, in a various kind, to forme
One thing, prodigiously, paints in the woods
A Dolphin, and a Boare amid' the floods.
So, shunning faults, to greater fault doth lead,
When in a wrong, and artlesse way we tread.
45 The worst of Statuaries, here about
Th'*Æmilian* Schoole,[15] in brasse can fashion out
The nailes; and every curled haire disclose,
But in the maine worke haplesse: since he knowes
Not to designe the whole. Should I aspire
50 To forme a worke, I would no more desire
To be that Smith; then live, mark'd one of those,
With faire black eyes, and haire;[16] and a wry[17] nose.

---

[13] on the calm side.
[15] a school for gladiators. Part of it was rented to a sculptor.
[16] Dark hair and eyes were considered beautiful.
[17] twisted.

55   Take therefore, you that write, a subject fit
      Unto your strength, and long be turning it:
      Prove what your shoulders will, or will not beare.
      His choise, who's matter to his power doth reare,
      Nor language nor cleare order will forsake:
60   The vertue and grace of which, or I mistake,
      Is now to speak, and even now to defer
      Much that mought[22] now be spoke, omitted here
      Till fitter season; now to like of this,
      Lay that aside, the Epicks office is.[23]
65   In using also of new words, to be
      Right spare, and wary: then thou speak'st to me
      Most worthy praise, when words that vulgar grew
      Are by thy cunning placing made meer[24] new.
      Yet, if by chance in uttering things abstruse,
70   Thou need new termes; thou maist, without excuse,
      Feigne words un-heard of to the girded Race
      Of the *Cethegi;*[26] and all men will grace
      And give, being taken modestly,[27] this leave,
      And those thy new, and late-coyn'd words receive,
75   So[28] they fall gently from the *Grecian* spring,
      And come not too much wrested. What's that thing
      A *Roman* to *Cæcilius* will allow,
      Or *Plautus,*[29] and in *Virgil* disavow,
      Or *Varius?*[30] Why am I now envy'd so,
80   If I can give some small encrease? when, loe,
      Cato's,[31] and *Ennius*[32] tongues have lent much worth
      And wealth unto our Language; and brought forth

[22] might.
[23] To enjoy this, lay that aside as the business of the epic. Horace wrote, "Lay it aside as [the excellence and charm that] the author of a long-promised poem shall say."
[24] entirely.
[26] M. Cornelius Cethegus, Consul in 204 B.C. Cicero reckons Roman oratory to begin with him. *Brut.* 15.
[27] if not overdone.
[28] if.
[29] two early writers of Roman comedy.
[30] epic and tragic poet; edited the *Aeneid.*
[31] the Censor; earliest important Latin prose writer.
[32] supposed father of Roman poetry.

Take, therefore, you that write, still, matter fit
Unto your strength, and long examine it,
55   Upon your Shoulders.[18] Prove[19] what they will beare,
And what they will not. Him whose choice doth reare
His matter to his power, in all he makes,
Nor language, nor cleere order ere forsakes.
The vertue[20] of which order, and true grace,
60   Or I am much deceiv'd, shall be to place[21]
Invention. Now, to speake; and then defer
Much, that mought now be spoke: omitted here
Till fitter season. Now, to like of this;
Lay that aside, the *Epicks* office is.
65   In using also of new words, to be
Right spare, and warie: then thou speak'st to mee
Most worthie praise, when words that common grew,
Are, by thy cunning placing, made meere new.
Yet, if by chance, in utt'ring things abstruse,
70   Thou need new termes; thou maist, without excuse,
Faine words, unheard of to the well-truss'd[25] race
Of the *Cethegi*; And all men will grace,
And give, being taken modestly, this leave,
And those thy new, and late-coyn'd words receive,
75   So they fall gently from the *Grecian* spring,
And come not too much wrested. What's that thing,
A Roman to *Cæcilius* will allow,
Or *Plautus*, and in *Virgil* disavow,
Or *Varius?* why am I now envi'd so,
80   If I can give some small increase? When, loe,
Cato's and *Ennius* tongues have lent much worth,
And wealth unto our language; and brought forth

---

[18] i.e., see whether you can sustain it.
[19] test, discover.
[20] culmination.

[21] i.e., properly.
[25] The earlier Romans had worn a kind of loin cloth beneath the toga.

New names of things. It hath beene ever free,
And ever will, to utter termes that be
85   Stampt[33] to the time. As woods whose change appears
Still in their leavs, throughout the sliding years,
The first-borne dying; so the aged Fate
Of words decay, and phrases borne but late
Like tender Buds shoot up, and freshly grow.
90   Our selves, and all thats ours, to death we owe:
Whether the Sea[34] receiv'd into the shore,
That from the North the Navy safe doth store,
A Kingly work; or that long barren Fen
Once rowable, but now doth nourish men
95   In neighbour-towns, and feels the weighty plough:
Or the wild River, who hath changed now
His course, so hurtfull both to grain and seeds,
Being taught a better way. All mortall deeds
Shall perish: so farre of[35] it is, the state
100   Or grace of speech, should hope a lasting date.
Much phrase that now is dead shall be reviv'd,
And much shall dye, that now is nobly liv'd
If custome please, with whom both choyse, and will,
Power, Art, and rule of speaking resteth still.
105   The deeds of Kings, great Captains, and sad wars,

What number[37] best can fit, *Homer* declares.
In verse unequal[38] match'd, first sowre laments,[39]
After mens wishes, crown'd in their events[40]
Were also clos'd:[41] but who the man should be,
110   That first sent forth the dapper Elegie

[33] stamped or fitted. Jonson may be practicing the idea of the passage and developing a new meaning for the word, as Horace had coined *cintutus* ("well-truss'd") at l. 71.

[34] Julius Caesar attempted to build a harbor at Ostia, to drain the Pomptine marshes (ll. 93–95), and to straighten the Tiber (ll. 96–98). See Plutarch, *Life of Caesar*, 58.

[35] far off: impossible.

[37] poetic meter.

[38] The lines of elegies are alternately of hexameter and pentameter.

[39] the elegy.

[40] happy outcomes of love affairs. The classical elegy was not limited to dirges.

[41] enclosed: limited by the poetic form.

New names of things. It hath beene ever free,
And ever will, to utter termes that bee
85 Stamp'd to the time. As woods whose change appeares
Still in their leaves, throughout the sliding yeares,
The first borne dying; so the aged state
Of words decay, and phrases borne but late
Like tender buds shoot up, and freshly grow.
90 Our selves, and all thats ours, to death we owe:
Whether the Sea receiv'd into the shore,
That from the North, the Navie safe doth store,
A kingly worke; or that long barren fen
Once rowable, but now doth nourish men
95 In neighbour-townes, and feeles the weightie plough:
Or the wilde river, who hath changed now
His course so hurtfull both to graine, and seedes,
Being taught a better way. *All mortall deeds
Shall perish:* so farre off it is, the state,
100 Or grace of speech, should hope a lasting date.
Much phrase that now is dead, shall be reviv'd;
And much shall dye, that now is nobly liv'd,
If Custome please; at whose disposing will
The power, and rule of speaking resteth still.
105 The gests[36] of Kings, great Captaines, and sad
                                          [Warres,
What number best can fit, *Homer* declares.
In Verse unequall match'd, first sowre Laments,
After mens Wishes, crown'd in their events
Were also clos'd: But, who the man should be,
110 That first sent forth the dapper Elegie,

[36] exploits.

All the Grammarians strive:[42] and yet in Court
Before the Judge it hangs, and waits report.
    Unto the Lyrick strings, the Muse gave grace
To chant the gods, and all their god-like race,[43]
115 The conquering champion, the prime horse in course,
Fresh Lovers businesse,[44] and the wines free source.[45]
    The *Iambicke* arm'd *Archilochus*[46] to rave,
This foot the socks[47] tooke up, and Buskins[48] grave
As fit t'exchange discourse, and quell the rings
120 Of popular noyses, borne to actuate[50] things.
If now the changes, and the severall hues
Of Poëms here describ'd, I can nor use,
Nor know t'observe; why (i'the Muses name)
Am I cald Poet? wherefore with wrong shame
125 Perversely modest had I rather owe
To ignorance still, then yet to learne, or know.
Yet Comick matter shunnes to be exprest
In Tragicke verse, no lesse *Thyestes* feast[52]
Abhorres low numbers, and the private straine
130 Fit for the Sock: Each subject should retaine
The place allotted it, with decent praise:
Yet sometime both[54] the Comœdy doth raise
Her voyce, and angry *Chremes*[55] chafes out-right,
With swelling throat: and, oft, the Tragick wight[56]
135 Complaines in humble phrase. Both *Telephus*[57]
And *Peleus*,[58] if he seek to heart-strike us,

[42] The identity of the inventor of the elegy has not survived.

[43] as in Pindar's writings.

[44] as in Alcaeus and Sappho.

[45] as in Anacreon.

[46] Archilochus of Paros (c. 650 B.C.), one of the earliest writers of iambic verse.

[47] emblem of comedy, with pun on foot.

[48] emblem of tragedy. The dialogue of Roman plays was written in iambic verse.

[50] stir up, arouse.

[52] Thyestes unknowingly ate his own children at the behest of his brother Atreus. The Greek story came to the Elizabethan stage via Seneca.

[54] omit.

[55] abusive old man in Terence's *Heautontimorumenos*.

[56] character.

[57] son of Hercules, wounded (and cured) by Achilles. Plays about him have perished.

[58] father of Achilles, a wanderer both in youth and old age. No plays about him survive.

All the Grammarians strive; and yet in Court
Before the Judge, it hangs, and waites report.
   Unto the Lyrick Strings, the Muse gave grace
To chant the Gods, and all their God-like race,
115 The conqu'ring Champion, the prime Horse in course,
Fresh Lovers businesse, and the Wines free source.
Th'Iambick arm'd *Archilochus* to rave,
This foot the socks tooke up, and buskins grave,
As fit t'exchange discourse; a Verse to win
120 On[49] popular noise with, and doe businesse in.
126 If now the turnes, the colours,[51] and right hues
Of Poëms here describ'd, I can, nor use,
Nor know t'observe: Why (i'the Muses name)
Am I call'd Poët? wherefore with wrong shame,
Perversly modest, had I rather owe
131 To ignorance still, then either learne, or know.
121   The Comick matter will not be exprest
In tragick Verse; no lesse *Thyestes* feast
Abhorres low numbers, and the private straine
Fit for the sock: Each subject should retaine
125 The place allotted it, with decent thewes.[53]
132 Yet, sometime, doth the Comedie excite
Her voyce, and angry *Chremes* chafes out-right
With swelling throat: and, oft the tragick wight
135 Complaines in humble phrase. Both *Telephus*,
And *Peleus*, if they seeke to heart-strike us

[49] above.
[51] rhetorical devices like meta-
phors.
[53] suitable attributes.

That are spectators, with his misery,
When he is poore, and banisht, must throw by
His Bombard-phrase,[59] and foot-and-half-foot words:
140 Tis not enough the labouring Muse affords
Her Poëms beauty, but a sweet delight,
To worke the hearers minds, still to the plight.
Mens count'nances, with such as laugh, are prone
To laughter: so they grieve with those that mone:
145 If thou wouldst have mee weep, bee thou first dround
Thy selfe in tears, then me thy harms will wound,
Peleus, or *Telephus.* If thou speak vile
And ill-pen'd things, I shall or sleep, or smile.
Sad language fits sad looks; stuft menacings,
150 The angry brow: the sportive, wanton things;
And the severe, speech ever serious:
For nature first within doth fashion us
To every Fortunes habit; she helps on,
Or urgeth us to anger; and anon
155 With weighty woes she hurles us all along;
And tortures us, and after by the tongue,
Her Truck-man, she reports the minds each throe,
If now the phrase of him that speaks, shall flow
In sound, quite from his fortune; both the rout,
160 And *Roman* Gentry, will with laughter shout.
It much will sway whether a god speak, than;
Or an *Heroe:* If a ripe old man,
Or some hot youth, yet in his flourishing course;
Whe'r some great Lady, or her diligent Nurse;
165 A ventring Merchant, or the husband free
Of some small thankfull land: whether he be
Of *Colchis*[64] borne: or in *Assyria*[65] bred;
Or with the Milke of *Thebes,* or *Argus*[66] fed:
Or follow fame, thou that dost write, or faine
170 Things in themselves agreeing: if againe

[59] bombastic phrase.
[64] a fierce race, as reported of Medea's people in the *Argonautica.*
[65] effeminate people.
[66] apparently two prominent, and contrasting, Greek tribes.

That are Spectators, with their miserie,
When they are poore, and banish'd, must throw by
Their bombard-phrase, and foot-and-halfe-foot words:
140 'Tis not enough, th'elaborate[60] Muse affords
Her Poem's beautie, but a sweet delight
To worke the hearers minds, still, to their plight.
Mens faces, still, with such as laugh, are prone
To laughter; so they grieve with those that mone.
145 If thou would'st have me weepe, be thou first drown'd
Thy selfe in teares, then me thy losse will wound,
Peleus, or *Telephus*. If you speake vile
And ill-penn'd things, I shall, or sleepe, or smile.
Sad language fits sad lookes; stuff'd menacings,
150 The angry brow; the sportive, wanton things;
And the severe, speech ever serious.
For Nature, first within doth fashion us
To every state of fortune; she helpes on,
Or urgeth us to anger; and anon
155 With weightie sorrow hurles us all along,
And tortures us: and, after by the tongue
Her truch-man,[61] she reports the minds each throw.[62]
If now the phrase of him that speakes, shall flow
In sound, quite from his fortune; both the rout,
160 And Roman Gentrie, jearing, will laugh out.
It much will differ, if a God speake, than,
Or an *Heroe*; If a ripe old man,
Or some hot youth, yet in his flourishing course;
Where[63] some great Lady, or her diligent Nourse;
165 A ventring Merchant, or the Farmer free
Of some small thankfull land: whether he bee
Of *Colchis* borne; or in *Assyria* bred;
Or, with the milke of *Thebes*; or *Argus*, fed.
Or follow fame, thou that dost write, or faine
170 Things in themselves agreeing: If againe

60 laboring.
61 interpreter.
62 throe.
63 whether.

Honour'd *Achilles* chance by thee be seiz'd;
Keepe him still active, angry, unappeas'd,[67]
Sharp, & contemning Lawes at him[68] should aime,
Be nought so 'bove him, but his bold sword claime.

175   *Medea*[70] make wild, fierce, impetuous:
Ino[71] bewaild; *Ixion*[72] trecherous;
Io[73] still wandring; griev'd *Orestes*[74] sad:
If something fresh, that never yet was had,
Unto the Stage thou bringst, and dar'st create

180   A meer[75] new person, look he keep his state
Unto the last, as when he first went forth,
Still to be like himselfe, and hold his worth.
    'Tis hard, to speake things common properly:
And thou maist better bring a Rhapsody[76]

185   Of *Homers* forth in Acts, then of thine owne
First publish things unspoken, and unknowne.
Yet, common matter thou thine owne maist make,
If thou the vile, broad-troden ring forsake.
For, being a Poet, thou maist feigne, create,

190   Not care, as[77] thou wouldst faithfully translate,
To render word for word: nor with thy sleight
Of imitation, leape into a streight[78]
From whence thy modesty, or Poëms Law
Forbids thee forth againe thy foot to draw.

195   Nor so begin, as did that Circler,[79] late,
I sing a noble warre, and *Priams* fate.

---

[67] basic to the story of the *Iliad*.

[68] that at him.

[70] She murdered her children.

[71] Athamas, her husband, maddened by Juno, killed their son; Ino threw herself and her other son into the sea.

[72] murdered his father-in-law to escape payment of bridal gifts. In heaven he tried to seduce Juno. As punishment Jove chained him in Hades to a perpetually rolling wheel.

[73] loved by Jupiter, who changed her into a heifer to avoid Juno's jealousy. Juno sent a gadfly which drove Io from country to country.

[74] pursued by Furies after he had murdered his mother Clytemnestra.

[75] completely.

[76] song: the sung performance of the epics.

[77] as though.

[78] difficulty.

[79] Horace's *scriptor cyclicus*: a writer of cyclic poems, continuing Homer's stories. The next line is quoted from such a work (unidentified).

Honour'd *Achilles* chance by thee be seiz'd,
Keepe him still active, angry, un-appeas'd,
Sharpe, and contemning lawes, at him should aime,
Be nought so'bove him but his sword let claime.[69]
175   *Medea* make brave with impetuous scorne;
Ino bewaild; *Ixion* false, forsworne;
Poore *Jö* wandring; wild *Orestes* mad:
If something strange, that never yet was had
Unto the *Scene* thou bringst, and dar'st create
180 A meere new person, looke he keepe his state
Unto the last, as when he first went forth,
Still to be like himselfe, and hold his worth.
      'Tis hard, to speake things common, properly:
And thou maist better bring a *Rhapsody*
185 Of *Homers*, forth in acts, then of thine owne,
First publish things unspoken, and unknowne.
Yet common matter thou thine owne maist make,
If thou the vile, broad-troden ring forsake.
For, being a Poët, thou maist feigne, create,
190 Not care, as thou wouldst faithfully translate,
To render word for word: nor with thy sleight
Of imitation, leape into a streight,
From whence thy Modestie, or Poëmes law
Forbids thee forth againe thy foot to draw.
195 Nor so begin, as did that Circler late,
I sing a noble Warre, and *Priam's* Fate.

[69] perhaps, but let him use his
sword.

What doth this promiser, such great gaping worth
Afford? the Mountains travail'd,[80] and brought forth
A trifling Mouse! O how much better this
200   Who nought assaies, unaptly, or amisse?
Speak to me, Muse, the man, who after *Troy* was sackt

Saw many towns, & men, & could their manners tract.[81]

He thinks not how to give you smoak from light,
But light from smoak, that he may draw his bright
205   Wonders forth after: As *Antiphates*,[82]
Scylla, Charybdis,[83] *Polypheme,*[84] with these.
Not from the brand with which the life did burne
Of *Meleager,*[85] brings he the returne
Of *Diomede,* nor *Troyes* sad wars begins
210   From the two Egges,[86] that did disclose the twins.
He ever hastens to the end, and so
(As if he knew it) rapp's[87] his hearer to
The middle of his matter: letting goe
What he despaires, being handled[88] might not show.
215   And so well faines, so mixeth cunningly
Falshood and truth, as no man can espy
Where the midst differs from the first, or where
The last doth from the midst disjoyn'd appeare.
Heare, what it is the people, and I desire.
220   If such a ones applause thou dost require,

[80] labored.
[81] treat (L. *tractare*). Jonson uses hexameter in this translation of the opening of the *Odyssey.*
[82] cannibal king of the Laestragonians (*Odyssey* 10).
[83] dangerous rocks and whirlpool (*Odyssey* 12).
[84] a Cyclops (*Odyssey* 19).
[85] uncle of Diomede whose life was to last until a brand taken from a fire at his birth should be consumed. The point is that to tell Diomede's story in the Trojan War (*Iliad*) one would find the long-antecedent story of Meleager quite beside the point.
[86] the ultimate origin of the Trojan War in the two eggs laid by Leda after her rape by Zeus disguised as a swan. From the eggs came Helen and Clytemnestra, and Castor and Pollux. Again, to begin here would be to trace the story too far back.
[87] carries.
[88] leaving out material which, if he handled it, might not be suitable.

What doth this Promiser such gaping worth
Afford? The Mountaines travail'd, and brought forth
A scorned Mouse! O, how much better this,
200 Who nought assaies unaptly, or amisse?
Speake to me, Muse, the Man, who after Troy *was*
                                          [*sack't,*
Saw many Townes, and Men, and could their manners
                                          [*tract.*
Hee thinkes not, how to give you smoake from light,
But light from smoake; that he may draw his bright
205 Wonders forth after: As *Antiphates,*
Scylla, Charybdis, Polypheme, with these.
Nor from the brand, with which the life did burne
Of *Meleager,* brings he the returne
Of *Diomede;* nor *Troyes* sad Warre begins
210 From the *two Egges,* that did disclose the twins.
He ever hastens to the end, and so
(As if he knew it) rapps his hearer to
The middle of his matter: letting goe
What he despaires, being handled, might not show.
215 And so well faines, so mixeth cunningly
Falshood with truth, as no man can espie
Where the midst differs from the first: or where
The last doth from the midst dis-joyn'd appeare.
Heare, what it is the People, and I desire:
220 If such a ones applause thou dost require,

That tarries till the Hangings[89] be tane downe,
And sits till the Epilogue says clap, or crowne:[90]
The customes of each age thou must observe,
And give their years and natures as they swerve,[91]
225 Fit dues. The child that now knows how to say,
And can tread firme, longs with like lads to play.
Soone angry, and soone pleas'd, is sweet, or soure,
He knowes not why, and changeth every houre.
   The unbearded youth, his Guardian being gone,
230 Loves Dogs, and Horses; and is ever one
I'th open field;[92] is waxe-like to be wrought
To every vice; as hardly to be brought
To endure Counsell: a provider slow
For his owne good, a carelesse letter-goe
235 Of Mony, haughty, to desire soone mov'd,
And then as swift to leave what he hath lov'd.
   These Studies alter now, in one growne Man;
His betterd mind seeks wealth, and friendships than,[93]
Looks after honours, and bewares to act
240 What straightway he must labour to retract.
The old man many evills doe girt round;
Either because he seeks, and having found,
Doth, wretchedly the use of things forbeare,
Or does all businesse coldly, and with feare:
245 A great differrer, long in hope, grown numbe
With sloth, yet greedy still of whats to come:
Froward, complaining; a commender glad
Of the times past, when he was a young lad,
And still correcting youth, and censuring.
250 Mans comming yeares much good with them doe
                                                    [bring,
   As his departing take much thence: lest then
   The parts of age to youth be given, or men

---

[89] curtains.

[90] (let us honor the) crown—a frequent ending to the plays of Jonson's period. Jonson adapts Horace to his own day.

[91] swarve: climb, grow.

[92] the Campus Martius in Rome, an athletic field.

[93] then.

That tarries till the hangings be ta'en downe,
And sits, till the *Epilogue* saies *Clap*, or *Crowne:*
The customes of each age thou must observe,
And give their yeares, and natures, as they swerve,
225 Fit rites. The Child, that now knowes how to say,
And can tread firme, longs with like lads to play;
Soone angry, and soone pleas'd, is sweet, or sowre,
He knowes not why, and changeth every houre.
    Th'unbearded Youth, his Guardian once being gone,
230 Loves Dogges, and Horses; and is ever one
I'the open field; Is Waxe like to be wrought
To every vice, as hardly to be brought
To endure counsell: A Provider slow
For his owne good, a carelesse letter-goe
235 Of money, haughtie, to desire soon mov'd,
And then as swift to leave what he hath lov'd.
    These studies alter now, in one, growne man;
His better'd mind seekes wealth, and friendship: than
Lookes after honours, and bewares to act
240 What straight-way he must labour to retract.
    The old man many evils doe girt round;
Either because he seekes, and, having found,
Doth wretchedly the use of things forbeare,
Or do's all businesse coldly, and with feare;
245 A great deferrer, long in hope, growne numbe
With sloth, yet greedy still of what's to come:
Froward, complaining, a commender glad
Of the times past, when he was a young lad;
And still correcting youth, and censuring.
250 Mans comming yeares much good with them doe
                                        [bring:
At his departing take much thence: lest, then,
The parts of age to youth be given; or men

To children, we must alwayes dwell, and stay,
In fitting proper adjuncts to each day.

255   The businesse either on the stage is done,
Or acted told:[94] but, ever, things that runne
In at the eare, doe stirre the mind more slow
Than those that faithfull eyes take in by show,
And the beholder to himselfe doth render.

260   Yet to the Stage at all thou maist not tender
Things worthy to be done within,[95] but take
Much from the sight, which faire Report will make
Present anon. *Medea* must not kill
Her Sons before the people: or the ill-

265   Natur'd, and wicked *Atreus* cooke to the eye
His Nephews intrailes: nor must *Progne*[96] flye
Into a Swallow there: nor *Cadmus*[97] take
Upon the stage, the figure of a Snake.
What so is shewne, I not believe, and hate.

270   Nor must the Fable,[98] that would hope the fate[99]
Once seene, to be againe call'd for, and play'd;
Have more, or lesse than just five Acts: nor lay'd
To have a god come in;[1] except a knot
Worth his untying happen there: and not

275   Any fourth man[2] to speak at all desire.
     An Actors part, and office too, the quire[3]
Must manly keep, and not be heard to sing
Between the Acts a quite cleane other thing
Than to the purpose leads, and fitly agrees.

280   It still must favour good men, and to these

---

[94] or reported. Horace is developing the classical principle of decorum.

[95] offstage.

[96] Procne, mother of Itys, whom she killed and served to Tereus, the father. When Tereus pursued Procne, she changed into a swallow.

[97] turned into a serpent when he asked the gods to remove him from the misfortunes of life.

[98] plot.

[99] feat: performance.

[1] the *deus ex machina*, god of the machine, used by classical dramatists to extricate themselves from plot difficulties.

[2] Classical drama had a maximum of three speakers on stage at any one time.

[3] the classical chorus. Its functions are outlined in the following lines.

To children; we must alwayes dwell, and stay
In fitting proper adjuncts to each day.
255　The businesse either on the Stage is done,
Or acted told. But, ever, things that run
In at the eare, doe stirre the mind more slow
Then those the faithfull eyes take in by show,
And the beholder to himselfe doth render.
260　Yet, to the Stage, at all thou maist not tender
Things worthy to be done within, but take
Much from the sight, which faire report will make
Present anone: *Medea* must not kill
Her Sonnes before the people; nor the ill-
265　Natur'd, and wicked *Atreus* Cooke, to th'eye,
His Nephews entrailes; nor must *Progne* flie
Into a Swallow there; Nor *Cadmus* take,
Upon the Stage, the figure of a Snake.
What so is showne, I not beleeve, and hate.
270　Nor must the Fable, that would hope the Fate
Once seene, to be againe call'd for, and plaid,
Have more or lesse then just five Acts: nor laid,
To have a God come in; except a knot
Worth his untying happen there: And not
275　Any fourth man, to speake at all, aspire.
An Actors parts, and Office too, the Quire
Must maintaine manly; not be heard to sing
Betweene the Acts, a quite cleane other thing
Then to the purpose leades, and fitly 'grees.
280　It still must favour good men, and to these

Be wonne a friend; it must both sway and bend
The angry, and love those that fear t'offend.
Praise the spare dyet, wholsome Justice, Lawes,
The open ports,[4] and sports that peace doth cause,
285   Hide faults, and pray to th' gods, and wish aloud
Fortune would love the poore, and leave the proud.
      The Hau-boy,[5] not as now with Latten[6] bound,
And rivall with the Trumpet for his sound,
But soft and simple, at few holes breath'd time,
290   And tune too, fitted to the Chorus Rime,
As loud enough to fill the Seats, not yet
So over-thick, but where the people met,
They might with ease be numbred, being a few
Chast, thrifty, modest folk, that came to view.
295   But as they conquer'd, and inlarg'd their bound,
The wider walls imbrac't their City round,
And they un-censur'd might at feasts, and playes,
Steep the glad Genius in the Wine, whole dayes,
Both in their Tunes the license greater grew,
300   And in their Numbers; for alas, what knew
The Idiot, keeping holy day, or drudge,
Clowne, townsman, base, and noble, mixt to judge?
Thus to his ancient art the piper lent
Gesture, and Riot, whilst he wandring went
305   In his train'd[8] Gown, about the stage, thus grew
To the grave Harp, and Violl voyces new;
The rash and headlong eloquence brought forth,
Unwonted language; and that sense of worth
That found out profit, and fore-told each thing,
310   Now differ'd not from *Delphick* ridling.[10]
      He too, that did in Tragicke Verse contend
For the vile Goat,[11] soone after forth did send

[4] gates (of Janus), symbolically opened in ancient Rome in times of peace.
[5] oboe.
[6] brass.
[8] with a train.

[10] The oracle at Delphi was famous for the obscurity of its statements.
[11] the prize at the dramatic festivals.

Be wonne a friend; It must both sway, and bend
The angry, and love those that feare t'offend.
Praise the spare diet, wholsome justice, lawes,
Peace, and the open ports, that peace doth cause.
285 Hide faults, pray to the Gods, and wish aloud
Fortune would love the poore, and leave the proud.
    The Hau'-boy, not as now with latten bound,
And rivall with the Trumpet for his sound,
But soft, and simple, at few holes breath'd time
290 And tune too, fitted to the *Chorus* rime,
As loud enough to fill the seates, not yet
So over-thick, but, where the people met,
They might with ease be numbred, being a few
Chaste, thriftie, modest folke, that came to view.
295 But, as they conquer'd, and enlarg'd their bound,
That wider Walls embrac'd their Citie round,
And they uncensur'd might at Feasts, and Playes
Steepe the glad *Genius* in the Wine, whole dayes,
Both in their tunes, the licence greater grew,
300 And in their numbers; For, alas, what knew
The Ideot, keeping holy-day, or drudge,
Clowne, Towns-man, base, and noble, mix'd, to judge?
Thus, to his antient Art the Piper lent
Gesture, and riot, whilst he swooping[7] went
305 In his train'd Gowne about the Stage: So grew
In time to Tragedie, a Musicke new.[9]
The rash, and head-long eloquence brought forth
Unwonted language; And that sense of worth
That found out profit, and foretold each thing
310 Now differ'd not from *Delphick* riddling.
319 Hee too, that did in Tragick Verse contend,
320 For the vile Goat, soone after, forth did send

[7] sweeping.
[9] For the ancients the lyre was
more antique than the flute.

The rough rude Satyrs[12] naked, and would trye,
Though sower, with safety[13] of his gravity,
315 How he could jest; because he mark't & saw
The free spectators subject to no law,
Having well eate and drunke: the Rites[14] being done,
Were to be staid[15] with softnesses, and wonne
With something, that was acceptably new.
320 Yet so the scoffing Satyrs to mens view,
And so their pratling to present were best,
And so to turne our earnest into jest,
As[16] neither any god, be brought in there,
Or semi-god, that late was seene to weare
325 A royall Crown, and Scarlet, be made hop,
With poore base termes, through every baser shop:
Or, whilst he shuns the earth, to catch the aire,
And empty clouds. For Tragedy is faire,
And farre unworthy to blurt out light Rimes;
330 But, as a Matron drawne at solemne times
To dance,[17] so she should, shame-fac'd, differ farre
From what th'obscœne, and petulant[18] Satyres are.
   Nor I, when I write Satyres, will so love
Plaine phrase, my *Piso's*, as alone t'approve
335 Meere raigning[19] words: nor will I labour so
Quite from all face of Tragedy to goe,
As not make difference whether *Davus*[20] speake,
And the bold *Pythias*,[21] having cheated weake
Simo, and of a talent cleans'd his purse;
340 Or old *Silenus*,[22] *Bacchus* Guard, and nurse.

[12] the satyr drama, which followed the Greek trilogies in a performance. Its chorus was made up of Satyrs.

[13] without damage to.

[14] for Dionysius, in whose honor the dramas were performed.

[15] soothed.

[16] so that.

[17] The Roman matron might properly dance only at religious festivals.

[18] wanton.

[19] established.

[20] type name for a slave in comedy.

[21] girl in a lost comedy who cheated Simo, her master.

[22] oldest and wisest of the Satyrs; tutor and companion of Bacchus.

The rough rude Satyres naked; and would try,
Though sower, with safetie of his gravitie,
How he could jest, because he mark'd and saw
The free spectators, subject to no Law,
325 Having well eat, and drunke: the rites being done,
Were to be staid with softnesses, and wonne
With something that was acceptably new.
Yet so the scoffing Satyres to mens view,
And so their prating to present was best,
330 And so to turne all earnest into jest,
As neither any God, were brought in there,
Or Semi-god, that late was seene to weare
A royall Crowne, and purple; be made hop
With poore base termes, through every baser shop:
335 Or, whilst he shuns the Earth, to catch at Aire
And emptie Clowdes. For Tragedie is faire,
And farre unworthy to blurt out light rimes;
But, as a Matrone drawne at solemne times
To Dance, so she should, shamefac'd, differ farre
340 From what th'obscene, and petulant Satyres are.
   Nor I, when I write Satyres, will so love
Plaine phrase, my *Piso's*, as alone, t'approve
Meere raigning words: nor will I labour so
Quite from all face of Tragedie to goe,
345 As not make difference, whether *Davus* speake,
And the bold *Pythias*, having cheated weake
Simo; and, of a talent wip'd his purse;
Or old *Silenus*, *Bacchus* guard, and Nurse.

I can, out of knowne stuff, a Fable frame,
And so, as every man may hope the same:
Yet he that offers at[24] it, may sweat much,
And toyle in vaine: the excellence is such
345   Of order, and connexion; so much grace
There comes sometimes to things of meanest place;
But let the Faunes,[25] drawne from the groves beware,
Be I their judge, they doe at no time dare,
Like men Town-born, and neare the place[26] rehearse,
350   Or play young tricks in over-wanton verse;
Or cracke out shamefull speeches, or uncleane.
The Roman Gentry, men of birth, and meane,[28]
Take just offence at this: nor, though it strike
Him that buyes Pulse[29] there, or perhaps may like
355   The nut-crackers[30] throughout, will they therfore
Receive, or give it any Crowne the more.
        Two rests,[31] a short, & long, th'*Iambicke* frame,
A foote, whose swiftnesse gave the verse the name
Of Trimeter, when yet it was sixe-pac'd,[32]
360   But meere *Iambicks* all, from first to last.
Nor is't long since they did with patience take[33]
Into their Birth-right, and for fitnesse sake,
The steady *Spondæes;* so themselves to beare
More slow,[34] and come more weighty to the eare:
365   Provided, ne're to yield, in any case
Of fellowship, the fourth, or second place.[35]
This foote yet in the famous Trimeters
Of *Accius,*[36] and *Ennius,*[37] rare appeares;

---

[24] attempts.

[25] with the Satyrs, companions of Dionysius.

[26] i.e., the Forum.

[28] of means.

[29] pulse: peas; *chiches blanch't:* scalded peas, eaten by the poor.

[30] i.e., noisy people at the performance.

[31] syllables (rather than pauses).

[32] with six feet.

[33] i.e., as substitute feet.

[34] Jonson intends "More slow" to be a spondee.

[35] Latin poetry did not permit the substitution of a spondee for an iamb in the second or fourth foot of a line.

[36] Roman playwright, c. 100 B.C.

[37] writer of tragedies, 239–170 B.C.

      I can out of knowne geare,[23] a fable frame,
350 And so, as every man may hope the same;
      Yet he that offers at it, may sweat much,
      And toile in vaine: the excellence is such
      Of Order, and Connexion; so much grace
      There comes sometimes to things of meanest place.
355 But, let the *Faunes*, drawne from their Groves, beware,
      Be I their Judge, they doe at no time dare
      Like men street-borne, and neere the Hall,[27] reherse
      Their youthfull tricks in over-wanton verse:
      Or crack out bawdie speeches, and uncleane.
360 The Roman Gentrie, Men of Birth, and Meane
      Will take offence, at this: Nor, though it strike
      Him that buyes chiches blanch't,[29] or chance to like
      The nut-crackers throughout, will they therefore
364 Receive, or give it an applause, the more.
371   Two rests, a short and long, th'*Iambick* frame;
      A foot, whose swiftnesse gave the Verse the name
      Of *Trimeter*, when yet it was sixe-pac'd,
      But meere *Iambicks* all, from first to last.
375 Nor is't long since, they did with patience take
      Into their birth-right, and for fitnesse sake,
      The steadie *Spondæes*; so themselves doe beare
      More slow, and come more weightie to the eare:
      Provided, ne're to yeeld, in any case
380 Of fellowship, the fourth, or second place.
      This foot yet, in the famous *Trimeters*
      Of *Accius*, and *Ennius*, rare appeares:

[23] material.   [27] Westminster (H&S).

So rare as with some taxe it doth engage
370   Those heavy verses sent so to the stage
Of too much hast, and negligence in part,
Or a worse crime, the ignorance of art:
But every Judge hath not the faculty
To note, in Poëms, breach of harmony;
375   And there is given too unworthy leave
To *Roman* Poets: shall I therefore weave
My verse at randome, and licentiously?
Or rather, thinking all my faults may spy,
Grow a safe Writer, and be wary-driven[38]
380   Within the hope of having all forgiven.
'Tis cleare, this way I have got off from blame,
But in conclusion merited no fame.
Take you[39] the *Greeks* examples, for your light,
In hand, and turne them over, day, and night.
385   Your Ancestors, old *Plautus* numbers prais'd,
And jests, and both to admiration rais'd,
Too patiently,[40] that I not fondly say;
If either you, or I know any way
To part scurrility from wit: or can
390   A lawfull Verse, by th'eare, or finger scan.[41]
      Thespis[42] is said to be the first, found out
The Tragœdy, and carried it about,
Till then unknown, in Carts, wherein did ride
Those that did sing, and act: their faces dy'd
395   With lees of Wine. Next *Æschilus*[43] more late
Brought in the visor, and the robe of state,
Built a small-timber'd stage, and taught them talke
Lofty, and great; and in the Buskin walk.
      To these succeeded the old Comœdy,[44]
400   And not without much praise; till liberty

[38] a coinage.
[39] the Pisos.
[40] tolerantly.
[41] i.e., by counting the rhythm on the fingers.
[42] originator of Greek drama by developing an actor apart from the chorus of Dionysius.
[43] supposed to have invented the masques worn by actors, the costumes, and the fixed stage.
[44] of Aristophanes.

So rare, as with some taxe it doth ingage
Those heavie Verses sent so to the Stage,
385 Of too much haste, and negligence in part,
Or a worse Crime, the ignorance of art.
But every Judge hath not the facultie
To note in Poëmes, breach of harmonie;
And there is given too, unworthy leave
390 To Roman Poëts. Shall I therefore weave
My Verse at randome, and licentiously?
Or rather, thinking all my faults may spie,
Grow a safe Writer, and be warie-driven
Within the hope of having all forgiven?
395 'Tis cleare, this way I have got off from blame,
But, in conclusion, merited no fame.
Take you the Greeke Examples, for your light,
In hand, and turne them over day, and night.
    Our Ancestors did *Plautus* numbers praise,
400 And jests; and both to admiration raise
Too patiently, that I not fondly say;
If either you, or I, know the right way
To part scurrilitie from wit: or can
404 A lawfull Verse, by th'eare, or finger scan.
311   *Thespis* is said to be the first found out
The Tragedie, and carried it about,
Till then unknowne, in Carts, wherein did ride
Those that did sing, and act: their faces dy'd
315 With lees of Wine. Next *Eschylus*, more late
Brought in the Visor, and the robe of State,
Built a small timbred Stage, and taught them talke
318 Loftie, and grave; and in the buskin stalke.
365   To these succeeded the old Comœdie,
And not without much praise; till libertie

Fell into fault so farre, as[45] now they saw
Her force was fit to be restrain'd by law:
Which law receiv'd, the Chorus held his peace,[46]
His power of fowly hurting made to cease.

405   Our[47] Poets, too, left nought unproved[48] here:
Nor did they merit the lesse Crowne to weare,
In daring to forsake the *Græcian* Tracts,[49]
And celebrating their owne home-born facts:
Whether the guarded[50] Tragœdy they wrought,

410   Or 'twere the gowned[51] Comœdy they taught.
Nor had our *Italy* more glorious bin
In vertue, and renowne of Armes, than in
Her language, if the stay,[52] and care t'have mended
Had not our every Poet like offended.

415   But you, *Pompilius* off-spring,[53] spare you not
To taxe that Verse, which many a day and blot[54]
Have not kept in, and (least perfection faile)
Not, ten times o're, corrected to the naile.[55]
Because *Democritus*[56] believes a wit

420   Happier than wretched Art, and doth by it
Exclude all sober Poets from their share
In *Helicon;*[57] a great sort[58] will not pare
Their nails, nor shave their beards, but seek by-paths
In secret places, flee the public baths.[59]

425   For so, they shall not onely gaine the worth,
But fame of Poets, if they can come forth,

---

[45] that.

[46] The chorus declined and then disappeared in later Greek comedy.

[47] Roman.

[48] untried.

[49] tracks, i.e., traditional subjects.

[50] *praetexta*: in a toga edged with purple, worn by magistrates. Roman rather than Greek.

[51] Roman rather than Greek.

[52] self-control.

[53] The Pisos claimed to be descended from Numa Pompilius.

[54] correction.

[55] a Latin metaphor taken from sculpture: to the most sensitive degree.

[56] the "laughing" epicurean philosopher of Abdera; Cicero reports him to have denied the value of poetry (*de Div.* 1.37.80).

[57] haunt of the Muses.

[58] number.

[59] i.e., the Roman beatniks disliked cleanliness and grooming.

Fell into fault so farre, as now they saw
Her licence fit to be restrain'd by law:
Which law receiv'd, the *Chorus* held his peace,
370   His power of fouely hurting made to cease.
405   Our Poëts, too, left nought unproved here;
Nor did they merit the lesse Crowne to weare,
In daring to forsake the *Grecian* tracts,
And celebrating our owne home-borne facts;
Whether the guarded *Tragedie* they wrought,
410   Or 'twere the gowned *Comœdy* they taught.
     Nor had our *Italie* more glorious bin
In vertue, and renowne of armes, then in
Her language, if the Stay, and Care t'have mended,
Had not our every Poët like offended.
415   But you, *Pompilius* off-spring, spare you not
To taxe that Verse, which many a day, and blot
Have not kept in; and (lest perfection faile)
Not ten times o're, corrected to the naile.
Because *Democritus* beleeves a wit
420   Happier then wretched art, and doth, by it,
Exclude all sober Poëts, from their share
In *Helicon*; a great sort will not pare
Their nailes, nor shave their beards, but to by-paths
Retire themselves, avoid the publike baths;
425   For so, they shall not only gaine the worth,
But fame of Poëts, they thinke, if they come forth,

And from the Barber *Licinus*[60] conceale
The head that three *Anticira's*[61] cannot heale.
O I, left-witted,[62] that purge every spring
430   For Choler![63] if I did not, none could bring
Out better Poems: but I cannot buy
My title at their rate. I had rather, I,
Be like a whetstone, that an edge can put
On steele, though 't selfe be dull, and cannot cut.
435   I, writing nought my selfe, will teach them yet
Their charge,[65] and office, whence their wealth to
                                         [fet,[66]

What[67] nourisheth, what formed, what begot
The Poet, what becommeth, and what not:
Whether truth will, and whether errour bring.
440   The very root of writing well, and spring[68]
Is to be wise, thy matter first to know,
Which the *Socratick* writing[69] best can show:
And, where the matter is provided still,
There words will never follow 'gainst their will.
445   He that hath studied well the debt, and knowes
What to his Country, what his friends he owes,
What height of love a Parent will fit best,
What brethren, what a stranger, and his guest,
Can tell a States-mans duty, what the Arts
450   And office of a Judge are, what the parts
Of a brave Chiefe sent to the warres, he can
Indeed give fitting dues to every man.
And I still bid the learned maker look
On life, and manners, and make those his booke:
455   Thence draw forth true expressions, for somtimes,
A Poëm, of no grace, waight, art in Rimes,

[60] some unknown barber.

[61] a town in Phocis where grew hellebore, used to treat madness.

[62] i.e., fool that I am.

[63] one of the four humors of the body (phlegm, choler, blood, and melancholy). Its excess was purged to return one to a proper mixture, or temperament, of the four.

[65] responsibility.

[66] fetch.

[67] whatever.

[68] root and spring of writing well.

[69] Plato and Xenophon.

And from the Barber *Licinus* conceale
Their heads, which three *Anticyra's* cannot heale.
O I left-witted, that purge every spring
430 For choller! If I did not, who could bring
Out better Poëms? But[64] I cannot buy
My title, at their rate, I'ad rather, I,
Be like a Whet-stone, that an edge can put
On steele, though 't selfe be dull, and cannot cut.
435 I writing nought my selfe, will teach them yet
Their Charge, and Office, whence their wealth to fet,

What nourisheth, what formed, what begot
The Poët, what becommeth, and what not:
Whether truth may, and whether error bring.
440   The very root of writing well, and spring
Is to be wise; thy matter first to know;
Which the *Socratick* writings best can show:
And, where the matter is provided still,
There words will follow, not against their will.
445 Hee, that hath studied well the debt, and knowes
What to his Countrey, what his friends he owes,
What height of love, a Parent will fit best,
What brethren, what a stranger, and his guest,
Can tell a States-mans dutie, what the arts
450 And office of a Judge are, what the parts
Of a brave Chiefe sent to the warres: He can,
Indeed, give fitting dues to every man.
And I still bid the learned Maker looke,
On life, and manners, and make those his booke,
455 Thence draw forth true expressions. For, sometimes,
A Poëme, of no grace, weight, art, in rimes

64 but since.

With specious places,[70] and being humour'd[71] right,
More strongly takes the people with delight,
And better stayes[72] them there than all fine noyse
460 Of empty Verses, and meere tinckling toyes.
The Muse not onely gave the *Greeks* a wit,
But a well compass'd mouth[73] to utter it,
Being men[74] were covetous of nought but praise.
Our *Roman* youthes they[75] learne more thriving wayes
465 How to divide into a hundred parts,
A pound, or piece,[76] by their long counting Arts;
There's *Albin's*[78] sonne will say, subtract an ounce
From the five ounces, what remaines? pronounce
A third of twelve, you may: foure ounces: Glad,
470 He cryes, good boy, thou'lt keep thine owne: now adde

An Ounce, what makes it then? the halfe pound just,
Six Ounces:[79] O, when once the canker'd rust,
And care of getting thus our minds hath stain'd,
Thinke we, or hope, there can be verses feign'd
475 In juyce of Cædar[80] worthy to be steep'd,
And in smooth Cypresse boxes to be keep'd?
Poets would either profit, or delight,
Or mixing sweet, and fit, teach life the right.
     Be briefe in what thou wouldst command, that so
480 The docill mind may soon thy precepts know,
And hold them faithfully; for nothing rests,
But flowes out, that ore swelleth in full brests.
Let what thou feign'st for pleasure sake, be neare
The truth; nor let thy Fable think, what e're

[70] beautiful passages.
[71] i.e., characterized.
[72] suits.
[73] smooth language.
[74] as (ideal) men (they).
[75] omit.
[76] of money.
[78] not identified in the make-believe school lesson which fol-lows.

[79] The Roman *as*, translated *pound*, was twelve *unciae* or *ounces*.

[80] Cedar oil was used on the back of book rolls to prevent decay. They were stored in boxes made of cypress wood.

With specious places, and being humour'd right,
More strongly takes the people with delight,
And better stayes them there, then all fine noise
460 Of verse meere-matter-lesse, and tinckling toies.
 The Muse not only gave the *Greek's* a wit
But a well-compass'd mouth to utter it;
Being men were covetous of nought, but praise.
Our Roman Youths they learne the subtle wayes
465 How to divide, into a hundred parts,
A pound, or piece, by their long compting arts:[77]
There's *Albin's* sonne will say, Substract an ounce
From the five ounces; what remaines? pronounce
A third of twelve, you may: foure ounces. Glad,
470 He cries, Good boy, thou'lt keepe thine owne. Now,
                                                [adde
An ounce, what makes it then? The halfe pound just;
Sixe ounces. O, when once the canker'd rust,
And care of getting, thus, our minds hath stain'd,
Thinke wee, or hope, there can be Verses fain'd
475 In juyce of *Cedar*, worthy to be steep'd,
And in smooth *Cypresse* boxes to be keep'd?
Poëts would either profit, or delight,
478 Or mixing sweet, and fit, teach life the right.
503   Be briefe, in what thou wouldst command, that so
The docile mind may soone thy precepts know,
505 And hold them faithfully; For nothing rests,
But flowes out, that ore-swelleth in full brests.
 Let what thou fain'st for pleasures sake, be neere[81]
The truth; nor let thy Fable thinke, what e're

[77] long counting: difficult be-   [81] near.
cause of the Roman numerals.

485   It would, must be: lest it alive would draw
     The child, when *Lamia'*[82] has din'd, out of her maw.
     The Poëms voyd of profit, our[83] grave men
     Cast out by voyces; want[84] they pleasure, then
     Our gallants give them none, but passe them by:
490   But he hath every suffrage can[85] apply
     Sweet mix'd with soure, to his reader, so
     As doctrine and delight together goe.
     This book will get thee *Sosij*[86] money; this
     Will passe the Seas; and long as Nature is,
495   With honour make the far-known Author live.
     There are yet faults, which we would well forgive,
     For, neither doth the string still yield that sound,
     The hand, and mind would; but it will rebound
     Oft-times a sharp, when we require a flat:
500   Nor always doth the loosed bow hit that
     Which it doth threaten:[87] Therefore, where I see
     Much in a Poëm shine, I will not be
     Offended with few spots, which negligence
     Hath shed, or humane frailty not kept thence.
505   How then? why, as a Scrivener, if h' offend
     Still in the same, and warned, will not mend,
     Deserves no pardon; or who'd play and sing
     Is laught at, that still jarreth in one string:
     So he that flaggeth[88] much, becomes to me
510   A *Chœrilus*,[89] in whom if I but see
     Twice, or thrice good, I wonder: but am more
     Angry, if once I heare good *Homer* snore.
     Though I confesse, that, in a long work, sleep
     May, with some right, upon an Author creep.
515   As Painting, so is Poësie: some mans hand
     Will take you more, the nearer that you stand;

[82] Lybian queen whom Jupiter loved. Juno destroyed her children, and she in turn ate the children of others.
[83] which our.
[84] if they lack.
[85] approval who can.

[86] Roman booksellers.
[87] aim at.
[88] lacks much or has many faults.
[89] an inferior epic writer who celebrated Alexander the Great.

It would, must be: lest it alive would draw
510 The Child, when *Lamia*'has din'd, out of her maw.
The *Poëms* void of profit, our grave men
Cast out by voyces; want they pleasure, then
Our Gallants give them none, but passe them by:
But he hath every suffrage, can apply
515 Sweet mix'd with sowre, to his Reader, so
As doctrine, and delight together go.
This booke will get the *Sosii* money; This
Will passe the Seas, and long as nature is,
With honour make the farre-knowne Author live.
520   There are yet faults, which we would well forgive,
For, neither doth the String still yeeld that sound
The hand, and mind would, but it will resound
Oft-times a Sharpe, when we require a Flat:
Nor alwayes doth the loosed Bow, hit that
525 Which it doth threaten. Therefore, where I see
Much in the *Poëme* shine, I will not bee
Offended with few spots, which negligence
Hath shed, or humane frailtie not kept thence.
How then? Why, as a Scrivener, if h'offend
530 Still in the same, and warned will not mend,
Deserves no pardon; or who'd play, and sing
Is laugh'd at, that still jarreth on one string:
So he that flaggeth much, becomes to me
A *Chœrilus*, in whom if I but see
535 Twice, or thrice good, I wonder: but am more
Angry. Sometimes, I heare good *Homer* snore.
But, I confesse, that, in a long worke, sleepe
May, with some right, upon an Author creepe.
As Painting, so is Poësie. Some mans hand
540 Will take you more, the neerer that you stand;

As some the farther off: this loves the dark.
This, fearing not the subtlest Judges mark,
Will in the light be view'd: this, once, the sight
520 Doth please, this ten times over will delight.
You Sir, the elder brother, though you are
Informed rightly; by your Fathers care,
And, of your selfe too understand; yet mind
This saying: to some things there is assign'd
525 A meane, and tolleration, which doth well.
There may a Lawyer be, may not excell;
Or pleader at the Barre; that may come short
Of eloquent *Mesala's*[90] powers in Court;
Or knowes not what *Cassellius Aulus*[91] can:
530 Yet, there's a value given to this man.
But neither men, nor gods, nor Pillars[92] meant
Poets should ever be indifferent.[93]
As jarring Musick doth at jolly feasts,
Or thick grosse oyntment, but offend the guests,
535 Poppy, with hony of *Sardus*;[94] 'cause without
These, the glad Meal, might have bin wel drawn out;

So any Poëm fancy'd, or forth-brought
To bettering of the mind of man in ought,
If ne're so little it depart[95] the first,
540 And highest; it sinketh to the lowest, and worst.
He that not knowes the games, nor how to use
The Armes in *Mars*, his field,[96] he doth refuse;
Or who's unskilfull at the Coyt,[97] or Ball,
Or trundling wheele,[98] he can sit still[99] from all:
545 Lest the throng'd rings should a free laughter take:
Yet who's most ignorant, dares Verses make.

[90] M. Valerius Messala Corvinus (64 B.C.–A.D. 9), orator, general, statesman.
[91] eminent jurist, contemporary of Cicero.
[92] posts in front of a bookseller's shop on which books were tied for customers to examine.
[93] merely average.

[94] Poppy seeds were roasted and served with honey as a delicacy. If the honey was bitter (as was Sardinian), it spoiled them.
[95] fall below first rank.
[96] the Campus Martius.
[97] quoit.
[98] hoop.
[99] aloof.

As some the farther off: This loves the darke;
This, fearing not the subtlest Judges marke
Will in the light be view'd: This once, the sight
Doth please; this, ten times over, will delight.
545   You Sir, the elder brother, though you are
Informed rightly, by your Fathers care,
And, of your selfe too, understand; yet mind
This saying: To some things there is assign'd
A meane, and toleration, which does well:
550 There may a Lawyer be, may not excell;
Or Pleader at the Barre, that may come short
Of eloquent *Messalla's* power in Court,
Or knowes not what *Cassellius Aulus* can;
Yet, there's a value given to this man.
555 But neither, Men, nor Gods, nor Pillars meant,
Poëts should ever be indifferent.
    As jarring Musique doth, at jolly feasts,
Or thick grosse ointment, but offend the Guests:
As Poppie, and *Sardane* honey; 'cause without
560 These, the free meale might have beene well drawne
                                                  [out:
So, any *Poëme*, fancied, or forth-brought
To bettring of the mind of man, in ought,
If ne're so little it depart the first,
And highest; sinketh to the lowest, and worst.
565   Hee, that not knowes the games, nor how to use
His armes in *Mars* his field, he doth refuse;
Or, who's unskilfull at the Coit, or Ball,
Or trundling Wheele, he can sit still, from all;
Lest the throng'd heapes should on a laughter take:
570 Yet who's most ignorant, dares Verses make.

Why not; being honest, and free-borne, doth hate
Vice, and is knowne to have a Knights estate.
    Thou, such thy judgement is, thy knowledge too,
550 Wilt nothing against Nature[1] speak, or doe:
But, if hereafter thou shalt write, not feare
To send it to be judg'd by *Metius*[2] eare,
And to your fathers, and to mine; though't be
Nine yeares kept by,[3] your papers in, y'are free
555 To change, & mend, what you not forth do set.
The word once out, never returned yet.
    Orpheus,[4] a Priest, and speaker for the gods,
First frighted men, that wildly liv'd in woods,
From slaughters, and foule life; and for the same
560 Was Tygers said, and Lyons fierce to tame:
Amphion[5] too, that built the *Theban* towers,
Was said to move the stones by his Lutes powers,
And lead them with his soft songs, where he would:
This was the wisedome that they had of old,
565 Things sacred from prophane to separate;
The publicke from the private; to abate
Wild ranging lusts, prescribe the marriage good,
Build townes, and carve the lawes in leaves of wood.[7]
And thus at first, an honour, and a name
570 To divine Poets, and their verses came.
Next these, great *Homer*, and *Tyrtæus*[8] set
On edge the Masculine spirits, and did whet
Their minds to wars, with rimes they did rehearse:
The Oracles too were given out in verse;
575 All way of life was shewn; the grace of Kings
Attempted by the Muses tunes, and strings:

---

[1] So Jonson translates *Minerva*.
[2] Maecius Torpa, critic who supervised the plays at the dedication of a theater erected by Pompey in 55 B.C.
[3] i.e., not published.
[4] mythological musician and oracle whose song could tame wild beasts.

[5] another musician, who built Thebes by the sound of his lyre.
[7] a very early way to preserve writing, as the laws of Solon were said to be inscribed.
[8] lame Greek schoolmaster who composed military songs for the Spartans, seventh century B.C.

Why not? I'm gentle, and free-borne, doe hate
Vice, and, am knowne to have a Knights estate.
Thou, such thy judgement is, thy knowledge too,
Wilt nothing against nature speake, or doe:
575   But, if hereafter thou shalt write, not feare
To send it to be judg'd by *Metius* eare,
And, to your Fathers, and to mine; though 't be
Nine yeares kept in, your papers by, yo'are free
To change, and mend, what you not forth doe set.
580   The Writ, once out, never returned yet.
479   *Orpheus*, a priest, and speaker for the Gods
First frighted men, that wildly liv'd, at ods,
From slaughters, and foule life; and for the same
Was Tigers, said, and Lyons fierce, to tame.
Amphion, too, that built the *Theban* towres,
Was said to move the stones, by his Lutes powers,
485   And lead them with soft songs, where that[6] he would.
This was the wisdome, that they had of old,
Things sacred, from profane to separate;
The publike, from the private; to abate
Wild raging lusts; prescribe the mariage good;
490   Build Townes, and carve the Lawes in leaves of wood.
And thus at first, an honour, and a name
To divine Poëts, and their Verses came.
Next these great *Homer* and *Tyrtæus* set
On edge the Masculine spirits, and did whet
495   Their minds to Warres, with rimes they did rehearse;
The Oracles, too, were given out in Verse;
All way of life was shewen; the grace of Kings
Attempted by the Muses tunes, and strings;

[6] wherever.

Playes were found out; and rest, the end, & crowne
Of their long labours, was in verse set downe.
Lest of the singer *Apollo*, and Muses fam'd
580 Upon the Lyre, thou chance to be asham'd.
'Tis now inquir'd which makes the nobler verse,
Nature, or Art. My judgement will not peirce
Into the profits, what a meer rude braine
Can,[9] or all toyle, without a wealthy vaine:[10]
585 So doth the one, the others helpe require,
And friendly should unto their end conspire.
He that's ambitious in the race to touch
The wished Goale, both did and suffered much
While he was young: he sweat, and freez'd again,
590 And both from wine and women did abstaine.
Who now to sing the *Pythian* Rites[11] is heard,
Did learne them first, and once a Master feard.
But, now, it is enough to say, I make
An admirable verse: the great Scab take
595 Him that is last, I scorne to be behind,
Or, of the things, that ne're came in my mind,
Once say I'me ignorant: Just as a Cryer,
That to the sale of wares calls every buyer,
So doth the Poet, that is rich in Land,
600 Or wealthy in monyes out at use,[13] command
His praisers to their gaine: but say he can
Make a greate Supper, or for some poore man
Will be a surety, or can helpe him out
Of an intangling suit, or bring't about,
605 I wonder how this happy man should know,
Whether his soothing friend speake truth, or no.
But, you, my *Piso*, carefully beware,
Whether y'are given to, or giver are,
You doe not bring to judge your verses one
610 With joy of what is given him over-gone:[14]

[9] can do.
[10] vein (of genius).
[11] At the Pythian games a flute performance represented in music the victory of Apollo over the Python.
[13] interest.
[14] overenthusiastic.

Playes were found out; and rest, the end, and crowne
500　Of their long labours, was in Verse set downe:
All which I tell, lest when *Apollo*'s nam'd,
502　Or *Muse*, upon the Lyre, thou chance b'asham'd.
581　　'Tis now inquir'd, which makes the nobler Verse,
Nature, or Art. My Judgement will not pierce
Into the Profits, what a meere rude braine
Can; or all toile, without a wealthie veine:
585　So doth the one, the others helpe require,
And friendly should unto one end conspire.
　　Hee, that's ambitious in the race to touch
The wished goale, both did, and suffer'd much
While he was young; he sweat; and freez'd againe:
590　And both from Wine, and Women did abstaine.
Who, since, to sing the *Pythian* rites is heard,
Did learne them first, and once a Master fear'd.
But, now, it is enough to say; I make
An admirable Verse. The great Scurfe[12] take
595　Him that is last, I scorne to come behind,
Or, of the things, that ne're came in my mind
To say, I'm ignorant. Just as a Crier
That to the sale of Wares calls every Buyer;
So doth the Poet, who is rich in land,
600　Or great in money's out at use, command
His flatterers to their gaine. But say, he can
Make a great Supper; or for some poore man
Will be a suretie; or can helpe him out
Of an entangling suit; and bring 't about:
605　I wonder how this happie man should know,
Whether his soothing friend speake truth, or no.
But you, my *Piso*, carefully beware,
(Whether yo'are given to, or giver are.)
You doe not bring, to judge your Verses, one,
610　With joy of what is given him, over-gone:

---

[12] scab. These are words said by
children at play: The Devil take
the hindmost.

For he'le cry good, brave, better, excellent!
Look pale, distill a dew was never meant
Out at his friendly eyes, leap, beat the ground!
As those that hir'd to weep at funeralls sound,
615 Cry, and doe more than the true mourners, so
The scoffer, the true prayser doth out-goe.[15]
Great men are said with many cups to plye,
And rack[16] with wine the man whom they would try,[17]
If of their friendship to be worthy or no;
620 When you make verses, with your judge doe so:
Looke through him, and be sure you take no mocks
For praises, where the mind harbours a Foxe.
If to *Quinctilius*[18] you recited ought,
He'd say, mend this my friend, and this, 'tis nought.

625 If you deny'd, you[19] had no better straine,
And twice, or thrice assay'd it, but in vain;
He'd bid blot all; and to the Anvill bring
Those ill-torn'd verses to new hammering.
Then, if your fault you rather had defend
630 Then change; no word nor work more would he spend
In vaine, but you, and yours you should love still
Alone, without a rivall, at your will.
A good and wise man will crye open shame
On artlesse Verse; the hard ones he will blame:
635 Blot out the carelesse with his turned[20] pen;
Cut off superfluous ornaments; and, when
They're dark, bid cleare 'hem; al thats doubtful wrote

Dispute;[21] and what is to be changed, note:
Become an *Aristarchus*:[22] And, not say,
640 Why should I grieve a friend this trifling way?

[15] surpass.
[16] ply.
[17] test.
[18] Quintilius Varius of Cremona, friend of Virgil and Horace.
[19] If you denied, (saying that) you.
[20] perhaps, reversed, or brought back (L. *transverso*).
[21] question.
[22] greatest ancient critic, second century B.C.

For hee'll cry, *Good, brave, better, excellent!*
Looke pale, distill a showre (was never meant)
Out at his friendly eyes, leape, beat the groun'.
As those that hir'd to weepe at Funeralls, swoune,
615 Cry, and doe more then the true Mourners: so
The Scoffer, the true Praiser doth out-goe.
    Rich men are said with many cups to plie,
And rack, with Wine, the man whom they would try,
If of their friendship he be worthy, or no:
620 When you write Verses, with your judge do so:
Looke through him, and be sure, you take not mocks
For praises, where the mind conceales a foxe.
    If to *Quintilius*, you recited ought:
Hee'd say, Mend this, good friend, and this; 'Tis
                                    [naught.
625 If you denied, you had no better straine,
And twice, or thrice had 'ssayd it, still in vaine:
Hee'd bid, blot all: and to the anvile bring
Those ill-torn'd Verses, to new hammering.
Then: If your fault you rather had defend
630 Then change. No word, or worke, more would he spend
In vaine, but you, and yours, you should love still
Alone, without a rivall, by his will.
    A wise, and honest man will cry out shame
On artlesse Verse; the hard ones he will blame;
635 Blot out the carelesse, with his turned pen;
Cut off superfluous ornaments; and when
They're darke, bid cleare this: all that's doubtfull
                                    [wrote
Reprove; and, what is to be changed, note:
Become an *Aristarchus*. And, not say,
640 Why should I grieve my friend, this trifling way?

These trifles into serious mischiefs lead
The man once mock'd, and suffered[23] wrong to tread.
  Those that are wise, a furious Poet feare,
And flye to touch him, as a man that were
645 Infected with the Leprosie, or had
The yellow jaundis, or were truely mad,
Under the angry Moon.[24] but then the boys
They[25] vexe, and carelesse follow him with noise.
This, while he belcheth lofty Verses out,
650 And stalketh, like a Fowler, round about,
Busie to catch a Black-bird; if he fall
Into a pit, or hole, although he call
And crye aloud, Helpe, gentle Country-men;
There's none will take the care to help him, then.
655 For, if one should, and with a rope make hast
To let it downe, who knowes, if he did cast
Himselfe there purposely, or no; and would
Not thence be sav'd, although indeed he could?
Ile tell you but the death, and the disease
660 Of the *Sycilian* Poet, *Empedocles*;[26]
He, while he labour'd to be thought a god
Immortall, took a melancholick,[27] odd
Conceipt, and into burning *Ætna* leap't:
Let Poets perish that will not be kept.[28]
665 He that preserves a man against his will,
Doth the same thing with him that would him kill.
Nor did he do this,[29] once; if yet you can,
Now, bring him backe, he'le be no more a man,
Or love of this his famous death lay by.
670 Here's one makes verses, but there's none knows why:
Whether h'hath pissed upon his Fathers grave:
Or the sad thunder-strucken thing he have,

[23] permitted.
[24] thought to cause madness.
Cf. lunatic: moon-struck.
[25] omit.
[26] Greek philosopher-poet who committed suicide by leaping into Etna. He desired to convince people of his divinity.
[27] one of the four humours noted above; its excess was thought to produce insanity.
[28] restrained.
[29] attempted suicide.

These trifles into serious mischiefes lead
The man once mock'd, and suffer'd wrong to tread.
  Wise, sober folke, a frantick *Poet* feare,
And shun to touch him, as a man that were
645 Infected with the leprosie, or had
The yellow Jaundies, or were furious mad
According to the Moone. But, then the boyes
They vexe, and follow him with shouts, and noise,
The while he belcheth loftie Verses out,
650 And stalketh, like a Fowler, round about,
Busie to catch a Black-bird; if he fall
Into a pit, or hole; although he call,
And cry aloud, Helpe gentle Countrey-men,
There's none will take the care, to helpe him then;
655 For, if one should, and with a rope make haste
To let it downe, who knowes, if he did cast
Himselfe there purposely, or no; and would
Not thence be sav'd, although indeed he could?
I'le tell you but the death, and the disease
660 Of the Sicilian Poët *Empedocles*,
Hee, while he labour'd to be thought a God
Immortall, tooke a melancholique, odde
Conceipt, and into burning *Aetna* leap'd.
Let Poëts perish, that will not be kept.
665 Hee that preserves a man, against his will,
Doth the same thing with him, that would him kill.
Nor did he doe this once; for if you can
Recall[30] him yet, hee'ld be no more a man:
Or love of this so famous death lay by.[31]
670   His cause of making Verses none knowes why
Whether he piss'd upon his Fathers grave;
Or the sad thunder-stroken thing he have

[30] call back: save.
[31] or lay aside his love of this
so notorious death.

          Polluted, touch't:[32] but certainly he's mad:
          And as a Beare, if he the strength but had
675   To force the Grates that hold him in, would fright
          All; so this grievous writer puts to flight
          Learn'd, and unlearn'd; holdeth whom[33] once he takes;
          And there an end of him with reading makes:
                Not letting goe the skin, where he drawes food,
680   Till, horse-leech like, he drop off, full of blood.

[32] A place struck by lightning was enclosed in a wall and consecrated. Thus, *Or the conse-* crated ground has been defiled because he touched it.
[33] whomever.

Defiled, touch'd; but certaine he was mad,
And, as a Beare, if he the strength but had
675   To force the grates, that hold him in, would fright
All; So this grievous Writer puts to flight
Learn'd and unlearn'd; holding, whom once he takes;
And, there an end of him, reciting makes:
Not letting goe his hold, where he drawes food,
680   Till he drop off, a Horse-leech, full of blood.

UNCOLLECTED POETRY

The circumstances of the publication of Jonson's writings resulted in the omission of a considerable body of his verse from his works collected in 1616 and 1640. In 1616 he printed all of the poetry written up to that time by which, presumably, he wished to be remembered. Some of the more important omissions from the *Epigrammes* and *The Forrest* may be easily explained, such as all of the songs from his plays with the exception of Volpone's "Come my Celia, let us prove" (*The Forrest* 5), for the plays were also printed in this volume. But Jonson had contributed four poems to the collection comprising *Love's Martyr* in 1601. Two of them appear in *The Forrest*, but the other two for some reason were not included. He also left out the long "Ode Allegorical" prefixed to his friend Hugh Holland's *Pancharis* (1603), the sonnet prefixed to Thomas Wright's book on the passions (1604), and the praise of his fellow playwright John Fletcher, prefixed to the *Faithfull Shepherdesse* about 1609. Perhaps by 1612 or 1613 when he arranged the copy for his *Works* of 1616 he had forgotten about these dedicatory tributes, for they are not inferior to work which he did print. The Holland piece, too, is not an epigram, and *The Forrest*, where it could have been printed, includes no dedicatory poetry; thus Jonson may not have found a logical place for it. The absence of his recently composed prefatory poems for Thomas Coryate's *Crudities* (1611) is explained by their slapstick nature: nothing in the 1616 volume reflects their low standards.

The omission of work in the 1640–41 collection of *Underwood* is easy to understand. When Jonson's friend, Sir Kenelm Digby, printed it he seems to have made no effort to go beyond the manuscripts which came into his hands after the poet's death. For example, *Under-wood* includes only two prefatory poems (to John Selden's *Titles of Honour*, 1614, and to Walter Raleigh's *History of the World*, 1614); it ignores many other pieces, such as the two prefixed to the first folio of Shakespeare's plays. Digby also lacked some manuscripts. Thus a considerable body of material written during Jonson's prime did not appear in 1640.

As should be expected, the *Uncollected Poetry* lacks the unity of the three collections of Jonson's verse printed in 1616 and 1640. Included here are all of the songs from the plays, the prefaces not printed elsewhere, a political poem delivered as part of the great welcome given King James upon his triumphal appearance in London in 1604, a marriage hymn from the masque given at the Lord Viscount Hadington's marriage (1616), and several pieces which survive only in manuscript. This heterogeneous group is arranged here so far as possible in chronological order. Other groupings would have been possible: the various prefaces, which show Jonson on friendly terms with almost all of the important writers of his day, including such younger playwrights as John Fletcher, his former servant Richard Brome, and Joseph Rutter; the religious poems, almost uniformly unsuccessful in comparison with similar writings of Jonson's contemporaries and successors; the songs from the plays, which show a side of Jonson often forgotten beside his polemical or satirical writing; and the magnificent group of intensely personal poems—the ode written to himself after the failure of the *New Inn* in 1629, the attacks on Milton's friend Alexander Gill and on his "Detractor," and the several bitter diatribes against his long-time collaborator and rival for court favors, Inigo Jones—diatribes of an old man bedridden by paralysis and in financial difficulties who refuses to compromise his principles under the most adverse circumstances.

UNCOLLECTED POETRY

1

WHen late (grave *Palmer*)[1] these thy graffs and
                            [flowers
(So well dispos'd by thy auspicious hand)
Weare made the objects to my weaker powers;
I could not but in admiracion stand.
5   First: thy successe did strike my sence with wonder;
That mongst so manie plants transplanted hether,
Not one but thrives; in spite of stormes & thunder,
Unseason'd frostes, or the most envyous weather.[2]
Then I admir'd, the rare and prescious use
10 Thy skill hath made of ranck dispised weedes;
Whilst other soules convert to base abuse
The sweetest simples,[3] and most soveraigne seedes.
Next, that which rapt mee, was: I might behold
How lyke the Carbuncle in *Aarons* brest[4]
15 The seaven-fold flower of Arte[5] (more rich then gold)
Did sparcle foorth in Center of the rest:
Thus, as a ponderous thinge in water cast
Extendeth circles into infinits,
Still making that the greatest that is last
20 Till th'one hath drownd the other in our sightes,
So in my braine; the stronge impression
Of thy rich labors worlds of thoughts created
Which thoughts being circumvolvd in gyerlyk mocion
Wear spent with wonder as they weare delated[6]

1: [1] from Thomas Palmer, *The Sprite of Trees and Herbes* (1598–99), BM Additional MS. 18040. Jonson's prefatory poem is to a book of emblematic treatment of trees and flowers. The work has not been published.
[2] Palmer suffered persecution as a Roman Catholic.
[3] herbs.
[4] Exodus 28:17ff. The meaning of the stones was allegorized in various ways.
[5] the seven liberal arts.
[6] dilated: spread abroad, with pun: set forth at length.

25 Till giddie with amazement I fell downe
In a deepe trance; * * * * *
* * * * * When loe to crowne thy worth
I struggled with this passion that did drowne
My abler faculties; and thus brake foorth
30   *Palmer thy travayles[7] well becum thy name*
    And thou in them shalt live as longe as Fame.
             BEN: JHONSON. GENT.

    Dignum laude virum Musa vetat mori.[8]

2. IN AUTHOREM[1]

THou, that wouldst finde the habit[2] of true passion,
    And see a minde attir'd in perfect straines;
Not wearing moodes, as gallants doe a fashion,
    In these pide[3] times, only to shewe their braines,

5 Looke here on *Bretons* worke, the master print:
    Where, such perfections to the life doe rise.
If they seeme wry,[4] to such as looke asquint,
    The fault's not in the object, but their eyes.

For, as one comming with a laterall[5] viewe,
10   Unto a cunning piece wrought perspective,
Wants facultie to make a censure[6] true:
    So with this Authors Readers will it thrive:

Which being eyed directly, I divine,
His proofe their praise, will meete, as in this line.
             BEN: JOHNSON.

---

[7] efforts.

[8] The Muse denies to death that man worthy of her praise. Horace, *Odes*, 4.8.28.

2: [1] prefixed to Nicholas Breton, *Melancholike Humours* (1600). Jonson had applied the theory of humours in *Every Man*

in his Humour and Every Man out of his Humour.

[2] dress; representation.

[3] pied: varicolored.

[4] twisted.

[5] side.

[6] judgment.

3.[1] MURDER

THose that in blood such violent pleasure have,
Seldome descend but bleeding to their grave.
                                    B. Johnson.

PEACE

WArres greatest woes, and miseries increase,
Flowes from the surfets which we take in peace.
                                    B. John.

RICHES

GOld is a sutor, never tooke repulse,
It carries Palme[2] with it, (where e're it goes)
Respect, and observation; it uncovers[3]
The knottie heads of the most surly Groomes,
5   Enforcing yron doores to yeeld it way,
Were they as strong ram'd up[4] as *Aetna* gates.
It bends the hams of Gossip Vigilance,
And makes her supple feete, as swift as winde.
It thawes the frostiest, and most stiffe disdaine:
10 Muffles the clearnesse of Election,
Straines[5] fancie unto foule Apostacie,
And strikes the quickest-sighted Judgement blinde.
Then why should we dispaire? Dispaire, away:
Where Gold's the Motive, women have no Nay.
                                    B. Johnson.

3: [1] from *England's Parnassus*, ed. Robert Allot (1600), a collection of "the choycest Flowers of our Modern Poets" which includes, besides these quotations from Jonson, passages from *Every Man in his Humour*, *Every Man out of his Humour*, and some of his lyrics—fourteen quotations in all.
  [2] recognition.
  [3] i.e., removes the hat as a mark of respect.
  [4] blocked up.
  [5] constrains, forces.

4. SONG[1]

SLow, slow, fresh fount, keepe time with my salt teares;
Yet slower, yet, ô faintly gentle springs:
List to the heavy part the musique beares,
    "Woe weepes out her division,[2] when shee sings.
5   Droupe hearbs, and flowers,
      Fall griefe in showers;
    "Our beauties are not ours:
        O, I could still
(Like melting snow upon some craggie hill,)
10   drop, drop, drop, drop,
Since natures pride is, now, a wither'd Daffodill.

5. SONG[1]

    O, That joy so soone should waste!
      or so sweet a blisse
        as a kisse,
    Might not for ever last!
5   So sugred, so melting, so soft, so delicious,
      The dew that lyes on roses,
        When the morne her selfe discloses,
        is not so precious.
    O, rather then I would it smother,
10   Were I to taste such another;
      It should bee my wishing
      That I might dye kissing.

4: [1] from *Cynthia's Revels* I.ii; sung by Echo. The play was first presented in 1600. Music is in Henry Youll, *Canzonets to Three Voyces* (1608).

[2] breaking up the time of slow notes into several quick ones.
5: [1] from *Cynthia's Revels* IV.iii.

Fig. 2 Song from *Cynthia's Revels*, Act I, Scene ii. From Henry Youll's *Canzonets to Three Voyces*, 1608.

FIG. 2 continued

FIG. 2 continued

6. SONG[1]

THou more then most sweet glove,
Unto my more sweet Love,
 Suffer me to store, with kisses
 This emptie lodging, that now misses
5 The pure rosie hand that ware thee,
  Whither then the kid, that bare thee:
   Thou art soft, but that was softer;
   Cupids selfe hath kist it ofter,
    Then e're he did his mothers doves,
10   Supposing her the Queene of loves,
     That was thy Mistresse,
     Best of gloves.

7. HYMNE[1]

QUeene and *Huntresse*, chaste, and faire,
Now the *Sunne* is laid to sleepe,
Seated, in thy silver chaire,
State in wonted manner keepe:
5 *Hesperus*[2] intreats thy light,
  Goddesse, excellently bright.

Earth, let not thy envious shade
Dare it selfe to interpose;[3]
Cynthias shining orbe was made
10 Heaven to cleere, when day did close:
  Blesse us then with wished sight,
  Goddesse, excellently bright.

6: [1] from   *Cynthia's   Revels*
IV.iii.
7: [1] from *Cynthia's Revels* V.vi;
sung to Diana, goddess of the

moon, of hunting, and of chastity.
 [2] the evening star.
 [3] Eclipses were thought to por-
tend evil.

Lay thy bow of pearle apart,
And thy cristall-shining quiver;
15 Give unto the flying hart
Space to breathe, how short soever:
Thou, that mak'st a day of night,
Goddesse, excellently bright.

8. AUTHOR

AD LIBRUM[1]

GOe little Booke,[2] Goe little *Fable*
unto the bright, and amiable
Lucy of *Bedford*; she, that Bounty
appropriates still unto that *County*:
5 Tell her, his Muse that did invent thee
to Cynthias fayrest Nymph hath sent thee,
And sworne, that he will quite discard thee
if any way she do rewarde thee
But with a *Kisse*, (if thou canst dare it)
10 of her white Hand; or she can spare it.

9. THE PHŒNIX ANALYSDE[1]

NOw, after all, let no man
Receive it for a *Fable*,
If a *Bird* so amiable,
Do turne into a Woman.

8: [1] inscribed in a copy of *Cynthia's Revels* (1601) presented to Lucy, Countess of Bedford. For her see *Epig.* 76.

[2] This address is used by Chaucer at the end of *Troilus and Criseyde* and by Spenser at the end of *The Shepheardes Calender*.

9: [1] This poem and the next appear in the appendix to *Love's Martyr: or, Rosalins Complaint* (1601). In the same section appear two other poems by Jonson, which he reprinted in *The Forrest* 10 and 11; see the notes there for the symbolism of the Phoenix and Turtle(-dove).

5   Or (by our *Turtles* Augure)
                  That *Natures* fairest Creature,
                  Prove of his *Mistris* Feature,
               But a bare *Type*[2] and *Figure*.

                  10. ODE ἐνθουσιαστικὴ[1]

               SP*lendor!*[2] O more then mortall,
               For other formes come short all
               Of her illustrate[3] brightnesse,
               As farre as Sinne's from lightnesse.[4]

5   Her wit as quicke, and sprightfull
               As fire; and more delightfull
               Then the stolne sports of *Lovers*,
               When night their meeting covers.

               Judgement (adornd with Learning)
10   Doth shine in her discerning,
               Cleare as a naked vestall[5]
               Closde in an orbe of Christall.

               Her breath for sweete exceeding
               The *Phœnix* place of breeding,[6]
15   But mixt with sound, transcending
               All *Nature* of commending.

               Alas: then whither wade I,
               In thought to praise this *Ladie*;
               When seeking her renowning,
20   My selfe am so neare drowning?

               Retire, and say; Her *Graces*
               Are deeper then their *Faces*:
               Yet shee's nor nice to shew them,
               Nor takes she pride to know[7] them.
                              Ben: Johnson.

[2] symbol.   [5] virgin.
10: [1] enthusiastic: inspired.   [6] Arabia, source of spices and
[2] i.e., superlative beauty.   perfumes.
[3] resplendent, lustrous.   [7] acknowledge.
[4] sc. of heaven.

11. SONG[1]

IF I freely may discover,
What would please me in my lover:
  I would have her faire, and wittie,
  Savouring more of court, then cittie;
5   A little proud, but full of pittie:
  Light and humorous in her toying.
  Oft building hopes, and soone destroying,
  Long, but sweet in the enjoying,
Neither too easie, nor too hard:
10 All extreames I would have bard.

Shee should be allowed her passions,
So they were but us'd as fashions;
  Sometimes froward, and then frowning,
  Sometimes sickish, and then swowning,
15   Every fit, with change, still crowning.
  Purely Jelous, I would have her,
  Then onely constant when I crave her.
  'Tis a vertue should not save her.
Thus, nor her delicates[2] would cloy me,
20 Neither her peevishnesse annoy me.

12. SONG[1]

LOve is blind, and a wanton;
In the whole world, there is scant
  One such another:
  No, not his *Mother*.[2]
5   He hath pluckt her *doves*, and *sparrowes*,[3]
  To feather his sharpe arrowes,

11: [1] from *Poetaster* II.ii (first performed in 1601). The two stanzas are sung by two different young men.
 [2] pleasure-giving parts.

12: [1] from *Poetaster* IV.iii. H&S question Jonson's authorship.
 [2] Venus, mother of Cupid.
 [3] which traditionally accompanied her.

And alone prevaileth,
Whilst sick *Venus* waileth.
But if *Cypris*[4] once recover
10   The wag;[5] it shall behove her
To look better to him:
Or shee will undoe him.

13. SONG[1]

WAke, our mirth begins to die:
Quicken it with tunes, and wine:
Raise your notes; you're out:[2] fie, fie;
This Drouzinesse is an ill signe.
5   We banish him the queere[3] of Gods,
That droops agen:
Then all are men,
For here's not one, but nods . . . .

HERM.	Then, in a free and lofty straine,
10		Our broken tunes we thus repaire;
CRIS.	And we answere them againe,
		Running division[4] on the panting aire:
AMBO.[5]	To celebrate this feast of *sense*,
		As free from scandall, as offence.
15 HERM.	Here is *beautie*, for the eye;
CRIS.	For the eare, sweet *melodie*;
HERM.	*Ambrosiack* odours, for the smell;
CRIS.	Delicious *nectar*, for the taste;
AMBO.	For the touch, a *ladies waste*;
20		Which doth all the rest excell!

[4] an island sacred to her; hence
Venus.
    [5] i.e., Cupid.
13: [1] from *Poetaster* IV.v. The
first part is sung by a group pre-
tending to be gods; Hermogenes
and Crispinus have the second

part.
    [2] i.e., of tune.
    [3] choir.
    [4] breaking up longer notes to
several short ones.
    [5] both.

14. ODE. ἀλληγορικὴ[1]

WHo saith our Times nor have, nor can
    Produce us a blacke Swan?
    Behold, where one doth swim;
      Whose Note, and Hue,
5 Besides the other Swannes[2] admiring him,
      Betray it true:
      A gentler Bird, then this,
  Did never dint the breast of *Tamisis*.[3]

Marke, marke, but when his wing he takes,
10   How faire a flight he makes!
      How upward, and direct!
      Whil'st pleas'd *Apollo*[4]
Smiles in his Sphære, to see the rest affect,[5]
      In vaine to follow:
15   This Swanne is onely his,
And *Phœbus* love cause of his blackenesse is.

He shew'd him first the hoofe-cleft Spring,[6]
    Neere which, the *Thespiad's* sing;
      The cleare *Dircæan*[7] Fount
20   Where *Pindar* swamme;
The pale *Pyrene*,[8] and the forked *Mount:*[9]
      And, when they came
      To brookes, and broader streames,
From *Zephyr's*[10] rape would close him with his beames.

14: [1] prefixed to Hugh Holland, *Pancharis* (1603), a poem about Owen Tudor, dedicated to James as King of Great Britain, France, and adjacent islands (see *Under.* 29, l. 30). Jonson terms this work an Ode Allegorical.

[2] Several other commendatory verses are prefixed to *Pancharis*.

[3] the Thames.

[4] as god of poetry as well as of the sun. The swan (because of its reputed song at death) was sacred to him.

[5] attempt, aspire.

[6] the Hippocrene, sacred to the Muses (Thespiads); caused by their horse, Pegasus, striking the ground with his hoof. Persius, Prologue to the *Satires*, l. 1.

[7] of Dirce, in Thebes, birthplace of Pindar, Greek poet.

[8] spring at Corinth sacred to the Muses. Persius, Prologue, l. 4: *pallidem Pirenen*.

[9] Parnassus. Persius, Prologue, l. 2: *bicipiti Parnaso*.

[10] the wind's.

25   This change'd his Downe; till this, as white
            As the whole heard[11] in sight,
            And still is in the Brest:
            That part nor Winde,
    Nor Sunne could make to vary from the rest,
30   Or alter kinde.[12]
        "So much doth Virtue hate,
        "For stile[13] of rarenesse, to degenerate.[14]

    Be then both Rare, and Good; and long
            Continue thy sweete Song.
35   Nor let one River boast
            Thy tunes alone;
    But prove[15] the Aire, and saile from Coast to Coast:
            Salute old *Mône*,[16]
            But first to *Cluid*[17] stoope low,
40 The Vale, that bred thee pure, as her Hills Snow.

    From thence, display thy wing againe
            Over *Iërna* maine,[18]
            To the *Eugenian* dale;[19]
            There charme the rout
45 With thy soft notes, and hold them within Pale[20]
            That late were out.
        "Musicke hath power to draw,[21]
        "Where neither Force can bend, nor Feare can awe.

    Be proofe, the glory of his hand,
50   (*Charles Montjoy*)[22] whose command

[11] herd (of swans).
[12] nature.
[13] sake, name.
[14] The quotation marks here and below indicate a tendentious statement.
[15] try.
[16] Anglesey, island off northwest Wales.
[17] Denbigh, Wales, where Holland was born.
[18] the Irish Sea.

[19] Ireland.
[20] Tyrone's rebellion, successful in driving the English from much of Ireland in 1599 and 1600 as it spread into the "Pale," the area within English jurisdiction.
[21] lead.
[22] As leader of the English forces, replacing Essex, he defeated Tyrone in Munster in 1601.

Hath all beene Harmony:
And more hath wonne
Upon the *Kerne*,[23] and wildest *Irishry*,
Then Time hath donne,
55   Whose strength is above strength;
And conquers all things, yea it selfe, at length.

Who ever sipt at *Baphyre* river,[24]
That heard but Spight deliver[25]
His farre-admired Acts,
60   And is not rap't[26]
With entheate[27] rage, to publish their bright tracts?[28]
(But this more apt
When him alone we sing)
Now must we plie our ayme; our Swan's on wing.

65 Who (see) already hath ore-flowne
The *Hebrid* Isles,[29] and knowne
The scatter'd *Orcades*;[30]
From thence is gon
To utmost *Thule*:[31] whence, he backes[32] the Seas
70   To *Caledon*,
And over *Grampius* mountaine,[33]
To *Loumond* lake,[34] and *Twedes* blacke-springing
[fountaine.[35]

[23] Irish foot soldier.
[24] supposed to be the Helicon, reappearing after a course underground. Thus, whoever tried to write poetry.
[25] state, utter. Perhaps reflecting the fact that as a friend of Essex Mountjoy had been close to his rebellion of 1600–1. Or perhaps owing to the fact that Penelope Devereux, beloved of Sidney and wife of Lord Rich, had become Mountjoy's mistress. After Essex's death Rich separated from her and then divorced her. Meanwhile, she and Mountjoy openly lived together (and finally were married by Laud).

[26] carried away.
[27] inspired by a god.
[28] tracks: careers.
[29] islands off the west Scottish coast.
[30] Orkney Islands north of Scotland.
[31] vaguely, some place north of England; probably here the Shetland Islands.
[32] turns back over the seas to Caledonia: Scotland.
[33] range dividing Lowlands from Highlands.
[34] Loch Lomond.
[35] the river Tweed in Scotland and northern England.

Haste, Haste, sweete Singer: Nor to *Tine*,
    Humber, or *Owse*,[36] decline;[37]
75   But over Land to *Trent*:[38]
        There coole thy Plumes,
And up againe, in skies, and aire to vent[39]
        Their reeking fumes;
        Till thou at *Tames* alight,
80   From whose prowde bosome, thou began'st thy flight.

Tames, prowde of thee, and of his Fate
        In entertaining late
        The choise of *Europes* pride;
        The nimble *French*;[40]
85   The *Dutch* whom Wealth (not Hatred) doth divide;
        The *Danes* that drench
        Their cares in wine; with sure
Though slower *Spaine*; and *Italy* mature.

All which, when they but heare a straine
90   Of thine, shall thinke the *Maine*[41]
        Hath sent her *Mermaides* in,
        To hold them here:
Yet, looking in thy face, they shall begin
        To loose that feare;
95   And (in the place) envie
So blacke a Bird, so bright a Qualitie.

But should they know (as I) that this,
        Who warbleth *Pancharis*,
        Were *Cycnus*,[42] once high flying
100   With *Cupids* wing;
Though, now by *Love* transform'd, & dayly[43] dying:
        (Which makes him sing
        With more delight, and grace)
Or thought they, *Leda's* white Adult'rers[44] place

---

[36] northern English rivers: Tyne, Humber, and Ouse.

[37] fly down to.

[38] river in central England.

[39] apparently, escape or get rid of.

[40] H&S suggest visits of Biron (1601) or the Duke of Neves (1602).

[41] ocean.

[42] Cygnus, constellation of the Swan in the northern hemisphere.

[43] as the constellation sets.

[44] Jupiter, who in the form of a swan raped her.

105 Among the starres should be resign'd
     To him, and he there shrin'd;
     Or *Tames* be rap't from us
     To dimme and drowne
In heav'n the Signe of old *Eridanus*:[45]
110   How they would frowne!
     But these are Mysteries
Conceal'd from all but cleare Propheticke eyes.

It is inough, their griefe shall know
     At their returne, nor *Po*,
115   *Iberus, Tagus, Rheine*,
          Scheldt, nor the *Maas*,
Slow *Arar*, nor swift *Rhone*; the *Loyre*, nor *Seine*,[46]
          With all the race
     Of *Europes* waters can
120 Set out a like, or second to our Swan.

15. A PANEGYRE, ON THE HAPPIE EN-
TRANCE OF JAMES, OUR SOVERAIGNE,
TO HIS FIRST HIGH SESSION OF PARLIA-
MENT IN THIS HIS KINGDOME, THE
19. OF MARCH, 1603[1]

MART. *LICET TOTO NUNC HELICONE FRUI*[2]

HEav'n now not strives, alone, our brests to fill
With joyes: but urgeth his full favors still.
Againe, the glory of our Westerne world
Unfolds himself: and from his eyes are hoorl'd
5   (To day) a thousand radiant lights, that stream
To every nooke and angle of his realme.[3]

---

[45] constellation in the southern hemisphere; also called river Po.

[46] various European rivers. The Iberus is in Spain, the Tagus in Spain and Portugal, the Scheldt in France and the Low Countries; the Arar is the Saone, in France.

15: [1] i.e., 1604 New Style.
[2] Martial, *Epig.* XI. vi. 2, written to the Emperor Nerva: "We may now enjoy full draughts of Helicon."
[3] Note the pronunciation to rime with "stream."

His former rayes did onely cleare the skie;
But these his searching beams are cast, to prie
Into those darke and deepe concealed vaults,
10   Where men commit blacke incest with their faults;
And snore supinely in the stall of sin:
Where *Murder, Rapine, Lust,* doe sit within,
Carowsing humane bloud in yron bowles,
And make their denne the slaughter-house of soules:
15   From whose foule reeking cavernes first arise
Those dampes,[4] that so offend all good mens eyes;
And would (if not dispers'd) infect the Crowne,
And in their vapor her bright mettall drowne.
      To this so cleare and sanctified an end,
20   I saw, when reverend *Themis*[5] did descend
Upon his state; let downe in that rich chaine,[6]
That fastneth heavenly power to earthly raigne:
Beside her, stoup't on either hand, a maid,
Faire *Dice,*[7] and *Eunomia;*[8] who were said
25   To be her daughters:[9] and but faintly knowne
On earth, till now, they came to grace his throne.
Her third, *Irene,*[10] help'd to beare his traine;
And in her office vow'd she would remaine,
Till forraine malice, or unnaturall spight
30   (Which Fates avert) should force her from her right.
With these he pass'd, and with his peoples hearts
Breath'd in his way; and soules (their better parts)
Hasting to follow forth in shouts, and cryes.
Upon his face all threw their covetous eyes,
35   As on a wonder: some amazed stood,
As if they felt, but had not knowne their good:
Others would faine have shew'ne it in their words:
But, when their speech so poore a helpe affords

---

[4] poisonous vapors.

[5] daughter of Heaven and Earth. Her name was usually taken to mean Justice or Righteousness.

[6] Cf. the interpretation of Macrobius from *Hymenaei* and

quoted in *The Forrest* 12, n. 12.

[7] Justice.

[8] Order.

[9] According to Hesiod, *Theogony* 901–3, the daughters of Themis by Zeus.

[10] Peace.

Unto their zeales expression; they are mute:
40   And only with red[11] silence him salute.
Some cry from tops of houses; thinking noise
The fittest herald to proclaime true joyes:
Others on ground runne gazing by his side,
All, as unwearied, as unsatisfied:
45   And every windore[12] griev'd it could not move
Along with him, and the same trouble prove.
They that had seene, but foure short daies[13] before,
His gladding looke, now long'd to see it more.
And as of late, when he through *London* went,
50   The amorous Citie spar'd no ornament,
That might her beauties heighten; but so drest,
As our ambitious dames, when they make feast,
And would be courted: so this Towne[14] put on
Her brightest tyre; and, in it, equall shone
55   To her great sister: save that modestie,
Her place, and yeares, gave her precedencie.
    The joy of either was alike, and full;
No age, nor sex, so weake, or strongly dull,
That did not beare a part in this consent[15]
60   Of hearts, and voices. All the aire was rent,
As with the murmure of a moving wood;
The ground beneath did seeme a moving floud:
Walls, windores, roofes, towers, steeples, all were set
With severall[16] eyes, that in this object met.
65   Old men were glad, their fates till now did last;
And infants, that the houres had made such hast
To bring them forth: Whil'st riper ag'd, and apt
To understand the more, the more were rapt.
This was the peoples love, with which did strive
70   The Nobles zeale, yet either kept alive

---

[11] perhaps, glowing.

[12] Note the etymology implied by the spelling and accepted in Jonson's time.

[13] James had made a triumphal progress through London on March 15.

[14] Westminster.

[15] harmony as well as agreement.

[16] various.

The others flame, as doth the wike and waxe,
That friendly temper'd, one pure taper makes.
Meane while, the reverend *Themis* drawes aside
The Kings obeying will, from taking pride
75   In these vaine stirres, and to his mind suggests
How he may triumph in his subjects brests,
"With better pompe. She tells him first, that Kings
"Are here on earth the most conspicuous things:
"That they, by Heaven, are plac'd upon his throne,
80   "To rule like Heaven; and have no more, their owne,
"As they are men, then men. That all they doe
"Though hid at home, abroad is search'd into:
"And, being once found out, discover'd lies
"Unto as many envies, there, as eyes.
85   "That princes, since they know it is their fate,
"Oft-times, to have the secrets of their state
"Betraid to fame, should take more care, and feare
"In publique acts what face and forme they beare.
"She then remembred to his thought the place
90   "Where he was going; and the upward race
.   "Of kings, præceding him in that high court;
"Their lawes, their endes; the men she did report:
"And all so justly, as[17] his eare was joy'd
"To heare the truth, from spight, or flattery voyd.
95   "She shewd him, who made wise, who honest acts;
"Who both, who neither: all the cunning tracts,
"And thriving statutes she could promptly note;
"The bloody, base, and barbarous she did quote;
"Where lawes were made to serve the tyran'will;
100   "Where sleeping they could save, and waking kill;
"Where acts gave licence to impetuous lust
"To bury churches, in forgotten dust,
"And with their ruines raise the panders bowers:[18]
"When, publique justice borrow'd all her powers
105   "From private chambers; that could then create
"Lawes, judges, consellors, yea prince, and state.

[17] that.   [18] As H&S note, Jonson was a
                    Catholic at this time.

"All this she told, and more, with bleeding eyes;
"For *Right* is as compassionate as wise.
Nor did he seeme their vices so to love,
110   As once defend, what *Themis* did reprove.
For though by right, and benefite of *Times*,
He ownde their crownes, he would not so their crimes.
He knew that princes, who had sold their fame
To their voluptuous lustes, had lost their name;
115   And that no wretch was more unblest then he,
Whose necessary good t'was now to be
An evill king: And so must such be still,
Who once have got the habit to doe ill.[19]
One wickednesse another must defend;
120   For vice is safe, while she hath vice to friend.
He knew, that those, who would, with love, command,
Must with a tender (yet a stedfast) hand
Sustaine the reynes, and in the checke forbeare
To offer cause of injurie, or feare.
125   That kings, by their example, more doe sway
Then by their power; and men doe more obay
When they are led, then when they are compell'd.
   In all these knowing artes our prince excell'd.
And now the dame had dried her dropping eyne,[20]
130   When, like an April *Iris*,[21] flew her shine
About the streets, as[22] it would force a spring
From out the stones, to gratulate[23] the king.
She blest the people, that in shoales did swim
To heare her speech; which still began in him
135   And ceas'd in them. She told them, what a fate
Was gently falne from heaven upon this state;
How deare a father they did now enjoy
That came to save, what discord would destroy:
And entring with the power of a king,
140   The temp'rance of a private man did bring,

[19] In the *Nicomachean Ethics* Aristotle argues that virtue is a habit.
[20] eyes.
[21] goddess of the rainbow.
[22] as though.
[23] praise.

That wan[24] affections, ere his steps wan ground;
And was not hot, or covetous to be crown'd
Before mens hearts had crown'd him. Who (unlike
Those greater bodies of the sky,[25] that strike
145   The lesser fiers[26] dim) in his accesse
Brighter then all, hath yet made no one lesse;
Though many greater: and the most, the best.
Wherein, his choice was happie with the rest
Of his great actions, first to see, and do
150   What all mens wishes did aspire unto.
    Hereat, the people could no longer hold
Their bursting joyes; but through the ayre was rol'd
The length'ned showt, as when th'artillery[27]
Of heaven is discharg'd along the skie:
155   And this confession flew from every voyce:
Never had land more reason to rejoyce.
Nor to her blisse, could ought now added bee,
Save, that shee might the same perpetuall see.
Which when time, nature, and the fates deny'd,
160   With a twice louder shoute againe they cry'd,
Yet, let blest Brittaine *aske (without your wrong)*
Still to have such a king, and this king long.

        Solus Rex, & Poeta non quotannis nascitur.[28]

16. TO THE AUTHOR[1]

IN Picture, they which truly understand,
    Require (besides the likenesse of the thing)
    Light, Posture, Height'ning,[2] Shadow, Culloring,
All which are parts commend[3] the cunning hand;

---

[24] won.
[25] the sun and moon.
[26] fires: stars and planets.
[27] thunder.
[28] "The king alone, and the poet, is not born every day." From the Latin poet Florus (H&S); cf. A. Riese, *Anthologia Latina* (1894) I. 202 (No. 252).
16: [1] prefixed to Thomas

Wright, *The Passions of the Minde in Generall* (2d ed., 1604), a study of the Renaissance theory of the passions. Wright was a Jesuit who may have converted Jonson during his imprisonment in 1598. The book is dedicated to the Earl of Southampton.
[2] intensifying the color.
[3] that commend.

5   And all your Booke (when it is throughly scan'd)
     Will well confesse; presenting, limiting,[4]
     Each subt'lest Passion, with her source, and spring,
So bold, as[5] shewes your Art you can command.
     But now, your Worke is done,[6] if they that view
10   The severall figures, languish in suspence,
     To judge which Passion's false, and which is true,
     Betweene the doubtfull sway of Reason', and
                                        [sense;
     Tis not your fault, if they shall sense preferre,
     Being tould there, Reason[7] cannot, Sense may
                                        [erre.
                                        B. J.

17

FOnd[1] Fables tell of olde
   How *Jove* in *Danaes*[2] lappe
Fell in a showre of Gold,
   By which shee caught a clappe;[3]
5   O, had it been my hap,
(How ere the blow doth threaten)
   So well I like the play,
   That I could wish all day
And night to be so beaten.

18. TO THE WORTHY AUTHOR M. JOHN FLETCHER[1]

THe wise, and many-headed *Bench*,[2] that sits
Upon the Life, and Death of *Playes*, and *Wits*,

[4] specifying.
[5] that.
[6] undone, ruined.
[7] there, (that where) Reason.
17: [1] foolish. From *Eastward Hoe* V.i, by George Chapman, Ben Jonson, and John Marston; performed c. 1604. Jonson probably wrote this part of the play. The song is done by Gertrude, one of the girls in it.

[2] Jupiter, in love with Danae, turned himself into a shower of golden rain which fell on her and made her pregnant with Perseus.
[3] apparently, good fortune.
18: [1] prefixed to John Fletcher, *The Faithfull Shepheardesse*, a pastoral tragi-comedy which cannot be exactly dated. It was not successful on its first performance.
[2] group of judges.

(Compos'd of *Gamester, Captaine, Knight, Knight's*
[*man,*
       Lady, or *Pusil,*[3] that weares maske, or fan,
5   *Velvet,* or *Taffata* cap, rank'd[4] in the darke
          With the shops *Foreman,* or some such *brave sparke,*
       That may judge for his *six-pence*)[5] had, before
          They saw it halfe, damd thy whole play, and more.
       Their motives were, since it had not to do
10   With vices, which they look'd for, and came to.
       I, that am glad, thy Innocence was thy Guilt,
          And wish that all the *Muses* blood were spilt,
       In such a *Martirdome;* To vexe their eyes,
          Do crowne[6] thy murdred *Poëme:* which shall rise
15   A glorified worke to Time, when Fire,
          Or moathes shall eate,[7] what all these Fooles admire.
                                            Ben: Jonson.

19. SONG[1]

       FOoles, they are the onely nation
       Worth mens envy, or admiration;
       Free from care, or sorrow-taking,
       Selves, and others merry-making:
5   All they speake, or doe, is sterling.
       Your Foole, he is your great mans dearling,
       And your ladies sport, and pleasure;
       Tongue, and bable are his treasure.
       Eene his face begetteth laughter,
10   And he speakes truth, free from slaughter;
       Hee's the grace of every feast,
       And, sometimes, the chiefest guest:

---

[3] pucelle: whore.
[4] associated or placed.
[5] price of admission.
[6] (I) do crown.
[7] Matt. 6:19–20.

19: [1] from *Volpone* I.ii (first
performed 1605). J. D. Rea, edi-
tor of the Yale edition of the play,
finds this to come from Erasmus'
The Praise of Folly.

Hath his trencher, and his stoole,
When wit waites upon the foole,
15   O, who would not bee
Hee, hee, hee?

20. SONG[1]

HAd old *Hippocrates*,[2] or *Galen*,[3]
(That to their bookes put med'cines all in)
But knowne this secret, they had never
(Of which they will be guiltie ever)
5   Beene murderers of so much paper,
Or wasted many a hurtlesse taper:
No *Indian*[4] drug had ere beene famed,
Tabacco, *sassafras*[5] not named;
Nor yet, of *guacum*[6] one small stick, sir,
10   Nor *Raymund Lullies*[7] great elixir.
Ne, had beene knowne the *Danish Gonswart*.[8]
Or *Paracelsus*,[9] with his long-sword.

21. SONG[1]

YOu that would last long, list to my song,
Make no more coyle, but buy of this oyle.
Would you be ever faire? and yong?
Stout of teeth? and strong of tongue?

20: [1] from *Volpone* II.ii. This and the next are singing commercials advertising a patent medicine.
[2] originator of Greek medicine.
[3] systematizer of Greek medicine.
[4] not identified.
[5] used sometimes as medicines.
[6] medicine prepared from a tree in the West Indies.
[7] Raymond Lull (1235–1315), Spanish priest. It is not clear what his elixir was.

[8] not certainly identified. Newdigate suggests Berthold Schwartz of Fribourg, who is supposed to have invented guns. Or perhaps it is Wessel Gansevoort of Groningen, Holland, like Lull a priest; late in life he directed the Nunnery of the Spiritual Virgins.
[9] (1493–1541) alchemical physician. In his sword hilt he carried various medicines by which he achieved some remarkable cures.
21: [1] from *Volpone* II.ii.

5   Tart of palat? quick of eare?
           Sharpe of sight? of nostrill cleare?
           Moist of hand? and light of foot?
           (Or I will come neerer to't)
           Would you live free from all diseases?
10   Doe the act, your mistris pleases;
           Yet fright all aches[2] from your bones?
           Here's a med'cine, for the nones.[3]

22. A SPEECH OUT OF LUCANE[1]

           JUst and fit actions *Ptolemey*[2] (he saith)
           Make many, hurt themselves; a praysed faith
           Is her owne scourge, when it sustaines their states
           Whom fortune hath deprest; come nere[3] the fates
5   And the immortall gods; love only those
           Whom thou seest happy; wretches flee as foes:
           Looke how the starres from earth, or seas from flames
           Are distant, so is proffitt from just aymes.
           The mayne comaund of scepters, soone doth perishe
10   If it begyn religious thoughts to cherish;
           Whole armyes fall swayd by those nyce respects
           It is a lycense to doe ill, protectes,
           Even states most hated, when no lawes resist
           The sword but that it acteth what it list.
15   Yet ware;[4] thou mayst do all things cruellie:
           Not safe; but when thou dost them thoroughlie:
           He that will honest be may quitt the Court,
           Virtue, and Soveraigntie, they not consort.
           That prince that shames a tyrants name to beare,
20   Shall never dare do any thing but feare.

² two syllables.
³ purpose.
22: ¹ ascribed to Jonson by W. D. Briggs, *Anglia*, XXXIX (1915), 247–48. It is a translation from Lucan's *Pharsalia* VIII. 484–95; the lines appear in Massinger's *The False One* I.i.302–

12 and in Jonson's *Sejanus* II. 178ff. (H&S).
² i.e., "O, Ptolomy": the man to whom the vicious speech is addressed.
³ near.
⁴ beware!

23. EPITHALAMION[1]

UP *youthes* and *virgins*, up, and praise
    The *god*, whose nights out-shine his daies;
      Hymen,[2] whose hallowed *rites*
    Could never boast of brighter lights:
5   Whose bands passe libertee.
Two of your troope, that, with the morne were free,
      Are, now, wag'd to his warre.
        And what they are,
        If you'll perfection see,
10   Your selves must be.
Shine *Hesperus*,[3] shine forth, thou wished *starre*.

What joy, or honors can compare
    With holy *nuptials*, when they are
      Made out of equall parts
15   Of yeeres, of states, of hands, of hearts?
        When, in the happy choyce,
The *spouse*, and *spoused* have the formost voyce!
      Such, glad of *Hymens* warre,
        Live what they are,
20   And long perfection see:
        And such ours bee.
Shine *Hesperus*, shine forth thou wished *starre*.

The solemne state of this one night
    Were fit to last an ages light;
25   But there are *rites* behind[4]
    Have lesse of state, but more of kind:[5]
      Loves wealthy croppe of kisses,
And fruitfull harvest of his *mothers* blisses.

23: [1] the concluding lines of *The Haddington Masque*, presented at Court on the night of February 9, 1608, in honor of the marriage of John Ramsey, Viscount Haddington (c. 1580–1626), to Elizabeth Radcliffe, daughter of the Earl of Sussex. She died in 1618 after bearing three children, all of whom died young.
[2] god of marriage.
[3] the evening star.
[4] yet to come.
[5] nature.

Sound then to *Hymens* warre:
30   That what these are,
Who will perfection see,
May haste to bee.
Shine *Hesperus*, shine forth thou wished *starre*.

Loves common wealth consists of toyes;
35   His councell are those *antique* boyes,
Games, laughter, sports, delights,
That triumph with him on these nights:
To whom we must give way,
For now their raigne beginnes, and lasts till day.
40   They sweeten *Hymens* warre,
And, in that jarre,
Make all, that married bee,
Perfection see.
Shine *Hesperus*, shine forth thou wished *starre*.

45   Why stayes the *Bride-grome* to invade
Her, that would be a matron made?
Good-night, whilst yet we may
Good-night, to you a *virgin*, say:
To morrow, rise the same
50   Your *mother* is,[6] and use a *nobler* name.
Speed well in *Hymen's* warre,
That, what you are,
By your perfection, wee
And all may see.
55   Shine *Hesperus*, shine forth thou wished *starre*.

To night is *Venus vigil* kept.
This night no *Bride-grome* ever slept;
And if the faire *Bride* doo,
The married say, 'tis his fault, too.
60   Wake then; and let your lights
Wake too: for they'l tell nothing of your nights:

---

[6] A wife, or matron: which is a name of more dignity, then *Virgin. D. Heins. in Nup. Ottonis Heurnii. Cras matri similis tuae redibis* (Jonson's note): Daniel Heinsius, "On the Marriage of Otto Heurnius"; Jonson translates the Latin in his text.

But, that in *Hymens* warre,
    You perfect are.
    And such perfection, wee
65   Doe pray, should bee.
Shine *Hesperus*, shine forth thou wished *starre*.

That, ere the rosy-fingerd *morne*[7]
    Behold nine moones, there may be borne
    A babe, t'uphold the fame
70   Of *Radcliffes* blood, and *Ramsey's* name:
    That may, in his great seed,
Weare the long honors of his *fathers* deed.[8]
    Such fruits of *Hymens* warre
    Most perfect are;
75   And all perfection, wee
    Wish, you should see.
Shine *Hesperus*, shine forth, thou wished *starre*.

24. SONG[1]

STill to be neat, still to be drest,
As[2] you were going to a feast;
Still to be pou'dred, still perfum'd:
Lady, it is to be presum'd,
5   Though arts hid causes are not found,
All is not sweet, all is not sound.

Give me a looke, give me a face,
That makes simplicitie a grace;
Robes loosely flowing, haire as free:
10   Such sweet neglect more taketh me,
Then all th'adulteries of art.
They strike mine eyes, but not my heart.

[7] Homer regularly so terms the morning.

[8] In August 1600 Ramsey had killed the Earl of Gowrie and his brother Alexander Ruthven, who perhaps had conspired against James's life.

24: [1] from *The Silent Woman* I.i (first performed 1609). K. F. Smith identifies the source in the *Anthologia Latina*; see *American Journal of Philology*, XXIX (1908), 133–56.
[2] as though.

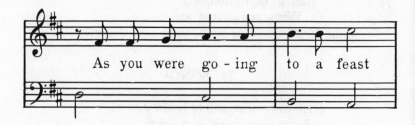

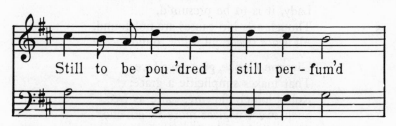

Fig. 3 Song from *The Silent Woman*, Act I, Scene i. Music by Henry Lawes, from *Select Ayres and Dialogues* published by John Playford, 1669.

FIG. 3 continued

25. MADRIGALL OF MODESTIE[1]

MOdest, and faire, for faire and good are neere
      Neighbours, how ere.—
No noble vertue ever was alone,
      But two in one.
5   Then, when I praise sweet modestie, I praise
      Bright beauties raies:
And having prais'd both beauty'and modestee,
      I have prais'd thee.

Silence in woman, is like speech in man,
10   Deny't who can.
         Nor, is't a tale,
That female vice should be a vertue male,
Or masculine vice, a female vertue be:
         You shall it see
15   Prov'd with increase,
I know to speake, and shee to hold her peace.

26. EPITAPH[1]

STay, view this stone: And, if thou beest not such,[2]
Read here a little, that thou mayst know much.
It covers, first, a Virgin; and then, one
That durst be that in Court: a vertu' alone
5   To fill an Epitaph. But she had more.
She might have claym'd t'have made the Graces foure;[3]
Taught Pallas[4] language; Cynthia[5] modesty;
As fit to have encreas'd the harmony

25: [1] from *The Silent Woman*
II. iii; sung by John Daw, servant
to Epicene, "suppos'd the silent
Woman."
26: [1] sent with a covering letter
to George Garrard at the news of
Cecelia Boulstred's death on Au-
gust 4, 1609. Cf. *Under.* 51,

where she is bitterly attacked;
these two poems cannot be rec-
onciled.
    [2] i.e., as was she.
    [3] traditionally three.
    [4] goddess of learning.
    [5] Diana, goddess of chastity.

Of Spheares, as light of starres; She was earthes Eye:[6]
10   The sole Religious house,[7] and Votary,[8]
With Rites not bound, but conscience. Wouldst thou
                                              [All?[9]

She was *'Sell Boulstred*. In which name, I call
Up so much truth, as could I it pursue
Might make the Fable of *Good Women*[10] true.

27

Here follow certaine other Verses, as *Charmes*, to
unlocke the mystery of the *Crudities*.[1]

A

HEre, like *Arion*,[2] our *Coryate* doth draw
All sorts of fish with Musicke of his maw.

B

HEre, not up *Holdborne*,[3] but downe a steepe hill,
Hee's carried 'twixt *Montrell* and *Abbevile*.[4]

C

5   A Horse here is sadled, but no *Tom* him to backe,[5]
It should rather have bene *Tom* that a horse did
                                              [lack.

[6] See the conception of the over-seeing eye in *Under*. 26.

[7] nunnery.

[8] worshipper.

[9] know all?

[10] Chaucer's *Legend of Good Women*.

27: [1] prefixed, with material from other writers, to Thomas Coryate, *Coryate's Crudities* (1611), a record of the author's travel on foot through Europe. The letters of each stanza are cued to the frontispiece (see Plate II, facing p. 223), which deserves study with Jonson's interpretation at hand. Jonson is regularly contemptuous of the author: *Epig*. 129, l. 17 and *Under*. 15, l. 128.

[2] famous musician of Lesbos who visited Italy. On his return, when some sailors were about to kill him for his money, he played and drew some dolphins to the ship; one carried him to shore on its back.

[3] to Tyburn (prison) (H&S).

[4] parts of the trip in France.

[5] ride on.

D

HEre, up the *Alpes* (not so plaine as to *Dunstable*)[6]
Hee's carried like a Cripple, from Constable to Con-
[stable.

E

A *Punke*[7] here pelts him with egs. How so?
10   *For he did but kisse her, and so let her go.*

F

REligiously here he bids, row from the *stewes*,[8]
He will expiate this sinne with converting *the Jewes.*

G

ANd there, while he gives the zealous *Bravado,*
A *Rabbin* confutes him with the *Bastinado.*[9]

H

15   HEre, by a *Boore* too, hee's like to be beaten
For Grapes he had gather'd before they were
[eaten.[10]

I

OLd Hat here, torne Hose, with Shoes full of gravell,[11]
And louse-dropping Case, are the *Armies* of his
[travell.

K

HEre, finer then comming from his Punke you him see,
20   F.[12] shewes what he was, K. what he will bee.

---

[6] proverb: plain as Dunstable Road (H&S).
[7] prostitute.
[8] brothels.
[9] beating.
[10] He stole the grapes in Germany; an armed "Boore" seized his hat in return.
[11] He hung up his shoes in Odcombe Church (Somerset County) after his return.
[12] Not meaning by F. and K. as the vulgar may peevishly & wittingly mistake: but that he was then comming from his Courtesan, a Freshman, and now having seene their fashions, & written a description of them, He will shortly be reputed a Knowing, proper, & well traveld scholer, as by his starchd beard, and printed ruffe may be as properly insinuated. (Jonson's note)

L

HEre *France*, and *Italy* both to him shed
　　Their hornes,[13] and *Germany* pukes on his head.

M

ANd here he disdained not, in a forraine land
　　To lie at Livory, while the Horses did stand.[14]

N

25　　BUt here, neither trusting his hands, nor his legs,
　　Beeing in feare to be robd, he most learnedly begs.[15]
　　　　　　　　　　　　　　　Ben. Jonson.

28

To the Right Noble Tom, *Tell-Troth* of *his trav-
ailes, the* Coryate *of Odcombe,* and his *Booke* now
going *to travell*[1]

T　Rie and trust *Roger*,[2] was the word, but now
H　onest *Tom Tell-Troth* puts downe *Roger, How?*
O　f travell he discourseth so at large,
M　arry he sets it out at his owne charge;[3]
5　A　nd therein (which is worth his valour too)
S　hewes he dares more then *Paules Church-yard*[4] durst
　　　　　　　　　　　　　　　　　　　　　　[do.

C　ome　forth　thou　bonnie　bouncing　booke　then,
　　　　　　　　　　　　　　　　　　　　[daughter
O　f *Tom* of *Odcombe* that *odde* Joviall Author,
R　ather his sonne, I should have cal'd thee, why?
10　Y　es thou wert borne out of his travelling thigh[5]

[13] both cornucopias and the horns of a cuckold.
[14] This happened at Bergamo.
[15] He begged in Germany to avoid being robbed.
28: [1]part of the preliminary matter of the *Crudities*. See previous poem, n. 1.
[2] i.e., any man.

[3] Coryate published the book at his own cost.
[4] area of book publishers in London.
[5] Bacchus was said to be born from Jove's thigh where he had been put upon the death of his mother, Semele.

A s well as from his braines, and claimest thereby
T o be his *Bacchus* as his *Pallas:*[6] bee
E ver his thighes *Male* then, and his braines *Shee*.

Ben. Jonson.

29. CERTAINE VERSES WRITTEN UPON CORYATS CRUDITIES,[1]

Which should Have beene Printed with the other
Panegyricke lines, but then were upon some occasions
omitted, and now communicated to the World

Incipit[2] *Ben. Jonson.*
To the London Reader, on the Odcombian *writer,*
Polytopian[3] Thomas *the Traveller*

WHo ever he be, would write a Story at
The height, let him learne of Mr. *Tom. Coryate*;
Who, because his matter in all should be meete,[4]
To his strength, hath measur'd it out with his feet.
5   And that, say Philosophers, is the best modell.
Yet who could have hit on't but the wise noddell[5]
Of our *Odcombian*, that literate Elfe?
To line out[6] no stride, but pas'd by himselfe?
And allow you for each particular mile,
10 By the scale of his booke, a yard of his stile?
Which, unto all Ages, for his will be knowne,
Since he treads in no other Mans steps but his owne.
And that you may see he most luckily ment
To write it with the selfe same spirit he went,
15 He sayes to the world, let any man mend it,
In five monthes he went it, in five monthes he pend it.
But who will beleeve this, that chanceth to looke
The Mappe of his journey, and sees in his booke,

---

[6] Minerva, born from Jove's head.

29: [1] from *Coryats Crambe . . . Now Served . . . as the Second Course to His Crudities* (1611). See No. 27, n. 1.

[2] Here begins.
[3] many-place; cf. Utopia.
[4] suitable.
[5] noodle: head.
[6] plan.

France, Savoy, Italy, and Helvetia,
20 The Low-countries, Germany and Rhetia[7]
There nam'd to be travell'd? For this our *Tom* saith:
Pies[8] on't, you have his historicall faith.
Each leafe of his journall, and line doth unlocke
The truth of his heart there, and tell's what a clocke
25 He went out at each place, and at what he came in,
How long he did stay, at what signe he did Inne.
Besides he tried Ship, Cart, Waggon, and Chayre,
Horse, foote, and all but flying in the ayre:
And therefore how ever the travelling nation,
30 Or builders of Story have oft imputation
Of lying, he feares so much the reproofe
Of his foote, or his penne, his braine or his hoofe,
That he dares to informe you, but somewhat meticu-
[lous,
How scabbed, how ragged, and how pediculous[9]
35 He was in his travaile, how like to be beaten,
For grapes he had gather'd, before they were eaten.[10]
How faine for his venery[11] he was to crie
[(*Tergum ô*)[12]
And lay in straw with the horses at Bergamo,[13]
How well, and how often his shoes too were mended,[14]
40 That sacred to *Odcombe* are there now suspended,
I meane that one paire, wherewith he so hobled
From Venice to Flushing, were not they well cobled?
Yes. And thanks God in his Pistle[15] or his Booke
How many learned men he have drawne with his hooke
45 Of Latine and Greeke, to his friendship. And seven[16]
He there doth protest he saw of the eleven.
Nay more in his wardrobe, if you will laugh at a
Jest, he saies. *Item* one sute of blacke taffata

[7] a district in the Alps.
[8] pox or pest.
[9] lousy.
[10] See No. 27, stanza H.
[11] love-making.
[12] O my back! See No. 27, stanza E.

[13] See stanza M.
[14] See stanza I.
[15] epistle.
[16] various scholars whom Coryate saw on his travels. In his Epistle to the Reader he gives twelve.

Except a dublet, and bought of the Jewes:
50   So that not them, his scabbes, lice, or the stewes,[17]
Or any thing else that another should hide,
Doth he once dissemble, but tels he did ride
In a Cart twixt Montrell and Abbevile.[18]
And being at Flushing enforced to feele
55   Some want, they say in a sort he did crave:
I writ he onely his taile there did wave;[19]
Which he not denies. Now being so free,
Poore *Tom* have we cause to suspect just thee?
No: as I first said, who would write a story at
60   The height, let him learne of Mr. *Tom Coryate.*

Explicit Ben. Jonson.

30. TO HIS MUCH AND WORTHILY ESTEEMED FRIEND THE AUTHOR[1]

WHo takes thy volume to his vertuous hand,
Must be intended still to understand:
Who bluntly doth but looke upon the same,
May aske, *what Author would conceale his name?*
5   Who reads may roave,[2] and call the passage darke,[3]
Yet may as blind men sometimes hit the marke.
Who reads, who roaves, who hopes to understand,
May take thy volume to his vertuous hand.
Who cannot reade, but onely doth desire
10   To understand, hee may at length admire.

B. J.

---

[17] brothels.
[18] See stanza B.
[19] i.e., wag like a dog.
30: [1] prefixed to *Cinthias Revenge: or Moenanders Extasie* (1613); anonymous, but on a few title pages appears the author's name: John Stephens. He also published in 1615 a series of satirical characters.
[2] shoot to determine the range.
[3] obscure.

31. TO THE MOST NOBLE, AND ABOVE HIS TITLES, ROBERT, EARLE OF SOMERSET[1]

THey are not those, are[2] present with theyre face,
   And clothes, and guifts, that only do thee grace
At these thy Nuptials; but, whose heart, and thought
   Do wayte upon thee: and theyre Love not bought.
5 Such weare true wedding robes, and are true freindes,
   That bid, God give thee joy, and have no endes.[3]
Which I do, early, vertuous *Somerset*,
   And pray, thy joyes as lasting bee, as great.
Not only this, but every day of thine,
10   With the same looke, or with a better, shine.
May she, whome thou for spouse, to day, dost take,
   Out-bee that *Wife*,[4] in worth, thy freind did make:
And thou to her, that Husband, may exalt
   Hymens amends,[5] to make it worth his fault.
15 So, be there never discontent, or sorrow,
   To rise with eyther of you, on the morrow.
So, be your Concord, still, as deepe, as mute;
   And eve'ry joy, in mariage, turne a fruite.
So, may those Mariage-Pledges, comforts prove:
20   And ev'ry birth encrease the heate of Love.

31: [1] Frances Howard, aged about twelve, had married in 1606 the young Earl of Essex, aged about fifteen. The husband then went abroad for his education. On his return Frances refused him, having begun an affair with Robert Carr, Viscount Rochester and in 1612 Earl of Somerset. She tried to dissolve her marriage with Essex, but Carr's friend Thomas Overbury opposed it. Carr had Overbury sent to the Tower, where Lady Essex procured his poisoning in September 1613. The marriage with Essex was then annulled, and on December 26 she and Carr were married, the celebration recorded in this poem. For the wedding Jonson also wrote *A Challenge at Tilt* and *The Irish Masque*. The couple was later charged with Overbury's murder.

[2] who are.

[3] ulterior motives.

[4] Overbury's poem *A Wife*, published the following year.

[5] alluding to the broken marriage with Essex.

So, in theyr number, may you never see
   Mortality, till you immortall bee.
And when your yeares rise more, then would be told,
   Yet neyther of you seeme to th'other old.
25 That all, that view you then, and late; may say,
   Sure, this glad payre were married, but this day.[6]
                                             Ben: Jonson.

32. A SPEACH PRESENTED UNTO KING JAMES AT A TYLTING IN THE BEHALFE OF THE TWO NOBLE BROTHERS SIR ROBERT & SIR HENRYE RICH, NOW EARLES OF WARWICK AND HOLLANDE[1]

TWo noble knightes, whome true desire and zeale,
Hath armde att all poyntes; charge mee humblye
                                             [kneele
Unto thee, king of men; their noblest partes
   To tender thus, their lives, their loves, their hartes!
5   The elder of these two, riche[2] hopes Increase,
Presentes a Royall Alter[3] of fayre peace;
And as an ever-lasting Sacrifice
His life, his love, his honour which ner dyes,
Hee freely bringes; and on this Alter layes
10 As true oblations; his Brothers Emblime sayes,
Except[4] your Gratious Eye as through a Glass
Made prospective,[5] behould hym, hee must passe

---

[6] i.e., only today.

32: [1] Sir Robert (1587–1658) and Sir Henry (1590–1649; created Earl of Holland 1624), sons of Lord Rich and Penelope Devereux, Sidney's Stella. The tilting took place before King James on March 24, 1613 (H&S). Robert was later important in Parliamentary naval affairs and in the American colonies; Henry supported Charles and was executed shortly after the king.

[2] with a pun on the family name.

[3] a symbolic or emblematic gift, described in the following lines.

[4] unless.

[5] able to magnify.

Still that same little poynte hee was, but when
Your Royal Eye which still creattes new men
15 Shall looke, & on hyme soe, then artes a lyer
Yf from a little sparke hee rise not fier.

Ben Johnson.

33. TO HIS FRIEND THE AUTHOR UPON HIS *RICHARD*[1]

WHen these,[2] and such, their voices have employd;
  What place is for my testimony void?[3]
Or, to so many, and so *Broad-seales*[4] had,
  What can one witnesse, and a weake one, add
5 To such a worke, as could not need theirs? Yet
  If Praises, when th'are full, heaping admit,
My suffrage brings thee all increase, to crowne
  Thy *Richard*, rais'd in song, past pulling downe.

BEN: JONSON

34. TO THE WORTHY AUTHOR ON THE HUSBAND[1]

IT fits not onely him that makes a Booke,
  To see his worke be good; but that he looke[2]
Who are his Test, and what their judgement is:
  Least a false praise do make theyr dotage his.
5 I do not feele that ever yet I had
  The art of uttring[3] wares, if they were bad;

33: [1] prefixed to Christopher Brooke, *The Ghost of Richard the Third* (1614). Brooke (d. 1628) was a lawyer and friend of Donne and William Browne.
[2] other congratulatory poems by Chapman, Browne, and others.
[3] empty.
[4] Great Seal of England; thus warranty, authorization.

34: [1] prefixed to *The Husband* (1614). The author is not known; the poem is a development from Overbury's successful work *A Wife*.
[2] consider.
[3] publishing.

   Or skill of making matches in my life:
    And therefore I commend unto the *Wife*,
   That went before, a *Husband*. Shee, Ile sweare,
10   Was worthy of a Good one; And this, here,
   I know for such, as (if my word will waigh)
    Shee need not blush upon the *Mariage-Day*.

             Ben: Jonson.

35. BEN JOHNSONS GRACE BEFORE KINGE JAMES

OUr Royall King & Queene, God Bless
Thee Pallzgrave[1] and the Ladye Besse
God bless pembrooke,[2] and the state
And Buckingham[3] the fortunate
God blesse the Counsell[4] & keep them save
And God bless mee, and God blesse Raphe.[5]

36

MY masters and friends, and good people draw neere,[1]
And looke to your purses, for that I doe say;
And though little money, in them you doe beare,
It cost more to get, then to lose in a day.
5   You oft have beene told,
    Both the young and the old;
    And bidden beware of the cutpurse so bold:

35: [1] Frederick Elector Pala-
tine, who married Elizabeth (the
Ladye Besse), James's daughter,
February 14, 1613.
 [2] William Herbert (1580–
1630), Lord Chamberlain under
James.
 [3] George Villiers (1592–
1628).

[4] Council of State.
 [5] according to Aubrey, the man
in the Swan tavern who served
Jonson canary wine. See H&S XI.
162f.
36: [1] from *Bartholomew Fayre*
III.v (first performed 1614);
sung by Nightengale, a ballad
singer.

Then if you take heed not, free me from the curse,
Who both give you warning for, and[2] the cutpurse.
10   Youth, youth, thou hadst better bin starv'd by thy
                                                    [Nurse,
Then live to be hanged for cutting a purse.

It hath bin upbrayded to men of my trade,
That oftentimes we are the cause of this crime.
Alacke and for pitty, why should it be said?
15   As if they regarded or places, or time.
              Examples have been
              Of some that were seen,
              In Westminster Hall, yea the pleaders between,
Then why should the Judges be free from this curse,
20   More then my poore selfe, for cutting the purse?
Youth, youth, thou hadst better bin starv'd by thy
                                                    [Nurse,
Then live to be hanged for cutting a purse.

At Worc'ter 'tis knowne well, and even i' the Jayle,
A Knight of good worship did there shew his face,
25   Against the foule sinners, in zeale for to rayle,
And lost (*ipso facto*) his purse in the place.[3]
              Nay, once from the Seat
              Of Judgement so great,
              A Judge there did lose a faire pouch of velvete.[4]
30   O Lord for thy mercy, how wicked or worse,
Are those that so venture their necks for a purse!
Youth, youth, &c.

At Playes and at Sermons, and at the Sessions,
'Tis daily their practice such booty to make:
35   Yea, under the Gallowes, at Executions,
They sticke not the *Stare-abouts* purses to take.

---

2 for, and: and moreover.
3 not identified.
4 H&S (X.199) identify as a
trick played by Sir Thomas More
on a judge who had lectured
victims of theft to be more care-
ful. More had a man cut the
judge's purse.

Nay one without grace,
At a far better place,
At *Court*, & in *Christmas*, before the Kings
[face.[5]

40 Alack then for pitty, must I beare the curse,
That onely belongs to the cunning cutpurse?

But O, you vile nation of cutpurses all,
Relent and repent, and amend and be sound,
And know that you ought not, by honest mens fall,
45 Advance your owne fortunes, to die above ground,
And though you goe gay,
In silkes as you may,
It is not the high way to heaven, (as they say)
Repent then, repent you, for better, for worse:
50 And kisse[6] not the Gallowes for cutting a purse.
Youth, youth, thou hadst better bin sterv'd by thy
[Nurse,
Then live to be hanged for cutting a purse.

37. TO MY TRULY-BELOV'D FREIND,
MR. BROWNE:
ON HIS *PASTORALS*[1]

SOme men, of Bookes or Freinds not speaking right,
May hurt them more with praise, then Foes with
[spight.
But I have seene thy worke, and I know thee:
And, if thou list[2] thy selfe, what thou canst bee.
5 For, though but early in these pathes thou tread,[3]
I find thee write most worthy to be read.

[5] done by John Selman at
Whitehall; he was hanged for the
crime on January 7, 1612 (H&S).
[6] go to.
37: [1] prefixed to *Britannia's
Pastorals. The Second Booke*
(1616), by William Browne.
The book is dedicated to the Earl
of Pembroke, who was also Jon-
son's patron. In Book II, Song
12, Browne praises Jonson among
other writers.
[2] enlist; engage yourself.
[3] In 1616 Browne was about
twenty-five.

It must be thine owne judgment, yet, that sends
  This thy worke forth: that judgment mine com-
                      [mends.
And, where the most reade bookes, on *Authors*
                      [fames,
10   Or, like our Money-Brokers, take up names
  On credit, and are cossen'd;[4] see, that thou
  By offring not more sureties, then inow,
  Hold thyne owne worth unbroke: which is so good
    Upon th'*Exchange*[5] of *Letters*, as[6] I wou'd
15 More of our writers would like thee, not swell
    With the *how much* they set forth, but th'*how well*.
                              BEN. JONSON.

38. TO MY WORTHY AND HONOUR'D FRIEND, MR *GEORGE CHAPMAN*, ON HIS TRANSLATION OF HESIODS WORKS, & DAYES[1]

WHose worke could this be, *Chapman*, to refine
Olde *Hesiods* Ore, and give it us; but thine,
Who hadst before wrought in rich *Homers* Mine?[2]

What treasure hast thou brought us! and what store
5 Still, still, dost thou arrive with, at our shore,
To make thy honour, and our wealth the more!

If all the vulgar Tongues, that speake this day,
Were askt of thy Discoveries; They must say,
To the Greeke coast thine onely knew the way.

10 Such Passage hast thou found, such Returnes made,
As, now, of all men, it is call'd thy Trade:
And who make thither else, rob, or invade.
                            Ben: Jonson.

4 tricked.
5 where business was transacted.
6 that.
38: 1 prefixed to George Chapman, *The Georgicks of Hesiod* (1618). Later the two dramatists and translators became enemies.
2 Beginning in 1598, Chapman had translated Homer.

39. CHARLES CAVENDISH TO HIS
POSTERITIE[1]

Ben: Jonson.
 Sonnes seeke not me amonge these polish'd stones:
 These only hide part of my flesh, and bones:
 Which, did they neere so neate, or proudly dwell,
 Will all turne dust, & may not make me swell.[2]
5 Let such as justly have out-liv'd all prayse,
 Trust in the tombes, their care-full freinds do
              [rayse;
 I made my lyfe my monument, & yours:
 To which[3] there's no materiall that endures;
 Nor yet inscription like it. Write but that;
10 And teach your nephewes[4] it to æmulate:
 It will be matter lowd inoughe to tell
 Not when I died but how I livd. Farewell.

40. ON THE AUTHOR, WORKE, AND
TRANSLATOR[1]

 WHo tracks this Authors, or Translators Pen,
 Shall finde, that either hath read Bookes, and Men:
 To say but one, were single.[2] Then it chimes,
 When the old words doe strike on the new times,
5 As in this *Spanish Proteus*;[3] who, though writ
 But in one tongue, was form'd with the worlds wit:

39: [1] Earl of Newcastle (c.
1553–1619). He left three chil-
dren and is buried at Bolsover,
Derbyshire. See *Under.* 55, 61.
 [2] with pride.
 [3] compared to which.
 [4] descendants.
40: [1] prefixed to James Mabbe,
The Rogue: or The Life of Guz-
man de Alfarache. Written in
Spanish by Matheo Aleman
(1622). Mabbe (1572–1642?)
later translated other Spanish
works.
 [2] slight, trivial.
 [3] sea god who could change his
shape.

And hath the noblest marke of a good Booke,
That an ill man dares not securely looke
Upon it, but will loath, or let it passe,
10　As a deformed face doth a true glasse.
Such Bookes deserve Translators, of like coate
As was the *Genius* wherewith they were wrote;
And this hath met that one, that may be stil'd
More then the Foster-father of this Child;
15　For though *Spaine* gave him his first ayre and Vogue,
He would be call'd, henceforth, the *English-Rogue*,
But that hee's too well suted,[4] in a cloth,
Finer then was his *Spanish*, if my Oath
Will bee receiv'd in Court; If not, would I
20　Had cloath'd him so. Here's all I can supply
To your desert, who'have done it, Friend. And this
Faire Æmulation, and no Envy is;
When you behold me wish my selfe, the man
That would have done, that, which you onely can.

　　　　　　　　　　　　　　　　Ben: Jonson.

41. TO THE READER[1]

THis Figure, that thou here seest put,
　　It was for gentle Shakespeare cut;
Wherein the Graver had a strife
　　with Nature, to out-doo the life:
5　O, could he but have drawne his wit
　　As well in brasse, as he hath hit
His face; the Print would then surpasse
　　All, that was ever writ in brasse.[2]
But, since he cannot, Reader, looke
10　　Not on his Picture, but his Booke.

　　　　　　　　　　　　　　　　　　B. J.

---

[4] pun: dressed, and adapted to.
41: [1] prefixed, with the next poem, to William Shakespeare, *Comedies, Histories, & Tragedies* (1623). This poem faces the engraving ("Figure," l. 1) of Shakespeare by Droeshout.
[2] a copper-zinc alloy used by engravers for books.

42. TO THE MEMORY OF MY BELOVED, THE AUTHOR MR. WILLIAM SHAKESPEARE: AND WHAT HE HATH LEFT US[1]

TO draw no envy (*Shakespeare*) on thy name,
    Am I thus ample[2] to thy Booke, and Fame:
While I confesse thy writings to be such,
    As neither *Man*, nor *Muse*, can praise too much.
5   'Tis true, and all mens suffrage.[3] But these wayes
    Were not the paths I meant unto thy praise:
For seeliest[4] Ignorance on these may light,
    Which, when it sounds at best, but eccho's right;
Or blinde Affection, which doth ne're advance
10   The truth, but gropes, and urgeth all by chance;
Or crafty Malice, might pretend this praise,
    And thinke to ruine, where it seem'd to raise.
These are, as[5] some infamous Baud, or Whore,
    Should praise a Matron. What could hurt her more?
15   But thou art proofe against them, and indeed
    Above th'ill fortune of them, or the need.
I, therefore will begin. Soule of the Age!
    The applause! delight! the wonder of our Stage!
My *Shakespeare*, rise; I will not lodge thee by
20   *Chaucer*, or *Spenser*, or bid *Beaumont*[6] lye
A little further, to make thee a roome:
    Thou art a Moniment, without a tombe,

42: [1] prefixed, with the preceding poem, to William Shakespeare, *Comedies, Histories, & Tragedies* (1623).
  [2] copious.
  [3] consent.
  [4] simplest.
  [5] as though.
  [6] All three are buried in Westminster Abbey; Shakespeare was buried in Stratford. W. Basse, in a poem printed in Donne's *Poems* of 1633, had written,

Renowned Spencer lye a thought
    more nye
To learned Chaucer, and rare
    Beaumont, lye
A little neerer Spenser, to make
    roome
For Shakespeare . . . .

And art alive still, while thy Booke doth live,
    And we have wits to read, and praise to give.
25   That I not mixe thee so, my braine excuses;
    I meane with great, but disproportion'd *Muses:*
For, if I thought my judgement were of yeeres,[7]
    I should commit[8] thee surely with thy peeres,
And tell, how farre thou didst our *Lily*[9] out-shine,
30   Or sporting *Kid*,[10] or *Marlowes* mighty line.
And though thou hadst small *Latine*, and lesse *Greeke*,
    From thence to honour thee, I would not seeke[11]
For names; but call forth thund'ring *Æschilus*,
    Euripides, and *Sophocles* to us,
35   *Paccuvius, Accius*,[12] him of *Cordova* dead,[13]
    To life againe, to heare thy Buskin[14] tread,
And shake a Stage: Or, when thy Sockes[15] were on,
    Leave thee alone, for the comparison
Of all, that insolent *Greece*, or haughtie *Rome*
40   sent forth, or since did from their ashes come.
Triúmph, my *Britaine*, thou hast one to showe,
    To whom all Scenes of *Europe* homage owe.
He was not of an age, but for all time!
    And all the *Muses* still were in their prime,
45   When like *Apollo* he came forth to warme
    Our eares, or like a *Mercury* to charme!
Nature her selfe was proud of his designes,
    And joy'd to weare the dressing of his lines!
Which were so richly spun, and woven so fit,
50   As,[16] since, she will vouchsafe no other Wit.
The merry *Greeke*, tart *Aristophanes*,
    Neat *Terence*, witty *Plautus*, now not please;

---

[7] i.e., over the course of many years: beyond the Elizabethans named back to the classical writers.

[8] unite, connect.

[9] best known for his prose comedies which precede Shakespeare's.

[10] best known for his *Spanish Tragedy*, which influenced Shakespeare. Jonson puns on his name with "sporting"; his plays are hardly playful.

[11] have a hard time finding.

[12] Roman tragic writers.

[13] Seneca, whose tragedies influenced the Elizabethan writers.

[14] representing tragedy.

[15] representing comedy.

[16] that.

But antiquated, and deserted lye
     As[17] they were not of Natures family.
55 Yet must I not give Nature all: Thy Art,
     My gentle *Shakespeare*, must enjoy a part.
For though the *Poets* matter,[18] Nature be,
     His Art doth give the fashion. And, that he,
Who casts[19] to write a living line, must sweat,
60   (such as thine are) and strike the second heat
Upon the *Muses* anvile: turne the same,
     (And himselfe with it) that he thinkes to frame;
Or for the lawrell, he may gaine a scorne,
     For a good *Poet's* made, as well as borne.
65 And such wert thou. Looke how the fathers face
     Lives in his issue, even so, the race
Of *Shakespeares* minde, and manners brightly shines
     In his well torned, and true-filed lines:
In each of which, he seemes to shake a Lance,[20]
70   As brandish't at the eyes of Ignorance.
Sweet Swan of *Avon!*[21] what a sight it were
     To see thee in our waters yet appeare,
And make those flights upon the bankes of *Thames*,
     That so did take *Eliza*, and our *James!*
75 But stay, I see thee in the *Hemisphere*
     Advanc'd, and made a Constellation there!
Shine forth, thou Starre of *Poets*, and with rage,
     Or influence, chide, or cheere the drooping Stage;
Which, since thy flight from hence, hath mourn'd like
                                                    [night,
80 And despaires day, but for thy Volumes light.
                                        BEN: JONSON.

[17] as though.
[18] subject matter.
[19] intends.
[20] The pun on Shakespeare's name had begun with Robert Greene's "Shake-scene" in his *Groat's-worth of Wit* (1592).

See also l. 37 above.
[21] For the Swan imagery applied to another poet, see No. 14 above to Hugh Holland. There, too, the swan turned into the constellation Cygnus (l. 99).

43

TRuth is the triall of it selfe,[1]
    And needs no other touch.[2]
And purer then the purest Gold
    Refine it neere so much.
5   It is the life and light of love,
    The Sunne that ever shineth
And spirit of that speciall Grace,
    That Faith and Love defineth.
It is the Warrant of the Word,
10   That yeeld's a sent[3] so sweete,
As gives a power to faith, to tread
    All false-hood under feete.
It is the Sword that doth divide,[4]
    The Marrow from the Bone,
15   And in effect of Heavenly love
    Doth shew the Holy one.
This blessed Warre, thy blessed Booke
    Unto the world doth prove.[5]
A worthy worke, and worthy well
20   Of the most worthie love.

                B. J.

43: [1] prefixed to *The Touchstone of Truth. Wherein Veritie, by Scripture Is Plainely Confirmed, and Errour Confuted* (1624), taken from the Dedication to be by James Warre, about whom nothing else is known. It is a compendium of Biblical quotation, directed against Catholics. There seems to be little reason why Jonson should be interested in such a book; this fact, plus the weakness of some of the lines, makes it very doubtful that he wrote this poem.
[2] test.
[3] scent.
[4] Heb. 4:12.
[5] establish.

44. OVER THE DOOR AT THE ENTRANCE INTO THE APOLLO[1]

WElcome all that lead or follow,
To the Oracle of Apollo—[2]
Here he speaks out of his Pottle,[3]
Or the Tripos,[4] his Tower[5] Bottle:
5   All his Answers are Divine,
Truth it self doth flow in Wine.[6]
Hang up all the poor Hop-Drinkers,[7]
Cries Old *Sym*,[8] the King of Skinkers;[9]
He the half of Life abuses,
10   That sits watering with the Muses.
Those dull Girls no good can mean us,
Wine, it is the Milk of Venus,
And the Poet's Horse[10] accounted:
Ply it, and you all are mounted.
15   'Tis the true Phoebeian[11] Liquor,
Chears the Brains, makes Wit the quicker,
Pays all Debts, cures all Diseases,
And at once three Senses pleases.
Welcome, all that lead or follow,
20   To the Oracle of Apollo.

44: [1] The Apollo was a room on the first floor of the Devil Inn, built in the summer of 1624. H&S (XI.294ff.) have a short history of its literary associations until the building was torn down in 1787.

[2] H&S suggest Rabelais's "Oracle of the Bottle," *Pantagruel* V.34. Apollo was god of poetry.

[3] a large tankard.

[4] tripod: a three-legged vessel; such had been employed at the shrine of Apollo at Delphi.

[5] i.e., in such a shape.

[6] *In vino veritas*.

[7] i.e., of beer or ale.

[8] Simon Wadlow, the tavern keeper (H&S).

[9] tapsters.

[10] Pegasus: poetic inspiration.

[11] i.e., of Phoebus Apollo.

45. TO THE MEMORYE OF THAT MOST HON-OURED LADIE *JANE*,[1] ELDEST DAUGHTER, TO *CUTHBERT* LORD *OGLE*: AND COUNTESSE OF *SHREWSBURY*:—

I Could begin with that grave forme, *Here lies*,
And pray thee *Reader*, bring thy weepinge Eyes
To see who'it is? A noble *Countesse*, greate,
In blood, in birth, by match, and by her seate;[2]
5   Religious, wise, chast, loving, gratious, good,
And number Attributes unto a flood:
But every *Table*[3] in this *Church* can say,
A list of Epithites: And prayse this way.
No stone in any wall here, but can tell
10   Such things, of every body, and as well.
Nay they will venter ones *Descent* to hitt,[4]
And Christian name too, with a *Heralds* witt.
But, I would have thee, to know something new,
Not usuall in a *Lady*; and yet true:
15   At least so *great* a Lady, she was *wife*
But of one *Husband*; and since he left life,[5]
But[6] *Sorrow*, she desir'd no other *friend:*
And her,[7] she made her Inmate, to the End
To call on *Sicknes* still, to be her Guest,
20   Whom shee, with *Sorrow* first did lodge, then feast,
Then entertaine, and as *Deaths* Harbinger;
So woo'd at last, that he was wonne to her
Importune wish; and by her lov'd *Lords* side
To lay her here, inclos'd, his second *Bride*.
25   Where spight of *Death*, next *Life*, for her Loves sake
This second marriage, will æternall make.

45: [1] She died January 7, 1625, and is buried in Westminster Abbey (H&S).
    [2] noble status.
    [3] tablet.
[4] to print one's ancestry.
[5] Cuthbert, Earl of Shrewsbury, had died in 1618 (H&S).
[6] except for.
[7] i.e., sorrow.

46

FResh as the Day, and new as are the Howers,[1]
Our first of fruits, that is the prime of flowers
Bred by your breath, on this low bancke of ours;
   Now, in a garland by the graces knit:
5   Upon this obeliske, advanc'd for it,
   We offer as a Circle the most fit
To Crowne the years, which you begin, great king,
And you, with them, as Father of our spring.

47. TO MY CHOSEN FRIEND, *THE LEARNED TRANSLATOR* OF LUCAN, THOMAS MAY, *ESQUIRE*[1]

WHen, *Rome*, I reade thee in thy mighty paire,[2]
And see both climing up the slippery staire
Of Fortunes wheele by *Lucan* driv'n about,
And the world in it, I begin to doubt,
5   At every line some pinn thereof should slacke
At least, if not the generall Engine cracke.
But when againe I veiw the parts so peiz'd,[3]
And those in number so, and measure rais'd,
As[4] neither *Pompey's* popularitie,
10   *Cæsar's* ambition, *Cato's* libertie,
Calme *Brutus* tenor[5] start;[6] but all along
Keepe due proportion in the ample song,
It makes me ravish'd with just wonder, cry
What Muse, or rather God of harmony

46: [1] fragment, perhaps from a masque addressed to King Charles early in his reign.
47: [1] prefixed to *Lucan's Pharsalia: or The Civill Warres of Rome, betweene Pompey the Great, and Julius Caesar*, trans. Thomas May (1627). May (1595–1650) also translated other classical writings.
[2] Caesar and Pompey.
[3] balanced.
[4] that.
[5] condition of mind.
[6] turn aside, swerve.

15   Taught *Lucan* these true moodes![7] replyes my sence
      What godds but those of arts, and eloquence?
      Phœbus, and *Hermes?* They whose tongue, or pen
      Are still th'interpreters twixt godds, and men!
      But who hath them interpreted, and brought
20   *Lucans* whole frame unto us, and so wrought,
      As not the smallest joint, or gentlest word
      In the great masse, or machine there is stirr'd?
      The selfe same *Genius!* so the worke will say.
      The *Sunne*[8] translated, or the Sonne of *May.*[9]
            Your true freind in Judgement and Choise
                                          BEN: JONSON.

              48. THE VISION OF
              BEN. JONSON, ON THE
              MUSES OF HIS FRIEND
              M. DRAYTON[1]

      IT hath beene question'd, *Michael,* if I bee
      A Friend at all;[2] or, if at all, to thee:
      Because, who[3] make the question, have not seene
      Those ambling visits, passe in verse, betweene
5   Thy *Muse,* and mine, as they expect. 'Tis true:
      You have not writ to me,[4] nor I to you;
      And, though I now begin, 'tis not to rub
      Hanch against Hanch, or raise a riming *Club*

[7] modes: scales.

[8] Phoebus Apollo: the sun god.

[9] Mercury, i.e., Hermes, son of Maia, with a pun on the author's name.

48: [1] prefixed to Michael Drayton, *The Battaile of Agincourt* . . . . *The Miseries of Queene Margarite* . . . . *Nimphidia* . . . . *The Quest of Cinthia. The Shepheards Sirena. The Moone Calfe. Elegies upon Sundry Occasions* (1627). Drayton was a contemporary dramatist and poet to whom Jonson had addressed nothing until this poem.

[2] In the *Conversations with Drummond* (1619), Jonson had told Drummond that he and Drayton were not friends.

[3] those who.

[4] For the first time, Drayton praises Jonson in his Letter to Reynolds, printed in his volume, p. 207.

About the towne: this reck'ning I will pay,
10   Without conferring symboles.[5] This's my day.
      It was no Dreame! I was awake, and saw!
      Lend me thy voyce, O *Fame*, that I may draw
      Wonder to truth! and have my Vision hoorld,
      Hot from thy trumpet, round, about the world.[6]
15   I saw a Beauty from the Sea to rise,
      That all Earth look'd on; and that earth, all Eyes!
      It cast a beame as when the chear-full Sun
      Is fayre got up, and day some houres begun!
      And fill'd an Orbe as circular, as heaven!
20   The Orbe was cut forth into Regions seaven.[7]
      And those so sweet, and well proportion'd parts,
      As it had beene the circle of the Arts![8]
      When, by thy bright *Ideas*[9] standing by,
      I found it pure, and perfect *Poësy*,
25   There read I, streight, thy learned *Legends* three,[10]
      Heard the soft ayres, between our Swaynes & thee,
      Which made me thinke, the old *Theocritus*,[11]
      Or Rurall *Virgil* come, to pipe to us!
      But then, thy'epistolar *Heroick* Songs,[12]
30   Their loves, their quarrels, jealousies, and wrongs,
      Did all so strike me, as I cry'd, who can
      With us be call'd, the *Naso*,[13] but this man?
      And looking up, I saw *Minervas* fowle,
      Pearch'd over head, the wise *Athenian* Owle:[14]
35   I thought thee then our *Orpheus*,[15] that wouldst try
      Like him, to make the ayre, one volary:[16]

[5] comparing contributions.

[6] This, and the lines which follow, suggest to J. W. Hebel, editor of Drayton, not praise but over-praise: satire. See *PMLA*, XXXIX (1923), 830–32. The fact that Drayton printed the poem in his volume suggests that he at least took it at face value.

[7] See the seven titles of the title page above.

[8] the seven liberal arts.

[9] *Idea; The Shepheards Garland*, 1593.

[10] *Piers Gaveston, Matilda*, and the *Tragicall Legend of Robert Duke of Normandy*, plays published in 1596.

[11] Both Theocritus and Virgil wrote pastoral poetry.

[12] *Englands Heroicall Epistles*, 1597.

[13] Ovid.

[14] *The Owle*, 1604.

[15] great classical musician; birds came to hear his music.

[16] bird cage.

And I had stil'd thee, *Orpheus*, but before
My lippes could forme the voyce, I heard that Rore,
And Rouze, the Marching of a mighty force,
40 Drums against Drums, the neighing of the Horse,
The Fights, the Cryes, and wondring at the Jarres
I saw, and read, it was thy *Barons Warres!*[17]
O, how in those, dost thou instruct these times,
That Rebells actions, are but valiant crimes!
45 And caried, though with shoute, and noyse, confesse
A wild, and an authoriz'd[18] wickednesse!
Sayst thou so, *Lucan?*[19] But thou scornst to stay
Under one title. Thou hast made thy way
And flight about the Ile, well neare,[20] by this,
50 In thy admired *Periégesis*,[21]
Or universall circumduction
Of all that reade thy *Poly-Olbyon*.[22]
That reade it? that are ravish'd! such was I
With every song, I sweare, and so would dye:
55 But that I heare, againe, thy Drum to beate
A better cause, and strike the bravest heate
That ever yet did fire the *English* blood!
Our right in *France!*[23] if ritely understood.
There, thou art *Homer!* Pray thee, use the stile
60 Thou hast deserv'd: And let me reade the while
Thy Catalogue of Ships,[24] exceeding his,
Thy list of aydes, and force, for so it is:
The Poets act! and for his Country's sake
Brave are the Musters, that the Muse will make.
65 And when he ships them where to use their Armes,
How do his trumpets breath! What loud alarmes!
Looke, how we read the Spartans were inflam'd
With bold *Tyrtæus*[25] verse, when thou art nam'd,

---

[17] *The Barrons Wars in the Raign of Edward the Second*, 1603, revised from *Mortimeriados*, 1596.

[18] legally sanctioned.

[19] author of the *Pharsalia*, a poem about the Roman civil wars.

[20] quite nearly.

[21] circumduction: leading about as a guide to describe a region.

[22] published in 1612 and 1622.

[23] *Battle of Agincourt* in this volume.

[24] *Agincourt*, ll. 345ff.

[25] classic Greek poet who roused the Lacedaemonians to war.

So shall our *English* Youth urge on, and cry
70   An *Agincourt*, an *Agincourt*, or dye.
This booke! it is a *Catechisme*[26] to fight,
And will be bought of every Lord, and Knight,
That can but reade; who cannot, may in prose
Get broken peeces, and fight well by those.
75   The miseries of *Margaret* the Queene[27]
Of tender eyes will more be wept, then seene:
I feele it by mine owne, that over flow,
And stop my sight, in every line I goe.
But then refreshed, with thy *Fayerie Court*,
80   I looke on *Cynthia*, and *Sirenas*[28] sport,
As, on two flowry Carpets, that did rise,
And with their grassie greene restor'd mine eyes.
Yet give mee leave, to wonder at the birth
Of thy strange *Moon-Calfe*,[29] both thy straine of
[mirth,
85   And Gossip-got acquaintance, as, to us
Thou hadst brought *Lapland*,[30] or old *Cobalus*,[31]
Empusa,[32] *Lamia*,[33] or some Monster, more
Then *Affricke* knew, or the full *Grecian* store![34]
I gratulate[35] it to thee, and thy *Ends*,[36]
90   To all thy vertuous, and well chosen Friends,
Onely my losse is, that I am not there:
And, till I worthy am to wish I were,
I call the world, that envies mee, to see
If I can be a Friend, and Friend to thee.

[26] here, book of instruction.
[27] in the present volume; she was wife of Henry VI.
[28] All three titles are in the present volume.
[29] idiot. The work is in the present volume.
[30] traditional haunt for witches.

[31] demon of the mines.
[32] ghost in Aristophanes' *Frogs*.
[33] monster who devoured children.
[34] i.e., of mythology.
[35] joy over it.
[36] the *Elegies*, last poem in this volume.

49

'Ο Ζεὺς κατεῖδε χρόνιος εἰς τὰς διφθερὰς[1]

T'Is a Record in heaven. You, that were
Her Children, and Grand-children, reed it heere!
Transmitt it to your Nephewes,[2] Freinds, Allies,
Tenants, and Servants, have they[3] harts, and eyes
5   To veiw the truth and owne it. Doe but looke
With pause upon it; make this page your booke;
Your booke? your volume! Nay, the state, and story!
Code, Digests, Pandects[4] of all fæmale glory!

Diphthera Jovis:[5]~

Shee was the light (without reflexe[6]
10   Upon her selfe) to all her sexe!
The best of Woemen! her whole life
Was the example of a wife!
Or of a parent! or a freind!
All Circles had their spring and end
15   In her! and what could perfect bee,
Or without angles,[7] it was shee!
All that was solid, in the name
Of vertue, pretious in the frame:
Or else Magnetique in the force,
20   Or sweet, or various, in the course!
What was proportion, or could bee
By warrant call'd just Symetry,
In number, measure, or degree
Of weight, or fashion, it was shee.

49:   [1] In the fullness of time Zeus observes the records. H&S identify this as a proverb in Stephens' *Thesaurus*. The poem is an epitaph on Katherine, Baroness Ogle, sister of the lady of No. 45. She died on April 18, 1629, and was buried at Bulsover (H&S).
[2] descendants.

[3] if they have.
[4] the Roman law code of Justinian.
[5] the hide (i.e., the record written on it) of Jove.
[6] reflection.
[7] The ancients considered the circle to be perfect, the straight or angled line imperfect.

25   Her soule possest her fleshes state
        In faire freehould,[8] not an Inmate:
        And when the flesh, here, shut up day,
        Fames heate upon the grave did stay;
        And howrely brooding ore the same,
30   Keeps warme the spice of her good name,
        Untill the dust retorned bee
        Into a *Phœnix*,[9] which is shee.

        For this did Katherine, Ladie Ogle, die
        To gaine the Crowne of immortalitye,
35   Æternities great charter; which became
        Her right, by gift, and purchase of the Lambe:
        Seal'd and deliver'd to her, in the sight
        Of Angells, and all witnesses of light,
        Both Saints, and Martyrs, by her loved Lord.
40   And this a coppie is of the Record.

50. ON THE HONOR'D POËMS OF HIS HONORED FRIEND, SIR *JOHN BEAUMONT*, BARONET[1]

        THis Booke will live; It hath a *Genius*: This
        Above his Reader, or his Prayser, is.
        Hence, then, prophane: Here needs no words expense
        In Bulwarkes, Rav'lins,[2] Ramparts, for defense,
5   Such, as the creeping common Pioners[3] use
        When they doe sweat to fortifie a Muse.
        Though I confesse a *Beaumonts* Booke to bee
        The Bound, and Frontire of our Poëtrie;
        And doth deserve all muniments[4] of praise,
10   That Art, or Ingine,[5] on the strength can raise.

---

[8] tenure for life.
[9] See the symbolism in *The Forrest*, 9, 10.
50: [1] prefixed to John Beaumont, *Bosworth-Field* (1629). Beaumont (1583–1627) was brother of the dramatist Francis.
[2] outworks of a fortification.
[3] foot soldiers.
[4] protections.
[5] wit; also, military device.

Yet, who dares offer a redoubt[6] to reare?
   To cut a Dike? or sticke a Stake up, here,
Before this worke? where Envy hath not cast
A Trench against it, nor a Battry plac't?
15 Stay, till she make her vaine Approches. Then
   If, maymed, she come off, tis not of men
This Fort of so impregnable accesse,
   But higher power, as spight could not make lesse,
Nor flatt'ry! but secur'd, by the Authors Name,
20   Defies, whats crosse to[7] Piety, or good Fame.
And like a hallow'd Temple, free from taint
Of Ethnicisme,[8] makes his Muse a Saint.[9]

Ben. Jonson.

51. TO MY WORTHY FRIEND, MASTER *EDWARD FILMER*, ON HIS WORKE PUBLISHED[1]

WHat charming Peales are these,
   That, while they bind the senses, doe so please?
   They are the Mariage-rites
Of two, the choicest Paire of Mans delights,
5   *Musique* and *Poesie:*
French Aire and *English* Verse here Wedded lie.
   Who did this Knot compose,
Againe hath brought the *Lillie* to the *Rose;*[2]
   And, with their Chained dance,
10 Recelebrates the joyfull Match with *France.*

---

6 a small field defense.
7 adverse to.
8 paganism.
9 There are several religious poems in the book. Newdigate observes that Beaumont was a Roman Catholic.
51: 1 prefixed to Edward Filmer, *French Court-Aires* (1629). Filmer, who died in 1669, translated the words from French originals.
2 The lily represents the French, the rose the English. See *Under.* 67.

They are a Schoole to win
The faire *French* Daughter to learne *English* in;
And, graced with her song,
To make the Language sweet upon her tongue.[3]

Ben: Jonson.

52

IT was a beauty that I saw[1]
So pure, so perfect, as the frame
Of all the universe was lame,
To that one figure, could I draw,
5   Or give least line of it a law!

A skeine of silke without a knot!
A fair march made without a halt!
A curious[2] forme without a fault!
A printed booke without a blot!
10   All beauty, and without a spot!

53. ODE TO HIMSELFE[1]

COme leave the loathed Stage,
And the more loathsome Age,
Where pride and impudence in faction knit,
Usurpe the Chaire of wit:
5   Inditing and arraigning every day,
Something they call a Play.

[3] from the *Canterbury Tales*, General Prologue, l. 265.
52:    [1] from *The New Inn* IV.iv (first performed 1629), sung by Lovel, "a compleat gentleman."
[2] beautifully wrought.
53:    [1] provoked by the poor reception of Jonson's *The New Inn* in 1629. On the title page of the play he blames everyone for the failure: "A Comoedy. As it was never acted, but most negligently play'd, by some, the Kings Servants, and censured by others, the Kings Subjects. 1629. Now, at last, set at liberty to the Readers, his Majesties Servants, and Subjects, to be judg'd."

Let their fastidious vaine
Commission of the braine,
Runne on, and rage, sweat, censure, and condemn:
10 They were not made for thee, lesse thou for them.

Say that thou pour'st'hem wheat,
And they would Akornes eat:
'Twere simple² fury, still thy selfe to wast
On such as have no taste:
15 To offer them a surfeit of pure bread,
Whose appetites are dead:
No, give them Graines³ their fill,
Huskes, Draffe⁴ to drinke, and swill:
If they love Lees, and leave the lusty Wine,
20 Envy them not, their pallat's with the Swine.

No doubt a mouldy Tale,
Like Pericles,⁵ and stale
As the Shrives⁶ crusts, and nasty as his Fish,
Scraps out of every Dish,
25 Throwne forth and rak'd into the common Tub,⁷
May keep up the Play Club.⁸
Broomes⁹ sweepings doe as well
There, as his Masters meale:
For who the relish of these guests will fit,
30 Needs set them but the Almes-basket of wit.

And much good do't yee then,
Brave Plush and Velvet men
Can feed on Orts;¹⁰ and safe in your scoene cloaths,
Dare quit upon your Oathes
35 The Stagers, and the stage-writes too; your Peers,
Of stuffing your large eares

² foolish.
³ refuse malt left after brewing.
⁴ dregs.
⁵ attributed at least in part to Shakespeare; printed in 1609 but evidently still popular in 1629.
⁶ sheriff's: the food served in jails.
⁷ refuse collected for the poor.
⁸ See below, No. 63,
⁹ with pun on Richard Brome, Jonson's former servant, now a playwright. See below, No. 59.
¹⁰ table scraps.

With rage of Commicke socks,[11]
Wrought upon twenty Blocks;[12]
Which, if they're torne, and foule, and patch'd enough,
40 The Gamsters[13] share your gilt,[14] and you their stuffe.

Leave things so prostitute,
And take th'Alcaike[15] Lute;
Or thine owne Horace, or Anacreons[16] Lyre;
Warme thee by Pindars[17] fire:
45 And though thy Nerves[18] be shrunke, and blood be
[cold,
Ere years have made thee old,
Strike that disdainfull heat
Throughout, to their defeat:
As curious fooles, and envious of thy straine,
50 May blushing sweare, no Palsi's in thy braine.[19]

But when they heare thee sing
The glories of thy King;
His zeale to God, and his just awe of men,
They may be blood-shaken, then
55 Feele such a flesh-quake to possesse their powers,
That no tun'd Harpe like ours,
In sound of Peace or Warres,
Shall truely hit the Starres
When they shall read the Acts of *Charles* his Reigne,
60 And see his Chariot triumph 'bove his *Waine*.[20]

[11] representing comedy.
[12] punning: molds and blockheads.
[13] of the Play Club above.
[14] punning: guilt and gild.
[15] Alcaeus was an early Greek lyric poet; Horace used his alcaic meter.
[16] Greek lyric poet, sixth century B.C.
[17] greatest Greek lyric poet.
[18] sinews (Latin *nervi*).
[19] Jonson had been paralyzed by a stroke in 1628.
[20] Charles's wagon: the Big Dipper, with pun on "wane."

54. ANOTHER [EPIGRAM] ON THE BIRTH OF THE PRINCE[1]

ANother Phoenix,[2] though the first is dead,
A second's flowne from his immortall bed,
To make this our Arabia to be
The nest of an eternall progeny.
5   Choise Nature fram'd the former but to finde
What error might be mended in Man-kinde:
Like some industrious workmen, which affect
Their first endeavours onely to correct:
So this the building, that the modell was,
10   The type of all that now is come to passe:
That but the shadow, this the substance is,
All that was but a prophesie of this:
And when it did this after birth fore-runne,
'Twas but the morning starre unto this Sunne;
15   The dawning of this day, when Sol did thinke,
We having such a light, that he might wink,[3]
And we ne're misse his lustre: nay, so soone
As Charles was borne, he and the pale-fac'd Moon
With envy then did copulate,[4] to try
20   If such a Birth might be produc'd i'the'sky.
What Heavenly favour made a starre appeare,
To bid wise Kings to doe their homage here,[5]
And prove him truely Christian? Long remain
On Earth, sweet Prince, that when great Charles shal
                                  [reign
25   In Heaven above, our little Charles may be
As great on Earth, because as good as he.

54: [1] Prince Charles, born May 29, 1630. See also *Under.* 67. H&S hesitate to accept the poem as authentic.

[2] Arabian bird, reborn from its ashes. "The first" was an earlier son Charles, born May 12, 1629; he died at birth.

[3] be eclipsed. See *Under.* 67, n. 7.

[4] Johnston notes the alchemical imagery: sol (gold) and luna (silver) were thought of as parents of the philosopher's stone.

[5] Cf. Matt. 2:1ff.

55

SHall the prosperity of a Pardon still
Secure thy railing Rhymes, infamous *Gill*,[1]
At libelling? Shall no *Star-Chamber* Peers,
Pillory nor Whip, nor want of Ears,
5 All which thou hast incurr'd deservedly:
Nor Degradation from the Ministry,
To be the *Denis*[2] of thy Father's School,
Keep in thy bawling Wit, thou bawling Fool.
Thinking to stir me, thou hast lost thy End.
10 I'll laugh at thee poor wretched Tike,[3] go send
Thy blatant Muse abroad, and teach it rather
A Tune to drown the Ballads of thy Father:[4]
For thou hast nothing left to cure his Fame,
But Tune and Noise the Eccho of thy Shame.
15 A Rogue by Statute, censur'd to be whipt,
Cropt, branded, slit, neck-stockt; go, you are stript.

55: [1] addressed to Alexander
Gill, friend of Milton and son of
the master of St. Paul's School,
which Milton had attended. Jon-
son had attacked the father in
Time Vindicated (1622). The
son had attacked Jonson's
Magnetic Lady. Later he was
jailed for hostility to Charles, and
was threatened with a fine, ear-
cropping, and removal from the
ministry. He was released Nov.
30, 1630. See D. L. Clark, *John
Milton at St. Paul's School* (New
York, 1948), pp. 84ff.
  [2] Dionysius, Tyrant of Syra-
cuse; deposed, he became a
teacher and thus is synonymous
with school tyrant (H&S). For
Gill as a flogger, see Clark, p.
62.
  [3] mongrel.
  [4] i.e., songs about him. For
examples see Clark, pp. 79ff.

56. AN EXPOSTULATION WITH INIGO JONES[1]

MR Surveyor, you that first begann
From thirty pound, in pipkins,[2] to the man
You are; from them leapt forth an Architect,
Able to talk of Euclide! and correct
5   Both him & Archimede! damne Architas,[3]
The noblest Inginere that ever was!
Controll Ctesibius![4] overbearing us
With mistooke[5] names, out of Vitruvius!
Drawne Aristotle on us! & thence showne
10   How much *Architectonice*[6] is your owne!
Whether the buylding of the Stage, or Scene!
Or making of the properties, it meane!
Vizors,[7] or Anticks![8] or it comprehend
Some-thing your Surship[9] doth not yet intend!

56: [1] dated by H&S as immediately after the performance of Jonson's masque *Chloridia* in 1631 and the publication of his *Love's Triumph*, where Jonson put Jones's name below his own on the title page, to Jones's irritation. Jonson then omitted Jones entirely from the title page of *Chloridia* and went on to write this and the next two poems. They seem to have angered King Charles. Jones (1573–1652), a Catholic, the son of a poor cloth worker, had for many years collaborated with Jonson on the production of court masques. In addition, he was an important architect. Feeling between the two men had been growing for some time. Besides these three poems, H&S consider that *Epigs.* 115 and 129 are directed against Jones; he is satirically treated as Lanthorn Leatherhead in *Bartholomew Fair*, as Iniquo Vitruvius in *Love's Welcome*, and as In-and-In Medley in *Tale of a Tub* (Jones managed to have the name Vitruvius Hoop struck out of this play).
[2] pots or pans. H&S interpret as articles used in trade.
[3] Pythagorean mathematician, c. 460–390 B.C.
[4] Alexandrian engineer, c. 250 B.C.
[5] i.e., mistranslated, from Vitruvius' *De Architectura*, the standard classical work on the subject.
[6] architectural knowledge.
[7] masks worn by the actors.
[8] grotesque parts.
[9] state of being superior.

15   By all your Titles, & whole style at ones,
      Of Tyre-man,[10] Mounte-banck[11] & Justice[12] Jones,
      I doe salute you! Are you fitted,[13] yet?
      Will any of these express your place? or witt?
      Or are you soe ambitious, 'bove your Peeres,
20   You would be'an Asinigo,[14] by your ears?
      Why, much good doo't you! Be what beast you will,
      You'will be as *Langley*[15] sayd, an Inigo[16] still.
          What makes your Wretchednes to bray soe loud,
      In Towne, & Court? Are you growne rich? & proud?
25   Your Trappings will not change you. Change your
                                                  [mynd.
      Noe velvet[17] sheath, you weare, will alter kynde.[18]
      A wodden Dagger, is a Dagger of Wood[19]
      Though gold or Ivory haftes would make it good.
      What is the cause you pompe it soe? I aske;
30   And all men eccho, you have made a masque!
      I chyme[20] that too: And I have mett with those,
      That doe cry up the Machine! & the Showes![21]
      The majesty of Juno,[22] in the Clouds!
      And peering forth of Iris, in the Shrowdes![23]

---

[10] assistant in dressing actors.

[11] a soapbox actor or charlatan; see *Epig.* 129.

[12] Beginning in 1630 Jones was Justice of the Peace for Westminster.

[13] properly titled; cast to the part.

[14] Spanish *asnico*, little ass, with pun on Inigo (H&S).

[15] Francis Langley, owner of Paris Garden and builder of the Swan Theater.

[16] pun on Italian *iniquo*, wicked (H&S).

[17] Scabbards so covered were popular.

[18] your nature.

[19] carried by the character Vice (Iniquity) in the morality plays.

See, *e.g.*, *Twelfth Night* IV.ii.136ff.

[20] echo mechanically.

[21] Jones contributed the machinery and staging for the masques.

[22] H&S show that this and the following lines are applicable to *Chloridia* (X.682). Jonson's attack on his own masque here suggests that Jones had a hand in the content as well as in the staging. The characters Juno, Iris, etc., all appear as extraneous material at the end of the masque. This was Jonson's last collaboration with Jones.

[23] up among the ropes used to handle the scenery and machinery.

35 The ascent of Lady Fame! which none could spy,
  Not they that sided her, Dame Poëtry,
  Dame History, Dame Architecture too,
  And Goody[24] Sculpture, brought with much adoo,
  To hold her up. O Showes! Showes! Mighty Showes!

40 The Eloquence of Masques! What need of prose,
  Or Verse, or sense, t'express Immortall you?
  You are the Spectacles of State! T''is true
  Court Hiero-gly-phicks![25] & all Artes afford,
  In the mere perspective of an Inch board![26]

45 You aske noe more then certeyne politique Eyes!
  Eyes, that can pierce into the Misteryes
  Of many Coulors! read them! & reveale
  Mythology, there, painted on slit-deale![27]
  Ô, to make Boardes to speake! There is a taske!

50 Painting, & Carpentry, are the Soule of Masque!
  Pack with your pedling Poëtry to the Stage,
  This is the money-gett, Mechanick Age!
  To plant the Musique where noe eare can reach!
  Attyre the persons as[28] noe thought can teach

55 Sense, what they are! which by a specious, fyne
  Terme of the Architects, is called *Designe!*
  But, in the practisd truth, *Destruction* is
  Of any Art, besyde what he calls his!
  Whither? ô whither will this Tire-man growe?

60 His name is Σκενοποίος[29] wee all knowe,
  The maker of the Propertyes! in summe,
  The Scene! the Ingine! but he now is come
  To be the Musique-Master! Fabler[30] too!
  He is or would-bee the mayne Dominus doo-

65 All,[31] i'the Worke! And soe shall still, for Ben:
  Be Inigo, the Whistle,[32] & his men!

---

[24] goodwife.

[25] symbols of court pretense, as the masque characters themselves are symbolic; see *Masque of Beauty*, n. 37.

[26] i.e., Jones's devices have no depth.

[27] board or plank.

[28] so that.

[29] preparer of scene properties.

[30] plot creator; see n. 22 above.

[31] i.e., master fac-totum.

[32] agent, parasite.

Hee's warme on his feete, now, he saies! & can
Swim without Corke! Why, thank the good Queen
[Anne.[33]

I am too fatt, to'envy him. He too leane,
70   To be worth Envy. Hence-forth I doe meane
To pitty him, as smiling at his Feat
Of Lanterne-lerry:[34] with fuliginous[35] heate,
Whirling his Whymseys, by a subtilty
Suckt from the Veynes of shop-phylosophy!
75   What would he doo now, giving his mynde that way,
In praesentation of some puppet-play?
Should but the king his Justice-hood employ
In setting forth of such a serious Toye!
How would he firke,[36] lyke Adam over-doo[37]
80   Up, & about! Dyve into Cellars too,[38]
Disguisd! and thence drag forth Enormity![39]
Discover Vice! Commit Absurdity!
Under the moral! shewe he had a pate
Moulded, or stroakt up to survey[40] a State!
85   Oh wise Surveyor! wyser Architect!
But wisest Inigo! who can reflect
On the new priming of thy old signe-Postes;[41]
Reviveing with fresh colours the pale Ghosts
Of thy dead Standards:[42] or (with miracle) see
90   Thy twice conceyvd, thrice payd-for[43] Imag'rye?
And not fall downe before it? and confess
Allmighty Architecture? who noe less

[33] wife of James I and strong
supporter of masques.
[34] some method of producing
artificial light.
[35] hitting at various tricks of
fire and illumination which Jones
used for scenic effects. H&S list
some examples from the collabo-
ration of the two (XI.153f.).
[36] hurry about.
[37] Justice of the Peace in
Bartholomew Fair (1614).
[38] in *Bartholomew Fair* II.i.1ff.

(H&S).
[39] wickedness.
[40] In 1615 Jones had been ap-
pointed the King's surveyor-
general: supervisor of construc-
tion.
[41] stage materials being reused
for a new production.
[42] upright posts being re-
painted.
[43] The set was used twice;
Jones collected three times.

A Goddess is, then paynted Cloth, Deal-boards,
Vermilion, Lake, or Cinnopar[44] affoards
95 Expression for! with that unbounded line,
Aymd at, in thy omnipotent *Designe!*
What Poësy ere, was painted on a Wall,
That may compare with thee? what story shall
Of all the Worthyes hope t'outlast thy one,
100 Soe the Materialls bee, of Purbeck[45] stone!
Lyve long the Feasting Roome.[46] And e're thou burne
Againe, thy Architect to ashes turne!
Whom not ten fyres, nor a Parlyament can,
With all Remonstrance, make an honest man!

57. TO INIGO MARQUESS WOULD BE[1]
A COROLLARY

BUt 'cause thou hear'st, the mighty king of Spaine
Hath made his Inigo Marquess,[2] wouldst thou fayne
Our Charles should make thee such? T'will not be-
[come
All Kings to doe the self-same deeds with some!
5 Beside, his Man may merit it, and be
A Noble honest Soule! what's this to thee?
He may have skill, & judgment, to designe
Citties, & Temples! thou a Cave for Wyne,[3]
Or Ale! He build a pallace! Thou, a shop,
10 With slyding windowes, & false Lights a' top![4]

---

[44] cinnabar: red coloring.
[45] limestone quarried in this area of Dorsetshire.
[46] at Whitehall, burned January 12, 1619, and rebuilt by Jones (H&S).
57: [1] See previous poem, n. 1. For the title, cf. Sir Politic Would-be in *Every Man in his Humour.*

[2] Philip IV made his architect Crescenzio a marquis for his work on the Escurial (H&S).
[3] See *Under.* 50.
[4] perhaps, build a shop with the same kind of flimsy construction you use for masques. H&S suggest the design for a new Whitehall.

He draw a Forum, with quadriviall[5] Streets!
Thou paint a Lane,[6] where Thumbe,[7] the Pygmy
[meets!
He some Colossus, to bestryde the Seas,
From the fam'd pillars of old Hercules!
15   Thy Canvas-Gyant, at some Channell[8] a'mes,
Or Dowgate torrent,[9] falling into Thames!
And stradling, shews the Boyes browne-paper fleet,
Yearly set out, there, to sayle downe the street!
Your workes thus differing; troth, let soe your style:
20   Content thee to be Pancridg-Earle[10] the whyle;
An Earle of show: for all thy worth is showe!
But when thou turnst a Reall Inigo,
Or canst of truth, the least intrenchment pitch,[11]
Wee'll have thee stil'd, the Marquess of New-Ditch.[12]

58. TO A FREIND AN EPIGRAM OF HIM

SIr Inigo[1] doth feare it, as I heare,
(And labours to seem worthy of that feare)
That I should write upon him some sharp verse,
Able to eat into his bones, & pierce
5   The Marrow! wretch! I quitt[2] thee of thy paine.
Thou'rt too ambitious: and dost fear in vaine!
The Lybian Lion[3] hunts noe butter-flyes!
He makes the Camell, & dull Ass his prize!
If thou be soe desirous, to be read,
10   Seek out some hungry painter, that for bread,

[5] with four roads meeting there.
[6] small, in contrast with a forum.
[7] Jeffrey Hudson, the Queen's dwarf, who participated in *Chloridia* (H&S).
[8] gutter.
[9] a drainage ditch. H&S refer to the artificial sea in the *Masque of Blackness*.
[10] a pretended honorary personage in the annual parade of a fraternal archery group (H&S).
[11] build a fortification.
[12] a drainage ditch.
58: [1] Inigo Jones; see the two previous poems.
[2] release.
[3] The poem is adapted from Martial, *Epig.* xii.61, where the phrase appears.

With rotten chalk, or cole, upon a Wall
Will well designe thee; to be viewd of all
That sit upon the Comon Draught;[4] or Strand;[5]
Thy Forehead is too narrow, for my Brand.

59. TO MY DETRACTOR[1]

MY verses were commended, thou didst say,
　　And they were very *good*: yet thou think'st nay.
For thou objectest (as thou hast been told)
　　Th'envy'd returne, of forty pound in gold.
5　Foole, doe not rate[2] my Rymes; I have found thy Vice
　　Is to make cheape, the Lord, the lines, the price.
But barke thou on; I pitty thee, poore Cur,
　　That thou shouldst lose thy noyse, thy foame, thy
　　　　　　　　　　　　　　　　　　　　　　[slur,
To be knowne what thou art, thou blatent beast,[3]
10　　But writing against mee, thou thinkst at least,
I now would write on thee: no wretch, thy name
　　Cannot worke out unto it such a fame:
No man will tarry by thee as hee goes
　　To aske thy name, if he have half a nose;
15　But fly thee, like the Pest! Walke not the street
　　Out in the Dog-dayes, least the Killer meete
Thy Noddle, with his Club; and dashing forth
　　Thy dirty braines, men see thy want of worth.

---

[4] privy.
[5] sewer.

59: [1] Jonson is replying to an attack upon *Under.* 79, to Lord Weston:

YOur Verses were commended,
　as 'tis true,
That they were very good, I
　meane to you:
For they return'd you *Ben*, I
　have been told,
The seld seene summe of forty pound in gold.
These Verses then, being rightly understood,
His Lordship, not *Ben: Jonson*,
　made them good.

They are signed "J.E."—probably John Eliot, otherwise undistinguished.
　[2] evaluate, or berate.
　[3] Cf. *Faerie Queene* V.xii and VI.

60. TO MY OLD FAITHFULL SERVANT: AND (BY HIS CONTINU'D VERTUE) MY LOVING FRIEND: THE AUTHOR OF THIS WORK, M. RICH. BROME[1]

I Had you for a Servant, once, *Dick Brome;*
   And you perform'd a Servants faithfull parts:
Now, you are got into a nearer roome,
   Of *Fellowship,* professing my old Arts.
5   And you doe doe them well, with good applause,
     Which you have justly gained from the *Stage,*
By observation of those Comick Lawes
   Which I, your *Master,* first did teach the Age.
You learn'd it well; and for it, serv'd your time
10   A Prentise-ship: which few doe now a dayes.
Now each Court-Hobby-horse will wince in rime;
   Both learned, and unlearned, all write *Playes.*
It was not so of old: Men tooke up trades
   That knew the Crafts they had bin bred in, right:
15   An honest *Bilbo*-Smith[2] would make good blades,
     And the *Physician* teach men spue, or shite;
       The *Cobler* kept him to his nall;[3] but, now
       Hee'll be a *Pilot,* scarce can guide a Plough.

                        BEN. JONSON.

60: [1] prefixed to Richard Brome, *The Northern Lasse* (1632). Brome (d. c. 1652) began work as Jonson's servant and wrote several plays. He recognized Jonson as his master in drama. In 1629 Jonson mentions him with some disparagement (see above, No. 52).
[2] Bilbao in Spain, source of fine swords.
[3] awl.

61. TO MRS. ALICE SUTCLIFFE, ON HER DIVINE MEDITATIONS[1]

WHen I had read your holy *Meditations,*
And in them view'd th'*uncertainty* of *Life,*
The *motives,* and true *Spurres* to all good *Nations.*
The *Peace* of *Conscience,* and the *Godly's* strife,
5   The *Danger* of *delaying* to *Repent,*
And the *deceipt* of *pleasures,* by *Consent.*
The *comfort* of weake *Christians,* with their *warning,*
From fearefull *back-slides;* And the debt we'are in,
To follow *Goodnesse,* by our owne discerning
10   Our great *reward,* th'*aeternall Crown* to win.
I sayd, who'had supp'd so deepe of this sweet *Chalice,*
Must *Celia* bee, the *Anagram* of *Alice.*

                            Ben. Jonson.

62. THE GHYRLOND OF THE BLESSED VIRGIN MARIE[1]

HEre, are five letters in this blessed Name,
   Which, chang'd, a five-fold mysterie designe,
The *M.* the Myrtle, *A.* the Almonds clame,
   R. Rose, *I.* Ivy, *E.* sweet Eglantine.

61: [1] prefixed to Alice Sutcliffe, *Meditation of Man's Mortalitie* (1634). The author was wife of John Sutcliffe, Groom of the Privie Chamber. Jonson's poem outlines the contents of the book.
62: [1] prefixed to Anthony Stafford, *The Femall Glory: or, The Life, and Death of our Blessed Lady* (1635). Stafford (1587–c.

1645) was author of several religious books. Jonson's authorship of this poem is doubtful; if he did write it H&S judge that he worked on it between 1598 and 1612, when he was a Catholic. A Ghyrlond is a garland, here the symbolic representation of it as worked out in the poem.

5   These forme thy Ghyrlond. Wherof *Myrtle* green,
           The gladdest ground[2] to all the numbred-five,
       Is so implexed,[3] and laid in, between,
           As Love, here studied to keep Grace alive.

       The second string is the sweet *Almond* bloome
10   Ymounted high upon *Selinis*[4] crest:
       As it, alone, (and onely it) had roome,
           To knit thy Crowne, and glorifie the rest.

       The third, is from the garden cull'd, the *Rose*,
           The Eye of flowers, worthy, for his scent,
15   To top the fairest Lillie, now, that growes,
           With wonder on the thorny regiment.[5]

       The fourth is humble *Ivy*, intersert,[6]
           But lowlie laid, as on the earth asleep,
       Preserved, in her ántique bed of V*ert*,[7]
20   No faith's more firme, or flat, then, where't doth
                                                    [creep.

       But, that which summes all, is the *Eglantine*,
           Which, of the field is clep'd the sweetest brier,
       Inflam'd with ardor to that mystick Shine,
           In *Moses* bush,[8] un-wasted in the fire.

25   Thus, Love, and Hope, and burning Charitie,[9]
           (Divinest graces) are so entermixt,
       With od'rous sweets and soft humilitie,
           As if they' ador'd the Head, wheron th'are fixt.

---

[2] foundation.
[3] entwined.
[4] from *Faerie Queene* I.vii.32 (and also appearing in Marlowe's *Tamburlane*). Selinus is in Sicily.
[5] group or kind.
[6] put between the others.
[7] green.
[8] Exod. 3:2ff.
[9] more usually Faith, Hope, and Charity.

THE REVERSE
ON THE BACKE SIDE

THese Mysteries do point to three more great,
30   On the reverse of this your circling crowne,
        All, pouring their full showre of graces downe,
The glorious *Trinity* in *Union* met.

Daughter, and Mother, and the Spouse of *God*,
      Alike of kin, to that most blessed *Trine*,
35   Of Persons, yet in Union (*One*) divine.
How are thy gifts, and graces blaz'd abroad!

Most holy, & pure Virgin, blessed Mayd,
      Sweet Tree of Life, King *Davids* Strength and
              [Tower,[10]
      The House of gold, the Gate of heavens power,
40 The Morning-star, whose light our Fal hath stay'd.

Great Queen of Queens, most mild, most meek, most
                   [wise,
      Most venerable. Cause of all our joy.
      Whose chearfull look our sadnesse doth destroy,
And art the spotlesse Mirrour to Mans eyes.

45 The Seat of Sapience, the most lovely Mother,
      And most to be admired of thy Sexe,
      Who mad'st us happy all, in thy reflexe,[11]
By bringing forth *God's* onely Son, no other.

Thou Throne of glory, beauteous as the Moone,
50   The rosie Morning, or the rising Sun,
      Who like a Giant hasts his course to run,
Till he hath reach'd his two-fold point of Noone.[12]

[10] Newdigate points out that the imagery of this stanza comes from the attributes of the Virgin in the Litany of Loretto, which is mentioned in Stafford's poem.

[11] i.e., indirectly.

[12] i.e., both hands point upward together.

How are thy gifts and graces blaz'd abro'd,
        Through all the lines of this circumference,
55   T'imprint in all purg'd hearts this virgin sence,
    Of being Daughter, Mother, Spouse of *God!*

                                                    B. J.

63. *TO MY DEARE SONNE, AND RIGHT-LEARNED FRIEND, MASTER* JOSEPH RUTTER[1]

    YOu looke, my *Joseph*, I should something say
    Unto the *world*, in praise of your *first Play:*
    And truely, so I would, could I be heard.
    You know, I never was of Truth afeard,
5   And lesse asham'd; not when I told the crowd
    How well I lov'd *Truth:* I was scarce allow'd
    By those deepe-grounded, understanding men,
    That sit to censure *Playes*, yet know not when,
    Or why to like; they found, it all was new,
10 And newer, then could please them, by-cause trew.
    Such men I met withall, and so have you.
    Now, for mine owne part, and it is but due,
    (You have deserv'd it from me) I have read,
    And weigh'd your *Play:* untwisted ev'ry thread,
15 And know the woofe, and warpe thereof; can tell
    Where it runs round, and even: where so well,
    So soft, and smooth it handles, the whole piece,
    As it were spun by nature, off the fleece:
    This is my censure. Now there is a new
20 Office of Wit, a Mint, and (this is true)
    Cry'd up of late: Whereto there must be first
    A *Master-worker* call'd,[2] th'old standerd burst

63: [1] prefixed to *The Shepheards Holy-day. A Pastorall Tragi-Comoedie*, by Joseph Rutter (1635). The book is dedicated to Sir Kenelm Digby and contains an elegy on the death of Lady Venetia Digby (see *Under.* 86).

[2] This person and the following ones cannot now be identified. Cf. the "Play Club" in Jonson's *Ode to Himselfe* (No. 53).

Of wit, and a new made: a *Warden* then,
And a *Comptroller*, two most rigid men
25   For order, and for governing the pixe,[3]
A *Say-master*,[4] hath[5] studied all the tricks
Of *Finenesse*, and *alloy:* follow his hint,
Yo'have all the *Mysteries* of *Wits new Mint*,
    The *valuations, mixtures*, and the same
30   Concluded from a *Carract*[6] to a *dramme*.[7]

Ben. Jonson.

64. AN EPIGRAM TO MY JOVIALL GOOD FREIND *MR. ROBERT DOVER*, ON HIS GREAT INSTAURATION OF HIS HUNT-ING, AND DAUNCING AT COTSWOLD[1]

I Cannot bring my *Muse* to dropp her *Vies*[2]
Twixt *Cotswold*, and the *Olimpicke* exercise:
But I can tell thee, *Dover*, how thy *Games*
Renew the Glories of our blessed *Jeames:*
5   How they doe keepe alive his memorie;
With the *Glad Countrey*, and *Posteritie:*
How they advance true Love, and neighbourhood,
And doe both *Church*, and Common-wealth the good,
In spite of *Hipocrites*, who are the worst
10   Of Subjects; Let such envie, till they burst.

Ben. Johnson.

[3] pyx: a box at the Mint where specimen coins were deposited for testing.
[4] assay-master.
[5] who hath.
[6] carat, for weighing precious stones.
[7] for other weights.
64: [1] prefixed to *Annalia Dubrensia. Upon the Yeerely celebration of Mr. Robert Dovers Olimpick Games upon Cotswold-Hills* (1636). Dover (c. 1575–1641) founded about 1604 the Cotswold games celebrated annually in Gloucestershire. They included various athletic events. The book contains 34 poems by Drayton, Feltham, Heywood, and others besides Jonson.
[2] comparisons (from card playing: bets).

65. MARTIAL. EPIGRAM XLVII, BOOK X

THe Things that make the happier life, are these,
Most pleasant Martial; Substance got with ease,
Not labour'd for, but left thee by thy Sire;
A Soyle, not barren; a continewall fire;
5   Never at Law; seldome in office gown'd;
A quiet mind; free powers; and body sound;
A wise simplicity; freindes alike-stated;
Thy table without art, and easy-rated:
Thy night not dronken, but from cares layd wast;
10   No sowre, or sollen bed-mate, yet a Chast;
Sleepe, that will make the darkest howres swift-pac't;
Will to bee, what thou art; and nothing more:
Nor feare thy latest day, nor wish therfore.

66

TO the wonders of the Peake,[1]
I am come to Add, and speake,
Or as some would say to breake
    My mind unto you,[2]
5   And I sweare by all the light
At my back, I am no spright,
But a very merry wight
    Prest in to se you.

I had somewhat else to say
10   But have lost it by the way:
I shall think on't ere't be day.
    The Moone comends hir

66: [1] titled by Gifford "A Song of the Moon"; probably part of some lost entertainment. The Peake is an area in Derbyshire (cf. l. 21).
[2] say what I think.

To the merry beards in Hall,[3]
Those turnd up, and those that fall,
15 Morts,[4] and mirkins[5] that wagg all,
Tough, foule, or tender.

And as either newes or mirth
Rise or fall uppon the earth,
She desires of every birth
20 Some tast to send hir
Specially the newes of Darby;
For if there, or peace or warr be
To the Peake it is so hard-by
Shee soone will heare it.

25 If there be a Coockold Major,
That the wife heades for a wager
As the standerd shall engage hir,
The Moone will beare it
Though shee chainge as oft as shee
30 And of Circle be as free
Or hir quarters lighter bee
Yet doe not feare it.

Or if any strife bety'de
For the breeches with the bride[6]
35 Tis but the next neighbour ride
And she is pleased
Or if't be the Gossipps happ
Each to pawne hir husbands capp,
At Pem Wakers[7] good ale Tapp
40 Hir minde is eased.

Or by chance if in their grease
Or theire Ale, they break the peace
Forfeitinge their drinking lease
Shee will not seise it.

---

[3] proverb: " 'Tis merry in hall when beards wag all" (H&S).
[4] women.
[5] both melkin (loose woman) and merkin (pudendum).
[6] as dominating the household.
[7] evidently a woman who served ale in the neighborhood.

67. ODE[1]

IF Men, and tymes were nowe
    Of that true face
As when they both were greate, and both knewe howe
    That fortune to imbrace,
5   By Cherishing the spirrits that gave their greatnes
                            [grace
    I then would rayse my notes
    Loud to the wondring throng
And better Blason them, then all their Coats,
That were the happy subject of my song.

10 But Clownish pride hath got
    So much the start
Of Civill virtue, that he now is not
    Nor can be of desert
That hath not Courtly impudence enough to laugh at
                             [Arte
15   Whilst like a blaze of strawe,
      He dyes with an ill sent,[2]
To every sence, and scorne to those that sawe
Howe soone with a selfe tickling he was spent.

Breake then thy quills, blot out
20   Thie long watch'd verse
And rather to the Fyer, then to the Rout
    Their labor'd tunes reherse
Whose ayre will sooner Hell, then their dull sences
                           [peirce
    Thou that dost spend thie dayes
25   To gett thee a leane face,
And come forth worthy Ivy or the Bayes,[3]
And in this Age, canst hope no other grace.

67: [1] attributed to Jonson by W. D. Briggs, *Athenaeum*, June 13, 1914, p. 828, on the basis of internal evidence alone; accepted as genuine by H&S.
[2] scent.
[3] poetic rewards.

Yet since the bright and wyse
    Mynerva deignes
30 Uppon so humbled earth to cast her eyes:
    Wee'll rip our ritchest veynes
And once more strike the Eare of tyme with those
                        [fresh straynes
    As shall besides delight
    And Cuning of their ground
35 Give cause to some of wonder, some despight
But unto more despaire to ymitate their sound.

Throw holye Virgen then
    Thy Christall sheild[4]
About this Ile and charme the rounde,[5] as when
40   Thou mad'st in open feild
The Rebell Gyants stoupe, and Gorgon Envye yeild:
    Cause Reverence, if not feare,
    Throughout their generall brests
And by their taking let it once appeare
45 Who worthie come, who not, to bee witts Pallace[6]
                         [guests.

68

THough I am young, and cannot tell,[1]
    Either what Death, or Love is well,
Yet I have heard, they both beare darts,
    And both doe ayme at humane hearts:
5   And then againe, I have beene told,
    Love wounds with heat, as Death with cold;
So that I feare, they doe but bring
    Extreames to touch, and meane one thing.

[4] Minerva gave Perseus a mirror which would help him kill the Gorgon (l. 41); he returned it with the Gorgon's head, and she affixed the head in her shield, which Jonson interprets to be the mirror (Christall).

[5] either outer boundary or the swinging stroke of a sword.

[6] with pun on Pallas (Minerva).

68: [1] from *The Sad Shepherd* I.v, which cannot be accurately dated. A musical setting is in John Playford's *Select Musicall Aires* (1652; another ed. 1653).

As in a ruine, we it call
10   One thing to be blowne up, or fall;
Or to our end, like way may have,
        By a flash of lightning, or a wave:
So Loves inflamed shaft, or brand,
        May kill as soone as Deaths cold hand;
15   Except Loves fires the vertue have
        To fright the frost out of the grave.

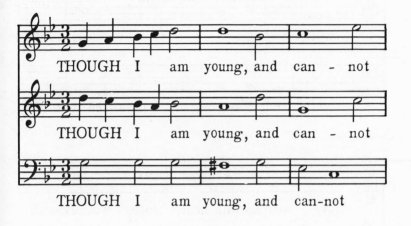

Fig. 4 Song from *The Sad Shepherd*, Act I, Scene v. Music by Nicholas Lanneare, from *Select Ayres and Dialogues* published by John Playford, 1653.

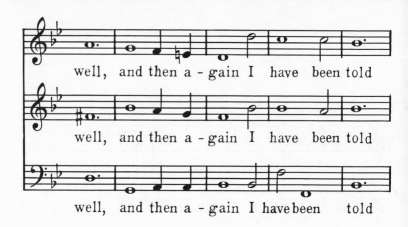

well, and then a - gain I have been told

well, and then a - gain I have been told

well, and then a - gain I have been told

love wounds with heat, love wounds with

love wounds with heat, love wounds with

love wounds with heat, love wounds with

heat, and death with cold.

heat, and death with cold.

heat, and death with cold.

Fig. 4 continued

THE MASQUE OF BEAUTIE

Except in periods of puritan ascendancy, masked dancing
has been popular in Western civilization; usually the maskers
have dressed in unusual costumes as they still do at Mardi
Gras. In Jonson's day Queen Anne, wife of James I, was es-
pecially attracted to this old form of entertainment, and she
was not so averse to the liberal expenditure which it requires
as had been her husband's predecessor, Elizabeth. During
James's reign the masque became the typical form of elabo-
rate entertainment at court, only to perish in the steady
progress toward bankruptcy of their son Charles.

In England during the latter years of Elizabeth's reign,
the masked ball developed an interruption to the dances
during which a group of the participants took simple acting
parts which included short speeches, suited to amateurs
whose main concern was the pleasure of the occasion. Be-
cause of the dress, the assigned parts would be adapted to the
costume theme; or as the little play grew in importance it
might in turn dominate the dress. Because of the social na-
ture of the occasion and the amateur performers, these little
plays never developed the elaborate plots or characterizations
of the stage proper; but they did develop elaborate cos-
tumes, scenery, a painted curtain, stage machinery, and
lighting—the last by open torches or candles which must have
presented a considerable fire hazard and which certainly
smoked the woodwork. Eventually the writing and staging of
these pageant-plays were turned over to professional writers,
stage designers, and choreographers. The English develop-
ment appears clearly in many of Shakespeare's plays, which
frequently employ masques or materials similar to them. For
example, in the early play *Love's Labor's Lost* a group of
women exchange masks at a dance as part of the plot; their

partners are disguised as Russians. Romeo and Juliet meet at a masked ball held by the Capulets. The *Midsummer Night's Dream* concludes with song and dance; the later comedy *As You Like It* has a true masque, that of Hymen, which sums up the several marriages which end the play. At the close of his career, Shakespeare occupies the fourth act of the *Tempest* with the masque of Ceres (fertility).

Throughout its development the masque retained its character of a dress ball in which the characters wore masks, sang, and danced. They were almost always conceived as allegorical, being developed to suit the particular occasion for which the masque was performed. If a very elaborate speaking part were required, a professional actor, often the author, took it.

Many writers were called upon to provide these entertainments, but undoubtedly the most popular and successful was Jonson. He wrote several entertainments for the court after James succeeded Elizabeth in 1603. Then in 1605 Queen Anne employed him to write his first court masque, *Blackness*, performed on Twelfth Night 1605 (i.e., January 6, 1606, by today's calendar). His stage designer for this and for his subsequent successes was the rising young architect Inigo Jones, with whom Jonson carried on an intermittent feud until they finally broke apart over the staging of *Chloridia* (see the "Expostulation with Inigo Jones" in *Uncollected Poetry*). From 1605 to 1634, Jonson wrote and helped produce some thirty-one masques which survive.

Queen Anne had suggested for the *Masque of Blackness* a group of twelve women from her court disguised as Negroes. Jonson developed the idea into a splendid pageant, with the masquers "placed in a great concave shell . . . curiously made to move on those waters, and rise with the billow; the top thereof was stuck with a *chev'ron* of lights. . . . On sides of the shell, did swim sixe huge *Sea-monsters*." He reports that the masquers were dressed in azure and silver, with pearls and jewels to contrast with the blackness of their faces. At the back was a painted drop designed by Inigo Jones to represent the sea. The speaking characters were Oceanus, Niger (an Ethiopian river), and Aethiopia.

The performance was highly successful, but Jonson was not invited to write another for the Christmas celebrations of the next two years because other festivities intervened. For Twelfth Night, 1608–9, however, Anne requested another masque which would continue and develop the successful *Blackness*. Jonson responded with *Beauty*, fulfilling the Queen's desires for a repetition of the Negro masquers, but he replaced the former speaking parts with Boreas and Vulturnus (two north winds) and January.

Beauty is a typical masque, both as to length and subject. It lacks only the anti-masque, developed at about this time as a means of contrast and incorporated into Jonson's later work. Today its speeches seem extremely formal, its action stilted, its characterization insignificant—all of these short-comings from the man who had recently produced *Volpone*. But the purpose of the masque was to afford a kind of entertainment quite different from that of the popular stage. The beauty of the spectacle and the enhancement of the beauty of the dress ball were uppermost. The allegorical significance of the several beautiful Ethiopians who came to the earthly center of beauty—the English court of a northern winter—was the main consideration, with its graceful praise of James and Anne. In his notes Jonson is careful to point out his use of various mythographers—Giraldi, Cartari, Conti, and Ripa were for him the most important—who had turned classical myth into Renaissance symbol.[1] Ultimately the relationships of the characters devolved upon the generalized scheme of love developed by such Italian Platonists as Marsilio Ficino and Pico della Mirandola.[2] The resulting entertainment certainly was very expensive, but it accomplished its purpose, with its spectacular staging by Inigo Jones and its fine music by Alphonso Ferrabosco, musical tutor to Henry, Prince of Wales. That Jonson was proud of his work is evidenced by the care with which he edited the text and by the explanations of the performance which he prints.

[1] See Allen H. Gilbert, *The Symbolic Persons in the Masques of Ben Jonson* (Durham, 1948) for quotations from these authors and for the meaning which they and Jonson attached to the allegorical characters.

[2] See D. J. Gordon, "The Imagery of Ben Jonson's *The Masque of Blacknesse* and *The Masque of Beautie*," *Journal of the Warburg and Courtauld Institutes*, VI (1943), 122–41.

THE SECOND MASQUE

Which Was of Beautie;

*Was presented in the same Court, at White-Hall,
on the Sunday night after the Twelfth Night.
1608.*

TWo yeares being now past, that her Majestie had inter-
mitted these delights, and the third almost come; it was her
Highnesse pleasure, againe to glorifie the Court, and com-
mand, that I should thinke on some fit presentment, which
should answere the former, still keeping them the same per-
sons, the daughters of Niger,[1] but their beauties varied,
according to promise, and their time of absence excus'd, with
foure more added to their number.

To which limits, when I had apted[2] my invention, and be-
ing to bring newes of them from the Sea, I induc'd *Boreas*,
one of the winds, as my fittest Messenger; presenting him
thus.

In a robe of Russet and White mixt, full, and bagg'd; his
haire and beard rough, and horride; his wings gray, and
full of snow, and ycicles: his mantle borne[3] from him with
wyres, and in severall puffes; his feet ending[4] in Serpents

---

[1] as Jonson explains in the
Masque of Blackness, a river in
Ethiopia, "of which the people
were called . . . Negro's." Such
was the character Niger in that
masque, accompanied by twelve
Negro nymphs, the masquers,
dressed in azure and silver.

[2] made fit.

[3] held out.

[4] So *Paus. in Eliacis* reports
him to have, as he was carved
in arcâ Cipseli (Jonson's note).

In the section on Elis in Greece,
Pausanias, *Description of Greece*
V.19, gives details of the chest
of Cypselus, Tyrant of Corinth;
Jonson found the material in
Vincenzo Cartari's description of
Boreas in *Le Imagini con la
Spositione dei Dei degli Antichi*
(1556ff.) Many of the details
are in Cesare Ripa, *Iconologie*
(1593ff.). See Gilbert. The
"Character" of Aquarius, which
rules at the new year, is ♒.

tayles; and in his hand a leave-lesse Branch, laden with ycicles.

But before, in midst of the Hall, to keepe the state of the Feast, and Season, I had placed *Januarie*,[5] in a throne of silver; his robe of ash-colour, long, fringed with silver; a white mantle; his wings white, and his buskins; in his hand a Lawrell bough; upon his head an *Anademe* of Lawrell, fronted with the signe *Aquarius*, and the *Character*. Who, as *Boreas* bluster'd forth, discover'd himselfe.

BOREAS

WHich, among these, is ALBION,[6] NEPTUNES sonne?

JANUARIUS

WHat ignorance dares make that question?
Would any aske, who MARS were, in the wars?
Or, which is HESPERUS,[7] among the starres?
5   Of the bright *Planets*, which is SOL? Or can
A doubt arise, 'mong creatures, which is Man?
Behold, whose eyes doe dart *Promethean* fire
Throughout this all; whose precepts do inspire
The rest with dutie; yet commanding, cheare:
10   And are obeyed, more with love, then feare.

BOREAS

WHat Power art thou, that thus informest me?

JANUARIUS

DO'st thou not know me? I too well know thee
By thy rude[8] voice, that doth so hoarcely blow;
Thy haire, thy beard, thy wings, ore-hil'd[9] with snow,

5 See *Iconolog. di Cesare Ripa* (Jonson's note).
6 England.
7 the evening star.
8 *Ovid. Metam. lib.* 6 neere the end see—*horridus ira, quae solita est illi, nimiumque do-* *mestica, vento, &c.* (Jonson's note): Ovid's *Metamorphoses* VI.685f., "rough with anger, which was the north-wind's usual and more natural mood."
9 covered.

15   Thy serpent feet, to be that rough *North-wind*,
      BOREAS, that to my raigne art still unkind.
      I am the Prince of Months, call'd JANUARIE;
      Because by me JANUS[10] the yeare doth varie,
      Shutting up warres, proclayming peace, and feasts,
20   Freedome, and triumphs; making Kings his guests.

BOREAS

      TO thee then, thus, and by thee, to that King,
      That doth thee present honors, doe I bring
      Present remembrance of twelve *Æthiope* Dames:[11]
      Who, guided hither by the *Moones* bright flames,
25   To see his brighter light, were to the Sea
      Enjoyn'd againe, and (thence assign'd a day
      For their returne) were in the waves to leave
      Their *blacknesse*, and true *beautie* to receive.

JANUARIUS

      WHich they receiv'd, but broke their day:[12] and yet
30   Have not return'd a looke of grace for it,
      Shewing a course, and most unfit neglect.
      Twice have I come, in pompe here, to expect
      Their presence; Twice deluded, have beene faine
      With other[13] *Rites* my Feasts to entertaine:
35   And, now the third time, turn'd about the yeare,
      Since they were look'd for; and, yet, are not here.

BOREAS

      IT was nor Will, nor Sloth, that caus'd their stay;
      For they were all prepared by their day,
      And, with religion,[14] forward on their way:

[10] See the offices and power of *Janus, Ovid. Fast.* I (Jonson's note): *Fasti* I, esp. 277–82.

[11] of the preceding *Masque of Blacknesse.*

[12] failed their appointment.

[13] Two marriages; the one of the Earle of *Essex,* 1606, the other of the Lord *Hay,* 1607 (Jonson's note). Essex had married Frances Howard; see *Uncol. P.* 31. Lord James Hay, Earl of Carlisle and favorite of James, married an heiress, Honora Denny, on January 6, 1607. Campion wrote a masque for the latter celebration; in 1617 Jonson wrote *Lovers Made Men* for one of the lord's entertainments.

[14] fidelity.

40   When PROTEUS, the gray *Prophet*[15] of the Sea,
      Met them, and made report, how other foure
      Of their blacke kind (whereof their Syre had store)
      Faithfull to that great wonder, so late done
      Upon their Sisters, by bright *Albion*,
45   Had followed them to seeke BRITANIA forth,
      And there to hope like favor, as like worth.
      Which NIGHT envi'd, as done in her despight,[16]
      And (mad to see an Æthiope washed white)
      Thought to prevent in these; lest men should deeme
50   Her colour, if thus chang'd, of small esteeme.
      And so, by malice, and her magicke, tost
      The *Nymphes* at sea, as[17] they were almost lost,
      Till, on an Iland, they by chance arriv'd,
      That floted[18] in the mayne; where, yet, she' had
                                              [giv'd[19]
55   Them so, in charmes of darknesse, as[20] no might
      Should loose them thence, but their chang'd Sisters
                                              [sight.
      Whereat the *Twelve* (in pietie mov'd, and kind)[21]
      Streight put themselves in act, the place to find;
      Which was the NIGHTS sole trust they so will doe,
60   That she, with labor, might confound them too.
      For ever since with error hath she held
      Them wandring in the *Ocean*, and so quell'd
      Their hopes beneath their toyle, as (desperat now
      Of any least successe unto their vow;

[15] Read his description, with *Virg. Geor. 4. Est in Carpathio Neptuni gurgite vates, Coeruleus Proteus* (Jonson's note): Virgil's *Georgics* IV.387f., "In Neptune's Carpathian flood dwells a prophet Proteus, of grey [caeruleus] color."

[16] Because they were before of her complexion (Jonson's note).

[17] so that.

[18] To give authoritie to this part of our fiction. *Plinie* hath a *chap.* 95 of his 2 booke. *Nat. Hist. de Insulis fluctuantibus. & Card. lib. I. de rerum. variet. cap.* 7. reports one to be in his time knowne, in the Lake of *Loumond*, in *Scotland*. To let passe that of *Delos*, &c. (Jonson's note): Pliny, *Natural History* II. 96 and Hieronymus Cardanus (1501–76) *De Rerum Varietate Libri XVII* (1557 *et seq.*).

[19] fettered.

[20] that.

[21] nature.

65   Nor knowing to returne to expresse the grace,
      Wherewith they labor to this Prince, and place)
      One of them, meeting me at sea, did pray,
      That for the love of my ORYTHYIA,[22]
      (Whose verie name did heat my frostie brest,
70   And make me shake my snow-fill'd wings and crest)
      To beare this sad report I would be wonne,
      And frame their just excuse; which here I have done.

JANUARIUS

      WOuld thou had'st not begun, unluckie *Wind*,
      That never yet blew'st goodnesse to mankind;
75   But with thy bitter, and too piercing breath,
      Strik'st horrors[23] through the ayre, as sharpe as death.

Here a second Wind came in, VULTURNUS, *in a blue
coloured robe and mantle, pufft as the former, but somewhat
sweeter; his face blacke, and on his head[24] a red Sunne,
shewing he came from the East: his wings of severall colours;
his buskins white, and wrought with gold.*

VULTURNUS

      ALl horrors vanish, and all name of *Death*,
      Be all things here as calme as is my breath.
      A gentler *Wind*, VULTURNUS, brings you newes
80   The *Ile* is found, and that the *Nymphs* now use

---

[22] The daughter of *Erectheus*, King of *Athens*, whome *Boreas* ravish'd away, into *Thrace*, as she was playing with other virgins by the floud *Ilissus*: or (as some will) by the fountaine *Cephisus* (Jonson's note). The story is found in Ovid, *Metamorphoses* VI.706ff.

[23] The violence of *Boreas*, *Ovid* excellently describes in the place above quoted. *Hâc nubila pello, hâc freta concutio, nodosaque robora verto, Induroque nives, & terras grandine pulso* (Jonson's note). *Metamorphoses* VI.690ff.:

"By force I drive on the gloomy clouds, disturb the sea, overturn gnarled oaks, pack down the snow, and strike the earth with hail."

[24] According to that of *Vir.—Denuntiat igneus Euros* (Jonson's note): Virgil, *Georgics* I.453, "a dark [dawn] threatens rain, a fiery one the Euros [east wind]." Ripa identifies the Greek Euros (east wind) with a similar wind, the *Vulturnus*, which according to Livy (XXII.43) had been adverse to Romans fighting Hannibal.

Their rest, and joy. The *Nights* black charmes are
[flowne.

For, being made unto their *Goddesse* knowne,
Bright ÆTHIOPIA, the silver *Moone*,
As she was HECATE,[25] she brake them soone:
85 And now by vertue of their light, and grace,
The glorious *Isle*, wherein they rest, takes place
Of all the earth for Beautie. There,[26] their *Queene*
Hath raised them a *Throne*, that still is seene
To turne unto the motion of the World;
90 Wherein they sit, and are, like Heaven, whirl'd
About the Earth; whil'st, to them contrarie,
(Following those nobler torches[27] of the Skie)
A world of little *Loves*, and chast *Desires*,
Doe light their beauties, with still moving fires.
95 And who to *Heavens* consent can better move,
Then those that are so like it, *Beautie* and *Love?*
Hither, as to their new *Elysium*,
The spirits of the antique *Greekes* are come,
Poets and *Singers*, *Linus*,[28] *Orpheus*, all
100 That have excell'd in knowledge musicall;[29]
Where, set in arbors made of myrtle, and gold,
They live, againe, these beauties to behold.
And thence in flowry mazes walking forth,
Sing hymns in celebration of their worth.
105 Whilst, to their songs, two fountaines flow, one hight
Of *lasting Youth*, the other *chast Delight*,

[25] She is call'd φωσφόρ
Ἑκάτη, by *Eurip. in Helena*,
which is *Lucifera*, to which name
we here presently allude (Jon-
son's note). The line from Eurip-
ides is in *Helena*, l. 569: "light-
bearing Hecate."

[26] For the more full and cleare
understanding of that which fol-
lowes, have recourse to the suc-
ceeding pages; where the *Scene*
presents it selfe (Jonson's note).

[27] the planets, which may move

contrary to the apparent motion
of the stars.

[28] son of Apollo and Terp-
sichore, who taught music to Or-
pheus, the greatest ancient mu-
sician.

[29] So *Terence* and the Ancients
calld *Poesy*, *Artem musicam* (Jon-
son's note). Terence calls poetry
the musical art in *Phormio*, Pro-
logue, l. 17, and *Hecyra*, Prologue,
l. 46.

That at the closes,[30] from their bottomes spring,
And strike the ayre to *eccho* what they sing.
But, why doe I describe what all must see?
110 By this time, neere the coast, they floating be;
For, so their vertuous *Goddesse*,[31] the chast *Moone*,
Told them, the fate of th'*Iland* should, and soone
Would fixe it selfe unto thy *continent*,
As being the place, by destiny fore-ment,
115 Where they should flow forth, drest in her attyres:
And, that the influence of those holy fires,
(First rapt from hence) being multiplied upon
The other *foure*, should make their beauties one.

Which now expect to see, great *Neptunes* sonne,
120 And love the miracle, which thy selfe hast done.

Here, a curtaine was drawne (in which the Night *was painted,) and the* Scene *discover'd, which (because the former was* marine, *and these, yet of necessitie, to come from the sea) I devised, should be an* Island *floting on a calme water. In the middest thereof was a seate of state, call'd the* throne of beautie, *erected: divided into eight squares, and distinguish'd by so many* Ionick *pilasters. In these* Squares *the sixteene* Masquers *were plac'd by couples: behind them, in the center of the* Throne *was a tralucent*[32] *Pillar, shining with severall*[33] *colour'd lights, that reflected on their backes. From the top of which* Pillar *went severall arches to the* Pilasters, *that sustained the roofe of the* Throne, *which was likewise adorn'd with lights, and gyrlonds; And between the* Pilasters, *in front, little* Cupids *in flying posture, waving of wreathes, and lights, bore up the* Coronice:[34] *over which were placed eight* Figures, *representing the* Elements of Beauty; *which advanced upon the* Ionick, *and being females, had the* Corinthian order.[35] *The first was*

---

[30] ends of musical phrases.
[31] Diana, goddess of both the moon and chastity.
[32] translucent.
[33] different.

[34] cornice.
[35] Vitruvius (Loeb ed. I.29) describes the Corinthian order of architecture as suited to gentler females.

SPLENDOR[36]

IN a robe of *flame* colour, naked brested; her bright hayre loose flowing: She was drawn in a circle of clouds, her face, and body breaking through; and in her hand a branch, with two *Roses*,[37] a *white*, and a *red*. The next to her was

SERENITAS[38]

IN a garment of bright *skie*-colour, a long tresse, and waved with a vaile of divers colours, such as the golden skie sometimes shewes: upon her head a cleare, and faire *Sunne* shining, with rayes of gold striking downe to the feet of the figure. In her hand a *Christall*,[39] cut with severall angles, and shadow'd with divers colours, as caused by refraction. The third

GERMINATIO[40]

IN greene; with a *Zone* of gold about her Wast, crowned with *Myrtle*, her haire likewise flowing, but not of so bright a colour: In her hand, a branch of *Myrtle*.[41] Her sockes of greene, and gold. The fourth was

[36] in part from Ripa's *Belleza* (Gilbert, q.v. for all of these characters).

[37] The *Rose* is call'd, elegantlie, by *Achil. Tat. lib.* 2. φυνῶν ἀγλάισμα, *the splendor of Plants*, and is every where taken for the *Hieroglyphick*, of Splendor (Jonson's note). Hieroglyphick means symbol, as Jonson interprets Achilles Tatius, II.i.

[38] Brightness of day, as described in Ripa (H&S).

[39] As this of *Serenity*, applying to the *Opticks* reason of the *Rainbow*, & the *Mythologists* making her the Daughter of *Electra* (Jonson's note). In his notes to the *King's Entertainment*, ll. 708–10 (H&S VII.107), Jonson says,

"*Electra* signifies Serenitie it selfe and is compounded of ἥλιος, which is the Sunne, and αἴθριος, that signifies serene. . . . She is also fained to be the mother of the rainbow (*Arist. in Meteorol.*)."

[40] Germination, i.e., Springtime.

[41] So *Hor. lib.* I. *Od.* 4. makes it the ensigne of the *Spring. Nunc decet aut viridi nitidum caput impedire myrto, aut flore, terrae quem ferunt solutae, &c.* (Jonson's note). From Horace *Odes* I.4: "Now [i.e., in the spring, the subject of the ode] we should adorn our anointed heads with green myrtle or with the first flowers that pierce the soft earth."

LÆTITIA[42]

IN a vesture of divers colours, and all sorts of flowers embroidered thereon. Her sockes so fitted. A *Gyrland*[43] of flowers in her hand; her eyes turning up, and smiling, her haire flowing, and stuck with flowers. The fift

TEMPERIES[44]

IN a garment of *Gold*, *Silver*, and colours weaved: In one hand shee held a burning *Steele*,[45] in the other, an *Urne* with water. On her head a gyrland of flowers, Corne, Vine-leaves, and Olive branches, enterwoven. Her sockes, as her garment. The sixth

VENUSTAS[46]

IN a *Silver* robe, with a thinne subtile vaile over her haire, and it: Pearle[47] about her neck, and forehead. Her sockes wrought with pearle. In her hand she bore several[48] colour'd *Lillies*.[49] The seventh was

DIGNITAS[50]

IN a dressing of state, the haire bound up with fillets of golde, the garments rich, and set with jewels, and gold; likewise her buskins, and in her hand a *Golden rod*.[51] The eight

[42] Gladness.

[43] They are every where the tokens of gladnesse, at al feasts, sports (Jonson's note).

[44] Mixture (in proper proportions).

[45] The signe of temperature, as also her girland mixed of the foure *Seasons* (Jonson's note). Temperature means a proper mixture.

[46]Loveliness.

[47] *Pearles*, with the *ancients*, were the speciall *Hieroglyphicks* of *lovelinesse, in quibus nitor tantam & laevor expetebantur* (Jonson's note).

[48] variously.

[49] So was the *Lillie*, of which the most delicate Citie of the *Persians* was called *Susae*: signifying that kind of flower, in their tongue (Jonson's note). For the pearls and lilies see Giovanni Pierio Valeriano, *Hieroglyphica* (1595).

[50] Dignity or Honor.

[51] The signe of *honor*, and dignitie (Jonson's note).

PERFECTIO[52]

IN a Vesture of pure *Golde,* a wreath of *Gold* upon her head. About her bodie the *Zodiacke,*[53] with the *Signes:* In her hand a *Compasse* of golde, drawing a *circle.*

On the top of all the *Throne,* (as being made out of all these) stood

HARMONIA[54]

A Personage, whose dressing had something of all the others, and had her robe painted full of *Figures.* Her head was compass'd with a crowne of *Gold,* having in it seven jewels[55] equally set. In her hand a *Lyra,* whereon she rested.

This was the Ornament of the *Throne.* The ascent to which, consisting of sixe steps, was covered with a multitude[56] of *Cupids* (chosen out of the best, and most ingenious youth of the *Kingdome,* noble, and others) that were the *Torch-bearers*; and all armed, with *Bowes, Quivers, Wings,* and other *Ensignes* of *Love.* On the sides of the *Throne,* were curious, and elegant *Arbors* appointed: and behinde, in the backe part of the *Ile,* a *Grove,* of growne trees laden with golden fruit, which other litle *Cupids* plucked, and threw each at other, whilst on the ground *Leverets*[57] pick'd up the

[52] Perfection, again described from Ripa.

[53] Both that, & the *Compasse* are known ensignes of *perfection* (Jonson's note).

[54] Harmony.

[55] She is so describ'd in *Iconolog. di Cesare Ripa,* his reason of 7. jewels, in the crown, alludes to *Pythagoras* his comment, with *Mac. lib. 2. Som. Sci.* of the seven *Planets* and their *Spheares* (Jonson's note). According to Macrobius, *Commentary on the Dream of Scipio* (trans. W. H. Stahl; New York, 1952, pp. 186–87), Pythagoras recognized the rationality of the music of the seven heavenly spheres and applied it to produce the mun-

dane musical scale.

[56] The inducing [introducing] of many *Cupids* wants not defence, with the best and most received of the *Ancients,* besides *Prop. Stat. Claud. Sido. Apoll.* especially *Phil. in Icon. Amor.* whom I have particularly followed, in this description (Jonson's note). From the *Icones* of Philostratus, Jonson took for the Cupids the number, the garden with golden fruit, the contest, and the hares (H&S).

[57] They were the notes of *Lovelinesse* and sacred to *Venus.* See *Phil.* in that place, mentioned (Jonson's note). A leveret is a young hare.

bruised apples, and left them halfe eaten. The ground-plat
of the whole was a subtle indented *Maze:* And, in the two
formost angles, were two *Fountaines,* that ran continually,
the one *Hebe's,*[58] the other *Hedone's:*[59] In the *Arbors,*
were plac'd the *Musicians,* who represented the *Shades* of the
olde *Poets,* and were attir'd in a *Priest*-like habit of *Crimson,*
and *Purple,* with *Laurell* gyrlonds.

The colours of the *Masquers* were varied; the one halfe
in *Orenge-tawny,* and *Silver:* the other in *Sea-greene,* and
Silver. The bodies[60] and short skirts *White,* and *Gold,* to
both.

The habite, and dressing (for the fashion) was most curi-
ous, and so exceeding in riches, as the *Throne* whereon they
sat, seem'd to be a Mine of light, stroake from their jewels,
and their garments.

This *Throne,* (as the whole *Iland* mov'd forward, on the
water,) had a circular motion of it owne, imitating that which
wee call *Motum mundi,*[61] from the *East* to the *West,* or the
right to the left side. For so *Hom. Ilia. M.*[62] understands
by δεξιὰ, *Orientalia mundi:* by ἀριστερὰ, *Occidentalia.*[63]
The steps, whereon the *Cupids* sate, had a motion contrary,
with *Analogy, ad motum Planetarum,*[64] from the *West* to
the *East:* both which turned with their severall lights. And
with these three varied *Motions,* at once, the whole *Scene*
shot it selfe to the land.

Above which, the *Moone* was seene in a *Silver* Chariot,
drawne by *Virgins,* to ride in the clouds, and hold them
greater light: with the *Signe Scorpio,* and the *Character,*[65]
plac'd before her.

The order of this *Scene* was carefully, and ingeniously
dispos'd; and as happily put in act (for the *Motions*) by the

[58] Of youth (Jonson's note).
[59] Of pleasure (Jonson's note).
[60] bodices.
[61] motion of the world.
[62] Homer, *Iliad* XII.239f.
[63] eastern parts of the world
. . . western parts of the world.

Homer is describing how birds fly
to the right, to the dawn; or to
the left, to darkness.
[64] to the motion of the planets.
[65] Its sign is ♏. H&S suggest
an error for Cancer ♋, the as-
trological "house" of the moon.

Kings Master Carpenter.[66] The Painters, I must needs say,
(not to belie them) lent small colour to any, to attribute
much of the spirit of these things to their pen'cills. But that
must not bee imputed a crime either to the invention, or
designe.

Here the loud *Musique* ceas'd; and the *Musicians*, which
were placed in the *Arbors*, came forth through the *Mazes*,
to the other Land: singing this full *Song*, iterated in the
closes by two *Eccho's*, rising out of the Fountaines.

SONG

> WHen *Love*, at first, did moove
> From out of *Chaos*,[67] brightned
> So was the world, and lightned,
> As now! *Eccho.* As now! *Ecch.* As now!
125   Yeeld *Night*, then, to the light,
> As *Blacknesse* hath to *Beautie*;
> Which is but the same duety.
> It was for *Beauty*,[68] that the World was made,
> And where she raignes, *Loves*[69] lights admit no shade.

[66] William Portington. See P. Cunningham, *Life of Inigo Jones*, in *Shakespeare Society Publications* (1848), p. 8.

[67] So is he faind by *Orpheus*, to have appear'd first of all the *Gods*: awakened by *Clotho*: and is therefore call'd *Phanes*, both by him, and *Lactantius* (Jonson's note). In Orpheus, *Argonautica* 15, Phanes is represented as the first principle of the world. Lilio Giraldi, *De Deis Gentium Varia et Multiplex Historia* (1548) equates him with Love; Hesiod had pictured Love as the first god to come out of Chaos (*Theogonia* 116–20) (H&S). Clotho is one of the Fates; she awakens Love in Spenser's *Hymne of Love*, l. 63.

[68] An agreeing opinion, both with *Divines* and *Philosophers*, that the great *Artificer* in love with his owne *Idaea*, did, therefore, frame the world (Jonson's note). The philosophers are Plato and his followers, who consider the world of perception to copy a world of Ideas. The divines are various church fathers and their followers who, influenced by neo-Platonism, interpreted the creative Word of the Gospel of John in much the same way.

[69] Alluding to his name of *Himerus*, and his signification in the name, which is *Desiderium post aspectum*: and more then *Eros*, which is onely *Cupido, ex aspectu amare* (Jonson's note). Again from Giraldi, who from Hesiod (*Theog.* 64) equates Love and Himerus (Desire).

130   *Ecch.* Loves lights admit no shade.
           Eccho. Admit no shade.

Which ended, *Vulturnus* the Wind spake to the River
Thamesis, that lay along betweene the shores, leaning upon
his Urne (that flow'd with water,) and crown'd with flowers:
with a blue cloth of *Silver* robe about him: and was per-
sonated by Master THOMAS GILES, who made the *Daunces.*

VULTURNUS

RIse aged *Thames,* and by the hand
Receive these *Nymphes,* within the land:
And, in those curious *Squares,* and *Rounds,*
135   Wherewith thou flow'st betwixt the grounds
Of fruitfull *Kent,* and *Essex* faire,
That lend thee gyrlands for thy hayre;
Instruct their silver feete to tread,
Whilst we, againe to sea, are fled.

With which the *Windes* departed; and the *River* receiv'd
them into the *Land,* by *couples* and *foures,* their *Cupids*
comming before them.

Their Persons were[70]

The QUEENE.	La. ANNE WINTER.
La. ARABELLA.	La. WINSORE.
Co. of ARUNDEL.	La. ANNE CLIFFORD.
Co. of DERBY.	La. MARY NEVILL.
Co. of BEDFORD.	La. ELIZ. HATTON.
Co. of MONTGOMERY.	La. ELIZ. GARRARD.
La. ELIZA. GILFORD.	La. CHICHESTER.
L. KAT. PETER.	La. WALSINGHAM.

These dauncing foorth a most curious *Daunce,* full of ex-
cellent device, and change, ended it in the figure of a *Dia-*
mant, and so, standing still, were by the *Musicians,* with a
second *Song* (sung by a loud *Tenor*) celebrated.

[70] H&S briefly identify them,
X.440–45. The Countess of Bed-
ford appears in *Epig.* 76; the
Countess of Montgomery in *Epig.*
104; and Lady Elizabeth Gilford,
who married November 8, 1596,
is celebrated in Spenser's *Pro-*
thalamium.

SONG

140 SO beautie on the waters stood,
When *love* had sever'd[71] earth, from flood!
So when he parted ayre, from fire,
He did with concord all inspire!
And then a *motion* he them taught,
145 That elder then himselfe was thought.[72]
Which thought was, yet, the child of earth,[73]
For *love* is elder then his birth.

*The song ended; they danced forth their second dance,
more subtle, and full of change, then the former; and so ex-
quisitely performed; as the Kings majestie (incited first by his
owne liking, to that which all others, there present wish'd)
requir'd them both againe, after some time of dancing with
the Lords. Which time, to give them respite, was intermitted
with song; first by a treble voyce, in this manner,*

SONG

IF all these Cupids, now were blind
As is their wanton *brother;*[74]
150 Or play should put it in their mind
To shoot at one another:
What prettie battaile they would make,
If they their objects should mistake
And each one wound his *mother!*

[71] As, in the creation, he is said, by the *ancients,* to have done (Jonson's note).

[72] Lucian, περὶ ὀρχήσεως (*Of Pantomime*), 7, traces dancing back to the creation of the uni-verse, coeval with Love, the be-ginning of all things (H&S).

[73] That is, borne since the world, and, out of those duller apprehensions that did not thinke

hee was before (Jonson's note).

[74] I make these different from him, which they fayne, *caecum cupidine,* or *petulantem* [blind or wanton with passion (or Cupid)], as I expresse beneath in the third song, these being chaste *Loves,* that attend a more divine beautie, then that of *Loves* commune *parent* (Jonson's note).

Which was seconded by another treble; thus,

155   IT was no politie of court,
              Albee' the place were charmed,
           To let in earnest, or in sport,
              So many *Loves* in, armed.
           For say, the *Dames* should, with their eyes,
160   Upon the hearts, here, meane surprize;
              Were not the men like harmed?

           To which a tenor answer'd.

           YEs, were the *Loves* or false, or straying;
           Or *beauties* not their beautie waighing:
           But here, no such deceipt is mix'd,
165   Their flames are pure, their eyes are fix'd:
           They doe not warre, with different darts,
           But strike a musique of like harts.

After which songs, they danc'd galliards,[75] *and* coranto's;[76]
*and with those excellent graces, that the musique, appointed
to celebrate them, shew'd it could be silent no longer: but by
the first tenor, admir'd them thus,*

SONG

           HAd those, that dwell in error foule,
           And hold that women have no soule,[77]
170   But seene these move; they would have, then
           Said, *Women were the soules of men.*
              So they doe move each heart, and eye
              With the *worlds soule,*[78] true *harmony.*

[75] a quick dance in triple time.
[76] another dance in triple time with a running or gliding step.
[77] There hath beene such a profane *paradoxe* published (Jonson's note). Cf. the opening lines of Donne's "To the Countesse of Huntingdon"; H&S give a short history of the idea (X.464).
[78] The *Platonicks* opinion. See also *Mac. lib.* 1 and 2. *Som. Scip.* (Jonson's note): "Thus the World-Soul, which stirred the body of the universe to the motion that we now witness, must have been interwoven with those numbers which produce musical harmony in order to make harmonious the sounds which it instilled by its quickening impulse. It discovered the source of these sounds in the fabric of its own composition"; Macrobius, *op. cit.,* p. 193.

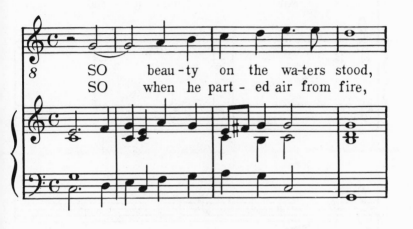

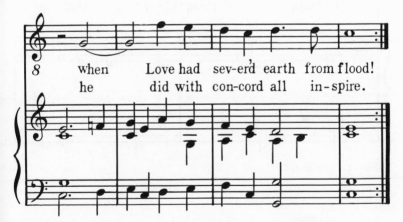

Fig. 5 "Song" from *The Masque of Beautie*. Published in Alfonso
Ferrabosco's *Ayres*, 1609.

FIG. 5 continued

el - der than him - self was thought.

Which thought was yet the child of

earth, for love is el - der than his birth.

FIG. 5 continued

Fig. 6 Another "Song" from *The Masque of Beautie*. Published in Alfonso Ferrabosco's *Ayres*, 1609.

Fig. 6 continued

IT was no pol-li-cie of

court, al -though the place be char-

med. To let in ear-nest or in sport

so ma-ny loves in

Fig. 6 continued

FIG. 6 continued

FIG. 6 continued

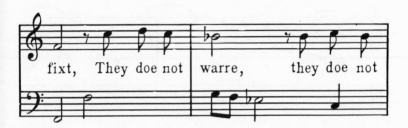

FIG. 6 continued

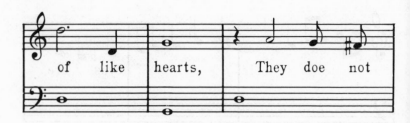

of like hearts, They doe not

warre with dif -

- f'rent darts But strike a

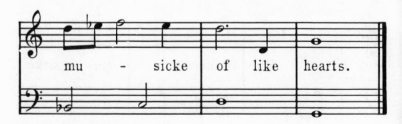

mu - sicke of like hearts.

Fig. 6 continued

*Here, they danc'd a third most elegant, and curious dance,
and not to be describ'd againe, by any art, but that of their
owne footing: which, ending in the figure, that was to pro-
duce the fourth,* JANUARY *from his state saluted them thus,*

JANUARIUS

YOur grace is great, as is your beautie, *Dames*;
175 Inough my *feasts* have prov'd[79] your thankfull flames.
Now use your seate: that seate which was, before,
Thought stray'ing, uncertayne, floting to each shore,
And to whose having every[80] *clime* laid clayme,
Each *land*, and *nation* urged as the ayme
180 Of their ambition, *beauties* perfect *throne*,
Now made peculiar, to this place, alone;
And that, by'impulsion of your destinies,
And his attractive beames, that lights these skies:
Who[81] (though with the'*Ocean* compass'd) never wets
185 His hayre therein, nor weares a beame that sets.
    Long may his light adorne these happy *rites*
As I renew them; and your gracious sights
Enjoy that happinesse, ev'en to envy, 'as when
Beautie, at large, brake forth, and conquer'd men.

*At which they danc'd their last dance, into their Throne
againe: and that turning, the* scene *clos'd with this full song.*

SONG

190 STill turne, and imitate the heaven
        In motion swift and even;
        And as his Planets goe,
        Your brighter lights doe so:
    May *youth* and *pleasure* ever flow.

---

[79] tried, demonstrated.
[80] For what countrey is it thinks not her owne beautie fayre,
yet? (Jonson's note).
[81] both the sun's and James's.

195   But let your state, the while,
              Be fixed as the Isle.
      CHO.   So all that see your *beauties* sphære,
              May know the'*Elysian*[82] fields are here.
      Ecch. Th'*Elysian* fields are here.
200   *Ecch. Elysian* fields are here.

   [82] heavenly.

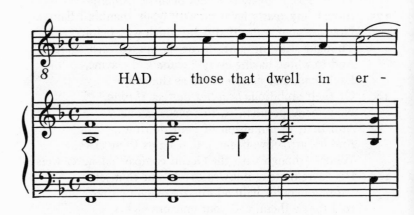

HAD   those that dwell in   er -

ror   foul,   and hold

FIG. 7   Yet another "Song" from *The Masque of Beautie.* Also published in Alfonso Ferrabosco's *Ayres,* 1609.

FIG. 7 continued

FIG. 7 continued

VARIANTS

VARIANTS

There seems to be no good reason to duplicate the complete textual apparatus which is found in Herford and Simpson's edition (referred to as H&S). The variants given here are confined to those which occur in texts published before 1700 and to manuscripts. For the latter, capital letters at the beginning of lines have been normalized and abbreviations have been expanded. Variations in spelling and punctuation are ignored unless they affect meaning. The use of i-j and of u-v conforms here to modern practice. Minor corrections of the original text are referred to H&S because it is the standard text today, even though it is repeating the emendations of earlier editors; but in cases where significant meaning is involved the earlier editor is named.

The editions of Jonson's works from which variants are given here are as follows:

1616   A folio volume of the *Works* which Jonson carefully supervised in its printing and hence the basic text. It includes the *Epigrammes* and *The Forrest*.

1640   Two folio volumes of the *Works* printed in 1640–41 by Sir Kenelm Digby. The first reprints the *Epigrammes* and *The Forrest* (with the addition of "To Edward Filmer" as *Epig.* 129; here it is *Uncol. P.* 51). The second volume includes the *Under-wood*, mostly poems written after 1613, the latest date to which any poem of the 1616 folio may be assigned, and the revised translation of Horace's *Art of Poetry*. The poems of the *Under-wood* are not numbered.

Q   A quarto volume, *Ben: Jonson's Execration against Vulcan. With divers Epigrams*, published by John Benson in 1640. Benson had surreptitiously acquired the manuscript. The volume includes twenty-one poems which appear, with variants, in the *Under-wood* of the 1640 folio, together with three others, two of which are printed here as *Uncol. P.* 53 and 54. The third, "So *Peleus,* when he faire *Thetis* got" (H&S, VIII.429) is omitted because it seems clear that Jonson did not write it.

D   A reissue in duodecimo (1640) by John Benson of his quarto edition of the same year. It includes Jonson's earlier translation of Horace's *Art of Poetry.*

1692   A folio edition of the *Works* which corrects some printing errors of the earlier editions.

Comparison has also been made with the editions of Peter Whalley (*Works,* 1756), of William Gifford (*Works,* 1816), of Francis Cunningham (*Works,* 1871), of B. H. Newdigate (*Poems,* 1936), of G. B. Johnston (*Poems,* 1955), and above all of Herford and Simpson (*Poems,* 1947, in *Works,* VIII). In the Textual Notes which follow the number before the decimal represents the number of the poem in the collection in which it appears, and the number after the decimal represents the line. Thus the first one refers to line 3 of the twenty-third poem of the *Epigrammes.*

Epigrammes. Text 1616 Folio

23.2	one] own Ashmolean MS. 47
39.13	fashion,] fashion; 1640
.14	times. Few] times few 1640
43.7	lest] least MS. (and Johnston)
55	printed in the Beaumont and Fletcher folios beginning with the first, 1647
92.14	twelve 1692] twelves 1616, 1640
.17	lock'd 1640] look'd 1616
.30	make] make not Gifford
94	printed in Donne's *Poems,* 1650ff.
96	printed in Donne's *Poems,* 1650ff.
102.3	the 1692] be 1616, 1640

108   in *Poetaster*, "Apologetical Dialogue," ll. 131–40

.6   profession; . . . once, . . . prove:] profession, . . . once . . . prove; *Poet.*

.8   dare now doe] dare, now, doe *Poet.*

       pen. *Poet.*] pen 1616

110   first printed in Clement Edmonds, *Observations* (1609)

111   first printed in Clement Edmonds, *Observations* (1609)

.13   helpe] Art 1609

115.10   sow] strow H&S *conj.*

124   MSS. variously attribute to Mrs. Boulstred, to "A Gentlewoman," or to Queen Elizabeth.

129   Before this poem 1640 inserts "To Edward Filmer," *Uncol. P.* 51.

130   first printed in Ferrabosco's *Ayres* (1609)

131   first printed in Ferrabosco's *Lessons for 1, 2, and 3 Viols* (1609)

.13   not] nor 1609

132   first printed in Josuah Sylvester, *Bartas his Devine Weekes* (1605)

133.30   the 1640] thee 1616

.161   are] is Gifford

.177   *Hol'borne* (three] *Hol'borne* (the three H&S Holborn-height Gifford Holborn bridge Cunningham

The Forrest. Text 1616 Folio.

3.25   friends;] friends, H&S from MSS.

.46   lent H&S from MSS.] lend 1616

5   first printed in *Volpone* III.vii.166–83

.2   may] can *Volp.*

.5   guifts] gifts *Volp.*

.7   if once we] if, once, we *Volp.*

       loose] lose *Volp.*

.8   'Tis, with us,] 'Tis with us *Volp.*

5.14	So removed] Thus removed, V*olp.*
.15	fruit] fruits, V*olp.*
.16	theft] thefts V*olp.*
6	ll. 19–22 first printed in V*olpone* III.vii. 236–39
.19	may] shall V*olp.*
.20	'hem] them V*olp.*
	they V*olp.*] thy 1616
10	first printed in an appendix to Robert Chester, *Love's Martyr* (1601); entitled *Praeludium.*
.2	use, H&S] use? 1616
.23	*Pegasus,* 1640] *Pegasus* 1616
11	also printed in the appendix to *Love's Martyr.*
.29	passions] passions still H&S from MSS.
.69	Peace] Peace, H&S
12.22	nor] not MSS.
.76	to notes] the notes H&S from MSS.
13.123	finde; 1640] finde? 1616

The Under-wood. Text 1640. All previous editions which have numbered the poems have considered that Nos. 1–3 are all parts of No. 1. Here they are treated as separate poems, so that the numbering throughout is in this edition two higher than in others.

1.34	*Union* Gifford] *Unitie* 1640
.42	meditate] mediate Gifford
.48	rest! 1692] rest? 1640
2.12	sweet, 1692] sweet. 1640
.18	done:] done? 1692
.20	slave?] slave: 1692
4.2.19	looke. H&S] looke, 1640
.22	with Gifford] which 1640
.3.11	draught.] draught H&S
.12	Armed,] Aymed, 1640 Aymed H&S
	shaft] shaft. H&S
.25	doe, H&S] doe 1640
.4.4	guideth. 1692] guideth 1640

.11–30 in *Divell is an Asse* II.vi with variants in punctuation.

.17 such a grace] such grace *Div.*

.23 fall o'the Snow] fall of Snow *Div.*

.5.23 in.] in? 1640

.45 thou] thou, H&S, 1692

.50 spi'd. 1692] spi'd 1640

.6.4 faire, H&S] faire. 1640

.7.7 gone:] gone 1640 gone, 1692, H&S

.12 long. H&S] long, 1640

.9.9 to] too 1692

.37 him] him; H&S from MS.

.10.6 understood. 1692] understood 1640

5.14 wake;] wake, 1640

7.10 straine:] straine, 1692

9.13 forborn, 1692] foreborne. 1640

12.6 fire: 1692] fire, 1640

.11 were, 1692] were, 1640

.13 forth:] forth 1640 forth, 1692

13.12 againe, 1692] againe; 1640

Aid; H&S] Aid, 1640

14.14 still. H&S from MS.] still 1640

.21 reprehend; H&S from MS.] reprehend 1640

.22 manners H&S] manners, 1640

.31 scant. H&S] scant, 1640

.36 he! 1692] he? 1640

.39 sloth:] sloth, 1640

.40 first] first, H&S

15.33 thankes,] thankes H&S

.42 Benefit] Benefit: 1640 Benefit; H&S
away,] away 1640 away: H&S

.47 *paragraph* 1640

.55 Land; 1692] Land 1640

.57 to, is] too, is 1640 to, as H&S

.62 -brokers, 1692] -brokers; 1640

.78 piece;] piece 1640 piece, H&S
place H&S from MS.] pace 1640

.80 borrowing; 1692] borrowing 1640
stopt] stopt, 1692

15.83   out of their] out their H&S from MS.
.86   reveale] reveal, 1692
.88   aloud] alow'd 1692
.89   wonder, why H&S] wonder! why? 1640
.100   health-sake] Healths-sake: 1692 health-sake H&S
.102   rites;] Rites: 1692 rites! H&S
.108   of discerning H&S from MS.] of a discerning 1640
.110   light. H&S] light 1640
.117   Beast: 1692] Beast, 1640
.122   none:] none? H&S
.123   that will H&S from MS.] that I will 1640 advance. 1692] advance 1640
.127   night?] night! H&S
.129   Christendome?] Christendome! H&S
.132   ought:] ought 1640 ought; H&S
.137   Arch,] Arch; 1692
.146   stature; 1692] stature, 1640
.148   fashion; 1692] fashion, 1640
16   first printed in John Selden, *Titles of Honor* (1614)
.1   write: 1614] write 1640
.3   care; 1614] care, 1640
.4   Truth . . . are 1640] Since, naked, but *Truth*, and the Graces are. 1614
.8   free, 1614] free. 1640
.12   Humanitie: 1614] Humanitie. 1640
.14   enemie. We 1614] enemie, we 1640
.17   farre otherwise] farre from this fault 1614
.22   such. 1614] such, 1640
.28   Vow. 1614] Vow, 1640
.37   T'instruct] To informe 1614
.41   urd'd! 1614] urg'd 1640
.48   Forme Act] Forme, Act, 1614
        sight.] sight? 1614
.56   manly] masculine 1614
.64   bound. 1614] bound 1640

.66   thine 1614] their 1640
         owne. 1614] owne, 1640

.73   love] love, 1614

.81   Gaine] gaine 1614 Graine 1640
         your two] two such 1614

17.11   nurse,] nurse 1692

.19   See,] See 1692

.30   stay:] stay 1640 stay, H&S from MS.

.31   swells. H&S from MS.] swells? 1640

.47   flowes. How H&S from MS.] flowes, how 1640

.53   more] more, H&S from MS.

.56   leese: H&S from MS.] leese 1640

.57   merit; H&S from MS.] merit 1640

.68   sick, H&S from MS.] sick 1640

.78   will.] will: H&S from MS.
         steele,] steele. H&S from MS.

.97   Mistresse,] Mistresse H&S

.108   suit,] suit H&S from MS.
         has] has, H&S

.122   increase] increase. H&S from MS.

.123   vices,] vices H&S from MS.

.133   waste, H&S from MS.] waste; 1640

.138   viewers] viewes H&S from MS.

.146   men;] men 1640

.148   Soule; H&S] Soule 1640

.160   both,] boote, H&S from MS.

.162   rimes H&S from MS.] rimes: 1640

.167   sufferers);] sufferers) 1640

.182   takst; H&S from MS.] takst 1640

.186   one; H&S] one, 1640

.192   sweare, H&S] sweare 1640

18.4   Gray.] Gray, H&S

19.4   Judge, 1692] Judge. 1640

.9   Band. H&S] Band, 1640

20.7   in't,] in't H&S

.11   blind: 1692] blind 1640

.21   thus,] thus; 1640

21.21   abuse:] abuse, 1640

22.2   sin] sin; 1640 sin, H&S

22.6   fit?] fit! 1692
   .11   outward fresh,] outward, fresh H&S
   .14   worse.] worse? H&S
24.17   rear'd, H&S] rear'd 1640
   .29   off-spring] offering Whalley
25.6   and destroys] and oft destroys H&S from MSS.
   .32   reproofe, H&S] reproof. 1640
   .35–6   also conclude the Apologetic Dialogue appended to *Poetaster.*
26   first printed opposite the frontispiece of Walter Raleigh, *History of the World* (1614)
   .1   neere H&S] neere 1614 ne're 1640
   .2   Historie, 1614] Historie 1640
   .3   Raising 1614] Razing 1640
               or 1614] and 1640
               fame, 1614] fame 1640
   .5   wise] High 1614
   .7   were] are 1614
   .8   When . . . dur'd.] And the reward, and punishment assur'd. 1614
   .9   Which . . . (lighted] This makes, that lighted 1614
   .10   Truth that] Truth, which 1614
   .12   meet] mete 1614
               things:)] things: 1614
27.26   rude. H&S from MS.] rude? 1640
   .54   clearest, H&S from MS.] clearest. 1640
28.2   wound:] wound, 1640
   .21   truth: 1692] truth 1640
               WROTH] WORTH 1640
   .32   sing? H&S] sing, 1640
30.5   it 1692] it. 1640
31   printed in *Recreation for Ingenious Headpeeces* (1645)
   .15   Art 1645] are 1640
   .21   bewail'd,] bewailed. 1640
32.4   *Epitome,* 1692] *Epitome* 1640
   .19   Land. Who H&S] Land, who 1640
34.12   thinke, yea] think yea, 1640
   .14   Punishment.] Punishment, 1640

35.18	skill] skill, H&S
36.16	this? 1692] this. 1640
38.2	Love 1692] love; 1640
.9	worlds H&S] world 1640
40.2	madde,] madde. 1640
.7	it. Helpe 1692] it, helpe 1640
.14	such a forme 1692] such forme 1640
.30	before. H&S] before, 1640
.32	can;] can, 1640
.35	now; 1692] now, 1640
.43	as Cunningham] is 1640
.50	unjust. H&S] unjust, 1640
.60	have. H&S] have? 1640
.69	pardons 1692] pardons, 1640
.78	die. H&S] die 1640
.79	mornes, H&S] mornes 1640
.91	I, 1692] I 1640
.115	away,] away; 1640
.117	heart;] heart 1640
.119–21	run: . . . Sun; . . . have;] run, . . . Sun, . . . have, 1640
41	by John Donne, entitled "The Expostulation" in *Poems* (1633)
.2	you? 1633] you. 1640
.8	perjuries? 1633] perjuries; 1640
.19	breake? 1633] break, 1640
.41	pitty; 1633] pittie 1640
.45	he] be 1640
.53	revive 1633] receive 1640
.62	wayes; 1633] wayes 1640
.65	soft 1633] lost 1640
42.9	me, 1692] me 1640
	Mrs.,] Mrs. 1640
.19	light, H&S] light 1640
.20	rarified 1692] ratified 1640
	sprite; H&S] spright 1640 Sprite; 1692
.25	Mistress] Masters 1640, perhaps from expansion of Mrs.
.38	belie 1692] belie. 1640
.48	not 1692] nor 1640

43.2	Heare, Mistress,] Heare Masters 1640
44.1	cold,] cold 1640
.5	Rithme] Rhyme 1692
.8	horse? H&S] horse 1640
.19	But then consent H&S] But then content 1640 Be then content Gifford
.21	not, H&S] not 1640
.44	force, H&S] force. 1640
.47	Chaires] Chaires; 1640
.66	see, 1692] see 1640
.73	Moore-fields! . . . night, 1640] Moore-fields, this other night! H&S
45	in Q,D, and several MSS.
.1	Lord] god Q,D
.2	had] have Q,D
.3	flame] flames Q,D
.4	an] one Q,D
.5	attempted, *Vulcan*, 'gainst H&S] attempted *Vulcan* 'gainst 1640 attempted ought against Q,D
.8	clos'd] close Q
.12	Bride, D] Bride. 1640, Q
.14	any . . . the] every . . . her Q,D
.16	Imposture] Impostures Q,D
	blasphemie, H&S] blasphemie? 1640 Blasphemy, Q,D
.23	honours] honour Q,D
.24	Glories] glory Q,D
	and] or Q,D
.27	then why] why then Q,D
.33	and] or Q,D
	fiftie] fittee 1640
.34	and] or Q,D
.35	pomp'd] pump'd Q,D
.36	*Eteostichs*] Ecrosticks Q,D
	flammes] flames Q,D
.39	on] or Q,D
.42	allay] a Lay Q,D

.45 might] would Q,D

.47 Executioner,] Executioner: Q,D

.50 thrift] thirst Q,D

.52 Geese, Q,D] Geese 1640

.53 poore] crispe Q,D

.54 me] them Q,D

.57 a] the Q,D

Rites doe] right doth Q,D

.58 make] sow Q,D

H&S note that for "consumption" several MSS.
read *propter viam:* a sacrifice made to Hercules
before one began a journey.

ever] every Q,D

.62 your . . . Nosthrill] thy . . . Nostrills Q,D

.63 in; enough Q,D] in enough 1640

.67 the] their Q,D

.68 the] their Q,D

.71 To] With Q,D

.73 Seales] Charmes Q,D

.74 Jemme] Jems Q

.78 so . . . doe] doe the times so Q,D

.79 Or] Our D

.82 Ball] Baal Q,D

.84 meale] meate Q

.85 accite] excite Q,D

.88 mastry] mistery Q mystery D

.89 All] And Q,D

.91 the] a Q,D

.92 could not doe Q,D] could do 1640

.94 song] Sung Q,D

.97 To] For Q,D

.99 Wherein] In which Q,D

succour] succours Q,D

.100 lent] sent Q,D

.102 With] And Q,D

Divinitie, Q,D] Divinitie; 1640

.105 thou dost] dost thou Q,D

.108 of] at Q,D

.110 Arts] Art Q,D

45.112	none.] none: Q,D none 1640
.121	with] by Q,D
.123	Wise-men H&S] wise men Q,D Wise man 1640
.124	My] Our Q,D
.126	of] on Q,D
.134	Flanck'd] Fenc'd Q,D
	forc'd] forkt Q
.139	nois'd] nos'd D
.142	lock't] rak'd Q,D
.144	the Q,D] in 1640
.145	fell] fall D
.146	And cry'd, it was] Twas verily Q,D
.148	ah] a Q,D
.157	his] thy Q,D
.158	shew'n too] too shew'd Q,D
.159	is] was Q,D
	true] right Q,D
.160	his] thy Q,D
.162	not she] she not Q,D
.165	those] them Q,D
.171	Chroniclers Q,D] Chronicles 1640
.172	Will] Would Q,D
.176	order] Orders Q,D
.181	forth] out Q,D
.183	Condemne] Confine Q,D
	the] some Q,D
.188	Burne] Waste Q,D
.189	were] more Q,D
.193	was unto] had beene to Q,D
.194	at] not Q
.195	and] which Q,D
.196	remaines yet] yet remaines Q,D
.201	Or] And D
	but *omitted* Q
.202	Who] That Q,D
.206	Make] Use Q,D
.207	receive] enjoy Q,D
.214	Evils] ills Q,D

.216	on] take Q,D
	B.B.'s] Bess Broughtons Q,D
46.4	Ambassadour, 1692] Ambassadour 1640
.32	were. 1692] were 1640
.53	men, H&S] men. 1640
.55	tame, H&S] tame 1640
.56	same; H&S] same 1640
.58	Guns,] Guns. 1640
.63	he] he not Gifford
.73	Clownes, 1692] Clownes; 1640
.82	become H&S] become, 1640
.88	late 1692] late? 1640
47.25	understand:] understand 1640
49.4	gold. H&S] gold, 1640
.7	eyes, H&S] eyes; 1640
.10	Drinke, 1692] Drinke 1640
.18	with] which 1692
.57	crack'd, H&S] crack'd 1640
.60	can, 1692] can 1640
.62	thence Gifford] then 1640
.70	shame; H&S] shame. 1640
.77	then, H&S] then 1640
50.4	new] now Gifford
.17	him, H&S] him 1640
51.11	cannot once] can at once H&S *conj.*
.25	Divine;] Divine 1640
52.22	Climes, H&S] Climes 1640
53.2	thee] the 1640
54	in Q,D, and MSS.
.4	skill] art Q,D
.7	here!] H&S from MS. here? 1640
	or] and Q,D
.8	when as] whereas Q,D
.9	Cheater! H&S] Cheater? 1640
Answer	
.5	lumpe] part Q,D
.11	described] describ'd but H&S from MS.
.13	whilst] since Q,D
.16	maistry] majesty Q,D

54.17	handling H&S from MS.] handling, 1640
.18	would] could Q,D
.19	But Q,D] Put 1640
.20	but] than Q,D
.22	Yet] But Q,D
	face,] face 1640
.24	will] would Q,D
55	in Q,D
.6	horse and you Q,D] horse; and you 1640
.11	Nay,] And Q,D
56.18	or] on H&S
57.5	braine, 1692] braine 1640
58.4	it. H&S from MS.] it, 1640
.7	tardie, H&S] tardie 1640
.23	rime H&S from MS.] rime, 1640
.25	man, H&S from MS.] man 1640
61	in Q,D, and MSS.
.7	such] This Q,D
.9	quick] swift Q,D
	dazeling] darling Q,D
.10	meet] men doe meet Q,D
.11	shot out] darted Q,D
.14	the] a Q,D
.15–16	is true / Valour! to sleight it,] tis true, / Next to dispise it Q,D
.17	the] all Q,D
.19	All] And Q,D
.20	All] and Q,D
.21–3	'mongst . . . fortune! *omitted* Q,D
.23	when, or] when Q,D
62.12	Arts, H&S] Arts. 1640
63.12	taske H&S] taske? 1640
.17	way H&S] way, 1640
65.1	WHo H&S] WAo 1640
67	text in Q,D, and MSS.
.1	birth, Q] birth? 1640 birth D
.2	spring, and earth] spring on earth Q,D
.8	come Q,D] *omitted* 1640
.9	there] still Q,D

	Hast] Haste Q,D
68	text in Q,D, and MSS.
.2	blessed'st] blessed Q,D
.3	why may] and why D
.4	prophanenesse) yet,] prophanenesse, as Q,D
.8	Man-kind] the world Q,D
.9	Isle, Q,D] Isle! 1640
.13	Glorie] Our thanks Q,D
.14	safetie to the Realme] health, both to our Land Q,D
69	text in Q,D, omitting the date and names of the Muses
.2	this] the Q,D
.7	thriftie] thirsty Q,D
.9	forth] out Q,D
.11	This . . . or] The . . . as Q,D
.13	our] the Q,D
.14	cleave] shake Q,D
.15	our] their Q,D
.18	daintie] learned Q,D
.26	Daughter] Daughtrr 1640
.29	Brothers] Fathers Q,D
.30	Fathers] brothers Q,D
.33	Isle] ground Q,D
.36	got] put Q,D
.39	his] the Q,D
.47	Summe] Make Q,D
.48	two and twenti'th] one and twenty Q,D
.49–54	omitted Q,D
70.11	lack:] lack, 1640
71.12	sight, 1692] sight. 1640
.14	faire 1692] farre 1640
72	text in Q,D, and MSS. entitled "Ode Pindarick" to the men
	The Turne] The turne of ten D
	The Counter-turne] The Counter-turne of ten D
	The Stand] The Stand, of twelve D
.12	sack,] sack? Q,D

72.15	hurried] hurld Q,D
.17	and] *omitted* Q,D
	fell] full Q,D
.41	So] Too Q,D
.44	fall'st 1692] fall'st 1640 tripst Q,D
.45	right] night Q,D
.50	in] and Q,D
.53	out] our 1692
.68	bald Q,D] bold 1640
.71	that] at Q,D
.73	beauties] beauty Q,D
.81	that] the Q,D
.84	*Ben* Q] *Ben.* 1640 *Ben:* D
.90	were] as Q,D
.91	long Q,D] Long 1640
.100	indentur'd Q,D] indenture 1640
.104	Orgies] Argues Q
.109	the tother] to th'other Q
.123	in deed H&S from MS.] indeed 1640, Q,D
73.4	Ingineers, H&S from MS.] Ingineers 1640
74	in Q,D, and MSS.; Q and D print as four-line stanzas through line 12; 13–18 are a six-line stanza; 19–20 are omitted.
.1	Day] birth day Q,D
	thou] the Q,D
.3	Discharge it] Discharging Q,D
.8	the other] another Q,D
.12	Made . . . else,] Made loftier by the winds all noises els Q,D
.13	*Rockets . . . Shoutes*] squibs, and mirth, with all their shouts Q,D
.14	that] the Q,D
.15	Had . . . routes] If they had leisure, at these lawfull routs Q,D
.16	On th'] The Q,D
76	in Q,D, in six-line stanzas, and MS.
.1	pleasure] pleasures Q,D
.6	yeare, the] yeare and Q,D
.7	The] That Q,D

	run, Q,D] run; 1640
.15	was] were Q,D
.16	Doth show] Have shew'd Q,D
.21	love] joy Q,D
.23	fruit shall] fruits that Q,D
.25	then our] the Q,D
.28	Shoot] Spring Q,D
.29	to his *Heire*] of the aire Q,D
.30	his] the Q,D
77.11	filled 1692] filed 1640
	Caroches H&S from MS.] *Cacoches* 1640
.17	Beavie H&S from MS.] Beautie 1640
.55	Day, 1692] Day 1640
.90	at, H&S from MS.] at 1640
.156	birth H&S] birth. 1640
.158	grace H&S] grace, 1640
.160	dare 1692] dare, 1640
.162	will] Johnston amends to wish
79	versions in Q,D, and MSS.
.2	now with] with some Q,D
.4	with] from Q,D
.6	or *Romano*] *Romans* famous Q,D
.10	I would] would I Q,D
	know] thinke Q,D
.12	the] his Q,D
.13	you Q,D] you, 1640
.16	they] these Q,D
.19	murmuring Subjects] froward Citizens Q,D
	the *omitted* Q,D
.20	worlds] world Q,D
.22	sweets . . . they] Fame and Honour you Q,D
.23	I looke] looke I D
	reverent] measuring Q,D
.25	as] like as Q,D
.26	or] and Q,D
.27	tune] voyce Q,D
.28	happ'ly] haply Q,D
80	texts in Q,D, and MS.
.2	read] take Q,D

80.3	honour] Honours Q,D
.4	could] would Q,D
.6	vertue] action Q,D
.8	that] those Q,D
.12	other] others Q,D
	dwelt] dwell Q,D
.13–14	Witnesse . . . *June*] Witnesse his birth-day, the eleventh of *June*, / And his great action done at *Scanderoone* Q,D
.15–16	*omitted* Q,D
.17–18	In . . . give.] That day, which I predestin'd am to sing, / For *Brittains* honour, and to *Charles* my King: Q,D
.21	cleare] cheare Q,D
.22	*Omen*] fortune Q,D
.27	shall] doth Q,D
.29	shall] will Q,D
.30	begg'd] made Q,D
.31	them] then Q,D
81.5	warpe] warpe. 1640
.20	Shep. at l. 22 1640
.24	Nym. at l. 26 1640
.31	Chor. at l. 29 1640
.35	Chor. at l. 33 1640
82.17	reduc'd, H&S] reduc'd 1640
.18	values H&S] value's 1640
83	by Sir Henry Wotton, *Reliquiae Wottonianae* (1651)
.9	flames] flame 1651
.15	Whilst] While 1651
.17	lead H&S from MS.] led 1640
85	texts in Q,D, and MSS.
	Jane Q,D] Anne 1640
	Winton] Winchester Q,D
.1	gentle] goodly Q,D
.6	you] I Q,D
.16	something] somewhat Q,D
.17	her Q,D] the 1640
.21	formes, good] titles, Q,D

.25 at that: the dotes] at, the Dotes thereof Q,D
.26 Thereof, no notion] No Nation Q,D
.29 Heaven] God Q,D
.31 these] those Q,D
.32 blaze] heat Q,D
.33 here, by] by Q by a D
.35 that] it Q,D
.38 rob] spoyle Q,D
.44 dazling] darling Q,D
.46 summe] heap Q,D
.56 world, all] world with my Q,D
.59 With] Which Q,D
.65 Who] That Q,D
.69 light] lights Q,D
.71 discourseth Gifford] discourses Q,D discovereth 1640
.74 beginnings] beginning Q,D
.75 doe] doth Q,D
.76 they . . . Crowne] the Elect of God Q,D
.78 you] yee Q,D
.79 grudge at] quarrell Q,D
.88 And] The Q,D
.90 with] and Q,D
.91 beginning there, to'ave] beginning to have Q,D
.92 should] can Q,D
.95 Contention, and brave] brave contention and Q,D
.96 the future] a future Q,D
86.9.2 sey'd] did 1692
.48 doome; H&S] dome. 1640
.123 the H&S] Tee 1640
87 facing the Latin text 1640
.23 may, H&S] may 1640
.25 floods,] floods? 1640
.51 East H&S from MSS.] bright 1640
.68 mere Gifford] more 1640
88 facing the Latin text 1640
89 facing the Latin text 1640
.9 I, H&S] I 1640

89.14   *Calais, Thurine* H&S] *Calais Thurine,* 1640
90–91   facing the Latin text 1640

Art of Poetry. D text

12 given	363 *Spondoees*
17 profest	384 night:
24 And Painter	386 rais'd;
25 Tree,	393 Courts
33 fire	461 not 1640 that
55 write	473 stain'd
57 beare,	481 rests
64 is,	518 mark
75 full	525 well,
76 came	529 can
99 Fate	531 not Pillars
100 date,	534 oyntment . . . guests.
103 will	577 the rest
106 declares	632 rivall
116 winds	653 helpe
299 gteater	658 could;
325 hop	671 h hath
352 Gentry;	

Art of Poetry. 1640 Folio text, printed opposite the Latin
text of Heinsius (1610). It is here rearranged to correspond
with the Duodecimo version since that agrees with modern
editions of Horace.

32 simply	432 the
61 differ	462 it.
167 Cholcis	463 praise;
180 person. Looke	472 whence
196 I sing a noble Warre, and *Priam's* Fate	480 and
284 cause	493 Tyrtoeus
322 gravitie.	514 suffrage

Uncollected Poetry.

1	from British Museum, Additional MS. 18040
.7	thunder
.20	sightes
2	text from Nicholas Breton, *Melancholike Humours* (1600)
3	text from Robert Allot, *Englands Parnassus* (1600)
.15	Apostacie.
.17	dispaire? Dispaire, away H&S] dispaire? Away 1600
4	text from *Cynthia's Revels* (quarto, 1601), I.ii
.5	flowers,] flowres; 1616
.6	showers] showres 1616
.11	pride is, now, 1616] pride, is now 1601
5	*Cynthia's Revels* IV.iii
.1	O, 1616] O 1601
.8	precious. 1616] pretious: 1601
.12	dye, 1616] dye 1601
6	*Cynthia's Revels* IV.iii
.2	Love,] Love; 1601 love, 1616
.3	store,] store 1616
.5	hand] hand, 1616
.6	kid, 1616] Kid 1601
	thee:] thee. 1616
.10	loves,] Loves 1601
.11	Mistresse, 1616] Mistris 1601
7	*Cynthia's Revels* V.vi
.1	Queene] Queene, 1616
.6,12,18	Goddesse, 1616] Goddesse 1601
.15	hart 1616] Hart, 1601
.16	breathe 1616] breath 1601
	soever: 1616] soever, 1601
.17	Thou,] Thou 1616
8	a special leaf of dedication found in the copy

	of *Cynthia's Revels* (1601) in the William Andrews Clark Memorial Library
9–10	text from *Love's Martyr* (1601)
11	text from *Poetaster* (quarto, 1602) II.ii
.6	Light] Light, 1616
	toying 1616] toying, 1602
.9	too hard 1616] to hard 1602
.10	extreames] extremes 1616
.16	Jelous] jealous 1616
12	*Poetaster* IV.iii
13	*Poetaster* IV.v
.3	notes;] notes, 1616
	fie, fie;] fie, fie, 1616
.4	Drouzinesse] drouzinesse, 1616
14	text from Hugh Holland, *Pancharis* (1603)
15	text from 1616; punctuation and spelling in Quarto 1603 differ slightly
16	text from Thomas Wright, *The Passions of the Minde in Generall* (1604)
.7	subt'lest] subject 1620 ed.
17	text from *Eastward Hoe* (quarto 1605) V.i
18	text from John Fletcher, *The Faithfull Shepheardesse* (quarto, n.d.)
.8	more.] more, Q
19	text from *Volpone* (1616; Quarto 1607) I.ii
.4	Selves] Themselves 1607
.9	Eene his] His very 1607
.14	waites] shall waite 1607
20	*Volpone* II.ii
21	*Volpone* II.ii
22	text from W. D. Briggs, *Anglia*, XXXIX (1915), 247–48; taken from MS.
23	text from *The Description of the Masque . . . Celebrating the happy Marriage of John, Lord Ramsey, Vicount Hadington. . . .* (Quarto, 1608), ll. 370-end (H&S VII. 261–63)
.6	free, H&S] free 1608

.36	*laughter* 1616] Laughters 1608
.61	nights: H&S] nightes. 1608
24–25	text from *Epicoene, or The Silent Woman* (1616 Folio)
26	text from MS. in Widener Library
27–28	text from Thomas Coryate, *Coryats Crudities* (1611)
29	text from *Coryats Crambe* (1611)
30	text from *Cinthias Revenge* (anonymous; 1613)
31	text from holograph in British Museum copy of 1640 Folio
32	text from Bodleian Library, Ashmole MS. 38
.3	thee, H&S] thee MS.
.5	Increase, H&S] Increase MS.
.6	peace;] peace MS.
.10	sayes, H&S] sayes MS.
.12	prospective, H&S]ˑprerspective; MS. perspective, Gifford
33	text from Christopher Brooke, *The Ghost of Richard The Third* (1614)
34	text from *The Husband* (anonymous; 1614)
35	survives in different forms in several MSS. This version is from Bodleian Library Ashmole MS. 38; Newdigate reprinted it.
36	text from *Bartholmew Fayre* (1631) III.v
37	text from William Browne, *Britannia's Pastorals* (1616)
38	text from George Chapman, *The Georgicks of Hesiod* (1618)
39	text from British Museum, Harleian MS. 4955
.3	neere H&S] neare MS.
.9	it. Write Newdigate] it write MS.
40	text from James Mabbe, *The Rogue* (1622)
41	text from William Shakespeare, *Comedies, Histories, & Tragedies* (1623)
42	text from No. 41
.29	didst] didstst 1623

43	text from *The Touch-stone of Truth* (anonymous; 1624)
.7	that eds of 1630, 1634] *omitted* 1624
.9	Warrant eds of 1630, 1634] Warre 1624
.10	sweete, H&S] sweete. 1624
.19	well H&S] will 1624
44	text from 1692
.14	it, H&S] it 1692
	H&S note that after l. 20 on the surviving wooden panel upon which the verses were inscribed is written, *O rare Ben Johnson!*
45	text from British Museum, Harleian MS. 4955
.1	lies, H&S] lies MS.
.4	seate] state Gifford
.16	life, H&S] life MS.
46	text from British Museum, Harleian MS. 4955, following the *Entertainment at the Blackfriars*
.1	Howers, H&S] Howers. MS.
.7	begin, H&S] begin MS.
47	text from *Lucan's Pharsalia* (trans. Thomas May; 1627)
48	text from Michael Drayton, *The Battaile of Agincourt* . . . . (1627)
49	text from British Museum, Harleian MS. 4955
.1	You H&S] you MS.
.5	Doe H&S] doe MS.
50	text from John Beaumont, *Bosworth-Field* (1629)
51	printed in 1640 as Epigramme 129
52	text from *The New Inn* (Octavo, 1631), IV.iv
53	text from Q,D; also in *The New Inn* (1631)
.11	thou 1631] *omitted* Q,D
.12	would] will 1631
.20	not,] not Q,D, 1631
.21	a] some 1631
.23	Fish, Q] fish- H&S
.27	Broomes Q] There, 1631
.28	There, . . . meale] As the best order'd meale 1631

.31	yee] you 1631
.36	stuffing] larding 1631
.37	rage of] their foule 1631
.39	they're . . . foule] they are torne, and turn'd 1631
.50	May blushing sweare] May, blushing, sweare 1631
.53	of] o're 1631
.54	may . . . then] may, blood-shaken, then, 1631
.56	That . . . ours,] As they shall cry, like ours 1631
.58	Shall . . . Starres] No Harpe ere hit the starres; 1631
.59	When . . . Acts] In tuning forth the acts 1631 *Charles* his] his sweet 1631
.60	And . . . *Waine*] And raysing Charles his chariot, 'bove his *Waine*
54	text from Q,D, following "An Epigram On the Princes birth" (*Under.* 67). Q,D also print another (not included here) which seems probably by Thomas Freeman; see H&S VIII.429
.7	workmen D] workman Q
55	first printed in a collection, *Wit & Drollery* (1656) and again in Langbaine, *An Account of the English Dramatic Poets* (1691), which text is followed here
.11	blatant H&S] blotant 1691
.13	nothing left MSS.] nought 1691
.14	thy H&S from MSS.] his 1691
56	text from British Museum, Harleian MS. 4955. H&S print Lord Ellesmere's copy
.5	Architas,] Architas MS.
.35	Fame] fame MS.
.58	besyde] by side MS.
.59	Whither . . . whither H&S] Whether . . . whether MS.
.78	serious] solemne H&S
.99	Worthyes H&S] worthies MS.
57	text as in No. 55

57.21	worth] worke H&S
58	text as in No. 55
.9	read, H&S] read; MS.
59	text from Q and D, following the verses quoted in note 1.
.1	didst] darst H&S from MS.
.7	barke] bawle H&S from MS.
.8	slur] stirre H&S from MS.
.10	writing] barking H&S from MS.
	thinkst] lookst H&S from MS.
.11	thee: no] thee? No H&S from MS.
.12	cannot] shall not H&S from MS.
	After line 12 H&S add four more lines from MS.
.14	a] his H&S from MS.
.18	see] smell H&S from MS.
60	text from Richard Brome, *The Northern Lasse* (1632)
61	text from Alice Sutcliffe, *Meditation of Man's Mortalitie* (1634)
62	text from Anthony Stafford, *The Femall Glory* (1635)
.13	cull'd, the H&S from W. T. Brooke] call'd the 1635
.40	stay'd. H&S] stay'd 1635
63	text from Joseph Rutter, *The Shepheards Holyday* (1635)
64	text from *Annalia Dubrensia* (1636)
.1	dropp her Vies H&S from conj. in *Macmillan's Magazine* XCII (Oct. 1905), 455] dropp Vies 1636
.3	thee, H&S] thee 1636
.7	advance H&S] advance, 1636
65	from holograph in Dulwich College, MS. I.135; printed by H&S as last of *Under.*
66	from British Museum, Harleian MSS. 4955; terminal punctuation (almost entirely missing) normalized
.1	Peake H&S] peake MS.

.8	in to H&S] into MS.
.14	turnd H&S] turne MS.
.21	Darby H&S] darby MS.
.37	if't H&S] it MS.
67	text from W. D. Briggs, *Athenaeum*, June 13, 1914, p. 828
.6	would] could H&S from MS.
.14	Courtly] Countrye H&S from MS.
.22	tunes Briggs] times MS.
.31	rip Briggs] ript MS.
.42	Cause] Canst MS.
.45	witts Pallace] wyse Pallas H&S from MS.
68	text from *The Sad Shepherd* (1640 Folio) I.v; also in Q,D
.6	heat Q,D] heart 1640
.10	or] and Q,D

The Masque of Beauty. Text from 1616 Folio; also printed in quarto, 1608, with *Blackness*. Minor variations of spelling and punctuation.

105	hight 1608] height 1616
110	the] thy 1608
following note 56 ingenious] ingenuous 1608
170	then] then, H&S

SELECTED BIBLIOGRAPHY

SELECTED BIBLIOGRAPHY

Besides the editions of the poems which are named in the introduction to the Variants, the reader may profitably consult several more specialized studies:

Allen, Don C. "Ben Jonson and the Hieroglyphics." *Philological Quarterly*, XVIII (1939), 290–300.

Briggs, W. D. "Studies in Ben Jonson." *Anglia*, XXXVII–XXXIX (1913–16).

Eccles, Mark. "Jonson and the Spies." *Review of English Studies*, XIII (1937), 385–97.

Evans, Willa M. *Ben Jonson and Elizabethan Music*. Lancaster, Pa., 1929.

Firth, Sir C. H. "Jonson and Raleigh's History of the World," in *Essays, Historical and Literary*. Oxford, 1938.

Fleay, F. G. *A Biographical Chronicle of the English Drama, 1559–1642*. London, 1891.

Gilbert, Allan H. *The Symbolic Persons in the Masques of Ben Jonson*. Durham, N.C., 1948.

Gordon, D. J. "The Imagery of Ben Jonson's 'The Masque of Blackness' and 'The Masque of Beautie.'" *Journal of the Warburg and Courtauld Institutes*, VI (1943).

Gordon, D. J. "Poet and Architect: the Intellectual Setting of the Quarrel between Jonson and Inigo Jones." *Journal of the Warburg and Courtauld Institutes*, XII (1949).

Johnston, G. B. *Ben Jonson: Poet*. New York, 1945.

Simpson, E. M. "Jonson and Donne." *Review of English Studies*, XV (1939), 274–82.

Swinburne, Algernon. *A Study of Ben Jonson*. London, 1889.

Talbert, Ernest W. "New Light on Ben Jonson's Workmanship." *Studies in Philology*, XL (1943), 154–85.

Talbert, Ernest W. "The Interpretation of Jonson's Courtly Spectacles." *PMLA*, LXI (1946), 454–73.

Trimpi, Wesley. *Ben Jonson's Poems: A Study of the Plain Style*. Stanford, 1962.

Walker, R. S. "Jonson's Lyric Poetry." *Criterion*, XIII (1933–34), 430–48.

Walton, Geoffrey. *Metaphysical to Augustan*. London, 1955.

Wheeler, C. F. *Classical Mythology in the Plays, Masques, and Poems of Ben Jonson*. Princeton, 1938.

Whipple, Thomas K. *Martial and the English Epigram from Sir Thomas Wyatt to Ben Jonson*. Berkeley, 1925.

Wilson, Edmund. "Morose Ben Jonson," in *The Triple Thinkers*, revised edition. New York, 1948.

INDEX OF FIRST LINES

INDEX OF FIRST LINES

Such pleasure as the teeming Earth,   230
Surly's old whore in her new silkes doth swim: 34

That Cod can get no widdow, yet a knight,   11
That I hereafter, doe not thinke the Barre,   170
That Love's a bitter sweet, I ne're conceive   181
That neither fame, nor love might wanting be   28
That, not a paire of friends each other see,   64
That Poets are far rarer births then kings,   33
That thou art lov'd of God, this worke is done,   246
That thou hast kept thy love, encreast thy will,   46
That we thy losse might know, and thou our love,   22
That whereas your royall Father   237
That you have seene the pride, beheld the sport,   216
Th'expence in odours is a most vaine sinne,   11
The humble Petition of poore Ben.   237
The Judge his favour timely then extends,   170
The ports of death are sinnes; of life, good deeds: 34
The Things that make the happier life, are these,   404
The wise, and many-headed Bench, that sits   347
The Wisdome Madam of your private Life,   206
Then his chast wife, though Beast now know no more,   13
There's reason good, that you good lawes should make: 12
These Mysteries do point to three more great,   401
They are not, Sir, worst Owers, that doe pay   154
They are not those, are present with theyre face,   363
They talke of Fencing, and the use of Armes,   214
This Booke will live; It hath a Genius: This   384
This Figure, that thou here seest put,   371
This is King Charles his Day. Speak it thou Towre   228
This morning, timely rapt with holy fire,   32
Those that in blood such violent pleasure have,   327
Thou art not, Penshurst, built to envious show,   77
Thou call'st me Poet, as a terme of shame: 7
Thou, Friend, wilt heare all censures; unto thee   214
Thou hast begun well, Roe, which stand well too,   45
Thou more then most sweet glove,   332
Thou, that mak'st gaine thy end, and wisely well,   5
Thou, that wouldst finde the habit of true passion,   326
Though Beautie be the Marke of praise,   158
Tho', happy Muse, thou know my Digby well;   239
Though I am young, and cannot tell,   407
Though thou hast past thy Summer standing, stay   231
Thy praise, or dispraise is to me alike,   25
Tilter, the most may'admire thee, though not I: 14
'Tis a Record in heaven. You, that were   383
'Tis growne almost a danger to speake true   106

INDEX OF SHORT TITLES
AND OF NAMES IN TITLES

INDEX OF SHORT TITLES
AND OF NAMES IN TITLES